C000203063

A Chronology of Ancient Greece

A Chronology of Ancient Greece

Timothy Venning

Pen & Sword
MILITARY

First published in Great Britain in 2015 by
Pen & Sword Military
an imprint of
Pen & Sword Books Ltd
47 Church Street
Barnsley
South Yorkshire
S70 2AS

Copyright © Timothy Venning 2015

ISBN 978 1 47383 428 6

The right of Timothy Venning to be identified as the Author of this Work
has been asserted by him in accordance with the Copyright, Designs and
Patents Act 1988.

A CIP catalogue record for this book is available from the British Library

Typeset in Ehrhardt by
Mac Style Ltd, Bridlington, East Yorkshire
Printed and bound in the UK by CPI Group (UK) Ltd,
Croydon, CRO 4YY

Pen & Sword Books Ltd incorporates the imprints of Pen & Sword
Archaeology, Atlas, Aviation, Battleground, Discovery, Family History,
History, Maritime, Military, Naval, Politics, Railways, Select, Transport,
True Crime, and Fiction, Frontline Books, Leo Cooper, Praetorian Press,
Seaforth Publishing and Wharncliffe.

For a complete list of Pen & Sword titles please contact
PEN & SWORD BOOKS LIMITED
47 Church Street, Barnsley, South Yorkshire, S70 2AS, England
E-mail: enquiries@pen-and-sword.co.uk
Website: www.pen-and-sword.co.uk

Contents

Contents

Section One

The Persian Wars c. 560 to 479

560?

Greece

First seizure of power in the unstable city-state of Athens by Peisistratus (born c. 596), son of Hippocrates, head of one of the three main contending factions (the hill villages) and a protégé/relative of the elderly statesman and constitutional reformer Solon (chief 'archon' in 594/3). Aristotle dates this first coup to the archonship of Comeas, i.e. 561/0.

Solon's political and economic reforms – probably carried out during his archonship – had stabilized Athenian politics for some years afterwards, by cancelling rampant debts that oppressed the poor and by admitting the three higher social classes to a share of political power, but turbulence has returned by the 560s. Peisistratus has risen to political prominence as a military commander by capturing the port of Nisaea from Athens' rival Megara in 564. He pretends that he has been attacked in his chariot out in the countryside and shows the city's council his injuries (self-inflicted) in order to be given an official bodyguard, and then uses this to seize power. This and other contemporary 'one-man' regimes in Greece are known as the age of the 'tyrants', but the word is not a pejorative one in its original context.

At around this time, the embryonic 'Spartan Alliance' in the central Peloponnese – nucleus of the later 'Peloponnesian League' – emerges. This commences with a rapprochement between Sparta and Tegea after years of conflict, allegedly at the suggestion of the oracle of Delphi and based on Sparta acquiring the 'bones of Orestes' (i.e. the son and successor of legendary ruler Agamemnon at Mycenae in the Argolid) to pose as the leader of the region. The Sparta/Tegea alliance is joined in the 550s (?) by most of Arcadia, Elis, and Sicyon, but Argos stays aloof.

559

?Expulsion of Peisistratus from Athens (anything from one year to five after his seizure of power), after quarrelling with his rivals Megacles the Alcmaeonid, head of the 'Paralia' coastal faction, and Lycurgus the head of the 'plain', the rural area around Athens. The faction-names may be based on the home region of the faction-leader rather than a distinct 'class' difference between wealthy lowland region farmers (the plain around Athens, i.e. Lycurgus' region, being the richest area) and poorer hillmen. Herodotus is unclear how long the first 'tyranny' lasted except that it was brief; Aristotle, however, dates the expulsion of Peisistratus to five years after 561/0, i.e. ?556.

Persia

?Accession of the creator of the Persian empire, Cyrus 'the Great', son of Cambyses, of the Achaemenid dynasty that rules the homeland province of the 'Persians' in southern Iran.

Probable union with the neighbouring northern state of Media, which Herodotus claims Cyrus takes from his hostile grandfather Astyages – though Herodotus' story is similar to that of the founder of Mycenae in Greece, Perseus, and his grandfather Acrisius of Argos.

c.556–5 or 551/0

Greece

Brief second period of rule by Peisistratus in Athens, involving his return to power in the company of a tall young woman called Phye? whom he has dressed up as the goddess Athene to convince the rural peasantry that he has divine support. She then escorts him by chariot from her village to Athens, in company with his ally Megacles. He forms an alliance with Megacles and marries his daughter, but avoids having children by her, annoying her father, and is expelled again. This implies that his elder sons Hippias and Hipparchus, the first an adult by 546 according to Herodotus, are already born by c. 558, by his first marriage, and he does not want to divide up his estates with a half-Alcmaeonid younger son to their detriment.

Around 555 Sicyon joins the 'Spartan Alliance' after the end of the 'tyranny' (benevolent) of Cleisthenes, father-in-law of the Athenian aristocrat Megacles (above). The date of Cleisthenes' death is uncertain; he probably ruled for around thirty years. By around 550 Corinth and Megara have also joined the alliance – Megara probably to protect herself against Athens after her defeat by Peisistratus in 564.

547

Persia/Greece

Croesus, king of Lydia in western Asia Minor, attacks the expanding Persian empire, crossing the River Halys Eastwards, after allegedly sending an enquiry to the oracle at Delphi about the war and being told that he will destroy a great empire – Persia, as he thinks, but, in fact, it means his own. He fights a drawn battle with the army of Great King Cyrus, ruler of eastern Asia Minor and Armenia as well as Persia/Media/Syria, then withdraws back to his capital, Sardes, for the winter. Unknown to him, Cyrus is planning to attack in winter contrary to the usual customs of war, and keeps his army mobilized.

546

Early – The Persian army arrives at and besieges Sardes, and Croesus brings his army out to fight but is routed, according to Herodotus by the smell of Cyrus' camels panicking his famous cavalry's horses. Croesus is forced to surrender a fortnight later, after Persian mountaineers scale a path up the rock of the citadel; Lydia is annexed to Persia. According to Herodotus and others, Croesus either plans to commit suicide or is punished by being put on a pyre with noble youths and some of his riches, but is (probably) spared by Cyrus as Herodotus thinks likeliest. (The date of this conquest of Lydia is presumed but unclear, and may follow the fall of Babylon in 539).

The annexation of Lydia by Persia is followed by the annexation of the adjacent Greek states of Ionia, who have to pay tribute but retain their autonomy; the inhabitants of the city of Phocaea, besieged by the Persian general Harpagus, evacuate themselves by sea to their colony in Corsica and the inhabitants of Teos move to found Abdera in Thrace.

Probable date of a major war between Sparta and Argos for the rule of the eastern Peloponnese over the region of Thyaea, which Sparta wins – according to Herodotus this war is underway when Croesus sends an unsuccessful appeal to Sparta, chief military power in Greece, for aid. Traditionally the war leads to a disputed 'battle of the champions' combat between 300 men from each city, which both claim to win as only two Argives and one Spartan survive, and then a large-scale battle won by Sparta. This conflict leads to the Spartan-led alliance of Peloponnesian states, traditionally known as the 'Peloponnesian League', dominating central Greece.

The preoccupation of Argos and Sparta with their war may be the occasion for the overthrow of the unstable oligarchic regime at Athens, for the second time, by the 'tyrant' Peisistratus. He and his sons return from about a decade (Herodotus and Aristotle agree on this length of time as ten years) in exile in Thrace, where they have set up a gold-mine and enlisted troops, land at Marathon in the East of Attica, and defeat their foes in battle at Pallene. They then occupy Athens, and Peisistratus becomes a benevolent dictator, 'national' unifier and expander of the annual festival of the 'Panathenaia', and patron of the arts. One of Peisistratus' main allies is the wealthy 'tyrant' Lygdamis of Naxos, in the Cyclades, who as a private citizen lent him men for his seizure of power and was helped to seize Naxos in return (i.e. after 546).

(Herodotus says that the main period of Peisistratid rule lasted for thirty-six years, to 511/10; thus it commenced in 547/6.)

Late 540s?

Seizure of power on the eastern Ionian island of Samos by the most notable pirate ruler and fleet-commander of the age, Polycrates, aided by Lygdamis of Naxos. Polycrates is also a patron of the age's major lyric poets, such as Anacreon of Teos (c. 570–485 BC), and a noted builder.

539

Persia

Cyrus' conquest of Babylonia, with his army defeating the dilettante astronomer king Nabonidus' army at Opis (October) and advancing on the defenceless city, which surrenders. The formal occupation of Babylon is on 12 October; the wealthy and powerful local cults are preserved intact in an alliance with the ancient priesthoods, and Cyrus makes his elder son Cambyses the new king of Babylon. Restoration of the Jewish exiles there to their homeland in Israel.

530/29

Death in battle in Central Asia of Cyrus 'the Great', campaigning against the 'Massegetae' nomads on the River Oxus, after a thirty-year reign in Persia; succeeded by his mentally unstable eldest son, Cambyses.

528/7

Greece

(Probably spring 527) Death of the benevolent 'tyrant' Peisistratus of Athens, probably aged around seventy, after an eighteen-year third period of rule; succeeded by his sons Hippias and Hipparchus. Both are probably over thirty by this time. They also hold family mines in Thrace and the town of Sigeum on the Hellespont.

527/6

Archonship of the obscure Onestorides in Athens.

526

Persia/Egypt

Cambyses invades Egypt, according to some stories after Pharaoh Amasis II 'insulted' him by only pretending to send his daughter to the Great King as a wife and sending a fake (?the daughter of his predecessor Apries) instead. Greek mercenaries fight on both sides in the war, with a Greek colony at Naucratis in Egypt supplying troops to the Egyptians; however, Amasis' leading Greek mercenary captain Phanes has defected to Persia and escaped an attempt to kidnap and repatriate him. The invasion is held up by the defiance of the fortress-city of Gaza on the Palestinian border; Amasis II dies six months before the fall of Egypt (i.e. November 526?), after a reign of forty-four years, and is succeeded by his son Psammetichus III.

526/5

Archonship of Hippias in Athens.

525

Early? – Fall of Gaza after a prolonged siege leads to the invasion of Egypt proceeding; Cambyses leads his army across the desert to the eastern mouth of the Nile and wins a major battle against Pharaoh Psammetichus at Pelusium. (The piles of bones are still visible when the historian Herodotus visits Egypt over sixty years later.) The city falls, followed by the capital up-river at Memphis where the defenders initially kill the crew of an Ionian ship (from Mytilene) who Cambyses sends to demand their surrender. The Pharaoh surrenders and is spared; Egypt is annexed as a Persian province and according to Herodotus Cambyses manically suppresses the local cults, killing the sacred bull of the god Apis to insult the Egyptians. This is at odds with the usual Persian respect for local religions – and archaeological evidence suggests that the current Apis cult bull died and was buried in a normal, honoured fashion c. 524.

525/4

Greece

Cleisthenes, head of the Alcmaeonid family and son of Megacles (by the daughter of the late 'tyrant' Cleisthenes of Sicyon), becomes the eponymous 'archon' of the year at Athens. This indicates that either Peisistratus or Hippias has recalled his family, despite their supposed permanent banishment from Athens arising from the 'curse of Cylon' (their part in murdering the would-be coup leader Cylon and his men in the sanctuary of a temple in 639 BC). Within a few years Cleisthenes and his family are banished again.

?(Story in Herodotus) The piratical tyrant Polycrates of Samos, ally of the Peisistratidae, is called on to send a naval contingent with Cambyses' army to Egypt and sends off shiploads of his political foes, with a secret request to the Great King to get rid of them; they realize what he intends, overthrow his commanders and revolt, and sail back to attack Samos. They fail to take the eponymous capital, and have to leave for exile.

524

Cimon, half-brother of Miltiades (I) the founder of the family's Athenian colony on the Chersonese, wins his third Olympic chariot-victory – a rare privilege and a sign of his wealth and prestige. His son Miltiades (II) is the eponymous 'archon' of the year 524/3 at Athens. Cimon's subsequent murder is rumoured to be at the hands of the jealous Peisistratids who fear a coup.

c. 522

Polycrates is lured to Sardes by the ambitious satrap Oroites, who covets Samos and its fleet as a gift for the Great King, to alleged talks on an alliance against the tyrannical Cambyses. Polycrates ignores warnings of the Persian being untrustworthy, allegedly including a dream by his daughter, and greedily believes a report from his envoy that he was shown a room full of treasure by Oroites; he is seized at Sardes, executed, and exposed on a cross but the island of Samos holds out against Oroites under the leadership of Polycrates' brother Maeandrius. The crisis probably leads to Polycrates' court poet Anacreon moving to Athens, according to Herodotus at the invitation of Hipparchus who sends a ship to fetch him.

522/1

Hippias' son, the younger Peisistratus, is eponymous 'archon' at Athens.

Persia

Spring? – Murder of Great King Cambyses' brother Bardiya/Smerdis, in secret in Persia on his orders sent back from Egypt; this is disputed though the next king, Darius, presents the 'Bardiya'/Smerdis who he killed as a pretender.

July? – Death of Cambyses in an accident on his way home to Persia from Egypt, in Syria; some portray it as suicide but a freak accident is more likely. Either the real Bardiya/Smerdis or ('official' version put out subsequently by the next ruler, Darius) a pretender who looks like him, a Magian priest called Gaumata, seizes power in Persia.

September – A conspiracy by seven great Persian nobles leads to the assassination of either the real or the fake Bardiya/Smerdis at Sikyavauvati, a fortress in the Nisean hills near Ecbatana; the leaders of the conspiracy include Ottanes (who Herodotus says has refused an offer of the throne), Megabyzus, Intaphrenes, and Gobryas. One of the plotters, the late Great King's distant cousin and honorary 'lance-bearer' Darius, son of the nobleman Hystaspes, becomes the new Great King and in effect founds a new dynasty but marries Cambyses' sister Atossa to increase his legitimacy. Several years of rebellion across the empire follow before his power is secured; initially Media, the Persian homeland, and Armenia are in revolt, plus Babylon.

November – Darius recovers Babylon.

521

Spring – Darius puts down the rebel 'king' Phraortes in Media, and then deals with a revolt in lowland Elam south-east of Babylonia; his generals recover Armenia to the north-west.

June – Darius' general Artavardiya defeats the rebels in the Persian homeland, who are led by Vahyazdata, at the battle of Parga.

c. 520

Persia/Greece

Oroites, the murderous satrap of Lydia and Ionia, is executed by arriving envoys from the new Great King Darius, particularly on account of his recent killing of Mitroates the governor of Dascylium and his failure to assist the new ruler.

Polycrates' and Maeandrius' exiled brother Syloson, who has gone to Persia to get aid and according to Herodotus met future ruler Darius while on the Egyptian expedition, persuades the new Great King Darius to let him become the new tyrant of Samos as a Persian vassal. He arrives with a Persian fleet under the senior noble (and 522 coup plotter) Otanes. Maeandrius proposes to abdicate his tyranny for a democracy and leave unmolested for exile, but his released captive brother Charilaus tries to put up a fight with some of the late tyrant's mercenaries and is defeated; the Persians massacre the populace and install Syloson as their puppet-ruler. Maeandrius ends up in Sparta.

Revolt of Babylon against Darius, according to Herodotus after the Persian expedition to Samos.

519

Greece

The southern Boeotian town of Plataea defects from the Thebes-led Boeotian League, and on advice from its putative helper Sparta allies with nearer Athens instead.

516

Hippias and Hipparchus send out the future general Miltiades (II), nephew of the eponymous founder of the family's colony on the Chersonese, to command the latter and protect the Athenian corn-trade route from the Black Sea; this may be another move to rid themselves of a potential political rival.

(or 515/14)? Seizure of the Athenian border fortress of Leipsydrium by the exiled Alcmaeonids, who use it to make attacks on Attica in an attempt to undermine Peisistratid rule; later they are driven out.

c. 515

Death of King Anaxandridas of Sparta; he is succeeded by his eldest son, Cleomenes, who is his son by his second wife who the King married thinking his first wife was barren; the elder son by Anaxandridas' first wife, the slightly younger Doreius, objects to this and soon leaves to found a new colony in Libya/Cyrene.

514

Spring – At the 'Great Panathenaia' festival in Athens, the tyrant Hippias' brother Hipparchus is assassinated by the famed 'tyrannicides', Harmodius and Aristogeiton. They are commemorated as heroes, especially with a statue-group on the Acropolis, after the fall of Hippias – but, in fact, their motive seems from Herodotus to have been personal rather than political. Allegedly Harmodius refused the advances of the homosexual Hipparchus, who in revenge banned his sister from taking part in the sacred procession of the 'maidens' attending the statue of Athene as she was 'not a virgin' so family honour had to be avenged. The assassins are killed, along with a number of suspects, and Hippias becomes notably more paranoid after this and the number of exiles increases; possibly the Peisistratids' poetic client, the famed Simonides of Ceos, leaves for Thessaly.

513

Persia

Expedition of Great King Darius over a 'bridge of boats' across the Bosphorus to invade Thrace – the first Persian penetration into Europe, with an Ionian Greek naval contingent led by Histiaeus, tyrant of Miletus, who has his own landed interests in Thrace. The 'bridge of boats' is built by Mandrocles of Samos, a Greek engineer. Darius and a large army advance across eastern Thrace to the Danube, and the local Getae submit. The Persian fleet sails into the Danube and transports the Persian army across to attack the nomad 'Scythians' on the plains of Wallachia, but the latter refuse to submit and withdraw in their horse-drawn wagons out of reach, burning the countryside. The Persians run short of supplies and are harassed by horse-archers, and eventually Darius has to give up and retire to the Danube and thence to Asia; before his arrival back at the Hellespont Scythian envoys have tried to lure its Ionian Greek protectors (including Miltiades of Athens ruler of the Chersonese) into demolishing the 'bridge of boats' there to cut Darius off. Behind him, some of the Propontis Greek states revolt, led by Chalcedon, which the Persians then sack, and the nomad Thracians attack the Persian bases in the region. This expedition arguably gives Miltiades, future victor of Marathon in 490, invaluable experience of Persian battle-tactics.

c.513

Greece

The exiled Alcmaeonids gain the contract for the rebuilding of the temple of Apollo at Delphi from the authorities, and use it to pressurize the Spartans to overthrow the Peisistratids; this duly has an effect on King Cleomenes, who plans an invasion on their behalf. ?Alliance between Hippias and the tyrant of Lampsacus on the Hellespont, as the Peisistratids' new link to the court of the Great King.

511/10

Sicily

?Cleomenes' half-brother Dorieus and his Spartans make a failed attempt to create a new colony in Sicily near Mount Eryx after leaving Cyrene, but are wiped out by local Siceliots.

Greece/Persia

Failed first invasion of Athens on behalf of the exiles by Cleomenes, king of Sparta; the Spartan army, led by Anchimolius, lands at the port of Phalerum but is driven back by the Peisistratids' hired 1000 Thessalian cavalry.

?Conquest of Thrace as a Persian province by the general Megabazus.

510

Greece

Summer – Second attack on Athens on behalf of the Alcmaeonids and other exiles by Cleomenes and the Spartan army; local help assists them in defeating the tyrant's Thessalian cavalry, and Hippias is blockaded on the Acropolis until his sons are captured and he is forced to agree to terms and leave Athens for his family's lands on the Hellespont at Sigeum. The pre-Peisistratid rule of the noble families is restored, but soon breaks down in feuding between the Alcmaeonids and the ambitious Isagoras, possibly a 'Philiad' and a friend of Cleomenes.

510/09

Sicily

Traditional date for the destruction of the famously rich and luxurious (hence 'sybaritic') Greek city-state of Sybaris in southern Italy by its neighbour Croton. According to Diodorus its new 'tyrant' Telys expels five hundred of the richest citizens, who flee to Croton as supplicants and persuade the city to help them; the Olympic wrestler Milo, possibly son-in-law to the locally resident philosopher/mathematician Pythagoras, leads the army of Croton to destroy the Sybarites' much larger army (Diodorus' figures are implausible) and the winners raze Sybaris to the ground. Strabo later (first century) claims a river is diverted over the site. Descendants of the evictees will attempt to restore Sybaris in 446/5, then join the new colony at Thurii.

508

Summer – Isagoras elected chief 'archon' at Athens, despite Cleisthenes rallying the support of the non-enfranchised classes who used to back the Peisistratids against the 'old' nobility. Isagoras declares that the Alcmaeonids must leave the city as they are still hereditarily guilty of the sacrilegious massacre of Cylon and his party in 639, and gets Cleomenes to send a herald agreeing to this; when they have left he calls in Cleomenes and Spartan troops to assist him (presumably against riots).

Cleomenes draws up a long list of 700 families to be banished as the Alcmaeonids' alleged co-conspirators in the 639 massacre, i.e. the opponents of his ally Isagoras; he proposes to replace the Areopagus council (?) with a new council of 300 consisting of Isagoras' faction, but there is a revolution led by the council and the Athenian people besiege Cleomenes and Isagoras on the Acropolis. After two days the besieged surrender, and Cleomenes' Spartans and Isagoras are allowed to leave but some of the oligarchic faction are arrested and executed. Cleisthenes and his faction are recalled, and envoys are sent to the Great King's satrap at Sardes, his brother Artaphernes, to seek a Persian alliance to warn off Sparta. The latter requires them to do homage with 'earth and water' as usual for a Persian vassal, but they are disowned on their return to Athens.

507

Cleisthenes as chief archon of Athens reforms the constitution, to negate aristocratic influence by creating new sub-divisions of the state as the basis for elections – one region each from the city ('asty'), coast ('paralia'), and inland ('mesogaia'), the three forming a new 'tribe' ('phyle') of which there are now ten in the state. These tribes are not based on one distinct geographical place, unlike the previous ones, so they are not dominated by the rich landed aristocrats. These new electoral areas are now used to elect the 'pool' of personnel from whom the new 'Council of Five Hundred' ('Boule') is chosen by lot; the council takes over the main administrative functions, certainly from the ex-archons' Areopagus council and possibly from Solon's 'Council of Four Hundred' if this still exists. In effect all the citizens have equal rights in politics as previously in justice; an equal chance at joining the government is provided by selecting which one of the ten committees (each of 50) in the 500 will govern the state when in the year, in rotation, by lot.

507/6

Archonship of Alcmaeon, from his name presumably a relative and ally of Cleisthenes, at Athens. This choice is probably to preserve the latter's new constitution from any 'comeback' by Isagoras and his oligarchic allies, and so provokes them into calling in Cleomenes again to aid a coup.

506

Spring – Cleomenes attempts to rectify his failure to help Isagoras earlier, by cozening the Peloponnesian League into sending troops to the Spartan army at the Isthmus for a campaign and not announcing the target until they have crossed the Athenian border to Eleusis. Meanwhile, his allies the Boeotian League, led by Thebes and hostile to Athens over the secession of Plataea, and Chalcis on Eretria attack Athens simultaneously from the north (via Oeonoe) and north-east. However, the Peloponnesians are unhappy at finding they are helping Sparta to restore an oligarchic faction at Athens as Sparta is supposed to be the foe of tyrants, and as the Athenian army arrives at Eleusis the Corinthians refuse to fight them. Cleomenes' co-ruler Demaratus agrees, refuses to go along with Cleomenes' plan, and withdraws his troops from the army. The army breaks up, and Cleomenes has to return home. At Sparta it is agreed that from now on only one king shall command in an overseas war at a time.

The Athenians head north-east for Euboea to deal with Chalcis, but coincidentally intercept the Boeotian army en route and defeat them, taking 700 prisoners; the same day they cross to Euboea and defeat the Chalcis army. The wealthy 'horse-owners' class of Chalcis are dispossessed and replaced by a colony of 4000 Athenian 'cleruchs' to control this state; these men keep their Athenian citizenship though living in another state. The Boeotian and Chalcis prisoners are ransomed at 50 drachmas a head, and a tenth of the money is used to commission bronze chains, which are hung up in a temple on the Acropolis as a trophy.

During this brief war, Thebes appeals to Athens' foe Aegina for help and the Aeginetan fleet attacks and burns the port of Phalerum in an unannounced, and thus generally disapproved of, act of war.

c. 505

Athens refuses a demand by Artaphernes, satrap of Lydia, on Darius' behalf to restore Hippias to power; the ex-tyrant goes to the congress of the Spartan-led 'Peloponnesian League' to ask them for help, and Sparta (probably via King Cleomenes) backs him, but Sosicles of Corinth persuades the allies to leave the plan alone. With a majority of the allies against backing Hippias, Sparta bows to their will. Hippias leaves Greece again and settles at Sigeum on the Hellespont, a family possession of the Peisistradae owned by his half-brother Hegistratus.

?At around this date King Cleomenes of Sparta attacks Argos, and during the course of a series of skirmishes between the two armies succeeds in driving the enemy troops into a supposedly sacred wood, which he blockades and then sets on fire; this may be the first sign of his later violent madness, and the insult to the gods is cited as reason for his later misfortunes.

501

Probable inauguration of the new board of ten generals ('strategoi'), commanding in rotation, to lead the Athenian army and fleet; the traditional annual commander, the 'polemarch', becomes largely honorary.

500

Aristagoras, tyrant of Miletus, interests his Persian overlords in extending their influence across the Aegean by aiding a faction of refugee oligarchs expelled from the island of Naxos; the Great King agrees to lend him troops for a naval expedition there to restore them to power as Persian vassals.

499

Spring–summer – Failure of a three-month siege of the eponymous 'capital' town of Naxos by Aristagoras, ruler of Miletus, and his Ionian/Persian army; the Persians blame him for making the expedition sound easy and he fears being reported to Darius and replaced.

Aristagoras is advised to start an Ionian revolt by his father-in-law and predecessor Histiaeus, now living at Darius' court in Susa. (According to Herodotus, Histiaeus tattoos his message on a slave's head, then waits while he grows his hair back and sends him to Miletus with a message to shave him.) Aristagoras, possibly realizing that he needs to use local anti-Persian feeling for his own benefit and pose as a national leader if he is not to be overthrown by his enemies as a Persian puppet, holds secret meetings of local notables to plan the war. He is advised by the geographer Hecataeus, who fears their being overwhelmed without outside help, to win control of the seas but does not take his advice to use the temple treasures of the shrine of Apollo at Didyma to pay for help. The Ionian fleet is still at Miletus after the Naxos expedition, and its captains are either suborned or arrested; Aristagoras announces the overthrow of the region's pro-Persian tyrants and proclaims his own abdication in the cause of democracy.

Winter – Aristagoras goes to Greece to ask for help, and visits Sparta but cannot interest its rulers – allegedly because he has to admit that the enemy capital is three months' march from the sea. Athens promises support (possibly due to anger over Darius backing the exiled Hippias), as does the city of Eretria on Euboea, and twenty Athenian and five Eretrian ships sail to join the rebel Ionian navy.

498

Spring/early summer – Once the promised ships have arrived from Greece, the Ionian navy sails into the mouth of the river Cayster in Lydia and lands at Ephesus, but Aristagoras stays at Miletus and sends his brother Charopinus instead; the rebels march upriver on and sack the satrapal capital of Lydia, Sardes, but satrap Artaphernes, Darius' nephew, holds the citadel. The sack of Sardes causes the revolt to spread to the Propontis, principally Byzantium, and to Caria to the south and on to Cyprus where Onesilus of Salamis leads the revolt and wins over most of the island except Amathus, which he attacks. Onesilus asks the Ionians for help.

Some months later, a Persian army under Daurises arrives in Lydia from inland and defeats the Ionian army at Ephesus, killing Eualcides the Eretrian commander; the Greeks flee to the coast. The Athenians and Eretrians go home. Darius sends Histiaeus to Lydia to advise Artaphernes on putting down the rebellion, as the latter has been pressing so that he would have the opportunity to defect; Daurises, Hymeas and Artybius (sons-in-law of Darius) gather large Persian armies ready to attack on three 'fronts'.

497

The piecemeal reconquest of Ionia commences; part of the coast in the north is reconquered by Daurises, who retakes Dardanus, Lampsacus, and Abydos on the Hellespont, and Hymeas.

Summer – Artybius and an army are taken by the Persian Phoenician fleet to rebel-held Cyprus to reconquer it. They land on the north coast without interception by the rebel fleet, and Artybius and the land-forces cross the island to attack Salamis, the main port on the east coast, with the fleet moving round to the east coast to cut it off from the sea. A land and sea battle follows near Salamis and Artybius is killed in combat, but some of the Cypriots desert led by Stesenor of Curium and the rebel land-army is defeated. The Ionian navy leaves Cyprus once the rebel-held towns are under siege.

Autumn – Daurises leads his army south to reconquer Caria in south Ionia and wins two major battles, the first against the locals at the river Marsyas and the second against a rescuing army of Ionians. While he is busy there, on the north-western 'front' Hymeas reconquers the southern Troad.

496

Fall of Soli on Cyprus to Persia after a four-month siege ends the rebellion there.

Hymeas and his north-western army in Ionia move south into Aeolis, but Hymeas dies; Artaphernes uses the army to take Cyme and Clazomenae. The army of Daurises is, however, heavily defeated in Caria and the other Persian army has to move south there to restore the situation.

Aristagoras leaves Miletus to set up a safer rebel base for himself in Thrace, but is killed at Myrcinus; Histiaeus arrives at Miletus seeking the return of his old command, is denied it by the citizens, and goes off to the Hellespont with a small fleet as a pirate. The Athenian colonial outpost in the Chersonese nearby is taken over by the future Athenian general Miltiades (II), nephew of its founding ruler Miltiades (I) and son of the Olympic chariot-victor Cimon.

495

Summer – As the Persian/Phoenician navy prepares to attack the main rebel centre at Miletus, the rebel cities and territories send envoys to a congress at the Panionium shrine and decide to base their fleet nearby at Lade to defend it. Three hundred and fifty-three ships assemble, commanded by Dionysius of Phocaea and centred on the fleets of Chios, Miletus, Samos, and Lesbos. The Persians send envoys promising a pardon for those who desert the rebels; these (including Aeces the ex-ruler of Samos) are officially defied, but soon the harsh training in ramming-tactics imposed on the fleet by Dionysius arouses discontent. As the Persian fleet, about twice the size of the Greek one, moves on Lade the Samian squadron sees the disorder of the Ionians, fears defeat, and flees except for eleven loyal ships, and the Lesbos squadron and others follow; the Chians (one hundred ships) lead the rebel defence, but lose about half their ships and abandon the fight. Dionysius takes three enemy ships and breaks out successfully to plunder off Phoenicia and then head for Sicily, and the rebel fleet disperses abandoning Miletus.

494

Siege, fall, and sack of Miletus; burning of the temple of Apollo at Didyma by the Persians. The inhabitants are deported to Susa by Darius. The Samians flee by sea to Italy rather than have Aeces put back as their ruler by Persia, and settle at Zancle (Messina), which the locals at Rhegium help them to take by evicting the current residents. The remaining rebel cities in Caria are either stormed or surrender; end of the Ionian rebellion. At around this time Histiaeus, having attacked Lesbos and Chios with his pirate ships, ventures onto the mainland in Mysia and is captured by Artaphernes' ally, the general Harpagus; he and Artaphernes impale Histiaeus so he will not be pardoned by Darius, and send his head to Darius who is not pleased.

494/3

Darius' son-in-law Mardonius, son of his 522 ally Gobryas, takes over the military command in Ionia, forces the Ionians to create a new league under Persian control where internal disputes will be dealt with by arbitration not war, and moves on via the Hellespont to Thrace to punish the restive tribes.

493/2

Mardonius conquers the Chersonese and also secures control of the Greek cities on the Propontis such as Byzantium. Miltiades has to flee the Chersonese, abandoning his base at Cardia with five ships, one of which the pursuing Persians take, and takes refuge in Athens to encourage resistance to Persia.

The non-aristocratic 'arriviste' Themistocles serves a term as chief 'archon' at Athens and commences the fortification of the Piraeus peninsula to protect Athens' adjacent harbours; this marks the switch of Athens under his direction to a increasingly naval orientation, in which she can stand out from land-bound Sparta.

The Athenian popular court (the assembly?) fines the playwright Phrynichus a thousand drachmas for his politically uncomfortable play 'The Fall of Miletus', a reminder of the recent horrors in Ionia.

Unsuccessful impeachment of Miltiades, on a charge of 'tyranny' in his rule as lord of the Chersonese – possibly a populist move against an ambitious rich aristocrat of uncertain political allegiances.

492

?Mardonius' fleet is sunk in a storm off Thrace as he is marching west; this probably brings a halt to any Persian plan for a land-based attack on mainland Greece, but King Alexander of Macedon becomes a Persian vassal around this time. The main military base of the Persian province of Thrace is at Doriscus.

491

Summer? – Aegina, Athens' naval rival on the Saronic Gulf, agrees a treaty with Persian envoys as a dependent ally of Darius and withdraws from its membership of the Peloponnesian League. Athens appeals to Sparta for help over this threat to Greek unity; King Cleomenes fails to win the backing of his co-king and long-term rival Demaratus, who is probably pro-Persian, but he goes to Aegina on his own to demand the surrender of the oligarchs that signed the Persian treaty; this is refused on the grounds that both kings are not present so this does not represent an official Spartan diplomatic initiative. He goes home to link up with Demaratus' half-brother Leotychidas and have Demaratus deposed in the latter's favour on a charge of being a bastard as his father, King Ariston, had public doubts over his paternity due to his marrying the baby's just-divorced mother barely nine months before it was born. Sparta asks the oracle at Delphi for advice, and the 'Pythia' priestess declares Demaratus to be a bastard – allegedly bribed by Cleomenes via a local friend of his.

With Leotychidas as his co-ruler, Cleomenes manages to persuade Sparta to attack Aegina. He and King Leotychidas lead an invasion, and the island is forced to surrender and ten members of its leadership are arrested; Cleomenes deports them to Athens for trial.

Autumn? – Cleomenes is accused by his enemies at Sparta of bribing the 'Pythia' at Delphi, and loses his nerve and flees to Thessaly; he moves closer to home, to Arcadia, to form a plot to invade Sparta and restore himself, and the worried Spartan government invites him home as king. Soon after his return, he apparently suffers a mental collapse (or so his critics claim in the 'official' story) and has to be placed under restraint; later he manages to get hold of a knife and kills himself (or possibly is murdered). His brother Leonidas succeeds him.

Sicily

?Hippocrates, the tyrant of Gela, is killed by Siceliots; he is succeeded by his brother Gelon, who deposes his young sons.

490

Greece

Aegina rallies support for its recent dealings with Darius at Sparta, probably with Demaratus, and succeeds in getting the 'ephors' to send Leotychidas to Athens to demand that the ten arrested pro-Persian oligarchs be released. Athens refuses on the grounds that both Spartan kings are not present so this is not an official Spartan request.

?Demaratus leaves Sparta for Persia in a rage to seek Darius' help after he is assured by his mother that he is legitimate and Leotychidas (who has just been abusing him at a public festival over his humiliating deposition) and Cleomenes cheated him out of his rights.

Persia/Greece

Darius sends a naval expedition across the Aegean to sack Athens and Eretria and demand submission there and along the route in reprisal for their support for the Ionian rebellion; the army is mustered in Cilicia and sails along the coast to Ionia. The Phoenician/Cilician/Ionian fleet is 600 vessels strong according to Herodotus, carrying a substantial army led by Darius' nephew, the successful 490s general/satrap Artaphernes, and admiral Datis. The exiled Athenian tyrant Hippias accompanies the expedition, and probably advises on tactics.

The expedition sails via Samos and lands on Naxos and sacks its principal town, deporting those who have not fled, but treats the sanctuary at Delos with respect as is usual for Persia's tolerance of other religions in its empire; after they leave Delos suffers a (rare) earthquake, seen by Herodotus as a sign of the crisis now coming to Greece; assorted Cycladean islands are forced to submit and supply troops to the expedition.

The Persians land at Carystus at the southern tip of Euboea, which resists; during the siege Eretria sends to warn Athens, which orders its 4000 colonists ('cleruchs') at Chalcis, at the narrows of the Euboea/mainland channel, to assist them; the Eretrians are divided over whether to resist or not, and the Athenians are sent off to safety in Attica on the advice of chief citizen Aeschines, and land at Oropus to warn their compatriots. After they leave, the Persians arrive and besiege the town for six days; on the seventh day traitors open the gates, and Eretria is looted, its temples are burnt, and its inhabitants are deported on the Persian fleet to Persia.

The Persian army lands on the bay of Marathon, on the East coast of Attica opposite Euboea, and disembarks the cavalry ready for a battle on the flat plain if Athens attacks; if not they will advance on the city, parallel to their fleet. Hippias lands on his home territory after twenty years, acting as the Persians' guide and in charge of the Eretrian prisoners. The Athenians hold a meeting of the assembly, decide to advance to Marathon, and send the runner Pheidippides to Sparta for help, a journey of one hundred and forty miles covered in one day. The Spartans reply that the feast of the Carneia is underway but they can come after the full moon, in six days, on the sixteenth day of the Athenian month 'Boedromion'. Pheidippides returns to Athens.

The Athenian army of around 10,000 'hoplites' plus 600 Plataean allies moves forward to the town of Marathon at the west end of its plain, inland from the Persian camp on the beach; the annually elected board of ten generals ('strategoi') is divided with five, led by Miltiades the ex-ruler of the Chersonese (who has served in the Persian army in Thrace), in favour of an attack and five in favour of waiting until the Spartans arrive. The overall commander, the 'polemarch' Callimachus of Aphidna, is summoned to give the deciding vote, and Miltiades intercepts and wins him over en route; an attack is ordered and as Miltiades has the only experience of fighting Persians his main supporter, Aristides, announces that when it is his day for the command on the rota he will give the command to Miltiades; the other three generals in favour of an attack agree to do this too.

('16th Boedromion, Athenian calendar) The Spartan army sets out for Athens as the moon sets.

('17th Boedromion', Athenian calendar) Battle of Marathon – a few nights after Aristides' plan at the generals' meeting, an Ionian delivers a message to the Greek camp that the Persians have 'sent away' their cavalry (probably meaning loading it on the fleet, i.e. ready to sail and march on Athens next day). The Athenians move into position under Miltiades' direction, the Athenians on the right wing and in the centre and their Plataean allies from Boeotia on the left wing; the line is extended so as to match the Persians' line and avoid them being enveloped. At dawn the Greeks attack and charge the Persian line, and the 'deeper' wings drive the Persians back with the aid of their better defensive armour and spears. The Persians hold out and push the Greeks back in the centre, but the Greek wings move in on them from the sides and drive the larger Persian army into a confused mass; the remaining Persian cavalry on the beach cannot identify a clear target to charge at in the melee. Eventually, the Persians break and flee to the safety of a marsh, north-east of the battlefield, and those who can embark on the ships do so; seven of the ships are captured. As identified from the burial mound at the site, 192 Greeks are killed, with probably around 6400 Persian casualties. The most notable Athenian casualties are Callimachus and the brother of the dramatist Aeschylus.

The Persian fleet sails off for Cape Sunion en route for Athens, and the Greeks note a flashing shield apparently signalling to them in the sunlight from up on the ridge inland – presumably a signal from traitors in Athens. They head back to Athens to defend it, with Pheidippides running ahead to announce the victory and memorably collapsing dead after doing so. The Greeks arrive at the Bay of Phalerum before the Persians do so, and the Persians see the enemy drawn up on the shore by a temple of Heracles and sail off for Asia Minor.

'18th Boemodromion' (Athenian calendar) Next day: 2000 Spartans arrive at Athens after a two-day march, early in the morning, and go on to view the battlefield.

489

?Miltiades leads an expedition of seventy ships across the Cyclades to punish those islands who 'medized' and levy fines on them. Paros, next to Naxos, holds out and refuses to pay up; Miltiades besieges the main town, but is wounded and gives up the siege on the twenty-sixth day. On his return to Athens he is prosecuted for accepting a bribe to leave Paros, and has to defend himself on a stretcher in court; the prosecutor is his political rival, the populist aristocrat Xanthippus (father of the later statesman Pericles) who is married to the late democratic leader Cleisthenes' niece Agariste. Miltiades has to pay a heavy fine, but dies before he can do so; his (teenage?) son Cimon does so instead.

487

Revolt in Egypt; Darius has to send his fleet there instead of back to Greece as planned.

Greece
The annual selection of the archons at Athens is changed from election to a choice by lot; this reduces the influence of the factions and clientage in selection. The institution of the annual 'ostracism' (i.e. a vote of the populace to expel an unpopular citizen for ten years, by secret ballot, if the public first decide there is a need for this) is either created or is first used in the year 488/7.

486

Persia
February/March? – Death of Great King Darius, probably in his sixties; succeeded by his son by Cyrus' daughter Atossa, Xerxes.
   June – Revolt against the Persian empire breaks out in Egypt.

Greece
Ostracism at Athens of the reputedly munificent and luxury-loving Megacles, nephew of the later reformer Cleisthenes and presumably as an Alcmaeonid an aristocratic rival of the democrats.

485

Ostracism at Athens of the statesman/general Xanthippus, married to Cleisthenes' niece and the father of the future leader Pericles (born mid-late 490s); due to his role in prosecuting Miltiades earlier this is possibly an oligarchic 'fight-back' by Miltiades' friends against the democrats or the Alcmaeonids.

Sicily
?The Gamoroi, an oligarchic faction ruling Syracuse, are expelled by rivals and flee to the city of Gela to get help from its tyrant, Gelon; he invades and takes Syracuse with them but then makes himself its ruler and transfers his base of power there. Leaving his brother Theron to rule Gela, he creates the new 'power' of Syracuse as the main city on the east coast and fortifies the mainland suburb of the small island citadel, Ortygia, to make it more secure.

483/2

Greece
Ostracism of Aristides by Athens, allegedly arranged by his main foe Themistocles and as such a triumph for the more radical democrats over the cautious moderates; he is, however, recalled later in time to command in the war in 480 by a vote to recall all the ostracized citizens arranged by Themistocles c.482/1.
   A new gold-mine is discovered at Laurium in southern Attica, and Themistocles carries a proposal that it should be used to build a larger fleet – this is now 200 warships. As the ships are to be manned by rowers from the lower classes, a larger fleet also reflects their increased political prominence.

482/1

Greece/Persia

Xerxes orders the assembly of a huge army and fleet for an invasion of Greece in 480, and a channel is cut through the 'neck' of the peninsula of Mount Athos in the Chalcidice to make sailing that route safer; food-dumps are to be assembled en route by allies.

481

Late summer? – The Greek states send enquiries to the oracle at Delphi about how to resist Persia; Sparta is told that it will either lose its city or its king and Argos is allegedly told to stay neutral.

September – Following a discouraging reply to a query about their fate to the oracle at Delphi, which says that Athens will be sacked, the Athenians vote to trust Themistocles' argument that the 'wooden walls' that will save them are the fleet, not the walls of the Acropolis; plans are made to evacuate Attica and the fleet is strengthened.

October? – The Greeks who are willing to fight Persia meet at Sparta, and set up a formal alliance; Sparta will command their army and fleet. Corcyra and Sicily are asked to send help; meanwhile, most of Boeotia and a few other states receive envoys, which are sent out by Persia and promise to submit. Reportedly an unsuccessful Greek request for help is sent to Gelon, ruler of Syracuse in Sicily, but he demands the command of all the Greek forces as his price for bringing 24,000 troops and is refused this.

480

Spring – The Greek states hold a congress at the Isthmus of Corinth to formalize their alliance and plans for the war. Thessaly sends to ask for a force to be sent to close the pass of the Vale of Tempe, without which they will be forced to submit to Persia; Euenetus the Spartan and 10,000 troops are sent there, but find that the Persians could easily use passes south from Macedon to the west and outflank them; a withdrawal is agreed, allegedly backed by local expert king Alexander of Macedon who warns that he will have to aid Persia.

The Persian army assembles at Sardes in Lydia, and advances on the Hellespont. Megabazus and Prexaspes bring the main Persian/Phoenician fleet up the Ionian coast parallel to the Persian army, while a major Ionian Greek contingent is commanded by Queen Artemisia of Halicarnassus; Xerxes' brothers Ariabignes and Achaemenes command the Egyptian and Ionian land-contingents, his cousin Artaphernes commands the Lydians, his brother-in-law Artochmes commands the Phrygians and Armenians, his wife Amestris' father Otanes commands the Persians, his brother Gobryas commands the Syrians, his brother Arsames commands the Arabians and 'Ethiopians' (Nubians?), his brother Hystaspes commands the Bactrians, Azanes the Sogdians from Central Asia, Pharnazathres the Indians, and Artabazus the Parthians. Xerxes arrives at Sardes from Susa.

Xerxes crosses the Hellespont on a 'bridge of boats' (360 ships supporting the upper, Northern passageway, and 314 the lower one) and invades Thrace, where the local tribes submit as do Macedon and Thessaly.

June–July? – The Persian 'host that drank the rivers dry', allegedly several million men strong but probably 300,000 or so at most, advance from their base at Doriscus in Thrace across Macedon into Thessaly, using up 'food-dumps' set up beforehand by their advance-forces and allies as far as possible; a fleet of 1200 ships (300 of them Greek Ionian ones), led by the Phoenician navy and squadrons from Cyprus and Egypt, heads along the northern Aegean shores parallel to this.

The Persian fleet waits at Thermae in Macedon while Xerxes, avoiding the Vale of Tempe coastal route into Thessaly, which could be blocked, has a road constructed across the hills west of Mount Olympus as an easier route.

The Greek congress held at the Isthmus of Corinth decides to defend the pass of Thermopylae into Phocis and Boeotia from Thessaly, and to station the fleet parallel to it at Artemisium at the north end of the Euboea channel. The designated army of around 6–7000 'hoplites', commanded by Spartan king Leonidas with 300 Spartan citizens, 1000 non-citizen Laconians, 2800 other Peloponnesians, 700 Thespians, and 400 Thebans, arrives at Thermopylae with Xerxes already approaching them across Trachis from Thessaly. The fleet under the Spartan commander Eurybiades consists of 271 ships, led by 147 from Athens; it moves into position at the cape of Artemisium, and backs into the narrow Euboean channel after a first clash between a reconnaissance squadron of ten Persian ships and three Greek ones off the island of Sciathos. As the Greeks pull back to the narrows of Chalcis, to the rear of their land-army's position at Thermopylae so presenting a danger of a Persian landing on the mainland, the Persians move south along the rocky coast of Magnesia in calm weather and drop anchor for the night, but are caught at dawn in a three-day storm with Easterly winds that blow them onshore; they lose up to 400 ships.

The Greeks hear of the storm, recover their nerve, and return to Artemisium to protect the parallel land-army at Thermopylae; the Persian survivors move south into the Bay of Pagasae and confront them.

(Four days before the start of fighting at Thermopylae – 12/13 September?) Xerxes' land-army arrives in the plain north of Thermopylae; the Persian navy is meant to arrive parallel to this, at sea, but is late due to the storm.

(Two days later – 14/15 September?) The Persian navy arrives at the Bay of Pagasae to refit before the battle; this forces Xerxes to postpone his planned simultaneous land and naval attacks. A two-day halt ensues for refitting.

(Two days later – 16/17 September?) At night, a Persian naval squadron is sent off at sea round the east side of Euboea, to take control of the south exit from the Euboea/mainland channel and stop the Greeks evacuating their fleet that way after a defeat. This is not noticed by the Greeks, but later in the day a Greek diver in the Persian navy called Scyllias arrives at the Greek naval base after a lengthy swim, to report on the squadron's move and on the extent of losses in the storm. A meeting of captains is held; most Greeks prefer to withdraw back down the channel once it is dark to attack the missing naval squadron as it arrives at the south end of the channel next day, but this is cancelled when it becomes apparent that the main Persian navy is not moving. One version has it (recorded by Plutarch) that the Euboeans bribe the Greeks not to desert them.

On land, the first attack develops against the Greek position, a repaired stone wall in the narrows of the pass at Thermopylae, which is only around fifty yards wide. This attack is pushed back; wave after wave of Persians make no visible impression on the defenders. Meanwhile, a force of Phocians has been sent by Leonidas to protect the path across the mountains to the south, which if taken by the Persians would 'turn' the Greek position.

Towards evening, the main Persian fleet moves out into the north end of the Euboea channel; the Greeks form a circle and dare the enemy to attack this, which they do; the Greeks row out and ram their attackers, who are pushed back but not decisively. Both sides hold their positions at dusk.

(That night) Another storm hits the Persian fleet, with southerly winds blowing the wreckage of the battle into the Persian ships; meanwhile, the storm wrecks the squadron of 200 Persian ships sent round the east side of Euboea so the Greeks cannot be taken in the rear.

(Next day – 17/18 September?) Second day of Persian infantry attacks on Thermopylae; fifty-five more Athenian ships join the Greek fleet. The Greeks attack again that evening and sink some Cilician ships; Xerxes still has more ships and he orders a Persian naval attack next day. That evening near dusk, the traitor Ephialtes of Malis informs the Persians at Thermopylae of the path round the south of the mountains to the rear of the Greek position. Xerxes orders his senior general Hydarnes and the crack regiment of the 10,000 'Immortals', the Great King's bodyguard, to take the path.

(Night) The 'Immortals' proceed along the path without being noticed.

(Next day – 18/19 September?) At first light, the 'Immortals' reach the Phocian position and are spotted; the defenders retire to a defensible hillock, but the Persians ignore them and march on. Leonidas is informed that the position at Thermopylae is untenable, and famously sends his army off to safety but proposes to hold the Persians back with his 300 Spartan citizens to protect their rear. The Thespians refuse to leave, and stay with Leonidas; he advances to a wider position in front of the narrowest part of the pass and (around 11 a.m.) the Persians attack. The Greeks are killed to the last man, apart from a regiment of Thebans who notoriously surrender – the only time a Spartan king will fall in battle until 371. Perhaps 20,000 Persians and 4000 Greeks are killed.

The naval battle rages all day off Artemisium, and the Greeks hold out with the Athenian captain Cleinias, father of the later statesman/general Alcibiades, distinguishing himself; however, losses are great, and half the Athenian ships are put out of action. Towards dusk news of the fall of Thermopylae arrives, and Eurybiadas announces withdrawal to the bay of Piraeus off Athens.

(Night) The fleet withdraws, leaving its camp-fires burning.

(Next day: 19/20 September?) A Persian force lands to find the camp at Artemisium empty; Xerxes marches on into Doris.

The Persians enter Boeotia via Phocis as the Greeks abandon the idea of a stand there with Chaeronea and Thebes both 'medizing'; Thebes leads the surrender but Plataea and Thespiae are sacked as their populace flee; a ?small Persian force heads for Delphi but retreats after rocks fall from the cliffs during a thunderstorm.

The Greek navy assembles in the Bay of Salamis, and Athens is evacuated onto the island as the Greek congress meeting at the Isthmus decides not to defend Attica to the fury of Athens. In accordance with Themistocles' decision of 481 that the 'wooden walls' that the oracle at Delphi says will save Athens are her fleet, not the wooden walls of the Acropolis, the city is abandoned; Argos and the neighbouring states stay neutral but Sparta, led by Pausanias the nephew of king Leonidas (now regent for his son Pleistarchus), starts to build a defensive wall across the Isthmus. Leonidas' brother Cleombrotus commands the army at the Isthmus, and Eurybiadas of Sparta commands the allied fleet at Salamis but the most forceful of his assistants are Themistocles and Aristides for Athens.

28 September (as calculated back from the coming eclipse) – Nine days after the end of the naval fighting at Artemisium, the Persian army marches into the evacuated Athens in the morning; the temples' treasurers and a force of volunteers hold out on the Acropolis, and Xerxes camps at the Areopagus and sends the defenders some of the exiled Peisistradae to offer terms of surrender but this is refused. Some Persians climb a path up the cliff onto the Acropolis, and the defenders either commit suicide by jumping off the rock or are overwhelmed; Xerxes burns the Acropolis and sends a victory message to Susa. The sight of the flames causes the Greek captains on Salamis to panic, and at a meeting before midday the majority propose to withdraw to the Isthmus sooner than be cut off and some leave immediately; Eurybiadas agrees, but is talked round by Themistocles who gets him to call a second meeting and steadies the captains' nerves but threatens to take the Athenians off to the west and found a new colony as a Corinthian jeers at him as now being 'stateless'. The Greek fleet is blockaded in the Bay of Salamis, with the exits east and west of the island guarded by the Persian fleet, which now arrives off Athens; at midday the Persian fleet puts out from the Piraeus to reconnoitre Salamis but withdraws after the Greeks do not move.

Late in the day, the Persian army starts to move west along the coast out of Athens, heading for the Megarid and thence the Isthmus; the Peloponnesians in the fleet want to move out to defend the Isthmus at sea, but the captains of Athens, Aegina, and Megara hold firm. Eurybiadas calls another meeting, and Themistocles quickly lures Xerxes to attack before the Greek fleet can break up by sending his slave Sicinnus to tell the Great King's admirals that the Greeks will retreat next day and he is prepared to assist the Persians.

28/9 September, night – Xerxes' commanders, convinced by Sicinnus, land a force of Persian marines on the island of Psyttalia in the middle of the eastern channel out of the Salamis narrows. The main Persian squadron moves to block the eastern exit, and a smaller one is sent round to the western exit; Aristides, arriving on Salamis from Aegina, spots this second force of Persian ships moving in on the western channel and tells Themistocles at the captains' conference, which has now begun. The latter gets Aristides to make his report, and talks the other commanders round to a battle next day; a ship from Tenos in the Persian navy arrives in secret to deliver the Persian battle-arrangements, which increases the Greeks' confidence. Before dawn, Themistocles addresses the marines on Sileniae beach about his tactics and they board the ships.

29 September, Battle of Salamis – 380 Greek ships against around 1200 Persian ships, with the main Greek line running north-south along the east coast of Salamis, facing the mainland where Xerxes sets up his throne on the promontory of Heraclea to watch the battle. The Corinthians protect the west entrance to the channel, in the Bay of Salamis north of the island. At dawn the Greeks assemble out of sight of the Persians and form up into columns for the advance south down the channel into their positions; the fastest, Aeginetan ships are in the vanguard and then the Spartans and Megarans, followed by the Athenians. As they move down the channel, they find the Phoenicians on the Persian right wing in a north-south line, closest to the shore and the Great King's throne, with the Ionians on the left (south) out to sea. As the Persians advance the Phoenicians take the lead, and the Persian left wing out to sea lags behind. The Phoenicians round the cape into the narrows, and the Greeks move down on them (moving South) with the Aeginetans in the lead; they then swing leftwards (east) to attack. The Athenians on the Greek left back water

to lure the Phoenicians in towards the narrowest part of the channel between Psyttalia and the mainland, then Themistocles orders an attack as the 'swell' starts to affect the heavy Phoenician ships. The Athenians ram them, and the Phoenicians are too tightly packed to manoeuvre; the Greeks all attack, and Aristides notices the Persian marines on Psyttalia and takes a force of Greek marines across from Salamis town to overpower them. The Phoenicians break first, and fleeing ships crash into those not yet engaged; the Persians are driven back, aided by a rising westerly wind, and eventually break off the battle to flee back to Phalerum bay off Athens leaving several hundred ships destroyed. The Greek losses of shipping are small, but many men have been killed and the Persian navy is still formidable but is now caught in an exposed bay with winter weather approaching. Xerxes thinks of erecting a boom to protect it from attack, but is told this is impractical and orders his fleet to withdraw out of reach to the Hellespont.

Early October to mid-November? – Xerxes marches back to the Hellespont in forty-five days, nervous that the Greeks will sail to the Hellespont and destroy his bridge of boats; he leaves a large occupation-force (60–70,000??) in Thessaly under his brother-in-law Mardonius and himself retires all the way to Susa; the Boeotians remain loyal to Persia ready for a new campaign in 479.

The Greek fleet advances across the Aegean to Andros without sighting the Persian navy, fails to force that island to pay compensation for 'medizing', but levies fines elsewhere; the leadership rejects Themistocles' proposal to sail to the Hellespont and destroy the bridge of boats, and allegedly Aristides urges them not to bottle up the Persians in Greece or they will fight more strongly. Themistocles then sends Sicinnus or a captive eunuch to Xerxes to claim credit for this decision. The Greek fleet returns to Salamis to set up trophies of victory and send captured ships' prows to Delphi; Aegina is awarded the prize for valour among the contingents, and Themistocles is invited to Sparta and feted there as a hero with a chariot and an honorary escort.

Sicily

Invasion of western Sicily by a large Carthaginian force in two hundred ships, led by the general Hamilcar; up to 300,000 men according to sources but probably fewer. The invasion is allegedly – or perhaps mostly – about restoring Terillus, Greek tyrant of Himera, who has been expelled by Theron of Akragas (father-in-law of Gelon of Syracuse) and who accompanies the invaders. It is not necessarily co-ordinated with Persia's attack on Greece, but presumably the Carthaginians have been informed by their mother-city, Tyre in Phoenicia, of its fleet's forthcoming role in the attack on Greece.

Hamilcar lands his army at Panormus, and plans to march along the north coast west to Himera to restore Terillus (?) and then east to Messina to link up with the tyrant Anaxilas of Rhegium, son-in-law of Terillus and foe of Carthage's enemy Gelon of Syracuse. Theron of Akragas blocks the Carthaginian advance on land and sea at Himera on the north coast, and Hamilcar leads his army to besiege him there in a three-day march from Panormus, camping to the west of the city. Gelon arrives with 50,000 infantry and 5000 cavalry, and relieves the siege by sending supplies into the city; he then camps at the eastern side of the city. According to Diodorus (but not the nearer-contemporary Herodotus), his patrols secure a messenger from pro-Carthage Selinus saying when their cavalry will arrive to aid the Carthaginians. At the appointed time a force of Gelon's cavalry turn up at the enemy camp pretending to be from Selinus, are admitted, and set fire to the Carthaginian fleet, possibly killing Hamilcar while he is conducting a sacrifice. The chaos, spotted in Himera, is the signal for the Syracusan army to attack the camp; Hamilcar is killed if still alive (Herodotus has him jump into the sacrificial fire as he is surrounded), and the Carthaginians' Iberian (Spanish) mercenaries rally but are driven back. The invaders hold onto a strongpoint and are blockaded there without access to water until they surrender. Carthage has to pay 7000 talents as ransom and agree to peace on Gelon's terms.

479

Persia / Greece

Winter – Sack of Olynthus in the Chalcidice by the local satrap Artabazus for a suspected plot; the population are rounded up and massacred. Successful revolt by Potidaea, which holds out; to the south, there is a guerrilla war in Phocis.

Spring – The Greek fleet of 110 ships musters at Aegina under King Leotychidas of Sparta and advances as far as Delos; meanwhile, Mardonius sends King Alexander of Macedon to Athens to offer independence, alliance and compensation if they leave the Greek league but these are refused. Sparta offers to protect and resettle the Athenians, but as their clients somewhere on the Peloponnese.

July – Mardonius invades Attica again, which is evacuated to Salamis, and sends to offer the Athenians alliance again; his envoy is received by the exiled Athenian 'Boule' on Salamis and refused, and the one councillor who backs alliance with Persia is immediately executed. Athens, Megara and Plataea (South Boeotia) all send a joint embassy to Sparta to ask them to invade Persian-occupied territories quicker and threaten to negotiate with Persia if this is not done, and the Spartan 'ephors' insolently keep them waiting through the 'Hyacinthia' festival before telling them at the end of it that the army at the Isthmus is already moving forward.

As the Greek army marches across the Isthmus Mardonius burns Athens and retires via Decelia to Boeotia to fight on more level ground suitable for his huge cavalry force. He sets up camp in the plain in South Boeotia below the ridge of Mount Cithaeron, with possibly 200,000 men and a huge stockaded camp; 1000 Phocians have to join the Persian army, and as they arrive Mardonius shows them how effective his cavalry is on manoeuvres as a warning.

In total, 5000 Spartan citizens, 5000 'periocoi', and 35,000 'helots' march from the Isthmus under Pausanias, regent for the young king Pleistarchus, and Aristides commands 8000 Athenians while Corinth sends 5000, Tegea 1500, 600 Plataeans, 3000 Megarans, and 500 from Aegina; the Boeotians except Plataea are fighting for Persia. There are 38,700 'hoplites' from twenty-four states, and 70,000 light infantry plus a few cavalry.

(Probably c. 10/20 August?) – The Greek navy advances from Delos to Samos to attack the Persians, after some Samian democrats led by Hegistratus came to the Greeks to say that the local regime under tyrant Theomestor is unpopular and the Greeks' arrival will start a revolution. The omens are taken on Delos and are said to be favourable to a Greek attack.

(Probably c. 20/23 August?) – At Plataea, Athens is given the Greek left wing, with Plataea next to them, then Megara and Aegina, and Sparta takes the right wing with Corinth and Tegea next to them. The Greeks advance from Mount Cithaeron to Plataea, but they are short of water up in the hills and Mardonius' cavalry prevents them from foraging on the plain and ambushes their supply-convoys coming across the passes from the Megarid. Mardonius waits for the Greek army to split up with the traditional quarrels, but suffers a reverse when Athenian infantry and archers sent to rescue the Megarans' camp from attacks kill his cavalry commander Masistius and routs a heavy cavalry ambush.

One night a horseman, believed to be King Alexander of Macedon, arrives at the Greek camp to say that the Persians have moved their best infantry from opposite the Spartans to opposite the Athenians and will attack at dawn; this may be either a move by him to betray Mardonius or a ploy by Mardonius to encourage the Greeks to fight. The Greeks move their infantry accordingly, but when next morning Mardonius sees the Spartans opposite his best infantry he declines battle again. The Persian cavalry attacks and blocks the main local spring at Gargaphia, and as a result Pausanias calls a council and decides to move that night to a new position. The army mostly starts to move once it is dark, but an obstinate Spartan officer called Amompharetus refuses to withdraw in the face of the enemy as it is cowardly and while Pausanias is arguing with him the news that the Spartans are still in position causes the Athenians and Tegeans to stay put too. At dawn Pausanias finally orders the Spartans to move off, via the foothills to avoid a cavalry attack, and Amompharetus and his company follow at a leisurely pace while the Athenians move off across the plain parallel to them.

(End of August) Battle of Plataea – the Persian cavalry makes for the expected Greek position, find it has been abandoned, and spot and attack Pausanias and Amompharetus on the march. Mardonius thinks the Greek army has broken up, and orders his infantry to charge them; the Greeks in the Persian army, led by the Boeotians, attack the Athenians who Pausanias tells too late to join up with his own troops, and the main Persian infantry attacks the Spartans and Tegeans. The Persians fire arrows at the Spartans before closing with them and waiting behind a 'wall' of their wicker shields, but the Spartan shields deflect the arrows and as the omens are declared favourable Pausanias orders a charge downhill onto the Persians. The Spartans break the Persian 'shield-wall' and drive the enemy back in hand-to-hand combat, the huge Persian infantry force being too closely packed to co-ordinate tactics easily, and the lack of Persian armour causes them severe casualties. Mardonius leads a cavalry charge by 1000 elite Median horsemen to crash into the Spartans, but is knocked off his horse and cut down and his men flee; the Persians are chased back to their camp, and the mass of men means that the untouched main Persian cavalry cannot get through them to tackle the pursuing Greeks. The Greek centre push forward down onto the plain where the Theban cavalry rally against them and 600 are killed and the rest flee back uphill, but the disintegrating Persian army forces the Boeotians, who are fighting the Athenians, to pull back as their elite force of 300 is destroyed. The Boeotians withdraw into Thebes, and Artabazus pulls back his cavalry and part of the centre, north across Booetia, abandoning the Persian camp which is so far holding out against the Spartans. The camp is overrun and looted, and the abandoned Persian infantry is destroyed; no prisoners are taken.

The Greeks agree to conduct solemn commemorative ceremonies and hold Games every year on the battlefield, and confirm the continuation of the League to liberate the rest of the Greeks, led by Sparta; 10,000 'hoplites', 1000 cavalry, and 100 warships are to be levied every year for the war.

(Late August; traditionally the same day as the battle of Plataea) Battle of Cape Mycale – The Greek fleet of 110 ships (Herodotus), commanded by King Leotychidas of Sparta with Xanthippus, the commander of the Athens contingent, among his senior officers, engages the main Persian fleet at Cape Mycale near Samos. The Persians have withdrawn there from their base on Samos to the mainland a few days before and (Herodotus) have sent their Phoenician contingent away. The Persians join a land army of 60,000 under Tigranes. According to Diodorus the overall Persian total of men is 100,000.

The Persians rely on their army on the beach, in a stockaded camp, to protect their beached fleet, and refuse to sail out to fight; Leotychidas fails to entice the Persians out, and sails his flagship inshore to have a herald shout encouragement to the Ionian contingent to defect when opportune and announce a password for this ('Hera'). He then sails on to land his men down the coast, while the nervous Persian commander disarms his Samian troops lest they defect and sends the Milesians away from his camp to protect its approaches. The Persians defend their camp on the beach, using their shields as a 'wall', and the Greeks advance eastwards on it – allegedly spurred on by a rumour of their land victory in Greece, which Leotychidas may announce before the battle. The Athenian/Corinthian/Sicyon/ Troezen troops (on the right wing, by the sea) arrive first, and defeat the opposing Persian infantry, storm the rampart, and break into the Persian camp; then the Spartans on the left wing, who have had further to go (inland), arrive. As the camp is overrun the Ionians mutiny and turn on the Persians. The latter are routed, around 40,000 men are killed, and their navy is burnt; naval commanders Artayntes and Ithamitres escape but Tigranes is killed; Artayntes is abused as a 'woman' for his incompetent cowardliness as the survivors retreat by Xerxes' brother, prince Masistes, and tries to kill him but is driven off by the Halicarnassan mercenary Xenagoras who Xerxes makes governor of Cilicia.

The Greek allies hold a meeting with the Ionians on Samos. The Spartans (who are not used to a long-term naval commitment and overseas allies) advise their new Ionian allies to evacuate their territory and move to places that the Greeks can defend, from which 'medizers' will be expelled to make room for them; the Athenians, however, offer to assist in protecting the defectors from Persia and accordingly Lesbos, Chios, and Samos (who have fleets) and other islands are taken into the Greek alliance – but not mainland states as yet.

Late Autumn – Leotychidas leads the fleet as it sails to Abydus to destroy Xerxes' bridge across the Hellespont, but it has been washed away by storms; Leotychidas and the Peloponnesians sail home, leaving Xanthippus and the Athenians/Ionians to besiege the Persian garrison in Sestus. After some weeks the garrison is starved out and breaks out to flee, and its commander Astyoches is captured with his son and executed by Xanthippus after local accusations that he looted the local treasures at the tomb of Trojan War hero Protesilaus for his own use; other prominent Persians are captured too but are ransomed, and general Oeobazus escapes into the Chersonese with some troops but is captured and sacrificed by local Thracians. The chains of Xerxes' bridge are taken back to Athens as a trophy of war.

Themistocles takes the lead in persuading the other Greeks of the alliance not to evict all states who 'medized' permanently from their counsels, as he fears this will give Sparta a permanent majority in votes.

The Mid-fifth Century 478 to 432

478

Late summer? (after the harvest) – The congress of the Greeks meets.

Pausanias leads a Greek naval expedition directed by the congress to Cyprus to destroy Persian/Phoenician shipping, and then goes to the Hellespont and on through the Propontis to reduce Byzantium. However, he does not pursue the war after that, and is increasingly living in luxury; his arrogance and dictatorial behaviour in command causes discontent among the Ionians, and the captains from the main Ionian islands with navies, Chios, Lesbos, and Samos, ask the Athenian commander Aristides to take over command and set up a new naval alliance led by Athens. This can protect them if Pausanias then turns on them. Aristides agrees if the Ionians will show that they are sincere, and they do so by driving Pausanias out of Byzantium in a mutiny. Sparta recalls Pausanias, and Aristides takes over command (officially until a new Spartan commander can arrive, but the Ionians are disinclined to accept the latter either).

(or 476) The Greek congress sends out an expedition by land under King Leotychidas of Sparta to punish the pro-Persians of 480–79 in Thessaly, especially the Aleudae dynasty of Pherae/Larissa, and drive out or gain the submission of all Persian allies in the region. The expedition gets as far as Pharsalus, defeats and expels local princes Aristomenes and Angelos, but cannot or will not expel the Aleudae who rally a strong force (especially cavalry) to oppose them. Leotychidas gives up and goes home, and the angry Spartan government impeaches and deposes him for allegedly accepting bribes; he is exiled and replaced by his grandson Archidamus as king. (Leotychidas dies in exile around 469, aged probably over seventy.)

Late? – Pausanias is accused of misbehaviour as the naval commander and acquitted, but allegations of intrigues with Persia are more difficult to disprove and he is sacked by Sparta as commander and as regent for the young King Pleistarchus, son of Leonidas; he withdraws to Byzantium, where he has made local allies, and sets himself up as its ruler. Sparta sends out Dorcis to command the Greek fleet in the Propontis, but the Ionians refuse to accept him or any other Spartan; the Spartan contingent goes home and probably this blow is blamed on an Athenian/Ionian plot from the later hostility of elements at Sparta to Athens in the mid-470s.

Sicily

Death of Gelon, ruler of Syracuse and Gela; succeeded by his brother Hieron.

478/7

Greece

Winter – Foundation of the new 'Delian League' by Athens and its partisans to replace the defunct Spartan-led alliance against Persia. It is centred on the sanctuary of Apollo at Delos, where the founding congress is held presided over by Aristides, and where the treasury is set up. It is led and dominated (due to naval predominance) by Athens; the 'Athenians and their Allies', as it is formally known, centres on an initial link of unbreakable friendship/offensive and defensive military alliance/oath-taking between Athens and the Ionian states, to which others later join. The state of Athens and the assembly of the Allies form the two parts of the institution, with Athens as 'hegemon' (commander) supplying the main fleet and army and arranging contributions of men and ships and providing the treasurers ('Hellenotamiae', 'treasurers of the Greeks'). Athens takes half of all proceeds of war; the allied congress, with one vote per state, decides policy with a majority vote binding on all; the state of Athens and the allied congress can propose policies on an equal status and have to agree for a policy to be enacted.

The annual tribute assessment is first arranged and assessed for the year 478/7; it amounts to 460 talents (including or excluding Athens?), and the assessments are carried out to general approval by Aristides 'the Just' of Athens.

477

Autumn? – The Delian League opens its naval operations with an expedition, led by Cimon, to besiege the Persian-allied/garrisoned town of Eion in coastal western Thrace.

476/5

Probable date of the Delian League expedition to the Hellespont to destroy Persian power there. Sestos on its western shore is captured and incorporated into the League; the fleet advances to Byzantium, blockades it, and forces the pro-Persian ruler Pausanias (ex-regent of Sparta) to flee to the Troad; Byzantium joins the League.

(Same campaign?) Athens' fleet under Cimon reconquers Eion from Persia, ending their possessions west of the Hellespont, and enslaves its inhabitants; it becomes an Athenian colony. Cimon also takes over the north-western Aegean island of Scyros for an Athenian colony and expels or enslaves its piratical indigenous residents; he claims to have found the bones of the Athenian hero-king Theseus, who traditionally died in exile there, and brings them back to Athens in a propaganda move.

475?

According to Thucydides, a formal debate on policy towards Athens take place at the 'Gerousia' in Sparta around now; some militants want a war on Athens to recover naval hegemony, but the elder statesman Hetoemaridas successfully persuades the meeting that Sparta has never held a successful naval role and it is not her real strength so it should be left to Athens, which is still well-disposed to Sparta.

475/3?

(Precise date unclear.) The town of Carystus in Euboea, a former Persian ally, is forced to join the Delian League, logically as an important port on the route north-east across the Aegean to the Hellespont.

473/2?

(Precise date unclear.) After the Carystus episode, the largest island in the Cyclades, Naxos, attempts to secede from the Delian League but is attacked and forced to stay in it by Athens.

Pausanias is recalled to Sparta to face arrest for intrigues with Persia and surprisingly accepts; he is placed under house-arrest and successfully argues that there should be a quick trial, probably aware of his foes' lack of hard evidence. He is acquitted due to lack of evidence, but the suspicious 'ephors' continue to spy on him as he lives in the city as a private citizen and he is accused of planning to raise the 'helots' in a revolution to make himself tyrant. Later, his servant tells the 'ephors' that he has been given a letter to take to Persia, which is handed over, and officials eavesdrop on Pausanias telling his servant about his mission; Pausanias flees to the sanctuary of the temple of Athene 'of the Brazen House'; to avoid execution, and is blockaded in the building and denied food; he starves to death, but is dragged out before he dies so Sparta cannot be accused of killing him in a holy place; nevertheless, it is claimed that the action 'curses' Sparta and its foes at Athens make the most of it. (The date of this is unclear, and depends on how long Pausanias was allowed to stay at Byzantium before his recall; it may be as late as c. 467.)

472

Production of Aeschylus' 'Persae' ('The Persians') in the annual theatrical festival at Athens. The wealthy citizen chosen to fund it as 'choregus' is the future leader Pericles, son of Xanthippus – appropriate given his father's role in the war which the play covers.

472/1

Ostracism of Themistocles by Athens, entailing exile of ten years and probably as a result of a clash with the more pro-Spartan, 'aristocratic' faction headed by his rival Cimon; he goes to Argos.

470?

At around this date, Themistocles is forced to flee from central Greece after Sparta demands his extradition from Argos for trial before the congress of the Greeks for an alleged plot with their late king Pausanias, supplying evidence from the latter's letters. He goes to Corcyra, and later to the court of Admetus, king of the Molossians in Epirus.

469/7

Greece/Persia

(Precise year unclear, probably 469/8.) A new Persian/Phoenician fleet is mustered in Pamphylia, in south Asia Minor, ready to transport troops to Ionia for an attack on the Greeks. It is attacked on the River Eurymedon near Phaselis by the fleet of the Delian League, probably two hundred ships, commanded by Cimon, which advances from its mustering-point at Cnidus. The Greek fleet lands troops to attack Phaselis first, but the Chians persuade the town to surrender and supply troops to the Greeks; before another Phoenician squadron can arrive from Cyprus, Cimon attacks the enemy fleet, which retreats into the river but is trapped and destroyed. Around two hundred Persian ships are sunk, including some from the Cypriot reinforcements, which are attacked too by Cimon in a second action some days after the battle; the Persian army on land is attacked by Cimon on the day of or that following the naval battle and destroyed after a fierce infantry clash, but Athenian losses are heavier there. End of the Persian domination of the eastern Mediterranean for some years, and of the threat of a naval attack on Greece – and after this date the Delian League comes to be seen more as an Athenian 'empire' run for Athens' benefit.

Following the victory, Cimon and his board of fellow-generals in Athens are given the unusual honour of being invited to act as judges at the 'City Dionysia' theatrical competition and give the first prize in the tragedy category to Sophocles, who submits his first entries. This is probably in spring 468.

467

Sicily
Death of Hieron, tyrant of Syracuse/Gela; succeeded by his more oppressive younger brother Thrasyboulus.

466

Revolt in Syracuse, aided by Gela, Akragas and Himera; Thrasyboulus is besieged in the walled areas of the city, the mainland quarter of Achradina and the island citadel of Ortygia, by the citizens and eventually agrees to leave for exile in Locroi, Italy; Syracuse becomes a limited democracy.

465

Greece/Persia
August – Assassination of Great King Xerxes, aged around fifty-three, by Artabanus, commander of the royal bodyguard, who probably aims at the throne. His eldest son, Darius, is either killed by Artabanus too (Aristotle) or is killed by Xerxes first at Artabanus' instigation. Xerxes' second son, Artaxerxes, secures the throne and executes Artabanus and his sons.

Greece

Thasos, the largest island in the northern Aegean, attempts to secede from the Delian League in a dispute with Athens over the latter trying to take over Thasos' mining interests in Thrace. Athens refuses to compromise and decides to attack Thasos and secure full control of the Thracian hinterland, thus banning any member-state from seceding from the League.

Autumn – The Athenian fleet under Cimon defeats that of Thasos, capturing thirty-three ships, and lands on Thasos; an Athenian colonizing expedition lands at the adjacent mouth of the river Strymon in western Thrace and sets up a colony at Ennea Hodi/'Nine Ways'.

464

The eponymous main town of Thasos is besieged, but the local Thracians attack the Athenian mainland expedition at Drabescus and inflict heavy casualties. The Athenians have to evacuate 'Nine Ways'.

Summer – With Thasos being starved out, its leaders send a secret embassy to Sparta to appeal for an attack on Attica. The chances of this are ended as a devastating earthquake hits Sparta, killing around 20,000 people, including many of the young men who are caught in a collapsing gymnasium. All but five of the houses in Sparta are destroyed (Plutarch). The 'helots' revolt and some of the 'Periocoi' join them, and an attack is quickly made on Sparta but King Archidamus has the alarm-trumpet sounded to summon the survivors from searching the ruins to collect weapons and fight off the attackers. The rebels retreat into the countryside, and Sparta sends Pericleidas as its envoy to Athens to appeal for military aid. The Athenian assembly debates this, and the 'hard-liner' democrat Ephialtes wants Athens to leave Sparta to collapse and rid them of a rival; Cimon urges Athens to send aid as Sparta helped to save her in 480–79 and they are the two 'yoke-fellows' (as in oxen pulling a plough) of Greece. The assembly votes help, and Cimon takes 4000 'hoplites' to aid Sparta; Plataea also sends help in memory of 479. The rebels are pushed back into Messenia.

(Thucydides states that the revolt lasts for ten years, i.e. to 455/4, or else from 468/7, but this is chronologically unlikely and his sketchy chronology of the 460s is dubious.)

463

Start of the blockade of the Messenian/'helot' rebels on Mount Ithome in Messenia as the lowlands are recovered by Sparta; the blockade is probably ineffective due to the limited numbers of men available to Sparta.

Persia

At around this date, probably early in the reign of Artaxerxes rather than while Xerxes is still alive as assessed by Plutarch, Themistocles arrives on Persian soil after having to leave Epirus when Sparta demands that King Admetus extradite him to face trial or face attack. Plutarch says that he crossed the Aegean to Ionia while the Athenian siege of Thasos was underway and so had to avoid being captured by his hostile countrymen, which dates it to 464/3; Thucydides prefers dating the voyage to the time of the siege of Naxos (i.e. late in the 470s) but this is less likely unless the sources that state he went to Persia before Xerxes died (465) are correct.

Themistocles lives secretly at Aegae in Aeolis at first, but then goes on to the royal court at Susa, presumably after exploring his likely reception there; he receives a favourable reception from the Great King and is appointed as the governor of Magnesia-on-the-Maeander in Lydia.

462

Greece

Summer – Surrender of Thasos after a prolonged blockade; the main town has its walls demolished, the fleet is confiscated, Thasos has to pay tribute to the League plus an indemnity, and the island's mining colonies in Thrace are seized by Athens. This undermines the League's reputation among neutrals, and encourages criticism of it as an Athenian 'empire'. Cimon returns in triumph to Athens, and fights off a charge laid against him by the democratic leaders, Ephialtes and the emerging young Alcmaeonid relative Pericles (the son of 509 reformer Cleisthenes' niece), that he has taken bribes from King Alexander of Macedon not to attack his country. He is also attacked for his pro-Spartan and anti-Persian stances.

August/September – There is a second appeal from Sparta to Athens for military aid, after Sparta fails to force the Messenians to surrender by the blockade of Mount Ithome. Cimon leads another expedition; in his absence the democratic leaders persuade the assembly to vote for constitutional reforms that strip the Areopagus of most of its judicial powers. These are shared between the Council of 500, the assembly, and the Heliaea (the assembly or a judicial panel of it, selected by lot, acting as a court and scrutinizing each year's officials). The news of the reforms reaches the allied Spartan/Peloponnesian/Athenian army at Mount Ithome, and undermines Cimon's usefulness to Sparta as it is now apparent that the constitution has shifted to a full democracy favouring his rivals. Possibly fearing democratic Athenians assisting the rebels, Sparta sends the Athenian contingent home and antagonizes Athens.

?Assassination of Ephialtes, by a Boeotian; there may be more to this than meets the eye, but any involvement by his rivals (Pericles?) is never proved.

461

Spring – Athens votes to hold an ostracism; Cimon loses the vote and is exiled for ten years, apparently for his pro-Spartan stance after the insult of the Athenian army being sent home in 462; Pericles assumes the main direction of Athenian politics for the next thirty years, but has some colleagues like the general Tolmides at first.

461

Sicily
Probable date of the start of a ten-year secession from the Greek-dominated state system of non-Carthaginian Sicily by the native Siceliots in the inland hills; this is led by Ducetius and the small, rural communities come together into an alliance.

460

Greece
Megara revolts against the Peloponnesian League in a dispute with her neighbour, Corinth, and joins an alliance with Athens; Athens is allowed to send troops to occupy the Megaran ports of Nisaea (the city's port on the Saronic Gulf) and Pegae (on the Gulf of Corinth) and constructs 'Long Walls' from Megara to Nisaea so Sparta cannot blockade it by land into surrender.

Persia/Greece
The anti-Persian allies, led by Athens, agree to assist a rebellion in Cyprus and to send a fleet of two hundred ships there.

A combined Greek naval expedition, led by Athens part of whose fleet (forty out of two hundred ships) leaves for Cyrpus, led by the Athenian Charitemedes; the campaign shows that the post-Cimon leadership shares his wide-ranging ambitions.

Part of it later sails to Egypt and lands in the Delta to aid the rebels there led by Inarus, a Libyan prince possibly of Pharoanic descent, against the Persians, who asks the Greeks on Cyprus for help. A naval victory on the Nile sees the Persian/Phoenician fleet routed with fifty ships sunk, and the Persian commander, prince Achaemenes (brother of Great King Artaxerxes), is killed; Inarus secures most of lower Egypt but the Persians send in reinforcements.

459

A large Athenian fleet remains in Egypt, aiding Inarus against the Persians.

?Death of Themistocles at Magnesia in Lydia, aged around sixty-five. This supposedly occurs after the outbreak of the rebellion in Cyprus/Egypt, and is possibly suicide by poison to avoid him being asked by the Persians to command their fleet against the Greeks.

459/8?

The Messene rebels at Mount Ithome have to surrender to Sparta at the end of the blockade but are allowed to leave for exile; Athens offers them sanctuary and later sends them to Naupactus on the Gulf of Corinth. (This date may be too early, if Thucydides is correct that the Messenian revolt and subsequent siege of Ithome lasted for ten years – but he may believe that the revolt starts in 468, not 464, see above).

458

Greece

Production of Aeschylus' 'Oresteia' at Athens; this has political overtones, as it shows the establishment of the Areopagus and thus backs up the judicial role of the recently diminished Areopagus.

An Athenian fleet lands troops at Halieis in the eastern Peloponnese, who are repulsed by Corinth and her ally Epidaurus; the fleet defeats the Peloponnesian fleet off Cecryphalia in the Saronic Gulf; it then defeats the Aeginan fleet, which receives Peloponnesian naval help to no avail, in a battle on the Saronic Gulf and lands troops on Aegina to blockade its capital. 300 Corinthian and Epidauran 'hoplites' join the defence of Aegina; Corinth then invades Athenian-occupied Megara to force Athens to bring her troops back from Aegina; the main Athenian army is away, but Tolmides leads out the reserves (the young and the aged) and routs the Megarans. He secures Megara, and twelve days after the first battle defeats an arriving Corinthian force too in an ambush.

Summer: A 'stele' commemorating the past year's military losses in Athens speaks of men killed in Aegina, Megara, Cyprus, Phoenicia, and Egypt– a sign of Athenian ambition but also of 'overstretch'?

?Death of the Agid king of Sparta, Pleistarchus son of Leonidas (who was a boy in 480 so is probably in his thirties); succeeded by his son Pleistoanax.

457

Greece

Spring? – Surrender of Aegina; she loses her independence and becomes a member of the Delian League under Athenian occupation so Sparta cannot use the island as a base to attack Athens; the eponymous capital's walls are demolished.

In total, 1500 Spartans and 10,000 troops from the Peloponnesian League under Nicomedes, regent for the young Spartan 'Agid' king Pleistoanax, head for central Greece – possibly the less aggressive other king, Archidamus, is kept out of command in case he agrees a truce. Their official role is to aid the small region of Doris against an attack by its pro–Athenian neighbour, Phocis, but due to its size it is probably designed to invade Boeotia next. The army marches via the Isthmus to Phocis to force it to evacuate Doris; meanwhile, an Athenian fleet of fifty ships goes round the Peloponnese to occupy the upper reaches of the Gulf of Corinth, taking Pegae, to stop the Peloponnesians from returning home by sea. More Athenians occupy Mount Gerania on their landwards route home to block that. Nicomedes leads his army into Boeotia, and links up with local oligarchs who supply troops; there is also contact with the anti–war, anti–democracy party in Athens who urge him to attack the city and help them overthrow the democracy before the Long Walls to the Piraeus are complete and a landward blockade becomes impossible.

June/July? – Nicomedes' diplomatic contacts with Athens fail to agree a truce, and an Athenian army marches into Boeotia aided by 1000 'hoplites' from Argos. They are defeated by the Spartans and Peloponnesians at the battle of Tanagra, where Athens' Thessalian cavalry deserts, but the victor's losses are too heavy to enable them to stay on in Boeotia; Nicomedes marches home via the Megarid.

(Two months later) Late summer – Myronides leads an Athenian army into Boeotia and defeats Sparta's allies there at the battle of Oenophyta; they dismantle the walls of pro–Spartan Tanagra and set up pro–Athenian (mostly democratic) regimes in most of Boeotia. The Boeotian League is dissolved to destroy the leadership of pro–Spartan Thebes, and the latter's oligarchs are overthrown by a democratic revolt; this is soon reversed once Myronides has gone home. Myronides also takes hostages from Phocis and Opuntian Locris, and possibly takes over Naupactus on the Ozolian Locris coast of the Gulf of Corinth as an Athenian naval base.

Completion of the 'Long Walls' between Athens and the Piraeus harbour, ending the city's vulnerability to blockade by land.

Persia

Autumn (originally thought to be 459) – The Great King sends his ambassador Megabazus to Sparta with an offer of money if Sparta will invade Attica and so force Athens to withdraw from Egypt and Cyprus to protect itself; this is turned down.

457/6

Greece

Recall of Cimon to Athens from exile, some years early, probably as part of a political truce between him and Pericles; Plutarch alleges that he tried to join the Athenian army before the battle of Tanagra a little earlier as a volunteer (i.e. while it was in Boeotia) but Pericles turned him away. His sister Elpinice is his 'go–between' with Pericles, according to Plutarch. At around this date Pericles starts to become the dominant figure in Athenian military affairs as well as political ones, eclipsing Tolmides and being elected 'strategos'/ general each year.

456

Tolmides is appointed the naval commander; he takes a fleet of fifty ships to Peloponnesian waters to raid the island of Cythera, then burns the Spartan docks at Gytheium, sacks the south-western Peloponnesian town of Methone, and moves on to the Ionian Islands where Zacynthus and Cephallonia join him. He invades the Gulf of Corinth to capture the Corinthian colony of Chalcis near Cape Rhium, and sets up a naval base at Naupactus on the Gulf's north coast where a colony of refugee Messenian rebels from the 464–1 revolt is established as a blow to Sparta. Another probable Athenian naval base is at Pegae. He then raids the territory of Sicyon further up the Gulf.

455

Greece/Persia
Spring – Artaxerxes invades Egypt in force by land and sea, defeats the Greek expedition, and blockades them at the island of Prosophis between the lower Nile and a canal. The main Egyptian elite of lower Egypt makes peace and surrenders, probably with control of most of the cities returning to Persia, but Inaros continues resistance.

Greece
Spring – Tolmides leads land-invasion of Boeotia to install democratic regimes and undermine Sparta's allies there; meanwhile Pericles with a fleet and 1000 lower-class, non-'hoplite' infantry/rowers go to the western Peloponnese and ravage its north-western coast before invading Acarnania, north-west of the Gulf of Corinth. All Acarnania except the city of Oeniadae goes over to Athens; probably this secures Athenian control of the waters around the Peloponnese, designed to inspire a 'helot' revolt in Soarta and/or a revolt in Messenia, also involves Athens taking over Troezen in the north-eastern Peloponnese at around this date.

454

Athens invades Thessaly, helped by Phocis and pro-Athenians in Boeotia, to aid its local clients by demanding the restoration of people exiled by the pro-Spartan rulers after the battle of Tanagra in 457. Pharsalus resists this and is unsuccessfully besieged; the Thessalian cavalry harasses the besiegers and the siege is abandoned.

The expedition to Thessaly returns to Athens; Pericles is sent with 1000 marines to Pegae to command the fleet in the Gulf of Corinth/western Peloponnese and later to bring it home. During the final stages of the campaign, as he leads the fleet west out of the Gulf of Corinth he lands to ravage Sicyon, defeating its army as this intervenes, and attacks Oeniadae too.

Greece/Persia
Midsummer – The Persians divert the waters of the canal to one side of Prosophis to lower the water-level and attack the island; most of the Greeks are either killed or surrender and 6000 prisoners are taken, but some escape across the desert west to Greek-ruled Cyrene.

Soon afterwards, a relief-expedition of around fifty Greek ships commanded by the new generals for the year 454/3 arrives at the eastern mouth of the Nile unaware of the disaster and lands; it is attacked by land and sea and heavily defeated, losing most of its ships (around one hundred are lost by the two Greek forces in Egypt this summer). This ends the Greek offensive and opens the way for the Persian/Phoenician navy to attack rebel Cyprus next.

454/3

Greece

Winter – Alliance between Athens and Phocis, thus protecting the western / northern flanks of Athens by providing a friendly state to the rear of pro-Sparta Megara and Boeotia. This then leads to Athenian backing for Phocis taking over leadership of the local Amphictyonic League and its council, which control the sanctuary at Delphi – alarming Sparta.

Between this date and c.448, Athens (presumably as directed by Pericles) re-shapes her League, to increase the number of states due to pay tribute and to convert the contributions of some larger states from ships to money, thus decreasing the number left with autonomous fleets able to stand up to Athens' – only Lesbos, Chios, and Samos are left with fleets. Other states that have seceded or do not pay tribute, e.g. Miletus, Colophon and Erythrae on mainland Ionia, are reduced to tributary status. At this point the Treasury of the League is transferred from Delos to Athens, allegedly on account of the Persian threat, and it comes totally under Athenian control; the assembly of the League ceases to meet so the League becomes a non-consultory adjunct to the power of Athens.

453/2

Persia

?Persian invasion of Egypt continues after the death of Inarus, probably with an invasion up the Nile towards Thebes; the new rebel leader/Pharoah, Amyrtaeus, loses control of most of Egypt and takes refuge in the swamps of the Delta. He is aided at first by Athenian/Greek naval dominance of the north-eastern Mediterranean, which brings in supplies. However, the Persian/Phoenician fleet returns from Egypt after the main war there ends (453?), and is used to launch a successful invasion of Cyprus within a year or two.

451

Greece

Thirty Years' peace between Sparta and Argos, which undermines Athens' hopes of using Argos as its main route to undermining Sparta in the Peloponnese – from now on Athens will be seen as the external 'aggressor', not the ally of a major local state. This probably precedes a five-year truce between Athens and Sparta agreed as a result of Athens losing its hopes of Argive help; from the time when the truce expires in late(?) summer 446 it is probably agreed in the summer.

451/0

Law of Pericles at Athens, confining the citizenship to the sons of Athenian mothers as well as fathers; possibly this is intended to provide a smaller and easily controllable body of voters, one less open to pro-Peloponnesian influences from overseas relatives. This may be aimed at the 'pro-Sparta' Cimon.

450

Greece/Persia
Cimon is appointed to the naval command against Persia as its command of Cyprus threatens a naval advance to the Aegean, probably as his terms for a political truce with Pericles. He is sent with a fleet to Cyprus, and wins a major victory over the Persians; he besieges them in their main naval base there, the city of Citium. Sixty ships are sent to Egypt to help the rebel Amyrtaeus in the Delta.

Perdiccas succeeds his father Alexander as king of Macedon.

450/49

5000 talents from the Delian League treasury is transferred for the use of Athens, probably allegedly for the 'sacred' work of rebuilding the temples in Athens destroyed by the Persians in 480 as the money is eventually used for this on the Acropolis.

449

Early – Death of Cimon in an epidemic at Citium, aged around fifty-five; the siege of Citium is abandoned and the Athenian/allied fleet fights off an attack by the Persian/Phoenician fleet off Salamis as it leaves. Negotiations between Athens and Persia follow.

Summer/Autumn – As part of the truce, Athenian forces leave Cyprus and Egypt.

Greece
Autumn – Sparta pushes its allies in the Amphictyonic League to declare a 'Sacred War' on Phocis over control of Delphi, and is 'invited' to send troops to help them which she does; Phocis is evicted from Delphi and it is declared an autonomous place.

448

Greece/Persia
Spring? – Conclusion of 'Peace of Callias' (the chief Athenian/Greek negotiator) at Susa with the Great King. The Greek envoys, led by Athens and probably aided by Argos, agree to abandon their allies in Cyprus and Egypt and the states of Ionia within three days' ride of the sea are guaranteed from any Persian control. The Greeks, in practice Athens and her navy, secure control of the seas west of Phaselis in south Asia Minor and west of Cyanae at the mouth of the Bosphorus. The seas are open to merchant shipping of both parties.

Greece
?Pericles sends twenty Athenian envoys around all the Greek states to try to sign up participants to a 'Panhellenic Congress' at Athens to restore all the temples wrecked by the Persians in 480, secure peace at sea for trade, and establish a universal peace treaty for the Greek states; these visit coastal Thrace, Ionia, the Aegean islands, and the Propontis as well as the main part of Greece. As Athens has the most notable temples destroyed in 480, which will be physically dominant at the congress and no doubt will be used for propaganda, and it led the resistance to Persia then with Sparta, the 'sub-text' is to establish

Athens as the leader of this pan-Greek initiative and undermine Sparta; in reply, Sparta and the Peloponnesian League refuse to attend and Pericles has to call off the congress. However, he goes ahead with restoring the temples on the Acropolis at Athens as planned, with the funds of the Delian League diverted to pay for the work as a 'sacred' act of piety to the gods; this leads to the arrangements for the building of the Parthenon and other new/restored temples on the Acropolis. Pheidias acts as chief architect, and constructs the 'chryselephantine' giant statue of Athene in the Parthenon.

447

Spring (or autumn 448) – Athens sends troops under Pericles to restore the control of the sanctuary at Delphi to Phocis. Once they have gone home, Sparta restores Delphian control again.

Autumn – The five-year Athens/Sparta truce expires.

Late autumn? – Exiled oligarchs seize Orchomenus and Chaeronea in west Boeotia from their new, Athenian-allied democratic regimes.

446

Tolmides and 1000 Athenians and allies invades western Boeotia, capture Chaeronea, and installs garrisons there, selling off the city's men as slaves; this temporarily brings Athenian power/democracy to the area and threatens the anti-Athenian neighbours in Locris and Boeotia. As he leaves with the main force he is attacked at Coronea by an army of oligarchic Boeotian exiles, who have called in Locris and the Euboean oligarchic regimes, and is defeated and killed. Many of his men are captured, and Athens calls a truce and agrees to evacuate Boeotia to get them back; the oligarchic regimes are restored across Boeotia.

Euboea then revolts against Athens.

July? – Pericles marches north with a large Athenian citizen army to cross the straits onto Euboea, but with the main Athenian army away Megara revolts, aided by neighbouring Corinth and Sicyon; all the Athenian troops in Megara are either killed or flee, and Spartan king Pleistoanax advances into the Ithmus to gather a Peloponnesian League allied army to invade Athens.

August/September – Pleistoanax invades Attica from Sparta's restored ally Megara, and camps on the plain of Eleusis; three Athenian regiments are cut off behind his advance at Pegae in the Megarid and have to march home via a detour north into Boeotia, and possibly the Boeotians join the Spartan army; surprisingly Pleistoanax withdraws rather than attacking Athens. Pericles now takes fifty shiploads of troops to Euboea, and puts down the rebellion there.

Negotiations between Athens (on behalf of her allies) and Sparta (with her League) lead to the 'Thirty Years' Peace' between them (October?), due to come into effect in midwinter 446/5; Athens abandons all its allies and positions in the Peloponnese including Troezen and parts of Achaea, leaving it to Spartan dominance, abandons Nisaea in the Megarid, and accepts Megara's independence/Peloponnesian League membership; Aegina stays in the Delian League but is guaranteed autonomy; all agree to avoid aggressive acts, and any other unnamed states can sign up to the treaty too if those party to it agree. Presumably, Delphi is confirmed as an autonomous shrine. Freedom of trade and arbitration of any dispute are agreed too, and oaths are taken to the treaty.

446/4

Sparta exiles King Pleistoanax for allegedly taking a bribe from Pericles – logically, a backlash among the 'war party' against the treaty with Athens and anger that Pleistoanax missed a chance to destroy Athens in 446. He is succeeded by his son Pausanias, probably still a minor, and remains in exile for around fifteen years.

444/3

Probable date of the foundation of the new Athenian colony in southern Italy at Thurii, unless this occurs two years or so earlier. Lampon and Xenocrates lead the expedition, with a site chosen by consultation with the oracle at Delphi; Peloponnesians as well as Athenians/Ionians are invited to join this 'panhellenic' project, and are represented in the city's ten tribes; it is to be a democracy. Tradition says that the historian Herodotus of Halicarnassus leaves Athens to become one of the early colonists.

443

Spring – A vote for an 'ostracism' is called in Athens, probably as the culmination of the political struggle between Pericles and the conservative leader Thucydides son of Melesias; the latter is ostracized and thus exiled for ten years, confirming Pericles' supremacy in Athens.

442

Sophocles produces his play 'Antigone' at Athens.

440

Summer – Samos refuses Athenian mediation in a dispute with Miletus over the control of Priene on the nearby mainland; as it does not pay tribute to the League and has a fleet it is a potential threat to Athens. Possibly Athens is seen as pro-Miletus (according to Diodorus). Pericles secures his appointment to lead an expedition of forty ships to Samos; he overthrows its oligarchic government and installs a more compliant democracy with a garrison, taking fifty leading citizens and fifty boys hostage and deporting them to Lemnos.

The Samian oligarchs go to satrap Pissuthnes of Lydia for assistance, and he lends them ships and 700 mercenaries to rescue the hostages from Lemnos and then return to Samos and overthrow the democracy. The Athenian garrison is handed over to Pissuthnes, and the leading city of Lesbos, Mytilene, offers support and asks Sparta for help. Samos sends to Sparta for help, and Sparta puts the question to the Peloponnesian League assembly; this body is won over to leaving Athens to punish Samos as its own ally by the pro-Athenian stance of Corinth, of which Corinth will remind Athens to no avail in 433.

Melissus' Samian fleet defeats an Athenian naval attack, before Pericles' main fleet arrives. Byzantium also revolts against Athens.

The dramatist Sophocles is one of the ten annual elected generals at Athens for 441/0, and so takes part in naval operations that summer, involving a visit to Chios.

439

Pericles leads the main Athenian fleet to Samos to blockade the Samians; the latter fail to receive the expected help from a Persian fleet and have to surrender. Samos loses its independent fleet, pays 1300 talents' reparations in twenty-six annual instalments, and becomes a dependant ally of Athens in the Delian League. Byzantium also surrenders.

?Pericles allows some dissident city-states in Caria to leave the League rather than fight them – at any rate, they disappear from its tribute-lists around this date.

438

Completion of the Parthenon, the 'Temple of the Maiden' (Athena), on the Acropolis in Athens, with its giant statue of Athene by Pheidias.

Euripides produces his play 'Alcestis', earliest dateable of his works, in the Athens city Dionysia tragedy competition.

?Pericles establishes a colony at Brea on the Thermaic Gulf in Macedon, close to the cities of the Chalcidice.

Spartocus deposes the 'Achaeanactid' dynasty of the Bosporan kingdom in the Crimea; foundation of his dynasty there, as allies of Athens.

437

?The sculptor Pheidias is prosecuted in Athens for embezzlement of official money during his contract-work on the Acropolis; he leaves for Olympia to build the gigantic statue of Olympian Zeus, one of the 'Seven Wonders of the World'.

437/6

Foundation of the Athenian colony of Amphipolis at the mouth of the River Strymon in eastern Macedonia, by the Athenian general Hagnon who in 439 assisted Pericles at Samos – Amphipolis controls the route to access the resources of Thrace and is a check on the nearby cities of Chalcidice.

(437 or 436) Pericles tours the Black Sea with a fleet, winning new local allies and expelling the tyrant of Sinope who is replaced with a democratic government of Athenian colonists. He may also found a colony at Astacus on the Propontis.

At around this time, or possibly as early as the late 440s, Pericles' mistress Aspasia, a famous 'hetaira' (high-class hostess/prostitute), is prosecuted by his enemies for 'impiety'; he persuades the jury to let her off. There is also a politically inspired prosecution by Diopeithes of the philosopher and scientist Anaxagoras for 'atheism', apparently aimed at his patron Pericles who advises Anaxagoras to leave Athens, which he does.

435

Quarrel between Corinth and its colony of Corcyra, as the democrats vs oligarchs strife in their mutual colony on the Adriatic coast, Epidamnus (north Albania), leads to the democrats' appeal to Corcyra for help. She refuses it, and the oracle at Delphi advises Epidamnus to go to Corinth. Corinth accepts and sends out a force of armed new colonists overland to help, assisted by her local colonies of the island of Levkas and mainland

Ambracia; Corcyra sends a fleet to demand that Epidamnus sends them home and readmits the expelled oligarchs. This is refused; Corcyra besieges Epidamnus with forty ships on behalf of the oligarchs.

Corinth asks her allies to contribute to a second force, with land in Epidamnus for the volunteers, and these come from Levkas, Ambracia, Megara, Thebes, Hermione (eastern Peloponnese), Troezen (ditto), Phlius (Achaea), and Elis. Corcyra sends delegates to ask Sparta and Sicyon for advice, and they urge her to press Corinth to accept arbitration. Corinth rejects this and asks her allies to send ships to help escort the colonists; Megara sends eight ships, Epidaurus five, Troezen two, Levkas eight, and Ambracia eight.

Summer – Thirty Corinthian and forty-five allied ships heads for the Ionian Sea with 2000 Corinthian 'hoplites', and are defeated by a fleet of eighty Corcyran ships near Actium; fifteen Corinthian ships are sunk. The same day Epidamnus surrenders to Corcyra. The Corinthian prisoners at Corcyra are put in chains, the others are executed, and the Corcyran fleet raids Elis; Epidamnus is recolonized by Corcyrans and its new arrivals from Corinth enslaved. Corinth rebuilds its fleet for a riposte, and hires many Peloponnesian and Aegean island sailors.

433

Early summer? – Corcyra sends envoys to Athens to ask for an alliance; Corinth sends to ask her to stay out of the war. The 449 peace treaty allows Athens to conclude a defensive alliance, as Corcyra is not an ally of Sparta; but Athens has no vital interests at stake and it would be safer to avoid entanglement. Pericles argues successfully in the assembly for a defensive alliance, which is approved on the second of two days' debates after the public mood had favoured non-intervention on the first day.

July? – Pericles, as head of the board of generals, sends out ten ships under Lacedaemonius (the son of the late general Cimon), Diotimus, and Proteas, a small commitment and ordered to intervene only if the Corinthian alliance lands on Corcyra or her territories. Possibly the choice of Cimon's son to command is due to Pericles tying this potential future opponent, son of a pro-Spartan and named after Sparta, to his policy – or to reassure Corinth and Sparta of a united Athenian stand.

August/September – Ninety Corinthian and sixty allied ships under Xenoclides defeat the Corcyran fleet of 110 ships off Cape Sybota, destroying seventy. The Athenian squadron on the Corcyran right wing avoids fighting the Corinthians opposite, but moves to protect the retreating Corcyran ships near them and clashes with the Corinthians as they approach Corcyra; the Corcyran left wing has defeated the Corinthians opposite them but this is negated by their centre's collapse. The Corinthians pull back from confronting the Athenians to hunt down Corcyran survivors in the water, and when they return to the offensive that evening an approaching Athenian squadron (under Glaucon and Andocides) is sighted and the Corinthians retreat again to their camp at Leukimme.

Next day the united Athenian and Corcyran squadrons offer battle outside the Corinthian squadron's anchorage at Sybota, but the Corinthians call a brief truce and accuse the Athenians of interference to be told that they can do what they like elsewhere but not by attacking an Athenian ally. The Corinthians leave, and their fleet goes home leaving Corcyra now linked to Athens.

Corcyra sends envoys to Athens to speak at an assembly debate, which is called to consider the threat now apparent of a war between Athens and the Peloponnesians, and hence Sparta; they offer their island's help for western bases in such a war, and Pericles apparently (following Thucydides' account) claims that war is likely in any case, coming from the Peloponnese, and it is as well to be well-prepared. But Corinth refrains from asking Sparta to assist her in attacking Athens or her colonies.

?Phormion is sent with an Athenian fleet to Acarnania, to help the locals expel the pro-Corinthian Ambracians from the disputed town of Amphilochian Argos.

432

Early (or late 433) – Corinth's Macedonian/Chalcidice coast colony of Potidaea, tributary to Athens, is ordered by Athens to demolish her seaward defences, give hostages to Athens, and send her Corinthian magistrates home and admit no more. Potidaea sends envoys to Athens asking for discussions, and these follow but Athens does not moderate her basic demands.

Spring/summer (or late 433) – Athens issues the 'Megarian Decree', proposed by Pericles: economic sanctions against her old foe Megara, which is excluded from trade with Athens and her empire. This increases Megaran bitterness after her unofficial involvement in Corinth's 433 Corcyra expedition, and arguably undermines Pericles' pro-peace ally ('guest-friend') King Archidamus at Sparta.

April/May? – Archestratus, commander of an Athenian force about to leave for the Chalcidice, is ordered to go to Potidaea, take hostages, and demolish the town's seaward defences so that Athens' will is carried out by force. The suspicious Potidaeans, fearing this sort of attack, send envoys to Sparta with the help of their founder, Corinth; Sparta's militant 'ephors' and the council ('Gerousia') agree to invade Attica if Athens attacks Potidaea. This arguably is the decisive move in Sparta setting up a 'trip-wire' to trigger war by helping one of her allies (Corinth), albeit in response to Athens already having made one interference in Corinth's colonial affairs. In Macedon, King Perdiccas is angry at Athenian interest in his rebel brother Philip and asks Corinth to encourage Potidaea to revolt against Athens and Sparta to start a war with her. He also gets the coastal Chalcidice settlers to concentrate their manpower at a new, walled inland town, Olynthus.

August? – Archestratus arrives in the Thermaic Gulf near the Chalcidice, with thirty ships and 1000 men; by this time the Potidaeans have declared war on Athens, and have been joined by other Chalcidice towns and cities and by nearby Bottiea. Archestratus joins Perdiccas' brother Philip and his Thracian sponsor Derdas to attack Macedon, and forces him to agree to become an Athenian ally.

(Forty days after the revolt of Potidaea.) 2000 Corinthian and Peloponnesian volunteers arrive at Potidaea in a mercenary force, commanded by Aristeus who signs an alliance with Chalcidice and Bottaiea.

July or August – The Corinthians complain to Sparta about Athens' conduct in attacking their colony at Potidaea, saying that this breaks the Thirty Years' Peace; Aegina also complains that their guaranteed autonomy has not been respected. Sparta invites all states who have complaints about Athens (not just their own allies) to send envoys to Sparta, and these men are invited before the Spartan citizen assembly. In reply, an Athenian embassy speaks too and reminds them of Athens' strength and asks for arbitration. The 'hard-line' 'ephor' Sthenelaidas urges the assembly to vote for war as Athens has committed many acts of aggression and the gods will be on Sparta's side, but King Archidamus urges caution and arbitration as the war would last for years. (Apocryphal account by Thucydides, of unknown reality.) The Spartan assembly then votes for war in a formal division, and the decision is put to an assembly of representatives of Sparta's allies which is now called; before the representatives arrive, the approval of the oracle of Apollo at Delphi is sought and given.

September? (six months before the attack on Plataea in spring 431, according to Thucydides) – Archestratus defeats Aristeus in battle on the isthmus between Olynthus and Potidaea, losing 150 men including the general Callias, and besieges Potidaea from the landward side. (Either this year or in 431 the philosopher Socrates is among the Athenian besiegers of Potidaea and is made famous by meditating at his guard-post in the middle of a snowstorm oblivious to the weather.)

September? (Possibly as early as August.) – The meeting of the Peloponnesian League congress proceeds at Sparta, with Corinth demanding war, and war is agreed. Pending a campaign in 431, Sparta sends envoys to Athens to claim that war would be just as avenging an act of sacrilege, which she should remedy by driving out the 'cursed' descendants of the temple-violator Cylon (639 BC), including Pericles. In reply, Athens tells Sparta to remedy its own temple-violating, namely in dragging rebel 'helots' (c. 465?) and King Pausanias (c. 478?) out of sanctuary.

Sparta requires the cancellation of the 'Megarian Decree', abandonment of the attack on Potidaea, and restoration of autonomy to Aegina as her terms for peace; the Athenian assembly votes to follow Pericles' advice and offer to accept arbitration but not any Spartan ultimatums. Sparta does not offer any concessions.

The Peloponnesian Wars 431 to 404

431

March – Dissidents in Plataea, in south Boeotia, who are in favour of the town entering the Theban-led Boeotian League, open the gates at night to 300 Theban 'hoplites'. Thebes is intending to send in 'back-up' and get the town to ask to enter the League. The coup is then challenged once the small number of the invaders is known, and before dawn the pro-Athenian majority of the population counter-attacks. The attackers are overwhelmed and 180 prisoners are taken; the main Theban force arrives too late, delayed by rain, to be told by a loyalist herald that Plataea will keep the peace if the Thebans leave but if they besiege Plataea it will be an act of war and the prisoners will be killed. The Thebans withdraw, and the prisoners are executed on a technicality; Plataea appeals to Athens for help, and the Athenian assembly agrees to send a garrison.

Production of Eurpides' tragedy 'Medea' in the Athens city Dionysia festival.

Athens and Sparta both send envoys around the Greek states asking for support against the other. Spartan king Archidamus assembles the army of the Peloponnesian League on the Isthmus of Corinth and marches on Attica. He sends a herald to Athens before he crosses the frontier, but the Athenian assembly accepts Pericles' proposal to vote to refuse any talks once a Spartan army has crossed the Isthmus (i.e. entered a demilitarized neutral zone). Pericles advises the Athenians to avoid fighting on land, relying on their walls to protect Athens and the Piraeus, and to use their strongest assets – their navy and their allies. They are due 600 talents of tribute from the allies each year, and have 6000 in reserve, so they are financially stable; they have 13,000 'hoplites' plus their existing garrisons of 6000, plus 1200 cavalry/mounted archers, 600 unmounted archers, and 300 triremes.

Archidamus attacks but fails to take the frontier town of Oenoe; he is criticized by his men for letting the enemy take away their moveables in Attica to safety during this delay. June: He advances to Eleusis where the countryside is ravaged, while on Pericles' advice the Attic rural population evacuates their stock and moveable possessions within the 'Long Walls' of Athens. The animals are sent on to Euboaea. The Spartans advance into the 'deme' of Acharnae and ravage the countryside, and Pericles restrains his angry countrymen from risking a battle with the superior Spartan army and sends out some cavalry to harass the attackers.

Late June – October? – A fleet of 100 Athenian ships led by Carcinus, Proteas, and Socrates raids around the Peloponnesian coasts, with 1000 'hoplites' and 400 archers on board; fifty Corcyran ships aid them. They head round the Peloponnese, raiding Pheia in Elis, to Acarnania at the north-west side of the Gulf of Corinth, and take Sollium and Astacus there; Cephallonia on the Ionian Islands goes over to Athens. At Methone in the south-west Peloponnese, the future Spartan general Brasidas saves the town from capture by leading 100 reinforcements there in time, brushing aside small enemy detachments in the area.

Athens occupies and depopulates the island of Aegina in the Saronic Gulf to stop it being used as a Spartan base for an attack on the Piraeus.

A second Athenian fleet led by Cleopompus operates in the straits of Euboaea, captures Thronium on the mainland and the island of Atalante, and heads on for Chalcidice where the Athenian navy is supplying the blockaders of rebel Potidaea. King Sitalces of Thrace, head of the 'Odrysian' kingdom, allies with Athens thanks to a mission by Athenian ally Nymphodorus of Abdera (Thrace) and persuades his neighbour, King Perdiccas of Macedon, to do so too. Therma is given to Perdiccas as a goodwill gesture.

Autumn: The Spartans go home from Attica; once they have left 13,000 Athenian troops raid and devastate the Megarid. At the end of the campaigning season, Pericles delivers his famous 'Fumeral Oration' over the bodies of the season's dead Athenians at the state's memorial service at the Ceramiecus cemetery. Possibly the version of the speech in Thucydides is partially accurate.

430

Late spring – King Archidamus of Sparta invades and ravages Attica again, staying in the state for around forty days; the rural populace evacuates into the city and behind the 'Long Walls' again, and a devastating plague breaks out. While this is underway, Archidamus moves south-east across Attica to the area of the goldmines at Laurium.

Early? summer – Pericles takes a fleet of 4000 citizen 'hoplites' and 300 cavalry to raid the eastern Peloponnese, aided by fifty ships from Chios and Lesbos; they leave Athens while the Spartans are still in Attica. They land and ravage the territory of Epidaurus and Troezen, then move south to Hermione and on to sack Prasiae in east Laconia. They return to find the Spartans gone but the plague still underway. There is criticism of Pericles in the city for bringing disaster on them by the war, and he replies with a defence of his policy to the assembly (as recorded, approximated, or invented by Thucydides).

Late? summer – The generals Hagnon and Cleopompus son of Cleinias, Pericles' colleagues, take the fleet on to the Chalcidice to open the siege of rebel Potidaea.

Sparta fails in a naval attack by Cnemus and 1000 'hoplites' on Zacynthus in the Ionian Islands, whose populace refuses to abandon Athens; a joint Spartan/Corinthian/Tegea embassy sets out by land for Persia to met up with the friendly satrap of Hellespontine Phrygia, Pharnabazus, and go on to the Great King, but only gets as far as Thrace; as they arrive at Thracian king Sitalces' court the Athenian envoys get Sitalces' son Sadocus, who has just been made an Athenian citizen, to help them kidnap the envoys en route to the Hellespont. They are sent to Athens. Athens, which has a particular grudge against the Corinthian envoy Aristeus for helping the revolt at Potidaea, has them quietly executed.

The pro-Spartan Ambracians, at the north-west end of the Gulf of Corinth, attack the town of Argos in Amphilochia, which has been taken from them earlier by Amphilochia aided by the Athenian general Phormion; this is repulsed.

Autumn? – Pericles is accused of incompetent leadership and prosecuted by his enemies, utilizing discontent at his military failures; he puts up a spirited defence of his policies but is deprived of his generalship for the rest of that year and fined ?fifteen talents.

Death of King Spartocus of the Bosporan kingdom (Crimea); succeeded by Satyrus.

430/29

Winter – Athens sends twenty ships under Phormion to Napuactus, on the northern side of the Gulf of Corinth near its entrance, to disrupt Peloponnesian/Corinthian shipping.

Surrender of Potidaea to the Athenian commanders besieging it – Xenophon, Hestiodorus, and Phanomachus. The citizens are allowed to leave with a small amount of possessions and money and settle elsewhere in Chalcidice; Potidaea is duly occupied by an Athenian colony. The assembly at home is discontented at such easy terms but gives way.

429

Sparta and its ally Ambracia, north-west of the entrance of the Gulf of Corinth, plan to overrun the nearer Ionian Islands and adjacent Acarnania to cut off Corcyra and close the Gulf of Corinth, trapping the Naupactus squadron; Cnemus and 1000 Peloponnesian 'hoplites' cross the Gulf northwards into Ambracia where he rallies an army of locals plus Epirots under Sabylinthus (regent for under-age king Tharrypus of the Molossians), 1000 from tribal Chaonia under Photius and Nicanor, and 1000 from Orestis in western Macedon; King Perdiccas is to send a Macedonian army of 1000 south-west to join them despite his official alliance with Athens, but Cnemus does not wait for them or for the Corinthian navy to join his allied Ambracian/Ionian shipping at Levkas. He marches on the pro-Athenian Acarnanians and heads for their capital, Stratus, in three separate columns, but his column of Epirots/Chaonians is ambushed by the locals as they push ahead. The rest of the army is unnerved and halts in camp, bombarded by Acarnanian slingers, and then retreats back to friendly Oeniadae where Cnemus' allies disperse.

March? – Pericles is elected as general again despite the setbacks of his military policies and the 430 prosecution; he takes up office in July

Early summer: King Archidamus of Sparta invades and sends messengers to Plataea in south Boeotia, near the current 'theatre of war' as the Spartans invade Attica, to offer her acceptance of her neutrality if she will abandon her Athenian alliance. Plataea protests at this attack on a town that is the site of the great victory over Persia in 479 and staunchly supported that war, and sends envoys to Athens with Archidamus' agreement; the assembly asks her to keep to the alliance and promises help as far as practicable. Plataea refuses the Spartan request, and evacuates her civilians (except for 110 women to cook the meals) as a garrison of 400 citizens is joined by eighty Athenians. Sparta blockades Plataea and builds a 'double wall' around it so that attacks from Athens cannot penetrate the besiegers' camp and reach Plataea. A huge mound is built to the height of the town walls to enable the Spartans to cross from this to the ramparts, but the Plataeans dig mines under it so it collapses, and then the Spartans pile tinder up to the walls and start a fire, which a storm puts out.

Xenophon leads 2000 Athenian 'hoplites' and 200 cavalry against local enemies of Athens in Chalcidice; they attack Spartolus, but are driven off as Olynthus and the Bottiaens aid the defence.

First naval battle off Cape Rhium: Phormion leaves the panicking Acarnanians to defend themselves despite an appeal, and waits at Naupactus for the main Peloponnesian fleet (led by Corinth) to head down the Gulf to attack him; their forty-seven triremes and other smaller ships appear on the south side of the Gulf, and he moves parallel on the north side, westwards from Naupactus, to block their crossing; the Peloponnesians halt for the night at Patras, then attempt to cross unnoticed in the dark but he catches them in the open sea north of Cape Rhium as dawn breaks. They form into a circle with their five best warships and their weakest small vessels in the centre, intending to fight a defensive battle against attempts to board them with their superior numbers of infantry aiding this. Phormion gets his ships to row round them in a circle and make several feints at attack, forcing them back into a tighter circle so they cannot manoeuvre, and as the expected easterly wind rises after dawn this causes chaos with the tightly packed enemy ships, which are blown into each other. The Athenians then row in to ram the outer ships, and the Peloponnesians are in too much chaos to fight back effectively; twelve ships are taken and the rest flee down the Gulf to land on its south-west end at Cyllene and link up with Cnemus who has evacuated his men from Ambracia on board the pro-Spartan Ionian squadron from Levkas.

Second naval battle off Cape Rhium: Sparta sends three commissioners, i.e. their future general Brasidas with Timocrates and Lycophron, to Cnemus and the fleet to order them to collect more ships then attack Phormion. The latter is still waiting for help from Athens (whose relief-fleet of twenty ships has stopped off in Crete to attack hostile Cydonia) when this reinforced Peloponnesian fleet, seventy-seven ships strong, arrives in the narrows of the Gulf East of Patras. The Peloponnesian army marches parallel to this fleet on the southern side of the Gulf. The twenty Athenian ships wait for them opposite Cape Rhium at Molycrium, west of Naupactus, on the northern shore of the Gulf; after a few days' mutual observation the Peloponnesians decide to head across the Gulf north-east to Naupactus as they are now nearer to it by sea than Phormion is, and lure him after them. At dawn they commence this manoeuvre, with a main 'column' four ships deep and twenty faster ships in the lead; Phormion heads back up the northern coast to Naupactus, and the Peloponnesians turn in towards him to trap him against the coast and then bottle his ships up for boarding; nine Athenian ships are caught in the trap and attacked, but the eleven faster ones row past them and head on for Naupactus; the advance Peloponnesian squadron of twenty ships chases them, and ten reach Naupactus and turn to face them, 'ram' (bows) – first; the eleventh ship is nearly caught by the leading Peloponnesian ship, but doubles round a moored merchant ship off Naupactus harbour and turns to ram the enemy; this disaster halts the other nineteen Peloponnesian ships, some of whom are in difficulties in the shallows off the port, and the rest of the Athenian squadron is able to build up speed as it rows out of Naupactus bay and charges them head-on. Six of the Peloponnesians are captured, and the Athenians go on to recapture their nine trapped ships and drive the enemy back in disorder to Cape Rhium.

(Some time after July.) Death of Pericles in a new outbreak of the plague shortly after the deaths of his two legitimate sons, Paralus and Xanthippus; he is aged probably in his mid-sixties; there is a leadership-vacuum in Athens.

Autumn/winter: Invasion of Macedon by King Sitalces of Thrace, in an unsuccessful attempt to replace Perdiccas by a pretender called Amyntas, nephew of the King and son of his hostile brother Philip. The Athenian envoy Hagnon accompanies them, but they take no towns and suffer from the cold and Perdiccas bribes Sitalces' nephew Seuthes (with the hand of his daughter Stratonice) to persuade him to abandon the war.

428

Winter (or late 429) – While Phormion is campaigning in Acarnania to take anti-Athenian towns, Cnemus and his commissioners, led by the imaginative Brasidas, plan a morale-boosting naval raid on the Piraeus; they land at the eastern end of the Gulf at the Isthmus, and carry their oars and cushions across it to spend a night at the harbour of Megara, launching a squadron of forty ships that their Megara allies have been building for Sparta since 430. They head out into the Saronic Gulf, where Athens has no reason to suspect the presence of any Peloponnesian ships, but as they practise their rowing off Salamis the sailors lose their nerve and land on and plunder the island instead. Salamis alerts Athens by signal, and at dawn the Athenians blockade the entrance to the Piraeus harbour with booms while the Peloponnesians are heading back by sea to Megara.

June – Revolt on Lesbos in the north-east Aegean against Athens, led by the town of Mytilene, which plans to dominate the island; its smaller local rival, Methymna, stays loyal to Athens, which sends troops by sea to set up a base there. The Athenians then build two fortresses at the mouth of the sea-inlet on which Mytilene lies to prevent any naval help reaching the rebel city; before Mytilene is fully besieged it sends for help to Sparta, twice, with reassurances that they have a large fleet which will help Sparta in Ionia.

Late August? – At the Olympic Games, envoys from Mytilene turn up to ask the Peloponnesian League representatives in council for aid (speeches recorded and possibly invented as apposite by Thucydides). They urge the Peloponnesians to use this chance to bring the two Ionian states of the Athenian League with large fleets, Lesbos and Chios, to the Spartan side and to attack Athens by sea and land at the same time so it will be kept busy and a general Ionian revolt will follow. It is agreed to admit Mytilene to the Peloponnesian League and Sparta musters its and its allies' army to invade Attica again. Their Corinthian Gulf fleet is to be pulled on rollers across the Isthmus of Corinth to attack Athens by sea.

The harvest causes the Peloponnesians to put their food-supply above a quick muster as priorities, and the army is only belatedly assembled; meanwhile Athens, with forty ships blockading Mytilene, puts another hundred ships to sea and summons all the available lower class citizens not yet enrolled to man it as sailors. This fleet then ravages the coast of the Peloponnese, and the Spartans put off their naval expedition to help Mytilene into 427.

427

May? –The oligarchs in Mytilene make a final attempt to rally as an arriving Spartan, Salaethus, persuades the popular assembly to arm the people and make a sortie; these 'hard-liners' are, however, met by an angry armed crowd, which threatens to surrender to Athens instead, and the oligarchs give in and negotiate with the Athenian commander Paches. It is agreed that the Mytileneans should be allowed to send envoys to Athens where the assembly will hear their excuses and then decide the fate of the city. A week after the embassy sails, a Spartan squadron of forty ships commanded by Alcidus arrives from the Peloponnese via Delos and Myconos at Embatum on the Ionian mainland, but he does not proceed to Lesbos to attempt a rescue.

With the annual Spartan invasion of Attica underway and the Attic countryside being burnt, the populace are angry and vengeful; meanwhile, Alcidus withdraws to Ephesus and into the southern Aegean, looting en route, and Paches is informed of his nearness by the Athenian state galleys *Paralus* and *Salaminia*, which spot him. He sails after Alcidus, cannot find him, and expels the pro-Spartan regime at Notium near Ephesus, executing their Arcadian mercenary commander Hippias, and installs Colophon loyalists there. He returns to Lesbos to round up the oligarchic leaders (interned by him on Tenedos) and Salaethus (in hiding but caught) and sends them to Athens.

June? – The Spartan fleet in the Aegean under Alcidus (forty ships) flees back to Cyllene on the mainland, and joins up with a squadron, which is en route to the Ionian Sea to aid local Corcyran oligarchs. Once it is clear that the Spartan threat to Ionia is over and their fleet has gone, the Athenian assembly votes to execute Salaethus, although he offers to ask Sparta to let the Plataeans go free; the fate of Mytilene is debated, and the ambitious demagogue Cleon (introduced by Thucydides at this point in his work as the leading influence on the assembly in 427, and much ridiculed by Aristophanes as the devious son of a tanner) urges the execution of every male in the city and the enslavement of the women and children. This is agreed, and a ship is sent to inform Paches; however, the next day the anger of the assembly has passed, and a motion is put by Cleon's enemy Diodotus to rescind the punishment as such harsh action will only embolden resistance to a pitiless opponent; Cleon defends the necessity of making examples in wartime to deter others, but the rescindment is narrowly voted for and a second ship hurries to Mytilene. It arrives just as Paches is reading the first despatch, and the citizens are reprieved but all the land on the island of Lesbos except the pro-Athenan town of Methyma is seized and handed to Athenian colonists. The residents can stay as tenants. Around 1,000 of the local enemies of Athens rounded up and sent there by Paches are executed, as urged by Cleon.

July? ('summer' according to Thucydides) – Shortly after the end of the Mytilene revolt, the besieged Plataeans have to surrender too – with only 200 of them and twenty-five Athenians left in the town, the rest having escaped the previous winter. The Spartan commander asks them to give up, as they are too weak to man the walls but if he has to storm the town it will count as 'occupied' and Athens can ask for it back easier than if it gives up voluntarily. The garrison asks for a trial before the Spartans not the vengeful Thebans, but the five Spartan judges who are sent only ask if they have rendered any service to Sparta and her allies in the war. The Plataeans remind the Spartans of the town's glorious services to Greece in 480–79, but the Thebans tell the Spartans about their countrymen who the Plataeans have killed in this war and the prisoners are condemned to death as they cannot prove any service to the Spartan cause. (Thucydides' account – speeches probably invented?) The Athenians are executed, the women are enslaved, and the town is razed and handed to Thebes.

Civil war breaks out on Corcyra, as angry oligarchs resist five of their leaders being fined by the democratic regime (led by Peithias) for alleged improper use of vines on sacred land – retaliation for a recent trial of Peithias on charges of working for Athens. The oligarchs break into a council meeting and kill Peithias and fifty-nine other democratic leaders. They take over the government as survivors escape to the Athenian envoy's ship in the harbour, then get a vote passed to declare neutrality in the war; envoys are sent to explain to Athens but are arrested; when a Spartan embassy arrives on a Corinthian ship they back the oligarchs; the latter attack the democrats, who initially flee to the acropolis and then resume an attack on the town, and there is fighting in the streets with both sides arming the slaves and starting fires. Then an Athenian squadron of twelve ships under Nicoatratus puts in at the town, and aids a democratic victory.

A few days later, a Spartan squadron of fifty-three ships commanded by Alcidas (aided by junior officer Brasidas, the future Spartan general) arrives at Sybota on the opposite shore of Epirus; they advance on Corcyra, and the Corcyran fleet of sixty ships sails out in hostile mode under democratic command, aided by the Athenian squadron; however, two of the ships mutiny and go over to Sparta and there is fighting in others, and the Spartans attack and take thirteen ships. The Athenian ships defeat the wing opposite them, who form a protective circle, and are able to escape as the rest of the Spartan ships come up but do not challenge them. Back in the town of Corcyra the two parties agree a truce after the Spartans land and start burning the south of the island; as a Spartan beacon on nearby Levkas warns Alcidas that a large Athenian fleet (sixty ships) is approaching he re-embarks and retires unmolested.

The Athenian fleet secures the town and harbour of Corcyra, and the democrats celebrate by massacring the remaining oligarchs; some escape to launch attacks from exile.

Summer – Nicias takes Minoa, the island off the coast of Megara, from which its port Nisaea is blockaded.

Death of King Archidamus of Sparta, after a reign of forty-one years, probably aged around sixty; succeeded by his eldest son, Agis. The second son, now in his early teens, is the future king Agesilaus.

Sicily

Laches and Chaeroaedes are sent with twenty Athenian ships to aid Leontinoi (of Ionian descent so supposedly distant kinsmen to Athens, as the Leontinoi envoys claim) against attacks by the local Dorian Greek colonies (kin to the Peloponnesians) especially Syracuse; the hope in this is to rally support to cut off corn-supplies to Sparta.

427/6 Winter

Pythodorus brings a first, small Athenian relief-fleet to Sicily at local request, with a further expedition to follow.

426

Greece

March? – Aristophanes wins first prize at the Athens city Dionysia theatrical festival with 'The Babylonians'.

Summer – Nicias and an Athenian fleet ravage the territory of Tanagra in Boeotia opposite Euboea, land to attack the town, and the ravage coastal Locris beyond; the main Athenian army simultaneously marches into Boeotia from the south-east. Later, he takes an expedition to the western Aegean island of Melos, a Spartan colony, to demand that it leave its Spartan alliance and join Athens but its inhabitants defy him.

The new Athenian general Demosthenes leads an expedition of thirty ships to Acarnania at the north-west entrance to the Gulf of Corinth, and enlists help from there and the islands of Zacynthus, Cephallonia, and Corcyra. He attacks the pro-Spartan island of Levkas, and is about to attack the island's eponymous town when the exiled Messenians at Naupactus successfully invite him to aid them in Aetolia. Over-running Aetolia would bring him via Phocis and Locris to pressurizing Boeotia from the west and surrounding it, and possibly this plan is drawn up at the same time as the attack by Nicias on Tanagra as a combined 'enveloping' move. If so, it is bold but depends too much on accurate co-ordination; Corcyra and Acarnania are not interested in attacking Aetolia and refuse to help, reducing the size of his army, and he is held up in hilly country by highly effective Aetolian skirmishers with missiles. His 'hoplites' cannot bring them to a proper battle, his men are picked off and lose heart, and the archers cannot hit rapidly moving targets; the Athenians flee the first serious clash, and Demosthenes has to retreat to Naupactus minus around half his men.

Sparta sends out a colony of soldiers to Heraclea in Trachis, near Thermopylae, to rally support in Locris and extend her influence into Thessaly, with potential as ships are built at Heraclea to raid Euboea and attack shipping in the Euboea channel; 500 of this force then join a Spartan expedition at Delphi after Demosthenes' retreat emboldens them and Aetolia (September?). Some 2500 Peloponnesian 'hoplites' under Eurylochus assemble at Delphi, and they and their allies invade north into Ozolian Locris; Oeneon and Eupalium are stormed and the Aetolians aid the succeeding attack on Naupactus. Demosthenes is away recruiting more men in Acarnania, and he brings 1000 'hoplites' to relieve Naupactus by sea. Eurylochus gives up and moves off to winter in Aetolia.

426/5

Winter – Warned that its neighbour Ambracia is about to co-ordinate an attack on it with Eurylochus, Acarnania asks Demosthenes and an Athenian squadron off the west coast of the Peloponnese for help. The Ambracians send 300 men to seize Olpae, and as Eurylochus heads west to help them the Acarnanians occupy Crenae to try to block his route; he evades them and joins the Ambracian army. This combined force of around 6000 camps at Metropolis, north of the city of (Ambracian) Argos, to await more Ambracian troops; the Athenian squadron then arrives offshore, and Desmothenes comes from Naupactus and camps just south of the enemy at Olpe.

Demosthenes has fewer 'hoplites', but he challenges Eurylochus to battle before the enemy reinforcements arrive and six days later Eurylochus marches south on Olpe. Eurylochus takes his left wing, the inland (east) side of his army, while the Ambracians and Peloponnesians are on his right wing; he is ambushed by a force of light infantry and Acarnanians hidden to the east of his advance-route by Demosthenes, and he is killed and his men flee; the Spartan/Ambracian right wing is winning, but is now left cut off with its general dead and flees. Menedais, commanding the survivors who are surrounded on a hill, agrees a truce with Demosthenes and arranges for the Athenians to let his Spartans/Peloponnesians go and abandon their local allies; the abandoned Ambracians run after them as they march off, the Acarnanians think that both groups of soldiers are attacking as they have not been told of the arrangements and set on them, and a skirmish follows. The Spartans/Peloponnesians are able to escape as agreed with Demosthenes but the locals are massacred; Demosthenes then intercepts and wipes out the arriving Ambracian reinforcements at dawn next day.

Athens thus wins the Ambracian campaign; but the Acarnanians refuse to let Demosthenes destroy Ambracia as now its army is destroyed it is harmless and they do not want any Athenian garrisons. They duly agree a hundred-year defensive alliance with Ambracia.

425

February – Aristophanes' 'The Acharnians' is put on at the Dionysia festival: a contrasting view of the opinions of urban and rural Athenians on the war.

Sicily

Late spring (corn beginning to ripen – Thucydides) – Syracuse and her ally Locroi each send ten ships on an attack on Messina, which they secure to force it to end its alliance with Athens and so hinder any Athenian invasion.

Greece

Late spring (ditto) – Sparta under King Agis invades Attica again.

Simonides' Athenians in Chalcidice take Eion, but are driven out by the locals.

A Spartan fleet of sixty ships heads for Corcyra to join a planned oligarchic revolt against alliance with Athens; the assembly at Athens votes to raise the annual tribute due from their alliance steeply to between 1000 and 1400 talents a year, minus around 200 talents in indemnities, as part of Cleon's call for new efforts for military success. Forty ships under Eurymedon and Sophocles are sent to Corcyra and then on to aid the force in Sicily, accompanied by Demosthenes who is not a general this year but is authorized to intervene in the Peloponnese if he judges it viable. The fleet puts in at the promontory of Pylos, on the north side of the north one of two entrances to the large natural harbour of Pylos, due to storms. Demosthenes suggests fortifying a position there as a base, and is ignored by the generals; however, more bad weather delays sailing, and the sailors voluntarily build a rough wall to block off the 'neck' of the peninsula for Demosthenes. Five days later the sea is calm enough for sailing, but five ships remain behind with Demosthenes; after the main fleet leaves the alarmed Spartans recall their army from Attica and their fleet from Corcyra to deal with this threat to their control of nearby Messenia.

The Spartan fleet of sixty ships arrives off Pylos, and plans are made to recapture the Pylos peninsula; Demosthenes sends two of his ships to the Athenian fleet at Zacynthus to recall it, and then his around 1000 men drive back assorted attempts by the Spartans on land to storm the wall and force the 'neck' of the peninsula; the Spartans also land men from their fleet on the island of Sphacteria, south of the peninsula across the northern entrance to the harbour, to cut off Demosthenes' retreat. Thrasymelidas, the Spartan admiral, tries to land his men on the peninsula to take Demosthenes in the rear; this is thwarted.

After three days of heavy fighting, the Athenian fleet (fifty ships) arrives; next morning they attack the Spartan fleet in the harbour through the latter's north and south entrances and disable a lot of ships, towing some out to sea as prizes. This maroons the Spartan garrison on Sphacteria. The Spartans at home send officials to the site, and successfully seek an armistice with the Athenian fleet, which can take over the beached Spartan fleet and any other Spartan warships in Laconia in return for letting supplies go to Sphacteria.

Sparta then sends to Athens for a general peace treaty and a defensive alliance in return for allowing the safe evacuation of Sphacteria – the best offer since 432. The Athenian assembly is persuaded by 'hard-liner' Cleon to demand the cession of Nisaea (port of her enemy Megara), Pegae, and Troezen (north-east Peloponnese) and Achaea (north Peloponnese) to Athens to dramatically improve her position on land in the north Peloponnese (all these places are one-time Athenian allies lost earlier in the century), plus the surrender of the garrison on Sphacteria. Cleon insists on conducting talks in public before the assembly, not in private as the Spartans want, and the Spartans give up and leave.

The Athenian fleet-commanders at Pylos allege Sparta has violated the local armistice, and seize the entire Spartan squadron; fighting resumes, with the Athenians blockading Sphacteria from the sea and the harbour and the Spartans smuggling food across by small boats and divers. The delay in securing Sphacteria worries the assembly at home into a less belligerent mood, and a proposal is made to send envoys to assess the situation; Cleon boasts that they need a general not an inspector and real generals would conquer Sphacteria easily, and Nicias (currently in office as a general) challenges Cleon to take over his own office and go out to achieve just that. Cleon tries to backtrack, but the public starts to shout for him to go and he has to give way and accept the offer of command; he boasts that he will achieve victory in twenty days, and only takes Demosthenes among the current board of generals to help him.

Cleon and the relief-expedition arrive at Pylos to find that some of Demosthenes' men have accidentally started a brush-fire on Sphacteria while landing for a meal – it has cleared the undergrowth so he can see the Spartans moving around better. Demosthenes then sends in a landing-party at dawn to take the beaches at the southern end of the island, aided by smoke from the fire, to secure a bridgehead and takes light infantry more than 'hoplites' so they can throw missiles better and keep the Spartan garrison back. The first batch of men to land (800) storms the main Spartan forward position at the southern end of the island, and then the rest land and fight the other Spartans under their commander, Epitidas, who tries to hold the level centre of the island; Epitadas is killed. The Spartans retreat to an old fort at the northern end of the island, protected by steep slopes, but after the local Messenians aiding Athens climb a cliff to their level they have to accept the Athenian generals' request to surrender. Some 292 prisoners, including 120 Spartan citizens, are taken as prisoners to Athens, where Cleon arrives in the stipulated twenty days from his departure. The blow to Sparta's prestige is severe.

Athens sets up a Messenian garrison at Pylos, to help encourage local revolt; the fleet goes on to Corcyra to help the democrats defeat the oligarchs, who are persuaded to surrender for the Athenian people to judge their fate but are the handed over to the democrats and killed.

Nicias and a part-Ionian naval expedition ravage the coast of Corinth and Epidaurus, then go on to take the eastern promontory of the Peloponnese, Methana, for another base.

Sicily
War between the Syracuse/Locroi alliance and pro-Athenian Rhegium, and several clashes in the Straits of Messina as Athens' enemies use Messina as a base to try to attack Rhegium; they also attack Naxos, which the local Siceliots help to resist.

424

Persia
Death of Great King Artaxerxes after a reign of forty-one years; succeeded by his eldest son, Xerxes II, who is soon assassinated and is replaced by his younger brother Ochus (as 'Darius II').

Greece

Winter – Athens refuses Spartan peace-offers, and captures a Persian envoy en route to Sparta from whose papers it is confirmed that the new Great King is still neutral; the Athenian fleet tours the eastern Aegean collecting the increased rate of tribute for the alliance and forces Chios to dismantle some disputed fortifications.

March? – Aristophanes' 'Knights' is put on at the Athenian city Dionysia festival; another attack on Cleon as a self-interested, low-born and greedy warmonger.

June/July? – The new Athenian generals set out on campaign; Nicias sails to Laconia and captures the island of Cythera off the southern approaches to Sparta, which is garrisoned so supply-convoys to Sparta can be attacked; Nicias raids the coast of Laconia from it unhindered.

A plot by the Mytilene rebels on Lesbos to fortify Antandrus as a base is prevented as the Athenian fleet under Demodocus and Aristides, collecting tribute locally and now at the Hellespont, arrives in time to occupy it first.

Sparta massacres 2000 potentially rebellious 'helots', and institutes regular roving patrols to watch out for a rebellion by others; it sends off 700 second-class citizens ('neodamodeis') and loyal freed 'helots' with Brasidas to aid King Perdiccas of Macedon who is attacking the Athenian-allied Chalcidice, and 1000 Peloponnesian allies join this army en route as paid for by Sparta. They march to Heraclea in Trachis to meet up with local allies, and cross Thessaly with help from firstly Pharsalus and then the Perrhaebians to Dium on the Macedonian border where Perdiccas joins them. Brasidas refuses Perdiccas' request to aid him against his local rival, Arrhabaeus of Lyncestis/Lyncus in west Macedon, and meets and attempts to reach agreement with him instead, which annoys Perdiccas, and marches to the Chalcidice to join his local allies and attack pro-Athenian Acanthus. Eucles, commanding for Athens at Amphipolis, and the historian Thucydides, commanding at Thasos, request but are denied help from Athens.

Late August? – Athens accepts an offer from the democrats at Megara to help them against the recently-readmitted oligarchic exiles there, by taking the city. An Athenian force under Demosthenes (light infantry) and Hippocrates (600 'hoplites') arrives at the island of Minoa at night, lands on the mainland, and lurks outside the Long Walls between Megara and Nisaea; at dawn the democrats open a gate in the latter, and Demosthenes enters to occupy the walls; the democrats fail to gain control of Megara and let the Athenians in, but the planned Athenian 'second wave' of 4000 'hoplites' and 600 cavalry arrives on time from Eleusis to join Demosthenes and blockade Nisaea. Next day, Nisaea surrenders, and Megara is blockaded. However, the Spartan general Brasidas is currently raising troops near Corinth, and he sends for help to the Boeotians to meet him at dawn in two days at nearby Tripodiscus ready to rescue Megara. He arrives at the rendezvous first with his 4000 men, before dawn, and hurries immediately to Megara, but is refused admittance; then the 2200 'hoplites' and 600 cavalry arrive from Boeotia at dawn, and he challenges the Athenians to battle but they are outnumbered and retreat to Nisaea. Megara now admits Brasidas, and around 100 democrats are arrested and executed.

The Athenian army leaves a garrison in Nisaea, and plans to respond to appeals for help from democrats in several Boeotian cities and help them to reduce pro-Sparta Thebes' regional power; it is arranged for exiles from Orchomenus to invade from the north-west with their Phocian allies and seize nearby Chaeronea while Demosthenes sails to Phocis via the Gulf of Corinth and is admitted to Siphae in the south-west and an army from Athens (the largest force) marches across the frontier in the south-east to seize the temple of Apollo at Delium to rally local dissidents.

November – The three attacks are co-ordinated for the same day, but the pro-Thebans in Boeotian cities are alert and Demosthenes, arriving from Naupactus on forty ships, fails to gain admittance to Siphae as a local Phocian has informed Sparta who alerted Boeotia; Chaeronea holds out too. Hippocrates and the main army, the city levy of Athens, seizes the temple at Delium as planned, and spends two days fortifying it; on the third day the main army is sent back into Attica while he finalizes the defence and installs the garrison of 300 men, but meanwhile the Boeotian army is mustering in strength at Tanagra nearby and due to the failure of the other two attacks those Boeotians dealing with these can get there too. Ten of the eleven commanding 'Boetarchs' want to leave the Athenians alone when they hear that the main army is withdrawing, but the eleventh, warlike Pagondas of Thebes, is the day's commander on the rota and persuades the troops to attack.

Battle of Delium – Pagondas and around 7000 Boetian 'hoplites', 1000 cavalry, 500 'peltasts', and over 500 light infantry, draw up behind a ridge out of sight of the marching Athenian army, while a small force moves to cut off the garrison at Delium. The Thebans are on their force's right wing, Haliartus and Coronea in the centre, and Orchomenus and Thespiae on the left wing. Hippocrates hears of the muster and heads back to his main army, leaving 3000 cavalry at the temple of Apollo garrison; Hippocrates arrives to find that the light infantry are already out of reach ahead and draws up his 'hoplites' and cavalry, but he is still addressing them and laying out their battle-front when the Thebans lead the charge over the ridge downhill onto them. The depth of the Theban right wing (twenty-five men deep not the usual eight of the rest of the army) catches the Athenians by surprise, and they are driven back; the Boeotian centre and right are defeated, but as the Athenians are chasing them Pagondas sends his cavalry round via the hidden ground behind the ridge to suddenly appear and attack them from the flank. The Athenians break and run, and the Boeotian cavalry is joined by some Locrian cavalry late-comers to chase them. Hippocrates and around 1000 'hoplites' are killed; in the retreat the future Athenian statesman/commander Alcibiades (born c. 448), related to Pericles and the Alcmaeonids, is one of the cavalry who help to protect the fleeing infantry and he saves the life of his mentor, the philosopher Socrates, an infantryman. Part of the army reaches Oropus on the coast and is evacuated next day by sea to Athens.

December? (or January 423) – Brasidas makes a surprise night march in the snow east from the Chalcidice to cross the river Strymon near Amphipolis, which is unaware of his approach; he is guided by the local settlers of the town of Argilus, enemies of Amphipolis; he takes the city's suburb outside the walls by surprise, but at dawn his allies inside the city fail to open the gates as they are opposed by a majority. The Athenian commander Eucles sends for help to Thucydides at Thasos, but when Brasidas offers to release his local prisoners and let any citizens who so wish leave in peace the locals surrender the town; Thucydides and his seven ships arrive from Thasos at Eion at the river-mouth too late by a few hours and can only receive refugees from Amphipolis, but manage to hold onto the town as Brasidas attacks.

423

Brasidas receives the allegiance of Myrcinus and takes Torone.

Thucydides returns home to Athens, but is tried for incompetence and exiled.

March – Sparta concludes a one-year armistice with Athens on the basis of the 'status quo'. Two days later, unaware of the agreement, the city of Scione in Chalcidice surrenders to Brasidas' Spartans; when the news arrives he has already garrisoned the place and admitted it to the Spartan alliance, and Athens refuses to include it in the truce; Sparta offers to submit it to arbitration as allowed by the truce, but Athens refuses and the belligerent Cleon persuades the assembly to authorize an expedition to Chalcidice and execute the inhabitants of Scione. Nearby Mende deserts Athens too, and Brasidas sends a garrison as he regards Athens as violating the truce; Athens votes to punish Scione similarly.

March? – Aristophanes' 'The Clouds' is put on at the Athens city Dionysia comedy competition, but comes last: a comic but vicious attack on the philosopher Socrates as a 'con-man' teaching young wastrels to abuse their elders and pervert the truth with clever logic. Plato later blames this for popularizing the image of Socrates as a socially destructive trouble-maker and so contributing to his execution in 399.

Summer – Brasidas joins Perdiccas for a Macedonian attack on the king's neighbour Arrhabaeus of Lyncestis/Lyncus who has summoned Illyrian help, but is left stranded as the Macedonian army is attacked and flees one night; he organizes his men for a disciplined fighting retreat east across Macedonia, but a force sent out to Thessaly by Sparta to link up with him is halted there by locals allied to the defecting Perdiccas (who now allies to Athens).

Nicias arrives in Chalcidice, bases himself at Potidaea, recaptures Mende, and attacks Scione.

422

Spring – End of the truce; Cleon raises an Athenian army of 1200 'hoplites', 300 cavalry, and thousands of allies, paid for by an annual revenue of around 500 talents of tribute collected from the Athenian alliance (which Cleon is remorseless in collecting despite the resulting disaffection, which will have drastic consequences once Athens' power starts to fail). They sail to the Chalcidice and take Torone on the central peninsula, with Brasidas arriving too late to relieve it; the men are taken off as prisoners to Athens and the women and children are enslaved.

Cleon then sails to Eion, fails to take Stagira/Stagirus, takes Galepsus, and tells King Perdiccas of Macedon and their Thracian ally Polles to join him in attacking Amphipolis. He waits for them to assemble before advancing, but his troops complain at his caution compared with Brasidas, so he agrees to make a reconnaissance to Amphipolis before the attack. The watching Brasidas (with around 2000 mostly local infantry and 300 Greek cavalry) sees his men on the move towards Amphipolis and hurries there to reinforce it first.

Thebes takes Panactum on the Athenian frontier, by treachery; Athens sends out Phaeax to Sicily to rally local support to the exiled democrats of the town of Leontinoi, who have had to leave following an oligarchic pro-Syracuse coup and the resulting Syracusan depopulation/evacuation of the now-empty town. The democrats are holding out against

Syracuse near their former town, and Phaeax gets Camarina and Agrigentum to help them but fails to interest Gela – this is the start of the move to war between Athens and Syracuse, completed in 415.

August? – Battle of Amphipolis: Cleon arrives to find the city apparently quiet and moves in on the east wall, apparently unmanned, with Brasidas visible within the city (sacrificing, so possibly anticipating a battle soon) but no sign of the large Spartan force, which is dispersed out of sight, behind the south and north gates and below the east wall. The Athenians note the human feet and the hooves of cavalry visible under the south gate and become nervous; Cleon is told, takes a look, and decides to retreat but as he marches off his column of men is exposed on its right-hand (west) side to a direct line of attack from the nearby south gate. The Spartans under Brasidas charge out of the south gate to attack them, and his lieutenant Clearidas emerges with more men from the north gate to attacks the rear. Cleon is killed as he joins a general Athenian flight, but their rear rallies on a nearby hillock and has to be overrun by the local Myrcinian/Chalcidian cavalry; around 700 Athenians are killed, with only seven Spartans – but Brasidas falls to a chance blow, unnoticed by the Athenians who thus do not rally, so both states' armies lose their main 'war-mongers' who would stand in the way of a quick peace. Brasidas is honoured as the 'founder' of Amphipolis and annual Games are instituted in his honour.

Nicias takes the lead in Athenian plans for peace, and Sparta is nervous of the approaching end of its thirty-year truce with Argos in 421 as Argos is demanding Cynuria back as the price for renewing it. With Brasidas dead, King Pleistoanax takes the lead in accepting the need for negotiations and has to deal with the danger that as he was controversially recalled from exile any military defeat will cause his enemies to say that this was wrong and the gods are punishing Sparta; peace-conferences follow.

421

'Peace of Nicias' agreed – Athens and the Spartan alliance take oaths to a fifty-year, annually renewable peace with no acts of aggression and arbitration of all disputes. They are to guarantee free access to and the neutrality of shrines. including Delphi; prisoners are to be returned; Sparta will return her gains in Chalcidice and Bottiaea if their autonomy is guaranteed by Athens, and Athens retains Nisaea (in Megara's territory) but returns Plataea to Boeotia. Athens evacuates Pylos, the island of Cythera, Methana, Pteleum and Atalante; Sparta returns its own Amphipolis and the Thebans' acquisition of Panactum. Athens can deal with Torone and two other Chalcidice towns as it pleases. Extra terms can be added if both alliances agree.

Sparta puts the treaty to the vote of a meeting of its allies, which passes it by a majority; those in favour then take the oaths to the treaty, but the leaders of the anti-treaty minority (Boeotia, Megara, Corinth and Elis) refuse to do so and stand aloof; thus Thebes still keeps Panactum, annoying Athens.

After the Spartan allies' meeting, the disgruntled Corinthian envoys return home via Argos and induce the latter to elect twelve envoys to negotiate an alliance with any state in Greece except Athens and Sparta, with the Argive assembly having to approve beforehand if they want to include those two states; these envoys win over democratic Mantinea and Elis to the idea of an alliance of Peloponnesian states against Sparta, and Corinth then joins; Megara and the Boeotians refuse, as does Tegea, which is a rival of Mantinea.

August? – Sparta takes over the southern Arcadian district of Parrhasia, to which Mantinea has a claim; Argos installs a garrison in Mantinea to protect it from Spartan attack. Meanwhile, both Athens and Sparta release their prisoners-of-war and Sparta pulls her garrison out of Amphipolis, but Athens holds on to Pylos as a bargaining-chip to induce Sparta to pressurize Boeotia over returning Panactum. The troops sent to Thrace with Brasidas return to Sparta; its second-class citizens ('neodamodeis') and 'helots' are enfranchised as promised.

421–20

Winter – The new, 'hard-line' 'ephors' Cleoboulus and Xenares negotiate secretly with Corinth and the Boeotian League against Athens; they ask for Boeotia to give Sparta Panactum, so they can offer this to Athens in return for Athens handing back Pylos to them, with the Boeotians formally allying with Argos (to influence them against Athens) and the two allies then entering alliance with Sparta.

420

February? – Sparta allies with the Boeotian League, thus entering alliance with a state still formally at war with Athens (these two are only at truce, not at peace by treaty), and intends to ask Boeotia for Panactum so that can be exchanged for Pylos with Athens. The Boeotians, however, raze Panactum to the ground before handing it over so it is militarily useless, and the threat of a Sparta-Athens-Boeotia alliance aimed at them causes the nervous Argos to send an embassy to Sparta for a fifty-year truce (not a formal alliance, which Sparta wants from them).

Nicias tries to preserve the Athens/Sparta treaty, despite Athenian fears of what Sparta is up to with their foe Boeotia and annoyance that Amphipolis and the Chalcidian defectors are still out of Athens' hands; Sparta sends envoys to Athens to return Athenian prisoners-of-war in Boeotian hands, who Boeotia has passed to them, and explain the issue of Panactum; the Athenian assembly is suspicious of them, and Alcibiades (now operating as pacific Nicias' 'hard-line' foe and critical of Spartan aims) sends to Argos privately to ask them to offer alliance with Athens and bring in Mantinea and Elis. Argos agrees and abandons its current talks at Sparta; this alarms Sparta into sending three envoys to Athens with full powers to settle disputes, but Alcibiades does not want them to calm the assembly so he asks them not to mention their powers to the latter and in return he will arrange for the handover of Pylos to Sparta. The assembly meeting thus sees the Spartans not offering to settle all the disputes themselves, and Alcibiades deviously accuses them of showing Sparta's untrustworthy inconsistency. An earthquake halts the meeting before he can bring the annoyed citizenry to a vote; next day it resumes and Nicias wins the public over to keeping the peace and sending an embassy to Sparta (including him), but this mission is authorized to require Sparta to break off its alliance with Boeotia (unless Boeotia makes a treaty with Athens) and hand over Panactum and Amphipolis. Sparta refuses these terms.

July – After the failure of Nicias' mission Athens makes an alliance with Argos, Mantinea and Elis, only defensive so not immediately threatening to Sparta, but requiring all to make peace together and to keep others' armies out of their territory – which is aimed at Sparta.

419

Early – The Boeotians cause offence to Sparta by occupying the latter's garrison at Heraclea in Trachis and expelling their commander, Agesippidas.

Alcibiades is elected as a general at Athens for the first time (March?, in office June/ July); he undertakes a summer expedition round the northern Peloponnese with Athenian and allied troops, persuading Patras to extend its walls down to the sea (i.e. to make it safe to defy Spartas as Athens can deliver food by sea) and building a fortress at Rhium in Achaea.

Argos attacks Epidaurus, over its alleged non-payment of offerings to an Argive shrine but (Thucydides) really at the behest of Alcibiades who wants an excuse to gain control of Epidaurus and provide an easier route for Athens to intervene locally. Sparta sends out an army under King Agis, but he goes home after unfavourable omens and then the sacred month of Carnaea makes it inauspicious for military operations. Once Sparta is inactive Argos raids Epidaurus to ravage the countryside, and the local states meet at Mantinea to discuss it; Corinth persuades them to offer to mediate, but this fails.

418

Early – Sparta installs a garrison at Epidaurus, and Argos complains of this aggression to Athens; skirmishes follow.

The ex-'helots' from Brasidas' army and their 'neodamodeis' superiors are settled at Lepraeum, which Elis claims.

Megara and Corinth return to the Spartan alliance, out of dislike of Argos; Agis summons the Peloponnesian League army to meet him at Phlius for a march into the Megarid. The Spartan contingent is unusually large at around 6000 'hoplites' and 400 cavalry, along with 5000 Boeotian 'hoplites' (led by 300 Thebans), 5000 lightly armed and 500 cavalry Boeotians, 2000 'hoplites' from Corinth, and others from Megara, Sicyon, Phlius, Epidaurus, and Arcadia – around 20,000 'hoplites' in all plus thousands of light infantry. Facing them are around 600 argive 'hoplites' plus 300 from Elis, nearly as many from Mantinea, and others from Cleonae and Orneae, a slightly smaller force and without cavalry. Agis leads the Spartan troops across the Argolid towards Phlius as planned, but the Argive coalition intercepts him on the man road near Nemea for a defensive stand. That night Agis leads a third of his army off across country to the west of the road, ready to start ravaging the countryside to the enemy's south at dawn, while the Corinthians support him by marching south around the Argive position on another route and the Boeotians march directly down the main road towards the Argives. The latter discover at dawn that Agis has gone round their army, march on to find the Boeotians ahead, and fear encirclement by the three enemy columns; the Argive commanders Thrasylus and Alciphron send to Agis to ask for a truce, and a four-month truce is agreed; Agis marches to Nemea and sends his allies, who wanted a battle and are disgruntled, home.

In total, 1000 'hoplites' and 300 cavalry, led by Laches and Nicostratus, arrive from Athens at Argos to discover a truce in effect but that this is unpopular and Thrasylus has nearly been lynched; the generals from Elis and Mantinea disagree with the Argive plan to send the Athenians home (a long-term truce will leave them to Spartan vengeance while Argos stands aside) and so does Athens' current ambassador to Argos, Alcibiades; the three of them persuade the Argives to accept that the truce is not binding (as not agreed with Argos' allies) and agree to them marching off to attack Orchomenus in Arcadia. The Eleans object to the next intended target, Tegea, as they prefer Lepraeum. The Elean troops go home; the Argive, Athenian and Mantinean troops head for Tegea. The latter calls for Spartan help, and Sparta sends out Agis but with a board of ten advisers to assist him (i.e. prevent any more unwanted truces). The Spartans and their Arcadian allies advance into Mantinean territory, and come up against the allied army drawn up in a strong defensive position. Agis halts, but the Argives fear that Corinth will send aid to the Spartans quickly and next day they descend the hillside and attack.

Battle of Mantinea – Mantinea is on the Argive right, Argive troops are in the centre, and Athens and their allies Cleonae and Orneae on the left, amounting to around 10,000; they catch the Spartans still marching into position in columns, but Agis swings his men round into a line with the Spartan citizens in the centre, the second-class citizens and a regional Laconian regiment from Sciritis on the left, and the Tegeans to the right. The Spartan left is driven into by the Argive charge as it is manoeuvring round to their left to avoid being outflanked and taken in the rear by the Mantineans opposite, as ordered by Agis, and is forced back; two Spartan regiments have been too slow to fill in the gap between the Spartan left and centre and this gap is exploited by the Argives, but the Spartan centre and right under Agis routs the Athenians and their allies; Agis then quickly halts the pursuit and manoeuvres back to take on the Argives who are routed too. Sparta is victorious and around 1000 of the enemy are killed.

Early winter (end of Carneia festival) – Argos surrenders as a Spartan envoy arrives with terms, and renews its old alliance with Sparta for fifty years; all Peloponnesian states are invited to join in a defensive alliance with them; Athens is to be excluded from the Peloponnese.

417

Spring – After aiding the (higher-class and less democratic) Argive 'hoplites' to impose a friendly oligarchy on Sicyon, Sparta overthrows the democracy at Argos with their help; it installs a compliant oligarchy at Argos; Perdiccas of Macedon and the Chalcidians sign up as their allies.

First ostracism in Athens for years after rising political tension among the democratic elders; the rising young 'imperialist' aristocratic demagogue Alcibiades, a relative of Pericles and pupil of Socrates, and his older and more moderate/cautious critic Nicias unexpectedly join forces to successfully rid themselves of a rival, the demagogue Hyperboulus.

Both Nicias and Alcibiades are elected as generals; Nicias is sent to assist King Perdiccas of Macedon against the Chalcidice and Amphipolis, but the King changes sides so Nicas has to return home.

Summer (Gymnopedia festival) – While the Spartans are busy with a festival at home, the Argos democrats stage a bloody coup; they are thence at odds with Sparta again, but when they attempt to build 'Long Walls' down to the sea so Athens can send supplies by sea the Spartan army under Agis arrives to demolish them.

Winter – Athens blockades the Macedonian coast.

416

Spring – Alcibiades leads a naval expedition of twenty ships to Argos to arrest three hundred leading anti-Athenians, who are deported.

Athens decides on a pre-emptive expedition to the obstinately neutral Melos, a western Aegean island near the Peloponnese and colony of Sparta, to bully her into line; thirty Athenian ships, six from Chios, and two from Lesbos arrive at the island with 1500 Athenian (1200 'hoplite' and 300 archers) and 1500 allied troops under Cleomedes and Tisias. Melos is blockaded, and the ruling oligarchy defies orders from the expedition's envoys to join the Athenian alliance or else. (Thucydides presents a 'verbatim' but probably invented account of the arguments by the two sides at the confrontation, with the Athenians saying that the weak should submit to the strong.)

Winter – The inhabitants of Melos are starved into surrender as a second Athenian force under Philocrates arrives and tightens up the slack siege-lines; they agree to entrust their fate to the decision of the Athenian assembly; the latter accepts Alcibiades' proposal to treat Melos as a conquered enemy state and kill all the men and enslave the women and children; an Athenian colony is set up there.

An appeal comes to Athens from Segesta on Sicily against her rival Selinus, a Spartan ally, and an embassy is sent to investigate the feasibility of an expedition there; Alcibiades, eager for a noteworthy success, encourages talk of taking on not only Selinus but her local patron Syracuse, richest city in Sicily and a colony of Sparta's ally Corinth, who the Segestans have pointed out have overrun Athens' ally Leontinoi and expelled the citizens.

Athens sends Macedonian exiles and some of their own cavalry to Methone to raid neighbouring Macedonia; Sparta sends to Chalcidice to try to persuade them to help Perdiccas and end their own truce with Athens.

415

Spring – The Athenian envoys return from Sicily, with sixty talents plus an over-optimistic offer of more from Segesta to help pay an expedition to attack its enemy Selinus; the assembly agrees to send sixty ships commanded by Nicias, Alcibiades, and the elderly but aggressive Lamachus to Sicily; at their next meeting five days later, to consider the logistics, Nicias asks to be excused as he opposes the project as too risky considering the need to concentrate the army and fleet at home against Sparta (and its allies Corinth and Macedon) and to aid Argos. Sicily is no threat and if overrun would be no use and tie down their troops; Nicias also blames Alcibiades for inexperience and rash ambition. Alcibiades, however, enthuses the audience, especially the ambitious and confident young (according to Thucydides), despite Nicias warning of the high cost; the expedition is backed and the generals are told to proceed to draw up their plans to help Segesta, re-establish Leontinoi if feasible, and advance Athenian interests. In total 3000 talents are voted as the state's contribution, and wealthy citizens volunteer to fit out ships and then serve as their commanders ('trierarchs').

Mid/late June – The 1500 infantry 'hoplites', 700 armed marines (from the lowest class, 'thetes'), and 50 cavalry assemble at the Piraeus, to sail on sixty triremes and forty troopships. However, the night before sailing, someone goes round Athens smashing up the busts of Hermes, the 'Herms' – the tutelary divine protectors of houses placed outside them – in the infamous 'Mutilation of the Hermae', which is taken as an ill omen. Rumour blames the known 'mocker of the gods' Alcibiades, who is said to have conducted a blasphemous parody of the sacred 'Mysteries' of Eleusis at a recent party and to have defaced other statues after parties, though opponents of his or of the expedition are more likely. Alcibiades offers to stay behind and undergo a formal trial, but this is voted down – possibly his enemies want to conduct a second vote once his 'war-party' friends have sailed and they can command an assembly majority. The expedition sails, joining the allied contingents at Corcyra – 134 triremes, 2900 infantry 'hoplites', and 1300 archers, slingers, and lightly armed skirmishers.

'Witnesses' come forward in Athens alleging that Alcibiades and his friends smashed the 'Herms' in a drunken frolic, and the assembly votes to recall him; the state galley *Salaminia* goes off to collect him.

Sicily

The fleet arrives at Rhegium after disappointingly securing very little local support in southern Italy and not even permission to land at Tarentum; news arrives that Segesta can only provide thirty talents after all so Athens will have to pay for the expedition itself; a council of war is held and Nicias proposes just helping Segesta against Selinus then going home, Alcibiades proposes offering help to the island's Greeks and Siceliots and securing a safe base like Messina, then attacking Syracuse if there is enough support; Lamachus proposes heading straight for the unprepared Syracuse to take it quickly. Alcibiades wins the vote, but the expedition cannot gain the help of Messina and it is agreed to send half the fleet (sixty ships) south towards Syracuse, calling in at Naxos; Catana, halfway down the east coast to Syracuse, is selected as a base but they have to camp outside as the city holds out. Some ships reconnoitre Syracuse and invite the inhabitants of Leontinoi living there to defect, and Alcibiades cleverly invites the leaders of Catane out to a meeting in the Athenian camp so as they return some soldiers can slip in with them and seize the gates; the anti-Athenians flee and the town is secured.

August – The *Salaminia* arrives at Rhegium and Alcibiades and his allies agree to return to Athens as ordered, on his own ship; however, en route at Thurii they 'jump ship', and hide, and the Athenian officials have to go on without him. He takes a ship to Argos; later he goes to Sparta to offer his services there to general shock in Athens and Sicily. He is impeached for blasphemy and condemned to death in his absence. Nicias and Lamachus are left in command in Sicily. Meanwhile, Syracuse rallies under the command of Hermocrates.

Winter – The Athenian fleet, based at Catane, cruises round northern Sicily and causes local resentment by a raid on a small town, Hyccara near Panormus/Palermo, to take and sell prisoners; Selinus, Gela and Camarina aid Syracuse in a raid on Catana, encouraged by a Catanian who alleges that the locals will help the attack but is actually an Athenian agent. While the Syracusan army is en route to Catana, the Athenians sail into the mouth of the Great Harbour of Syracuse and land on its south-west shore, cut off by the river Anapus from assault from the city to the north. They fortify it, and the Syracusans hurry home and attack the camp; the Athenians (centre) and Argives and Mantineans (right wing) drive the Syracusans back, but the retreating locals are saved from rout by their cavalry and reach the city safely. The exposed Athenian camp near the temple of Olympian Zeus, west of the harbour, is then evacuated for the winter; the Athenians camp at Naxos and pressurize the local cities to back them and send to Athens for reinforcements.

Syracuse appoints a new board of three generals, headed by Hermocrates; they start to extend their walls round the mainland quarter of Achradina, north of the harbour, out westwards along the ridge towards the plateau of Epipolae. Hermocrates secures the help of Camarina in person, despite an Athenian appeal to them.

414

Syracuse sends ambassadors to Corinth and Sparta to gain help, and Alcibiades persuades the latter to back them by sending out a capable commander; he also wins over Sparta to distracting Athens nearer home by invading Attica and setting up a permanent base there in the town of Decelea near the Boeotian border, which will mean that Athens has to keep part of its army at home and Sparta can ruin its agriculture by raiding.

Most of the inland Siceliots agree to support Athens, but Messina does not; Athens also sends to Carthage and Etruria.

March/April? – 280 more infantry arrive from Athens with 300 talents to pay for allies and horses; the Athenians sail south to land one morning at Leon on the Bay of Thapsus, just north of Syracuse and close to the northern slopes of the Epipolae ridge, without opposition or being noticed. Hermocrates is holding military manoeuvres on the plain south of the ridge, and the Athenians scramble up the north side of it to seize the plateau and drive him back as he hurries his men up the ridge from the south. Diomilus and around 300 Syracusans are killed.

The Athenians build a small round fortress on Epipolae, about halfway between the north slope down to the sea (at Trogilus) and the south slope down to the harbour; they start to construct a wall north–south to connect these two points and so cut off Syracuse from the land. The Syracusans construct an east–west wall across the south side of the ridge to halt this wall's work southwards and save the south end of the ridge for them; the invaders storm it and so take over the south end of the ridge; the Syracusans, driven back onto low ground south of the ridge, then construct a palisade/ditch east–west across the low ground near the harbour and Lamachus leads an attack on it while the sick Nicias leads the defence of the round fort at Epipolae. The attack on the palisade is pushed back and Lamachus is killed in single combat with an officer called Callicrates; a general clash follows, the Syracusans attack west across Epipolae, and Nicias fires his stores of siege-materials and engines at the round fort to stop the Syracusans over-running the fortification. Then the Athenian fleet appears offshore as it arrives from Thapsus Bay near Leon to occupy the harbour, and the Syracusans withdraw into the city. Syracuse is blockaded and the work on the walls is hurried on; Etruria and the Siceliots send help to the Athenians. Syracuse deposes its generals and opens negotiations.

Gylippus, the Spartan general sent to Sicily, lands at Tarentum in Italy, gets no help from Thurii despite his father having been a citizen there, and proceeds to Himera in southern Sicily; Nicias despises him and fails to send out enough ships to intercept him. Gylippus rallies Himera, Selinus and Gela to send help to Syracuse and assembles an army of around 3000, while Gongylus of Corinth sails direct to Syracuse to tell the defenders that help is coming; Gylippus marches on Syracuse, climbs up the Epipolae ridge from the west, and forces his way across the ridge's northern side where the Athenian wall is not yet finished; he and his army enter Syracuse.

Gylippus leads the defence to build a counter-wall across the northern end of Epipolae to stop the Athenian wall reaching the sea, and his cavalry drive back the Athenians; the

Syracusan counter-wall blocks the Athenians' wall in a burst of work the following night, thus saving the north side of Epipolae for Syracuse. He captures the Athenian supply-base at Labdalum at the northern end of Epipolae, and Nicias moves his camp to the safer Plemmyrium at the south side of the Great Harbour but is resented by the sailors as it is far from the springs.

With the Syracusan cavalry now controlling the hinterland, Gylippus goes off to round up more local reinforcements; twelve more relief-ships arrive at the smaller city 'Lesser Harbour', between the mainland and the Ortygia island citadel, and Nicias fails to intercept them.

Greece

Athens combines with its new ally, King Perdiccas of Macedon, to attack Amphipolis.

Argos persuades Athens to send thirty ships to raid eastern Laconia – extending the 'proxy' confrontation in Sicily to Greece and so giving Sparta an excuse to attack Athens. The attack rallies the Peloponnesian League to the cause of renewed war, as urged by Sparta.

November? – Nicias sends an appeal to Athens for either a second large expedition or recall, as otherwise they cannot win in 413 with the enemy likely to be reinforced from inland and from the Peloponnese and his own local allies unreliable; he asks to be recalled himself. The assembly votes to send out Eurymedon quickly, with ten ships, and a larger expedition under Demosthenes in 413, and refuses to give up the war.

Death of King Perdiccas of Macedon after a thirty-six year reign; succeeded by his son Archelaus.

?(or 413) Alcibiades seduces Timaea, the wife of King Agis, while he is away on campaign; the resulting boy is acknowledged by the King as his son, Leotychidas, but rumours spread.

413

Early spring. King Agis invades Attica, and takes and fortifies the town of Decelea in northern Attica as advised by Alcibiades.

Sicily

Sparta sends 600 second-class citizens and 'helots' led by Eccritus, 500 Corinthians under Alexarchus, 300 Boeotians under Xenon and Nicon, and 200 from Sicyon to Sicily; a Corinthian squadron covers their voyage and attacks the Athenian fleet in the Gulf of Corinth at Naupactus to keep them occupied.

May/June – Sixty-five ships take around 1500 Athenian infantry under Demosthenes to Sicily, and they join with Charicles' Gulf of Corinth ships to raid eastern Laconia and take a mainland promontory opposite the island of Cythera to put pressure on Sparta.

At night, Gylippus takes his army by land round the harbour to attack Plemmyrium at dawn, which will coincide with a Syracusan fleet assault (thirty-five ships) across the Great Harbour on the Athenian fleet and Syracusan naval reinforcements (forty-five ships) coming round from the Lesser Harbour to assist them. A naval battle rages, while Gylippus and his men storm Plemmyrium and take its three forts and supplies; the Athenian navy rallies to push the less organized and initially successful Syracusans back, but they have lost control of the south side of the harbour and now Syracuse can bring in supplies and ships at will. Syracuse also now attacks and sinks some Athenian supply-ships en route to the siege off Italy and sends an envoy to the Peloponnese to collect volunteers.

Greece

Demosthenes sails to the Ionian Islands to take on volunteers, and Eurymedon arrives from Syracuse to warn him of the fall of Plemmyrium. He helps the Gulf of Corinth fleet harass the Corinthian squadron, then goes on to Italy while the local Athenian ships under Conon, based at Naupactus, fight a drawn battle with the Corinthians.

Sicily

Demosthenes arrives at Thurii as pro-Athenians take over the city.

July – The Syracusan fleet sails out into the Great Harbour towards the Athenians, but avoids battle; however, it keeps the invaders busy manning their ships to reduce the help that can be given on land, where the Syracusans attack the Athenian double-wall (facing inwards, inland, and outwards to the city) that protects the Athenian position on the southern part of Epipolae. After two days of naval inaction, the Athenians (seventy-five ships) attack the Syracusan fleet (eighty ships) but are routed as Gylippus' ingenious new 'rams' at the Syracusan ships' bows are used to smash the bows of the Athenian ships. Seven are sunk and many others damaged as Syracusan javelineers rain missiles onto the enemy ships, and the Athenians flee back to their anchorage where Nicias organizes their 'screen' of merchantmen there to drive back the attackers with lumps of iron dropped onto them. Just in time before a second attack on the anchorage, Demosthenes and his seventy-three ships and 5000 'hoplites' arrive at the harbour to save the Athenians and the Syracusans retreat.

Demosthenes disembarks his troops, and insists on an immediate attack despite Nicias' efforts; he organizes an attack on Gylippus' wall on Epipolae to try to cut the city off; this is repulsed. A night-time attack up the hill onto the western end of the ridge at Euryalus secures the nearby fort, but as the Athenians press on along the ridge the enemy counter-attacks, led by the Boeotians, and there is confusion in the dark; the Athenians' reinforcements are pushing up the hill at Euryalus but the terrain crams them into a narrow space and their retreating compatriots rush back into this, causing chaos in the poor moonlight. The Athenians either flee back downhill, fall over the cliffs, or are rounded up and slaughtered on the ridge by the Syracusan cavalry at dawn; Nicias blames Desmothenes for the disaster.

Demosthenes proposes to withdraw and head home, but Nicias refuses and claims that Syracuse is short of money and nearly exhausted (is he also afraid of being put on trial for the disaster?) and Demosthenes and Eurymedon propose to go to Thapsus or Catana to regroup but he opposes that too. A delay of some weeks ends (mid-August?) when Gylippus brings the Sicilian reinforcements and the Peloponnesian army sent out by Sparta to Syracuse, the latter having been blown off-course to Libya and delayed, and Nicias then agrees to withdraw.

27 August – An eclipse of the moon occurs on the eve of sailing, and the augurs say that the army must wait for twenty-seven days; Nicias agrees as do the majority of the troops so the evacuation is halted.

Mid-September (14 or 15?) – After capturing eighteen Athenian ships in the Great Harbour, the Syracusans are emboldened to create an improvised boom across the harbour-entrance and trap the enemy fleet. All the Athenian ships that can be manned (110) are sent out to break it, but they are surrounded at the boom by flank attacks and are sunk or driven back. The army watches from on shore. Back at the beach, the army protects the survivors; Demosthenes urges a second attempt next day but the demoralized sailors refuse to fight.

Nor do the army retreat that night, as while the Syracusans are celebrating and the road is open Nicias believes a fake message from Hermocrates saying that the Syracusans are manning strongpoints on the passes on the road to Catana and he will not proceed through unknown country in the dark.

(c. 16 September) Next day, the demoralized army is rested in its camp while the rested Syracusans proceed out to block the local passes; the march commences the next day, and the Athenians (around 45,000) are harassed as they head for Catana. After five days of demoralizing struggle with the Syracusans harassing them, they halt to camp as their supplies run out. The Athenians then sneak out of their camp leaving their fires burning at night to gain some distance.

(c. 17 September) Demosthenes' rearguard detachment is surrounded next day and he surrenders on a promise of their lives being spared and is seized before he can fall on his sword.

(c. 18 September) Nicias and his men are surrounded next day, but fight their way out; Nicias offers to surrender hostages and leave Sicily but is ignored. Next day ('26th of the month Carneius' in Syracuse, according to Plutarch – around 20 September) they reach the River Assinarus, and as the troops rush in a disorganized mass to the river to drink the enemy closes in and massacres them. Nicias is taken alive, and Gylippus wants to keep him and Demosthenes alive but the Syracusans and Corinthians insist on execution; 7000 survivors are put in the prison-quarries on the ridge near Achradina at Syracuse and used as slaves there, most dying, though the Athenian allies are later taken out to be sold off as slaves.

Greece
The news reaches Athens, which goes into mourning; with 200 warships sunk and around 40,000 light infantry/sailors and 4000 'hoplites' and cavalry dead her power is permanently shattered and the news leads to plans for revolt among many of her allies; on land she is blockaded by King Agis from Decelea.

413–12

A board of ten emergency commissioners ('probouloi') are given supreme powers at Athens to co-ordinate a drastic shipbuilding programme to replace the lost ships; they include Hagnon and the dramatist Sophocles. Cape Sunion is fortified.

412

Winter – Sparta builds a fleet of a hundred ships to conduct an offensive Aegean campaign and break up the Athenian empire, while King Agis leaves Decelea and tours central Greece collecting financial contributions to pay for it, looting in defiant Malis. Euboea and Lesbos (to Agis at Decelea) and Chios and Erythrae (to Sparta directly) get in touch and propose to join them and abandon Athens, and satraps Pharnabazus of Hellespontine Phrygia and Tissaphernes of Lydia offer support; the two satraps each want Sparta to send a fleet to their regions so a choice has to be made.

March/April – Election of new board of Athenian generals for the next year – a mixture of future democrats (Srombichides, Diomedon and Leon) and oligarchs (Phrynichus) in their political actions in 411.

Sparta's allied Peloponnesian League council decides to support the Chios revolt plan and negotiate with nearby Tissaphernes for his financial aid for it, not to follow Pharnabazus' idea for an expedition to the Hellespont; this marks the victory of Alcibiades and his ally, 'ephor' Endius, over Agis in Spartan policy. An envoy is sent to Chios to check that the island has as many ships to aid Sparta as the rebel envoys say. However, the League insists on waiting until the Isthmian Games are over (July) and only then transferring its fleet across the Isthmus of Corinth by rollers to the Saronic Gulf ready to sail. News leaks out to Athens, which sends an envoy to Chios to investigate; the first Spartan squadron sent out to join the planned revolts, twenty-one ships under Agis' nominee Alcimenes, bringing the new Ionia regional commander-to-be Astyochus, is intercepted by an Athenian squadron off Epidaurus and defeated; it is beached at Spiraeum near Epidaurus and halts there, and Alcamenes is killed and some ships burnt in an Athenian raid on the camp. Alcibiades proposes to go to Asia Minor to arrange a treaty with Tissaphernes – possibly to get him away from his enemy in Sparta, Agis.

Spring – Alcibiades and the Spartan general Chalcideus sail with five ships to the eastern Aegean, and on Chios anti-Athenian oligarchs revolt; Chalcideus and his fleet arrive at Corycus nearby as the plotters seize the island's ruling council at a meeting, and he and Alcibiades are brought to the meeting to announce that Sparta controls the nearby seas and other locals are ready to revolt too. Erythrae, and nearby Clazomenae revolt too, followed by Miletus to the south as Chalcideus and Alcibiades land there; the two go to Sardes, and negotiate the first Spartan-Persian treaty with Tissaphernes, whereby Persia aids a revolt in Ionia and in return is guaranteed the ancestral possessions of the Great King – which in Persians terms means that Sparta will abandon all Ionia to them, though this is fudged in the language to hide the Spartan betrayal of their supposed allies.

Four more Spartan ships arrive at Chios, from the squadron blockaded at Epidaurus, with Astyochus who takes up his command; Athens has to use up her reserve state fund of 1000 talents to fund her navy-building programme after the Chios revolt, and cannot prevent a squadron of ships from Syracuse arriving in the Peloponnese to join the Spartan fleet.

Eight ships from Athens under Strombichides arrive quickly at Samos to secure the island, and when a second fleet of twenty ships under Thrasycles arrives they try to stop a Spartan force heading for rebellious Miletus but arrive too late and just set up a nearby base at Lade. The Spartan navy (twenty-five ships) is blockaded at Miletus from the Athenian base at Lade, and a rebel Chian squadron arrives to help and plans attack on the Athenians at Lade but Chalcideus sends them home to protect their own island. En route home they are mauled by Diomedon's squadron, arriving from Athens. The Athenians at Samos are then joined by Leon too, bringing their squadron up to forty-six ships, and the democratic-minded Athenian crews instigate a successful revolution on Samos to overthrow the local oligarchic regime who might prefer Sparta.

Athens grants autonomy to Samos to encourage local Ionian loyalty. The Chian rebels and Spartan help under Deinidias attack Lesbos, and Methymna and Mytilene revolt; the Athenian fleet proceeds to Lesbos to recapture Mytilene, and Astyochus' Spartan fleet from Miletus breaks past the blockaders and comes to the rebels' help too late so Astyochus goes back to Miletus; the Athenians take Clazomenae and land on Chios to ravage the countryside. In the skirmishes that follow between the two main fleets around Miletus, Chalcideus is killed.

Autumn? – A larger force of forty-eight ships under Phrynichus brings 1000 Athenian infantry, 1500 Argive infantry, and 1000 allies to the eastern Aegean; they land near Miletus, and the locals and Spartans are joined by Tissaphernes and his mercenary infantry and Persian cavalry for a sortie; the Athenians win the battle, though the Milesians rout the Argives, and besiege Miletus.

The main Spartan fleet of thirty-three Peloponnesian (under Therimenes) and twenty-two Sicilian ships (under Hermocrates, victor in 413) arrives off Miletus; the news reaches the Athenians on the evening of their victory. Therimenes halts a few miles away to reconnoitre, and Alcibiades brings him the news from Tissaphernes and urges an attack. The outnumbered Athenian admiral Phrynichus withdraws to Samos, and the Spartans set up their naval base at Miletus. The Argive contingent then goes home at the end of the campaigning season, and its city does not send out any replacements for 411.

The Spartan fleet sacks Iasus, catching a small Athenian force there under Amorges unawares and handing him to Tissaphernes as a hostage, and sells its inhabitants as slaves,

Late – Tissaphernes delivers the first tranche of money for the Spartan fleet to Miletus; meanwhile, Alcibiades' ally Endius ends his term of office in Sparta, thus opening him to vengeance from the cuckolded King Agis and his allies.

412–11

Winter (possibly November 412 /January 411) – Rebels against Athens on Euboaea capture Oropus and urge Sparta to send its Ionian fleet to help a general revolt, without success.

There is trouble over Astyochus' inactivity, which is reported to Sparta while Pedaritus, Spartan commander on Chios, refuses to let his ships aid a Lesbos revolt so cautious Astyochus leaves that alone. A second, revised Spartan agreement is made with Tissaphernes (called the 'treaty of Therimenes' after its Spartan negotiator) for him to pay the fleet's expenses and treat the Spartans as full friendly allies. The new board of eleven Spartan commissioners ('xymbouloi') led by 'high-profile' Olympic victor Lichas arrive to advise Astyochus and send some of his ships under Clearchus off to the Hellespont. Charminus and an Athenian squadron from Samos are sent to Cnidus to deal with an arriving Spartan squadron from Greece under Antisthenes (January? as the latter left Sparta at the midwinter solstice) but are unluckily caught en route by Astyochus, who is on his way to collect Antisthenes' fleet and escort it to Chios, and defeated. Astyochus joins Antisthenes and at Cnidus they stay in harbour declining a challenge from the main Athenian fleet; the Spartan commissioners arrive too, to meet Tissaphernes at Cnidus, but cancel the agreement with him over it being too humiliating to agree to Persia's reoccupation of Ionia. He leaves angry.

Persia is offended, and now Alcibiades arrives at the Great King's court to say that Athens would be a better ally; Tissaphernes is summoned there for consultations and Alcibiades urges Persia to play Athens and Sparta off against each other and keep the latter short of money for their fleet to prevent their predominance. The Athenian fleet at Samos besieges rebel Chios, and Pedaritus the Spartan commander is killed in a sortie; the Spartan fleet, now aiding the oligarchs at Rhodes to fight off an Athenian attack, ignores their appeals for help.

Alcibiades joins Tissaphernes in Sardes, and sends to the naval commanders at Samos to say that he will win over Tissaphernes to aid Athens if they help to install a friendly oligarchy at Athens, which he and Persia can deal with and he will then return; they send envoys to him to discuss it, and on the latter's return put it to the assembly of the fleet; most men back them as they are tempted by the prospect of Persian money, but the senior admiral Phrynichus tells his fellow-officers later that he does not trust Alcibiades or Persia. The officers send Peisander to Athens to announce the plan and suggest that the survival of the state is more important than its constitution and they need the Persian money and Alcibiades' talents. Peisander and ten others are chosen by the assembly to negotiate with Alcibiades and Tissaphernes, implying Alcibiades' recall and an oligarchy; they also agree to sack obstructive Phrynichus. Meanwhile, on Samos Phrynichus has apparently been writing to Astyochus the Spartan commander at Miletus, warning him of Alcibiades and Tissaphernes planning an alliance and a Persian/Athenian accommodation, with the result that Astyochus goes to Lydia to inform Tissaphernes of the plan now being known to Sparta – a plan by Phrynichus to discredit Alcibiades and ruin his Persian treaty and his recall?

411

January ('Lenaia' festival) or March ('City Dionysia' festival) – First performances of Aristophanes' plays, 'Lysistrata' (topical satire on war-weary women forcing their menfolk to give up fighting by a 'sex strike') and 'Thesmophoriazusae'/'Women Celebrating the Thesmophoria Festival'.

March? – Peisander's embassy goes from Athens to Sardes or Magnesia in Lydia, but Tissaphernes sets his terms of alliance too high and Alcibiades, acting as his spokesman in the talks, backs this, presumably to preserve his own influence. The satrap wants Athens to abandon Ionia, the nearer islands as well as the mainland, to Persia and let its fleet sail there unhindered.

April – Tissaphernes renews his treaty with Sparta, agreeing to mutual moves on war and peace and to his paying the Spartan fleet until the Persian (Phoenician) one arrives and then loaning money to Sparta instead; all the Great King's territory on the mainland is to remain his, implying Spartan abandonment of currently Greek mainland Ionia to its Persian ex-rulers. Meanwhile, during Peisander's mission his anti-democratic allies in the now open and hotheaded oligarchic 'clubs' in Athens start to put pressure on the Athenian democracy by violence and assassinate the democratic leader Androcles and others; an alliance of the (mostly extremist) clubs and the more moderate majority of oligarchic supporters takes over control of debates in the 'Boule' and assembly and urge a constitution limiting political participation to the wealthier citizens who are fitted to pay for and serve in the war – probably a government by '5000'. A reign of terror against their opponents silences opposition.

April/May? – Dercyllidas' Spartan force, sent north from Miletus, assists anti-Athenian revolt at Abydos on the Hellespont, threatening the Athenian supply-route to the Black Sea; Pharnabazus of Hellespontine Phrygia aids his attack. Astyochus in the south-eastern Aegean still avoids tackling the Athenian fleet, which is blockading Chios. Athens sends Strombichides from Samos to recover rebel Lampsacus and blockade Abydos.

Late May? – Peisander returns to Athens, with some Ionian oligarchic regime volunteers enrolled by him as troops. En route, some of his embassy have been installing oligarchic regimes in allied cities and islands, e.g. at Thasos. The oligarchic party convene the assembly and propose setting up a board of ten to revise the constitution by a named date; the assembly agrees on a compromise of the board of ten who served after the Sicilian disaster plus twenty others, all over forty so experienced. (Aristotle, confirming basic details by Thucydides.) One of the board of ten is the dramatist Sophocles.

The assembly wants the new board to refer to the constitution of Cleisthenes (509), i.e. a moderate oligarchy as in existence until the 460s, but Peisander's allies control the board's agenda; at the arranged assembly meeting (at Colonus outside the city walls so potentially dangerous if Spartans attack) to announce their decisions they announce the deposition of the current magistrates and the election of a 'board of five' who will then select a hundred trusted allies before the hundred then each choose three men to join them. The 'Four Hundred' will then govern the state and select a new electoral body/assembly of 'Five Thousand' (qualifications not stated) who will help them to govern for the rest of the war. (Thucydides implies that the extremists only intended the 'Five Thousand' as a smokescreen for a narrow oligarchy.) The assembly agrees, and the oligarchic 'hard-liners' then arrange a coup.

A few days later ('14th Thargelion' – probably 9 June) they and the Ionian troops assemble on the Agora in arms, as the unaware citizens go home from manning the walls, and the 'Four Hundred' and their bodyguard of 120 youths, all armed, take over the Council Chamber and evict the Boule.

Antiphon, assisted by Peisander and Phrynichus, emerge as the 'hard-line' leaders of the new regime, the 'Ten'; with Theramenes leading their moderate allies; there are some executions and exiles and an offer is sent to Agis at Deceleia for talks but is ignored; when the King marches on Athens the citizens man the walls and resist him. Envoys are sent to Sparta and to the fleet at Samos; meanwhile, the defection of Peisander's new oligarchic regime at Thasos, which appeals to Sparta for help (July), undermines his reputation.

The news of oligarchic plotting in Athens alarms and infuriates the men of the fleet at Samos (where most of the rowers are of the lower social classes and pro-democracy), and Thrasyboulus and Theramenes lead them in resistance; before the actual coup in Athens (i.e. June) allies of the oligarchs in Athens on Samos start to kill potential local opponents, starting with the exiled Athenian demagogue Hyperboulus, and the fleet aids the democrats of Samos in suppressing the oligarchic conspiracy in street-battles; it sends the state galley *Paralus* to Athens to announce their victory over the plotters, but the ship arrives to find the city in the hands of the oligarchs; the crew are arrested, but some escape back to Samos to announce the coup.

News of the Athens coup and exaggerated stories of atrocities, mainly due to escaped *Paralus* crew-member Chareas, alarms the fleet; the fleet's assembly denounces the coup and elects a new board of generals headed by Thrasyboulus and Theramenes. The assembly of the fleet takes an oath to democracy, which all are compelled to participate in. The Athenian regime's envoys hear of this revolution at Delos en route to Samos, and halt. The fleet sends to Sardes to ask Alcibiades to return and lead them, as proposed by Thrasyboulus; he is elected as their general and arrives before the belated arrival of the oligarchs' envoys from Delos.

Hearing of the revolution on Samos, Spartan general Astyochus sets out with his fleet to attack the disorganized Athenian fleet but goes back to Miletus after he hears that Strombichides and his squadron have arrived from the Hellespont to join them. However, a few weeks later Helixus of Megara and some Spartan ships get away safely to the Hellespont to stir up revolt around the Propontis, which is probably the decisive factor in the Athenian fleet deciding to recall Alcibiades quickly.

August? – Amidst mutiny from the underpaid sailors at Miletus and fighting with local anti-Spartans, the new admiral Mindarus and the next year's reinforcements arrive at the Spartan fleet's base.

The Athens oligarchs' envoys address the Samos fleet reassuringly and say that they can later join the 'Five Thousand' whose members will be rotated, but are nearly lynched and Alcibiades has to rescue them; he sends the envoys back with a message that the 'Four Hundred' should abdicate and restore the legal 'Boule', the 'Five Hundred', but the 'Five Thousand' can stay if they continue and pay for the war.

The new Athens regime's envoys to Sparta are arrested en route by the defecting sailors of the state galley *Paralus*, who are taking them there, and interned at Argos; Argos defects from Sparta to the cause of the democrats at Samos.

Theramenes and Aristocrates rally the moderates in the oligarchy to press for restoring the Five Hundred council, setting up the Five Thousand quickly, and coming to terms with Alcibiades, and their 'hard-line' rivals send an urgent second mission to Sparta, led by Antiphon, Peisander and Phrynichus; while they are away the other extremists fortify a headland position (Eetionea) by the harbour at Piraeus ready to assist any landing Spartan troops; when the envoys return Phrynichus is assassinated after a council meeting as he leaves the council chamber building.

September – A Spartan fleet sails into the Saronic Gulf to raid Aegina; fearing an attack on the Piraeus, Aristocrates leads the moderates' men to pull down the fortification of Eetionea at the Piraeus. The extemists' general Alexicles is arrested, and Theramenes persuades the rest of the Four Hundred to send him and his fellow-moderate Aristarchus with troops to intervene; they let the demolition go ahead as moderate soldiers arrest their extremist officers at the confrontation. The moderates now seize the Piraeus and march on the city, and the extremists who still control Athens send out a delegation to agree to announce the names of the 'Five Thousand' quickly and thence have the Four Hundred council elected from that body.

The two factions agree to meet a few days later at the theatre of Dionysus for an assembly to discuss the list of the new 'Five Thousand'. This is halted as another Spartan fleet is spotted at sea off Athens on the day of the meeting, and the citizens man their fleet and sail after it to join their guard-ships off Euboea where the Spartans are heading. One of the two Athenian squadrons, thirty-six ships at Eretria, is mauled badly by the Spartans (under Agesandridas) in a surprise attack aided by signals to the latter by the Eretrians to indicate that most of the Athenian sailors are on shore foraging.

The assembly is convened at Athens at the usual Pnyx venue, a return to pre-coup procedure, and dismisses the illegal 'Four Hundred' and establishes the proposed 'Five Thousand'; the extremists flee to Deceleia to seek Agis' help. The moderates under Theramenes are thus in control of Athens, and vote to recall Alcibiades and work in alliance with the democrats at Samos; the war is resumed. The new constitution is finalized, with the precise terms not certain – probably ten representatives, one from each tribe, select the finalized '5000' (i.e. 500 from each tribe) on the basis of being aged over thirty and from the upper three property-classes. The 5000 are then divided into one, executive council and the other three councils as a consultative assembly, with the executive council chosen annually by lot. This is, in effect, government by about half the male citizen population, but it is still unacceptable as a permanent solution by the democrats at Samos.

The Persian Phoenician fleet arrives at Aspendus in southern Asia Minor but does not enter the Aegean – increasing Spartan distrust of Tissaphernes?

September? – After Mindarus replaces the timid and unsuccessfully inactive Astyochus in command of the Spartan fleet at Miletus, he heads for northern Ionia to seek better financial support from Pharnabazus; currently Alcibiades is visiting Tissaphernes again with thirteen ships, and one Athenian squadron is at Sestos in the Hellespont watching the Spartan squadron at Abydos and the rebels in the Propontis (led by Byzantium) so Mindarus has more confidence in being able to move his fleet without disaster. He moves north to Chios, and the Athenian fleet at Samos moves after him up to Lesbos; he evades attack and reaches the Hellespont safely to join the Spartan squadron there. The Athenians at Sestos are attacked unawares and lose four ships; Thrasyboulus and Thrasyllus take the main fleet north from Lesbos to join the survivors, and reach Elaeus; they have seventy-six ships, Mindarus has eighty-six.

Battle of Cynossema – The Athenians head north up the west side of the Hellespont for Sestos, just as the Spartans are moving south down the east side towards Dardanus; near the promontory of Cynossema (south of Sestos), Mindarus and the leading Spartan ships suddenly turn west across the channel to attack Thrasyboulus' rear squadron, with the leading Athenian ships under Thrasyllus already being out of sight round the promontory of Cynossema up-channel. Thrasyboulus has to call his centre back to aid his rearguard; the Spartan centre attacks the opposing Athenian centre, denuded by the ships that Thrasyboulus has called downstream to help his rearguard, and drives it back but becomes ragged in formation in the pursuit; Thrasyboulus rallies his ships and breaks the ragged Spartan centre, driving it north to the Cynossema promontory. Thrasyllus reappears round the promontory (or the Spartans are driven round it into his view) and drives in on the Spartan ships from the north, routs Mindarus' squadron, and rescues the Athenian centre. Sparta's Syracusan allies flee, and Sparta loses the battle and twenty-one ships; Athens loses fifteen. The Spartans get away safely, but have to abandon the Propontis where Athens now retakes rebel Cyzicus.

The Peloponnesian fleet that has won the clash off Eretria is wrecked in a storm en route to the Hellespont to aid Mindarus; the Athenians take heart, and Alcibiades persuades Tissaphernes not to call in the Phoenician fleet to aid Sparta and then fortifies Cos as a base before taking over command at Samos for the winter.

November – Dorieus' Spartan squadron at Rhodes avoids Alcibiades and the Samos fleet, and heads north to the Hellespont; it is spotted by Athenian lookouts, and their fleet at Sestos comes out to challenge him; he pulls to shore on the east side of the channel at Rhoetum, waits for them to give up and leave, then re-floats and heads on to Abydos; he is caught and has to beach his ships at Dardanus, short of Abydos, but Mindarus arrives with the main Spartan fleet from Abydos to rescue him and Pharnabazus brings aid by land. The seventy-four Athenian ships, commanded by Thrasyllus and Thrasyboulus, are outnumbered but win a fierce battle as Alcibiades comes in view with his squadron towards evening and the Spartans flee. Thirty of their ships are taken.

410

Thrasyllus and Theramenes are joined by Alcibiades at Sestos; Thrasyllus reports their successes to Athens, and retakes oligarchic Paros and raids rebel Euboea en route.

He is sent back with more ships and with Theramenes as a new commander.

Alcibiades fails in a mission to win over Tissaphernes when the latter arrives at the Troad, is interned by him at Sardes under house-arrest, and has to escape back to Sestos.

Spring – Alcibiades brings his fleet up the Propontis to aid Cyzicus, which Sparta and Pharnabazus have retaken. He catches Mindarus holding manoeuvres out at sea, and possibly (Diodorus, denied by Xenophon) lures him out to sea with a feigned retreat so other squadrons can suddenly move up and attack the Spartans. He defeats the Spartan fleet of sixty ships, drives it ashore, and lands to capture it and then defeat the joint Spartan and Persian army; Mindarus is killed. Alcibiades takes Cyzicus. Sparta's position in the Propontis is seriously affected and her fleet sends home for help.

June – Democracy is restored in Athens by vote of the assembly as the 'Five Thousand' lose support, Sparta offers peace on the basis of the 'status quo', sending Alcibiades' old friend Endius who was 'ephor' in 413/12, but Athens refuses in a vote of the assembly; this is primarily due to the rise of a group of vengeful democratic extremists, led by Cleophon, who organizes prosecutions of the extremist oligarchic leaders remaining in the city in violation of the presumed amnesty and drives the future leader of the 'Thirty' in 404–03, Socrates' pupil Critias, into exile. The 'Decree of Demophnatus' (July) proposes execution for anyone who in future tries to undermine democracy, and is passed.

Theramenes sails around the Aegean evicting oligarchic regimes installed by the 'Four Hundred' and fining places, which have deserted Athens; Conon takes a squadron to Corcyra to aid the democrats in another local civil war.

Theramenes aids King Archelaus of Macedon in an attack on the coastal town of Pydna.

New Athenian officials and military commanders are elected from both the defunct regime and the Samos fleet democrats in July. Thrasyllus is elected as a general for 410/09, and Thrasyboulus is sent out with infantry and cavalry reinforcements to the war in the Hellespont.

409

Early – Sparta recaptures the Athenian position at Pylos off the Messenian coast, after an Athenian relief-squadron under Anytus is forced to sail home after losses in a storm.

Sparta's ally Megara recaptures its port of Nisaea from Athens; Leotrophides and Timarchus lead 1000 infantry and 400 cavalry from Athens to recapture it, but despite a successful battle at 'The Horns' near the frontier this is not accomplished.

Cratesippidas brings twenty-five more ships to the Spartan fleet at Miletus, and aids an anti-Athenian coup on Chios.

408

Sicily

Spring – A Carthaginian and local mercenary army commanded by Hannibal (grandson of Hamilcar, killed in 480) invades Greek territory, collects local support from the Siceliots, sacks Selinus, and attacks Himera; the Syracusans send Diocles to relieve it, but Hannibal evades him, captures the city of Himera, and tortures and executes 3000 prisoners.

Greece

Spring – Thrasyllus attacks Abydos in the Hellespont by sea while Alcibiades takes the cavalry by land; Pharnabazus arrives by land and fights Thrasyllus' men as they land, but is then caught by Alcibiades in the rear and routed; the city does not fall but the rift between the soldiers of the two generals is mended by their success.

Theramenes sails to Chrysopolis on the Bosphorus and attacks Spartan-occupied Chalcedon (where Hippocrates commands), and Alcibiades and Thrasyllus arrive from Lampsacus to join him; Alcibiades fights off the Chalcedonians' Bithynian allies as he ambushes a column of the city's valuables being evacuated into Bithynia, and Chalcedon is besieged with a palisade built across the landward side of the Athenian camp from the Bosphorus to the Propontis so Pharnabazus, who arrives, cannot intervene easily. Hippocrates is killed in a sortie, Pharnabazus retreats, and Alicbiades leaves the surrender-negotiations to Thrasyllus and Theramenes as he heads off on raids; Pharnabazus helps to negotiate the terms whereby Chalcedon surrenders and rejoins the Athenian alliance with overdue tribute paid but is not occupied, and he offers to help an Athenian embassy go to the Great King.

Alcibiades collects Thracian troops from the Chersonese, and returns to the Bosphorus via a surprise night-time attack on recalcitrant Selymbria where his allies open the town gates and he does not pillage the town but requires the locals to pay tribute and accept a garrison.

Summer–autumn? – Byzantium is besieged, Clearchus commanding its Spartan garrison; the starving citizens soon have enough of the arrogant Spartan's refusal to negotiate, and Alcibiades arranges for his allies in the city to spread rumours that he has to leave on urgent business, then has his ships sail off and land-army move back out of sight of the walls one night; some of his ships then return suddenly to attack Spartan shipping at the harbour, and while the defenders are dealing with this his land-troops arrive and put ladders up the walls. Fighting is fierce, but when Alcibiades' herald announces that the Byzantines will not be harmed they give up and the Spartans are overwhelmed. Byzantium rejoins the alliance and pays tribute, but no garrison is installed.

Athens' embassy to the Great King sets out, but has only reached its promised sponsor Pharnabazus at Gordium in Phrygia by winter. A rival Spartan embassy under Boetius, meanwhile, reaches Susa to seek an increase in Persian military and financial commitment.

Sicily

Autumn – Hannibal goes home, leaving a garrison in Himera. Hermocrates raises an army of mercenaries, lands in Sicily, bases himself at Selinus, and marches west to raid Carthaginian territory with the help of refugees from Himera; he reaches the ruined city, and recovers the bones of the dead from Diocles' expedition and sends them back to Syracuse as a goodwill gesture. He does not escort them himself as he is still exiled. But he is not recalled to Syracuse as he expected, though his enemy Diocles is exiled as the latter's abandonment of the bodies of the fallen is used against him; later Hermocrates marches on the city with 3000 men as friends inside it invite him to aid a coup, seizes the Achradina gate and enters, but is killed in street-fighting with the democrats. Among those of his men who escape the debacle and flee into exile but are listed as dead by their friends so they are not proscribed is the future tyrant Dionysius (born 430?).

407

Greece

Spring – The Spartan embassy returns from Susa after gaining promises of support from Darius II, and tells the Athenians who they encounter on their way home; the Spartans are accompanied by Darius' younger son Cyrus (born c. 435?), who is to take over as satrap of Lydia (and overlord of the other satrapies in the region as 'karanos') at Sardes and assist the Spartans. Tissaphernes is demoted to the satrapy of Lydia; possibly Cyrus' mother Parysatis gained him this command as part of a plan to replace her disliked elder son Arsaces (later Artaxerxes II) with Cyrus as the heir.

The new Spartan naval commander, the ambitious Lysander (socially inferior as ?the son of a 'helot' mother and a 'new man' of talent, and possibly the lover of king Agis' brother Agesilaus as Plutarch says), succeeds Cratesippidas and sails to the eastern Aegean via Rhodes and Cos; he makes friends with Cyrus when the latter reaches Sardes (June?), securing some money for troops from him, and moves the Spartan base from Miletus in southern to Ephesus in central Ionia. He also encourages the aristocrats and oligarchs of Ionia to support him financially by promising to overthrow the local democracies when Sparta takes over the region, and wins money from them.

Thrasyboulus and thirty ships subdue rebels in the northern Aegean, led by Thasos and the Thracian town of Abdera, while Alcibiades and the other admirals return to Athens. Alcibiades does not return directly with the others, but goes to Samos and on to Caria to collect money and then heads for the Peloponnese to check on shipbuilding at the Spartan port of Gytheium – he is probably waiting to see if his allies or critics are successful in the annual generalship elections (usually in March, but in 407 probably April/May). He and his allies Thrasyboulus and Adeimantus are elected, but not Theramenes (as he was too close to the discredited oligarchs of 411 at a time of democratic upsurge?) nor Thrasyllus. Once he is sure of a warm welcome, Alcibiades leads his squadron of twenty ships to the Piraeus ('25th Thargelion', when the great statue of Athena is covered up as part of the Panathenaic festival – in mid-June) and is honoured by the populace, although there is unease at him returning on what is seen as the unluckiest day of the year; he clears himself of the charges laid against him in 415 and has his property restored by popular vote after making an explanatory speech to the assembly on the Pnyx.

Alarmed at Lysander's success with Prince Cyrus, Athens decides to send an embassy to the latter to win his goodwill; however, she chooses Tissaphernes of Caria as the local expert to help the embassy, and relations between him and Cyrus are not good. The embassy gets nowhere at Sardes, possibly undermining Alcibiades' usefulness to Athens as a conduit to his Persian friends.

September – Alcibiades escorts the procession of the Eleusinian Mysteries to Eleusis by road, the first time it has gone that way since King Agis took over Decelea, to show his piety after the scandals of his alleged 'desecration' of the Mysteries earlier and the 'herm'-breaking incident; a few weeks later he leaves Athens with his naval command, and attacks Andros but cannot take it; he loots Cos and Rhodes, then goes via the Athenian headquarters at Samos to friendly Notium, the port of the Ionian city of Colophon south of Ephesus. By now Lysander, with ninety ships and raised rates of pay for his sailors, outnumbers Alcibiades, but Lysander evades battle; stalemate follows.

Sicily
Syracuse sends envoys to Carthage to demand that they cease interfering on the island; the Carthaginians raise a huge army for an attack in reply.

406

Greece
Early? – After several months of inaction at Notium, Alcibiades heads off, possibly to assist Thrasyboulus who is besieging Phocaea; in his absence he leaves Antiochus, the pilot of his own trireme, in command of the main fleet of around eighty ships – a very unusual choice for the era and much-criticized later. Antiochus ventures too close to Ephesus with his ship in some sort of attempt to provoke Lysander out to fight, without close support, and is killed as Lysander and three Spartan ships pounce on and sink his ship; the rest of the Athenian fleet is routed, losing twenty-two ships, and Alcibiades returns and tries to provoke another battle to repair the disgrace but Lysander stays in port. Alcibiades has to return to Samos.

Back in Athens, some attack Alcibiades for arrogance and Thrasyboulus the son of Thraso accuses him of giving drunken sailors high commands and living a life of debauchery (Plutarch); he is sacked as naval commander and Conon is told to leave the siege of Andros and replace him; Alcibiades retires to a fortress in the Thracian Chersonese.

March – New generals/admirals are elected in Athens for the next year: Conon, Diomedon, Pericles (son of the late leader Pericles), Leon, Erasinides, Archestratus, Protomachus, Thrasyllus, and Aristogenes. Conon is currently commanding the fleet at Samos, since Alcibiades left, and hands over sole command when the next archonal year commences in early July. Meanwhile, Callicratidas replaces Lysander in command at the Spartan fleet headquarters at Ephesus for 406–5, probably arriving in April 406. Lysander's supporters undermine him by spreading stories that he is too young and inexperienced, but he wins them over although Lysander has deviously handed back the unspent part of his subsidy from Cyrus to its loaner so Callicratidas cannot use it and will thus achieve little, although Callicratidas is legally entitled to it. Callicratidas has to go to Cyrus for it, and leaves empty-handed after a quarrel, according to Xenophon complaining that Greeks should not fawn over barbarians and he would prefer the more dignified policy of peace with Athens.

Sicily
Hannibal and the younger Hamilcar, son of Hanno, return to Sicily with a large army (100,000 according to Timaeus, thrice that according to others) including African, Iberian (Spain), and Italian (Campanian) mercenaries and found the city of Therma ('the Hot Springs') as a base for the devastated Himera region, while Carthage asks Athens to keep Sparta and Corinth from intervening. The Spartan mercenary Dexippus, currently in Gela, is sent with a mercenary army to lead the defence of wealthy Akragas, the Carthaginians' main target, while the Syracusan commander Daphnaeus collects a large Sicilian/ mercenary army and marches to relieve Akragas. Akragas refuses to surrender despite a Carthaginian offer of their becoming a friendly neutral without a garrison; Daphnaeus and his army rout the Carthaginian force sent to block a river to their advance and hurry to the city, but Daphnaeus will not press ahead to the panicking Carthaginians' camp as his men are too disorganized and the city's garrison fails to emerge to aid them; recriminations over

this missed opportunity after Daphnaeus' arrival leads to most of the city's commanders being executed by the assembly, and Dexipus is accused of taking a bribe to help Carthage.

Hannibal intercepts some corn-supplies for the besieged sent by sea by alerting his ships in Motya in the west of Sicily to pounce on them, but later dies of the plague in an epidemic; this is blamed on his men demolishing the tomb of local ruler Theron and the besiegers carry out human sacrifice to appease the gods. Daphnaeus, who has taken command in Akragas as Dexippus and his mercenaries leave for Messina, loses heart as he is not relieved by the eastern Greek cities, and evacuates Akragas with many inhabitants also fleeing (early winter?).

Greece

Callicratidas puts out an appeal for money, collects enough from his Ionian allies at Miletus and Chios, and sails with 140 ships to attack the fortress of Delphinium on Chios; he takes it, occupies the island of Teos, and then heads north to Lesbos to take the pro-Athenian city of Methymna by assault but free its inhabitants rather than enslaving them; Conon is outnumbered at sea until reinforcements under the other new generals arrive, and stays at Samos. The Methymna assault makes Conon move his seventy ships closer, to the Hekatonnesoi islands off the Asian mainland, opposite the northern side of Lesbos on which Methymna stands.

Callicratidas attacks, and Conon has to retreat as he is outnumbered by about two to one; he reaches the harbour of Mytilene on Lesbos (halfway down the Eastern shore) and is blockaded there. The Methymnans join Callicratidas to attack Mytilene on land too; one of the two ships that Conon sends for help gets through to Athens, while the Spartan success impresses Cyrus into sending funds to Callicratidas.

June–July – Athens has to raise a relief force of rowers from all social classes as the best rowers are trapped on Lesbos, and with money short the coins dedicated to the Olympians in the Acropolis temples and treasuries on the Acropolis are used and the statues of Nike ('Victory') are melted down; the relief force sets out under the board of eight generals, and the under-twenty and over-fifty citizens are left behind to man the city walls. The fleet calls at Samos, collects ten more ships there plus some allied ships, and heads to Lesbos; around 150 ships approach Mytilene, while Callicratidas leaves a small blockading force under Eteonicus there and takes around 120 ships south to Cape Malea, the south-east corner of Lesbos. The Athenian fleet has drawn up for its midday meal on the mainland shore opposite, by the Arginusae islands, as the Spartans spot them, and Callicratidas attacks at dawn next day after a planned night-time attack was prevented by a thunderstorm.

Battle of Arginusae – Callicratidas commands his right wing, and Thrasondas of Thebes the left wing; opposite Callicratidas are Aristocrates (the far Athenian left wing) and Diomedon (centre left), with Pericles and Erasinides behind them; the Athenian allies are in their centre, backing onto the island of Garipadasi, and Thrasyllus and Protomachus are on the Athenian right wing with Aristogenes and Lysias behind them. The Athenians are in three wings of sixty ships each, with each of their eight generals commanding fifteen ships. The Athenians sail out into the open sea from the Arginusae islands, their line stretching beyond the Spartan one on both wings, and the Athenian left wing starts to outflank the Spartans further; Callicratidas launches each half of his fleet against the overlapping Athenians opposite, risking having a weak centre against the Athenian allies, and heavy fighting follows with the Spartan outnumbered. Callicratidas is killed and then his left wing flees, with the Athenian allies then moving in to help the pursuit after leaving most of the fighting to the Athenians. Seventy-seven of the Spartan fleet (two-thirds) are sunk, and the survivors are leaderless and helpless to stop Athens; the victors lose twenty-five ships, and twelve of these are still afloat or survivors are clinging to wreckage as the other ships pursue the Spartans south. The Athenians do not bother to stop to pick up the survivors, and once the enemy has escaped the generals hold a conference at the Arginusae islands to decide whether to deal with Eteonicus and his blockaders at Mytilene before they can escape (Erasinides' idea) or stop to pick up the survivors first (Diomedon). Thrasyllus proposes dividing the fleet up between the two tasks, and Theramenes and Thrasyboulus (only assistant officers commanding individual ships that year) are given the role of leading the rescue by part of the fleet while the generals take the rest to Mytilene. A storm breaks out as the rescue-work commences, and probably threatens to swamp the Athenian ships as they abandon the rescue-work; the generals then arrive at Mytilene to be told by Conon that Eteonicus and his squadron have got away to Chios safely.

The Athenian fleet arrives at Samos and events are reported to Athens; anger at the loss of men who could have been rescued alive and the dishonour to the dead of not recovering their bodies mounts, and the returning Theramenes and Thrasyboulus manage to deflect the people's anger from themselves to the absent generals, possibly maliciously but equally possibly arguing that they could not do a rescue successfully as they were not given orders until the sea was already dangerously rough. The assembly votes to recall and prosecute the generals, but Aristogenes and Protomachus flee into exile when they hear the threat; the others return to clear themselves.

October – Erasinides is accused of embezzling as he submits his accounts and condemned and then the other five returnees are tried by the 'Council of 500' for abandoning their sailors; they are remanded for trial before the assembly as Theramenes accuses them of effective manslaughter by abandonment. The trial sees a reasoned defence blaming the storm for catching the generals unawares, and they are winning sympathy when the time for the day's proceedings runs out. The next day is the 'Apaturia' festival of the family in Athens, and the relatives of the dead at Arginusae attend the assembly in mourning attire to stir up anger that their relatives died due to avoidable incompetence, not an act of the gods in the storm; there are subsequently some allegations that this was politically inspired or encouraged – by Theramenes to deflect criticism from himself according to Diodorus. The assembly listens to the proposal of Callixeinus that they should accept that the procedure of establishing guilt or innocence by evidence was completed the previous day and proceed to voting and then sentence, and the heated atmosphere leads to the generals being convicted and sentenced to death; their property is to be confiscated and a tenth of it dedicated to Athena. Six of the eight accused in Athens are executed, though the public has regrets later and the episode is used to tarnish the reputation of their democracy.

Winter – With the surviving Spartan ships and crews at Chios in a bad way, Sparta offers to withdraw from Decelea and establish peace on the basis of the 'status quo'; Athens refuses.

?Deaths of Athens' two leading dramatists, the tragedians Sophocles (aged around eighty) in Athens and Euripides (about a decade younger?) at the court of King Archelaus in Macedon.

Sicily

Midwinter solstice (Diodorus) – Fall and looting of Akragas; the temples are sacked despite the usual custom, and allegedly some of the refugees burn themselves to death in a temple rather than be killed or enslaved.

405

Greece

Early – Lysander takes thirty-five ships from the Peloponnesian states to Ephesus (probably as it is closer to the Hellespont than his usual headquarters at Miletus) and orders Eteonicus to bring the main fleet there from Chios; he constructs new ships there and orders others from Antandrus. He goes to see Cyrus to collect more money, but is told that all the money allotted to the war by his father Darius II has been spent and he is shown the accounts to prove it. Cyrus lends him money from his own treasury to pay the Spartan crews' arrears of pay, then appoints Lysander as his acting stand-in as local satrap while he has to report to Persepolis to explain why he has executed two of his cousins for showing disrespect to him. In fact, Darius may be (terminally) ill too by this point; satrap Tissaphernes also goes to Persepolis, with, but watching, Cyrus.

January? – Aristophanes' satirical play 'The Frogs' wins first prize for comedy at the 'Lenaia' festival in Athens.

March? – Euripides wins the first prize at the Athens city Dionysia theatrical festival with 'The Bacchae' – posthumously, as he has recently died in Macedon where he had been living at the court of King Archelaus.

Cyrus leaves for Persepolis; Lysander goes to Miletus to collect the Spartan ships there, probably around 120, and at the city he undermines his predecessor Callicratidas' reconciliation with the democrats despite official goodwill to them, stirring up his oligarchic friends from his earlier residence there (probably as unpopular oligarchs are more dependent on his goodwill than democrats, so they will obey him). During the 'Dionysia' festival (February or March?) he organizes a coup at Miletus, and forty are killed in their homes and three hundred in the marketplace; others flee to Pharnabazus, who gives them sanctuary at Blauda in Lydia.

Lysander storms Iasus in Caria for returning to its old Athenian alliance and kills the men and sells the other inhabitants as slaves; he does the same at Cedriae on the Ceramic Gulf, then sails over the Aegean to Aegina; he lands in Attica, and Agis arrives across country from Deceleia to join him. As the Athenian fleet returns from Samos, he slips away across the Aegean evading them, possibly to Rhodes, and heads north for the Hellespont. Landing at his base of Abydos, he raises more men from the locals then heads by sea to Lampsacus while Thorax takes an army by land; the town is taken and plundered but the inhabitants are allowed to leave (an inducement to local quick surrenders to speed up his campaign).

Sicily

Spring – Himilico razes Akragas to the ground and heads for Gela as refugees fleet east, many of them to Syracuse as the strongest walled city there; panic and recriminations spread. The majority of the Akragans end up resettled at Leontinoi, while the city's loot is still in Carthage when it falls to Rome in 146.

Dionysius leads criticisms of the generals' incompetence and leads demagogic pressure in the assembly, which results in their dismissal; he is fined for causing riots but this is paid by his rich ally and later subordinate, Philistus. He is on the new board of generals that is chosen. He has his political allies from Hermocrates' faction recalled, and they assist him as he enrols mercenaries for his new army and sets off for Gela with around 2000 men.

Dionysius takes charge of the defence of Gela, inflaming local fears to have the rich charged as potential traitors and their property confiscated so he can use it to pay his mercenaries. He pays his men more than his rival Dexippus the Spartan does, so the latter's men start deserting to him and Dexippus has to obey him. He later returns to Syracuse to complain about the incompetence and suspicious inactivity of the city's other generals, and has the assembly dismiss them and elect him as sole general with supreme powers ('strategos autocrator') – in effect, tyrant. He doubles the mercenaries' pay and enrols 1000 of the refugees from the west as his personal bodyguard, and then appoints his own supporters to the city's military commands and marries the daughter of Hermocrates to cement his alliance to that faction. Dexippus is sent home to Sparta despite the expected imminent Carthaginian attack, and Daphnaeus is executed as a traitor. While rallying the troops at Leontinoi for an attack, Dionysius fakes an attack on himself (like Peisistratus at Athens in the 550s) so he can persuade the assembly to vote him a personal bodyguard of 600 men.

April – Himilco besieges Gela; Dionysius advances with a Syracusan/mercenaries / inland Siceliot/southern Italian army to relieve it, and he decides not to blockade the attacker's camp but launch an attack. He fails to co-ordinate his troops and it is a disaster, as part of his army lands from his ships to attack the enemy camp on the shore and his Italian troops skirt the city to arrive in position in time but he cannot get his mercenaries through the city quickly enough to aid them; he arrives to find the enemy winning the battle. He has to withdraw back inside the city, and that night evacuates it. He heads back to Syracuse as his army breaks up and the southern Italian Greeks march off to Messina, and the (mostly aristocratic/wealthy) Syracusan cavalry mutinies but cannot get at Dionysius for his mercenaries protecting him. They ride off ahead of him back to Syracuse, take over the city, and start killing his supporters, sacking his house and ?raping his wife. Dionysius is evacuating the population of Camerina when he hears, and he hurries back to Syracuse with 700 mercenaries in a forced march of forty-five miles that day. He arrives at midnight, sets fire to the gate at the quarter of Achradina to gain access, and takes the city back, slaughtering his opponents; at dawn his main army arrives to help him. The rebels flee to Aetna, and the Camarinans and exiled Gelans abandon Dionysius' cause.

The Carthaginian army arrives at Syracuse, but is quickly destroyed by plague; Himilco loses around half his men and sends a herald to Dionysius proposing terms which he accepts. Carthage is to have western Sicily and to be overlord of unfortified Selinus, Himera, Akragas, Gela, and Camarina, while Leontinoi, Messina, and the Siceliot towns and tribes are to be autonomous. Carthage is left the strongest power on Sicily, but Syracuse survives as a medium-seized power and Dionysius quickly gains a stranglehold on the politics of Syracuse with his ruthlessness.

Greece

The Athenian fleet of around 180 ships leaves Athens in pursuit of Lysander, and hears of the fall of Lampsacus at Elaeus, west down the Hellespont; they sail up the west shore to Sestos, then camp on the beach at Aegospotamai ('Goats' Creek'), an insignificant open roadstead opposite Lampsacus (on the eastern shore) with no harbour about twelve miles from Sestos. There are six generals in command – Adeimantus, Cephisodorus, Conon, Menander, Philocles and Tydeus – alternating the command day by day. After four days of sailing into the harbour-mouth of Lampsacus each morning to challenge Lysander and being ignored, they apparently think he is too cautious to fight and relax; however, the exiled Alcibiades is living in a fortress nearby on the Chersonese and turns up to tell them to move to safer Sestos and propose that he brings the local Thracian kings Medocus and Seuthes to help attack Lysander. The generals send him packing, allegedly fearing he will take the credit if they win or simply disbelieving him.

On the fifth day at Aegospotamai, that day's commander Philocles sets out with thirty ships on an unknown mission, possibly a personal attempt to lure Lysander out to fight an inferior force so the stalemate will be broken; possibly (Diodorus) Lysander has bribed men in the camp to tell him the plan. As Philocles sails towards Sestos, Lysander moves out of Lampsacus after him, but after a successful clash he quickly swoops on the rest of the Athenian fleet, which is still drawn up on the beach with many men not on board. (This suggests that the rest of the generals were unaware of any ploy by Philocles to lure Lysander into a quick battle.) Eteonicus lands a Spartan force to attack the camp, while Lysander attacks the ships at will; ten Athenian ships escape, one commanded by Conon who fears prosecution by the assembly so he heads to Cyprus, and many sailors escape on land and eventually reach the base at Samos but over 150 ships are captured or destroyed.

Lysander takes his ships, 3–4000 prisoners, and the loot back to Lampsacus, and sends the Milesian privateer Theopompus with the news and richest loot back to Sparta; the fates of the prisoners are put to the vote of the Spartan-allied fleet assembled at Sestos, and they vote to execute all the prisoners except for captured admiral Adeimantus. Captured general Philocles, who is hated for his mutilating or throwing prisoners overboard, is executed.

The state galley *Paralus* delivers the news to a stunned Athens, which next day votes to fight on and block all but one harbour. Lysander takes over the Propontis, whose city-states abandon Athens, and cuts off corn-supplies to Athens; he allows all captured Athenian citizens to go free provided they go back to Athens, so that they will increase its population and make starving it out easier.

Sthenelaus is appointed the Spartan governor of Byzantium and Chalcedon to control the Bosphorus and its trade and stop any ships heading for Athens; he garrisons the local cities with his own nominees, without waiting for sanction from Sparta (which accepts this only later), and heads to Lesbos to force its transfer to alliance with Sparta; Eteonicus does likewise in Thrace, and the democrats at Samos hold out by massacring their opponents before Lysander arrives. He leaves forty ships to blockade them, and goes on to Melos and Aegina to carry out the propaganda coups of restoring the inhabitants who Athens evicted.

October – Lysander arrives off Attica, and King Pausanias leads the full army of all the Peloponnesian states except Argos to invade Attica and camp at the 'Academy' outside the city. Agis joins them from Decelea. Athens is blockaded and starved out, by both Spartan kings at once in a break from the Spartan tradition of always keeping one king at home.

November? – Lysander heads off to resume the siege of Samos. The Peloponnesian allies are restive at the long siege, so the Spartans hold a conference to debate what to do with Athens and Thebes and Corinth demand that the city be razed; as a result of or independently of this, Athens sends an embassy to Agis at Decelea offering to abandon their empire and become a Spartan ally if they can keep their Long Walls and the Piraeus. Agis says he is not empowered to act and they must approach the 'ephors' at Sparta; the embassy is sent on to them, but the 'ephors' meet the Athenians on the frontier at Sellasia and tell them to go back and fetch better terms, including the demolition of most of the Long Walls (i.e. too much of it to be repaired quickly). Back at the assembly, Archestratus proposes to accept this but is imprisoned and the Athenians vote to ban any such offers.

December? – Theramenes persuades the Athenians to let him try to negotiate; he sails off to Samos to consult Lysander.

404

March? – After around three months at Samos, Theramenes returns to say that Lysander also insists he must negotiate with the 'ephors' – possibly he has delayed his return in order that the prolonged blockade will reduce his countrymen to a more humble frame of mind, or else to work on Lysander to moderate his desire for a harsh settlement. If so, it works; Theramenes is sent with a mission to Sparta on his return to Athens, and Lysander does not argue against his proposals. Both Lysander and the 'ephors' may also fear the results of crushing Athens and making the unreliable Thebes supreme in the region. It is agreed that Athens should keep her 'ancestral' constitution – an ambiguous term, open to different interpretations but implying a moderate but non-democratic regime (pre-460s or post-509 as the basis?). Some of the Spartan allies, led by Erianthus the Theban commander at Aegospotamai, still want Athens razed and her population enslaved but according to Xenophon the 'ephors' swing opinion against this with a reminder of Athens' service in the common cause in the Persian Wars. Theramenes has to accept the destruction of the Long Walls and defortification of Piraeus.

Before Theramenes returns from Sparta, his supporters have his foe the 'hard-liner' demagogue Cleophon, who led the resistance to surrender on any terms earlier, arrested and executed; when he does return those who lead complaints at the terms are charged and imprisoned for allegedly endangering the people.

Persia

March – Death of Great King Darius II, aged probably around sixty; he is succeeded by his elder son Artaxerxes II Mnemon, aged around forty, though stories have it that his wife Parysatis tried to persuade him to choose her favourite, younger son Cyrus instead. Cyrus returns to Asia Minor, possibly after an aborted plan to arrest him by his brother (and Tissaphernes?), which encourages him to think he is unsafe and plan a revolt.

Greece

April – Athens surrenders; Sparta requires her to disband her empire and demolish her walls to and round the Piraeus, cutting her off from her harbour and making her at the risk of blockade if she defies Sparta.

September ('16th Munychion', the anniversary of the battle of Salamis, according to Plutarch) – The Long Walls and the walls of Piraeus are pulled down by the Spartans under Lysander, to the sound of flutes played by the flute-girls in the Spartan camp for celebration.

The Athenians agree to set up a board of thirty to re-codify the laws; the latter swiftly turn into a despotism and put off completing their codification. They round up and execute all the informers who profited in recent years, which is generally approved of. They send to Sparta to send a garrison and offer to pay for it, and this is agreed; Callibius is appointed governor of the garrison installed on the Acropolis and the 'Thirty' flatter him into agreeing to help them arrest their enemies; the board of thirty's leader Critias, Plato's mother's cousin and a pupil of Socrates (and probably the dramatist of that name), tells Lysander that the democracy needs to be replaced as it would be an unreliable ally for Sparta and he agrees.

Critias leads the tyranny of the board of thirty as the 'Thirty Tyrants', the most extreme oligarchs, in Athens. They are to have the power of life and death over the rest of the citizens. They restrict civic rights, e.g. the membership of juries, to 3000 reliable supporters – the 'Three Thousand' – despite opposition by the moderate Theramenes. They set up civic governments of the 'Eleven' in Athens and the 'Ten' in Piraeus. Everyone else is at their mercy, and they start to purge their enemies with the 'Eleven' acting as a 'kangaroo court' to condemn anyone who they dislike or regard as a potential threat. At a military rally for the citizen army, the weapons of all except the 'Three Thousand' are seized by the oligarchs and their Spartan allies and impounded in the Spartan base on the Acropolis, and the oligarchs arrange a purge of the wealthiest resident 'metics' (aliens) with each nominating a man to be arrested and executed; the money is then used to bolster their regime.

Around 3000 Athenians are executed according to Plato, and many more go into exile – mostly in Thebes. Theramenes does his best to halt the terror, so Critias personally accuses him to the new Council of time-serving, changing his allegiances for his personal advantage, treachery, and being behind the execution of the admirals after the battle of Arginusae; Theramenes defends himself capably and the Council are impressed, but Critias strikes his name off the list of the Thirty so the latter can condemn him. Theramenes takes refuge at the Council chamber's altar, but Critias has his attendant thugs drag him outside and execute him.

Persia

Successful revolt in Lower Egypt of Amyrtaeus, probable grandson of the Amyrtaeus who Athens assisted in revolt c. 455; his fifth regnal year at Memphis opens in September 399 so his revolt gains Memphis before September 404. Upper Egypt remains under Persian control until c. 399.

The Hegemonies of Sparta and Thebes: 403 to 360

403

Winter – Thrasyboulus and around seventy Athenians in exile in Thebes, backed by that city, cross the frontier and seize the hilltop fortress of Phyle overlooking the Attic plain; the Thirty march on it with their '3000' loyalists and the city's (wealthy) cavalry, but are hampered by heavy snow; after a raid on their camp they give up and retire to Athens. Around 700 men now rally to the democrats. The Thirty send for the Spartan garrison, who march to Phyle and camp a few miles away but are routed in a surprise dawn attack with 120 killed.

The Thirty decide to fortify Eleusis as a base in case they have to flee Athens, and go there with the Athenian cavalry to hold a meeting of the populace to allegedly have a census but really to round up those they suspect, who are sent out of the city to be seized by waiting troops and deported to Athens. Once there, Critias holds a public meeting of the '3000' in the Odeum with a large Spartan military contingent on hand and forces them to condemn the accused to death, thus making them complicit in his massacres and less likely to defect.

Alcibiades heads for the Great King's court to encourage his support and save his career, in the manner of Themistocles, and visits Pharnabazus in Phrygia en route; reportedly the alarmed Lysander asks Pharnabazus to kill him, which the latter does using his brother Margaeus and a 'hit squad', or else it is done at the satrap's own initiative. Alternatively, the killing is a private feud with the brothers of Alcibiades' latest mistress. The house that he is staying at in a village is set alight and he is killed charging out with his sword aged around forty-five; he is given a private funeral by his final mistress, local girl Timandra.

Thrasyboulus and the democrats march on the Piraeus by night and seize control from the 'Ten'; the Thirty and their allies attack the town, and Thrasyboulus abandons the walls as he does not have enough men to man the circuit (he has around 1000) and defends the road up onto Munychia hill instead; in the battle Critias, leader of the Thirty, is among the dead along with around 70 others. The Thirty retreat back to the city, and next day as the 'Three Thousand' are losing heart and quarrelling they leave the 'Ten' in command and withdraw to their base at Eleusis. They are able to hold out there, and the 'Three Thousand' temporarily rule Athens; both appeal to Sparta for aid as the democrats raid around Athens at will, and Lysander asks the Spartan 'Gerousia' to make him governor of Athens so he can aid the oligarchs. They agree and he advances to Eleusis to summon Peloponnesian support.

King Pausanias, jealous of Lysander's power and ambitions, persuades the 'ephors' to send him to command the Spartan/Peloponnesian army instead and warns that Lysander could take Athens for his personal fief and loot it to gain money for his personal gain, posing a threat to the Spartan constitution; Pausanias supersedes Lysander at Eleusis, and the latter is reduced to commanding Pausanias' left wing as he leads out the army to confront the democrats at Piraeus. Some clashes follow, but Pausanias is better-disposed to the democrats and to conciliating Athens than Lysander is and he does not press his military advantage; he asks the democrats to send envoys to him who will receive a fair hearing, and urges the 'Three Thousand' to realize that he does not want to attack Piraeus and they should reconcile with their foes. The two 'ephors' with the army back Pausanias, and a truce is agreed; both parties in Athens send delegates to Sparta with the oligarchs proposing that the two factions dismantle their fortifications and let Sparta adjudicate, and Sparta agrees and sends a fifteen-man mediation mission.

The settlement is brokered by the Spartan mission, with amnesty for all and free residence in Athens without prosecution for all except the survivors of the Thirty, the 'Ten' and the 'Eleven', who must leave (i.e. for Eleusis) plus any who wish to go to Eleusis for their safety. Pausanias sends his army home, and Thrasyboulus leads his troops into Athens to sacrifice to Athena on the Acropolis.

403/2

The oligarchs at Eleusis march on Athens armed in a further clash, but are met by the citizen army and agree to a conference; the democrats arrest and execute their generals at this, and their leaderless oligarchs in the Eleusis army agree to ask the others at the town to give in, in return for amnesty. Peace returns to Athens.

401

Spring – Sparta demands that its neighbour Elis free some local cities that it has made 'periocoi' (i.e. non-citizens of Elis banned from the political process) and pay its share of the costs of the recent war; Elis refuses and claims it conquered the towns and so is entitled to them. Sparta is also dissatisfied over a recent ban from the Olympics by Elis and a refusal to King Agis' request to sacrifice at the temple of Zeus in Olympia for success in the Peloponnesian War as it was against fellow-Greeks. Agis invades but withdraws quickly on the excuse of an earthquake implying divine disfavour.

Elis rallies support against her punishment among Sparta's allies, sending envoys around to collect military help.

Persia
Spring – Prince Cyrus of Persia recruits a large Greek mercenary army (largely Peloponnesian), by sending envoys around the Greek cities, to assemble at Sardes for an unnamed campaign. It amounts to around 13,000 men and is commanded by Clearchus the Spartan, who has been assembling a contingent for him at the Chersonese with the excuse of a local campaign against the Thracians. The Athenian Xenophon (born c. 430), later historian of the expedition and probably discontented with the new democratic regime given his literary admiration for Sparta, is one of the recruits: Cyrus' friends Aristippus the Thessalian and Proxenus the Boeotian also collect troops from their home areas with Cyrus' money. The excuse given is to help satrap Tissaphernes with an expedition against Ionia, particularly Miletus whose exiles have asked him for help, but, in fact, Cyrus is planning to overthrow his brother after the threat posed by his near-arrest earlier. Cyrus blockades Miletus, and fools his brother into sending him money for the war.

Cyrus tells his recruits that he is to attack the hill-tribe brigands in Pisidia, southern central Asia Minor; Xenias brings around 4000 men and Proxenus about 1500 infantry and 500 cavalry; Cyrus leads them all off from Sardes along the 'Royal Road' to the River Maeander (three days) and to Celaenae in Phrygia; the suspicious Tissaphernes decides the army is too large to tackle just the Pisidians and hurries to the Great King to warn him. Cyrus halts at Celaenae for thirty days, and Clearchus joins him with 1000 infantry, 800 Thracian light infantry skirmishers, and 200 Crean archers; other contingents arrive, and Cyrus holds a review of his army with Games; then he proceeds up the River Cayster to Thymbrion, with the satrap/king Synnesis of Cilicia's wife Epyaxa (?Cyrus' mistress) joining him. They go on to Iconium in Isauria, then via Lycaonia (where the queen leaves to go home) into Cappadocia as Menon's troops proceed overland into Cilica to hold the loyalist Synessis back.

Cyrus sends an embassy to Sparta asking for its support against his brother; as a result Sparta orders its admiral Samius to assist Cyrus, and he links up his squadron with Cyrus' Asia Minor fleet and sails parallel to the rebel army along the south coast to Cilicia; as a result Synessis, satrap/king of Cilica, is unable to bring his troops to Artaxerxes' aid and block Cyrus' route.

Cyrus enters Cilicia unchallenged as the passes are open, and Synessis evacuates Tarsus where his wife and Menon occupy the city before Cyrus arrives; Epyaxa persuades her husband to obey a summons to Cyrus and pledge allegiance and money.

Clearchus' troops start to murmur about what Cyrus intends and refuse to march into the interior of Asia against the Great King who is now said to be the real target, and Clearchus takes his lead from them; Clearchus persuades them not to risk trouble by antagonizing their employer who can hinder them if they try to leave; delegates are elected to go with Clearchus to Cyrus and ask his intentions with a demand for more money if he is proposing a more risky expedition than he told them, and Cyrus raises their pay by 50 per cent but will not confirm his destination except that a hostile Persian force under satrap Abrocomas of Syria is blocking his route towards the Euphrates.

Cyrus leads his army for four days to the River Pyramus, then two days to Issus on the Gulf at the north-eastern corner of the Mediterranean; a day's march brings them to the Syrian Gates pass over the Amanus mountains into Syria, and Abrocomas abandons his garrison in the pass as the rebel fleet moves south to outflank him; he retires to join the Great King in Mesopotamia and Cyrus crosses the pass. Cyrus occupies Myriandrus, where he stays for a week and his senior Greek commanders Xenias (the Arcadian) and Pasion desert and sail home. A twelve-day march follows to Thapsacus at the crossing of the Euphrates, where Cyrus finally tells his officers that he is marching against his brother who is around Babylon. The officers tell the troops, who are angry and have to be paid extra; Menon persuades his men to cross the river on their own initiative to 'show willing', impress Cyrus to their future benefit, and shame the others into following; this has the desired effect.

The army marches for nine days to the river 'Araxes', and for five days across the desert to the river 'Mascas' at Corsote; after a three-day rest they go on for thirteen days on the left (north) bank of the Euphrates, downstream towards Babylon; the loyal troops burn the countryside ahead of them and avoid battle. One of Cyrus' Persian officers, Orontas, proposes to take a cavalry force off to deal with the enemy but, in fact, to defect to Artaxerxes, but his letter to the Great King is intercepted and he is arrested and executed. Cyrus holds a midnight review of his army as he approaches the convergence of the Euphrates and Tigris ahead of Babylon, expecting a battle at daybreak, and receives defectors at dawn as the army is drawn up; there are 10,400 Greek 'hoplites' and 2500 'peltasts', and up to '100,000' Persians (Xenophon). Aborcomus, Tissaphernes, Gobrias and Arbaces command the Great King's army – around a million according to Xenophon.

The rebels advance to and across the defensive ditch, which has been dug near the 'Median Wal' from Euphrates to Tigris to hold him up; the Great King's army evades battle. On the third day, the rebels are finally told by an arriving defector that the enemy is advancing.

Battle of Cunaxa – Clearchus is on the rebel right wing by the Euphrates, with the Greeks; then Cyrus is in the centre, and his ally Ariaeus is on the left. Cyrus orders an advance, though his smaller army is outflanked on the Greeks' wing by the loyalists. The Greeks charge and break through the Persians opposite them, and Cyrus with his 600 personal cavalry in their centre moves against Artaxerxes so the Great King cannot cut the Greeks off and surround them. Cyrus is killed in combat attacking his brother's escort, and his head is cut off; his troops break, and Ariaeus and his troops flee their camp back to the previous night's position. The Greeks are moving forward and chasing the wing opposite them oblivious of their leader's death, but later hear that the Persians have taken their camp; the Great King draws up his army ready for battle again, and after some manoeuvres his men attack the Greeks but are chased off; the Greeks proceed to a useful local hill, which they occupy for the night as evening is encroaching, and camp.

Next morning, with the Persians still keeping back, witnesses confirm that Cyrus is dead and Ariaeus sends a message saying that he is heading back to Ionia and they should join him; Clearchus takes command of the Greeks and sends him a message offering to make him Great King as Cyrus is dead and Artaxerxes defeated, and the Great King sends messengers that Cyrus is dead so he is the victor and they should hand in their weapons and negotiate terms. The Greeks decide to refuse, and head back under cover of darkness to join Ariaeus; the latter still intends to retreat up the Euphrates to Asia Minor. The march commences with the Great King's men avoiding a clash and following at a distance; Tissaphernes arrives with envoys a few days later to negotiate, and the Greeks (led by Clearchus) say that they were not invading the Great King's territory in hostility as Cyrus deceived them about his purpose and now they want a safe exit home but they will attack any who hinder them. A truce is negotiated, with the Greeks not being molested but having to pay for their supplies and leave the countryside which they cross alone as if on friendly territory. Tissaphernes promises to escort them back to Ionia, as he is marching his contingent back to his own province.

After a twenty-day delay, Tissaphernes returns with his colleague Orontas and the two armies march up the Tigris to the 'Wall of Media', though the ex-rebel Ariaeus and his men join Tissaphernes and Orontas and mutual Greek/Persian suspicion grows. A few days later they all reach Sittace on the Tigris, where the Greeks are warned via a message to Proxenus and Xenophon from Ariaeus of impending treachery by the locals and Tissaphernes; Clearchus does not believe it; they post guards on the bridge over the nearby canal in case of an attack but none materializes. A few days later, up the river at Opis an illegitimate brother of Artaxerxes and Cyrus arrives belatedly from Persia with a contingent for the recent war, and then a ten-day march follows up the Tigris to the town of Caenae.

At the river Great Zab, Tissaphernes summons Clearchus to a meeting and convinces him of his good intentions despite continuing rumours of treachery; he returns in good spirits and accuses his doubters of malevolent intentions; Clearchus suspects his rival Menon of stirring up trouble to undermine his authority and get elected as the new commander, and persuades five of the generals and around twenty captains to come with him to a second meeting with the satrap; generals Proxenus and Menon join him with Agias the Arcadian and Socrates the Athenian, and at Tissaphernes' tent the Persians suddenly seize and kill them all. Seeing the dust of the Persian cavalry as they attack the Greeks' escort, the Greek army immediately stands to arms; Ariaeus comes over to say that the treacherous Clearchus has been killed but Proxenus and Menon are alive and under arrest as honoured hostages and the Greeks should hand over their weapons and await their late employer Cyrus' brother's orders as their new master. They refuse to believe him unless they have it confirmed by the two Greek officers, who he cannot produce; as the Greeks are in camp that night, Xenophon (by his own account) decides to take command if nobody else will and lead the survivors to safety, not trusting any Persians and getting out of their country as soon as possible. He calls together the surviving officers for a night-time meeting, and they agree to follow his advice and elect him and other new officers; next morning the army assembles, receives their new leaders' report, and accepts Xenophon's advice on the need for a retreat to the coast and how to confuse the Persians by not making their destination or intentions clear.

The army sets out up the Tigris for the Armenian mountains, rather than risking attack by the huge Persian army in the plains to the west en route for the upper Euphrates and Persia; it marches in formation, fighting off the army of Tissaphernes in a number of skirmishes, and reaches the foothills of Cardousia (Kurd territory) where native guides are questioned and it is decided that the safest route is north over the mountains to the Black Sea despite the need to fight their way through the native tribes. With Chirisophus commanding the vanguard and Xenophon the rearguard, they reach the cover of the hills at night by a forced march before the Persians can catch them; the locals abandon their villages, which are plundered for food.

Midwinter 401/400

Harassed by the local tribesmen, the Greeks struggle on across Cadousia into Armenia through the mountains, and are intercepted by the local satrap of western Armenia, Tiribazus, who professes a willingness to let them pass if they leave the villages alone and escorts them at a distance; later they hear from the locals that he plans to ambush them in a narrow pass so they attack his camp by surprise and loot it. They cross the mountains in heavy snow through the regions of the 'Chalybes' and the 'Phasians' (a generic term for the tribes around Phasis i.e. Colchis, the region south of modern Batumi) and have some help from villagers who loan them guides but are harassed by others and suspect them all; the fierce 'Taochi' defy them. They refuse to give up their provisions, and man hilly strongpoints to throw stones on them and when their positions are stormed commit suicide by throwing themselves off the cliffs. Seven days of fighting with the 'Chalybes' follow, and the Greeks gain no food and have to live off what they seized from the 'Taochi'; finally the Greeks cross a river and climb over a pass, and the advance-guard starts shouting so Xenophon hurries up from the rear thinking it is another attack. The shout is 'Thalassa, thalassa' – 'The sea, the sea' – and they are in sight of the coast.

The Greeks cross the country of the 'Macones' to the coastal city of Trapezus/ Trebizond, after fighting their way through a hostile local force in a pass, and camp there for thirty days.

400

Chirisophus goes off by sea to contact Anaxibius, the commander of the Spartan navy, and get ships from him, and Xenophon organizes the army to borrow a few local ships from Trapezus and set up a fortified camp; they raid the local tribes for supplies, and as no help arrives they eventually put the sick and elderly on the ships and the rest march parallel to them along the coast west to Cerasus near Sinope. At the review they hold there they are numbered 8600. They cross the tribal lands of the Mossynoeci, who they help to fight rival tribesmen, to Harmene the port of Sinope where Chirisophus arrives with one ship but no more; they cross the Paphlagonian coast to Heraclea; the army has no money for supplies apart from a little made by selling prisoners, and defies its new elected commander Chirisophus by proposing to blackmail the nearby city of Heraclea into handing over money for them so he resigns. The citizens refuse and lock their gates on the army, and the Achaeans and Arcadians defy the new commander Xenophon and march off on their own rather than, as Peloponnesians, obeying an Athenian. The army crosses in three separate forces into Thrace, and the Arcadians are surrounded on a hill near 'Port Calpe' (the mouth of the Bosphorus) by hostile local Thracians but Xenophon, arriving last of the groups, rescues them. Pharnabazus sends troops under Spithridates across the Bosphorus to attack them, but the reunited army drives the latter off. However, Cleander, the Spartan governor of Byzantium, has a poor reception from some defiant soldiers when he arrives with some ships to negotiate and sees mutinous men refusing to hand over sheep which they have looted, and threatens to report their behaviour to Sparta and have them declared public enemies. Xenophon calms Cleander down.

Late summer? – Pharnabazus tries to lure the Greeks into fighting for him rather than have them attacking his Bithynian province, and appeals to Anaxibius, commander of the Spartan fleet at Byzantium, to arrange this; the troops are received at Byzantium by governor Cleander who is now a friend of Xenophon, but the Thracian chieftain Seuthes also wants to hire the army; admiral Anaxibius, nervous of having the unreliable troops within Byzantium lest they take it over (in alliance with Sparta's foes in the city?), orders the troops out of Byzantium and off by land along the Propontis to the Chersonese. Anaxibius' replacement as fleet-commander, Pollis, is now en route (i.e. it is autumn as this is the usual time for Sparta to change commands) and so is the new governor of Byzantium, Aristarchus, who he tells to sell off left-behind soldiers from the 'Ten Thousand' as slaves. Anaxibius asks Xenophon to collect the army at Perinthus and ship it to Bithynia as Pharnabazus wants it quickly, i.e. during Anaxibius' command so he not his successor will be the one to be rewarded for it by the satrap. Aristarchus does not want the troops to go to Pharnabazus and tells Xenophon not to do this when the latter goes to Byzantium, so Xenophon decides he is unreliable and concludes negotiations with Seuthes the Thracian instead. The 'Ten Thousand' move west into inland Thrace and join Seuthes to fight for him in a tribal war.

Tissaphernes takes over all the Persian satrapies and Greek cities of Ionia, as ordered by the Great King, and besieges Cyme; one of the refugees is local fleet-commander Tachos, father of the later Persian admiral Glos, who flees with his household and ships to Egypt where King Psammetichus kills him and takes over his ships.

The cities of Ionia appeal to Sparta for help; it sends out the general Thibron with 1000 troops to Ephesus.

Greece

Sparta attacks Elis again, having persuaded a congress of her allies meeting at Sparta to declare war too so they are obliged to send contingents; Boeotia and Corinth refuse to assist her, but Athens sends troops. Aetolia refuses to help Sparta, and sends aid to Elis instead. Agis invades via Aulon. The countryside of Elis is ravaged but the main city is not attacked apart from the suburbs where a gymnasium is wrecked probably due to Agis' moderation and Spartan hopes of the oligarchic faction there. The latter under Xenias try to stage a coup while Agis is at Cyllene and start a massacre, but are unsuccessful in targeting the democratic leader Thrasydaeus as a 'look-alike' is killed by mistake and the real Thrasydaeus leads his friends to drive the oligarchs out. Agis installs them and a garrison at Epitalium to put pressure on the Eleans.

(or 401) Summer – Death of King Agis of Sparta, who falls ill at Heraeum on his way back from Delphi at the end of the summer's campaign in Elis after going to the sanctuary to dedicate his spoils. He dies a few days later reaching Sparta, aged probably in his forties. The 'ephors' listen to rumours that 'his' son Leotychidas, aged around fifteen, is not his but Alcibiades' as the King avoided his wife, Timaea's, bedchamber for weeks after an earthquake shook Sparta on his wedding night and seemed to be a bad omen and then refugee Alcibiades had an affair with his wife in the interim. Agis has recognized Leotychidas as his son recently after years of doubts, to no avail. The boy is set aside, and Agis' lame younger brother Agesilaus (born around 440) is made king despite a prophecy that a lame king will bring bad luck to Sparta, which Diopeithes tries to use to block his selection; Lysander argues that the word 'lameness' means Leotychidas' illegitimacy, not Agesilaus' limp.

399

Spring – Thibron enlists the 6000 survivors of the 'Ten Thousand', led by Xenophon, as mercenaries for Sparta's war with Persia and sends envoys to Seuthes to arrange this; he asks various Greek states for military aid, and Athens sends some pro-oligarchic cavalrymen who are under political suspicion. Thibron occupies some northern Ionian cities as others throw out their pro-Persian garrisons, and advances south to central Ionia. Xenophon and his men sail across the Hellespont to Lampsacus and march south to Pergamon, where they join Thibron as he arrives.

Thibron takes Magnesia easily, and marches on to attack Tralles; he has to retreat as Tissaphernes brings up a large army, and evacuates Magnesia as too lightly walled but fortifies a nearby hilltop.

Summer – The ruling democrats at Elis under Thrasydaeus send envoys to come to terms with Sparta to preserve their regime; they agree to enter the Spartan alliance, demolish two contentious fortresses at Cyllene and Phea, get rid of their fleet, and free eight towns of 'periocoi' (including Phrixa and Epitalium) from their control. Sparta forces them to give up Epeum too, although Elis claims that they bought it from the previous occupiers, and lets Elis keep control of the Olympia sanctuary.

Dercyllidas is appointed land commander of the Spartan army in the Chersonese to succeed Thibron; he fortifies its 'neck' to keep the Thracian tribes back and protect the cities.

Anytus and Melytus, the latter submitting the formal charges to the relevant 'archon', accuse Socrates of corrupting the city's youth (i.e. by his encouraging them to question their elders and the established social customs /politics) and 'impiety' towards the city's gods. He is supposed to have stopped believing in the established gods and introduced his own gods (possibly a muddled misinterpretation of his references to his personal 'daemon' or guardian spirit), and probably his criticisms of democracy and past associations with his controversial pupils Alcibiades and Critias have led to suspicion that his influence is behind their anti-democratic actions. If politics is involved, this probably violates the amnesty agreed in 403 for alleged backers of the 'Thirty Tyrants'. The 'archon' decides that there is a case to answer, and Socrates defends himself against the charges with Melytus as prosecutor; he is found guilty. When asked to select his punishment, he ironically proposes a public pension and the right to attend daily dinners at a state building at public expense with other civic benefactors for the service he has done to the state; an alternative suggestion is a fine of 500 drachmas as he claims he is a poor man. Melytus advocates giving him the death penalty, and the majority of the jury agree; he is sentenced to drink poison (including hemlock). He refuses a suggestion by his pupils that he should flee the city, although his wealthy pupil Crito has offered to bribe the prison guards to let him escape and possibly most people expect him to do this. Famously, he holds a dinner party for his most trusted followers, led by his intellectual heir Plato, and continues his usual rigorous discussions as he drinks the poison and it takes effect.

Death of King Archelaus of Macedon, in a hunting-accident; he is succeeded by his under-age son Orestes, with the late king's brother Aeropus as regent.

Sicily
Dionysius of Syracuse prepares for war with Carthage in order to strike before she is ready, and poses as the liberator of all Greeks in Sicily from them (and probably also due to a recent plague in Africa decimating their army and tax-base); he builds a large new fleet, has pioneering catapults and other siege-engines constructed, and hires mercenaries in Greece especially in Laconia. Around this time he makes a present of disputed territory to his usual enemies of Messina to win them over, and chooses a new noble bride, Doris, from the city of Rhegium across the Straits of Messina as part of a 'charm offensive'; he also marries a well-connected Syracusan woman called Aristomache, and after the two weddings are celebrated at the same time he whips up the Syracusan assembly with a litany of all the crimes that Carthage has committed against the Greeks.

Persia/Egypt
?Nepherites succeeds Amyrtaeus as rebel pharoah, for a brief reign of around a year.

398

Greece
Dercyllidas attacks Aeolis, where the late satrap Zenis' wife Mania has succeeded to his rule by agreement with their overlord Pharnabazus of Hellespontine Phrygia but has been

murdered by her son-in-law Meidias; he quickly takes Larisa, Hamaxitus and Colonae and besieges Cebren while Ilium/Troy and other locals expel their pro-Persian garrisons at his request; Cebren surrenders as the citizens turn on its obstinate commander who gives in, and Dercyllidas heads for Scepsis where Meidias has to surrender too as the citizens mutiny. The tyrant's garrison are removed, and Meidias becomes a Spartan ally and is taken along as a hostage to ensure that Gergis, his home-town, surrenders too; he is then deposed from his rule of the region.

Herippidas the Spartan comes to the aid of the locals in Trachis who are being plundered by the citizens of Heraclea; he takes the town, kills 500 of the inhabitants, and installs a Spartan garrison. He then ravages around Mount Oeta. This is probably designed as a warning to hostile local Aetolia after they aided Elis in 399.

Dercyllidas winters at the Hellespont (Asian side) in order to avoid burdening the Greeks of Aeolis with supplying his army, and plunders Bithynia; the Thracians under Seuthes send him troops.

Sicily

Dionysius picks a showdown with Carthage and sends a herald to her senate to order her to evacuate all of Greek western Sicily or face war.

Carthage refuses, and while she assembles an army Dionysius invades western Sicily, aided by his propaganda offensive about 'liberation', which causes cities to rise in his support. Assorted Carthaginian garrisons and allied regimes are expelled or killed. He arms the local volunteers, and marches on the Carthaginian base at Motya with up to 80,000 infantry and 3000 cavalry while his fleet under his brother Leptines, joined by rebel coastal towns' ships, sails parallel at sea; Eryx surrenders to Dionysius but Entella, Segesta, Solus, and Panormus/Palermo remain loyal to Carthage.

Motya is on an island six 'stades' off the coast so Dionysius, like Alexander 'the Great' at Tyre in 333, has to construct a causeway out to his target while his ships blockade it at sea. But his communications are stretched, and the Carthaginian general Himilco arrives with a relief-fleet and sends a squadron of ten ships on a surprise night attack to Syracuse; the merchant marine on which Dionysius is relying to supply his besiegers by sea is mostly sunk so no supplies can get through quickly. Then Himilco and his main fleet of 100 ships attack the Syracusan fleet at the mainland bay at Motya, but can only destroy the merchant ships there as Dionysius' catapults open fire from the beach to protect his warships. Himilco blockades the bay entrance, but Dionysius moves his ships on rollers across the headland to the next bay and launches them and his catapults keep Himilco back from overwhelming the first few to be launched; Himilco has to retire to Carthage.

Autumn? – The causeway is completed; the walls of Motya are undermined by battering rams and siege-towers transport more rams across to the level of the ramparts while the catapults fire missiles to drive the defenders back off the walls, and eventually the ramparts are breached. But the defenders have built emergency walls inside the city between tightly packed houses to block the streets, and the Greeks can only advance slowly; eventually the inner city too is overrun and the garrison and inhabitants are massacred in a conflagration. Dionysius sends his heralds to tell the survivors to flee to the temples, which his men will respect, and then rounds them up and sells them as slaves.

As winter is coming and he is short of supplies, Dionysius installs a garrison at Motya and withdraws his main army; he leaves his brother Leptines to take Segesta and Entella.

397

Winter? – Segesta drives off a Syracusan assault by bombarding their camp with flaming material and burning the tents.

Himilco lands with a huge new Carthaginian army of at least 100,000 infantry (Timaeus) at Panormus, though Leptines manages to sink around forty of his four hundred ships as he tries to intercept them at sea; the rising wind saves the others. Himilco retakes Eryx and Motya; he wins over the inland Siceliot tribes against the threat of Syracusan rule and advances by land along the north coast on Messina, while his fleet proceeds parallel at sea. As he camps at Peloris, the Messinans send a force out to attack him but the Carthaginian navy hastens to the city to get there before the inhabitants' army can return; Messina is sacked and occupied although the women and children have mostly been evacuated already to Italy. Dionysius has to retreat from near Segesta on Syracuse, and moves his army to Catana to meet the advancing Himilco whose navy has taken Messina; he has around 30,000 infantry troops and 3000 cavalry.

Some 200 Carthaginian ships overwhelm the Syracusan navy under Leptines in battle opposite Mount Etna during an eruption, while Dionysius and the army watches from the shore and Himilco takes an inland route to avoid them and the eruption. Leptines loses around 100 ships; the Carthaginians sail on to the Great Harbour at Syracuse, and Dionysius has to retire to the city to avoid being outflanked by them. Himilco arrives to launch a siege and sends some of his navy to Sardinia and Africa for supplies; he builds a fortress at Plemmyrium at the Southern entrance to the harbour.

Greece

Spartan alliance with new king Psammetichus of Egypt; the latter supplies regular shiploads of grain to feed her Asia Minor expedition.

Early – Dercyllidas has his role as land-commander for another year confirmed as Spartan envoys meet him at Lampasacus; they investigate complaints of his looting Greek Ionian allies in 398, and the future historian Xenophon (as commander of the 'Ten Thousand' contingent) defends his own men's actions. During an eight-month truce with Pharnabazus, Dercyllidas occupies the Chersonese and drives Thracian raiders off.

Spring–summer – Dercyllidas in the Troad; he besieges the city of Atarneus for eight months in reprisal for its attacks on its pro-Spartan neighbours.

Dercyllidas as land commander and Pharax as naval commander are ordered by the 'ephors' to attack Caria and its satrap Tissaphernes; the Persians have a small fleet based in Caria at Caunus. Dercyllidas launches a land attack, but as he marches south, Tissaphernes and Pharnabazus evade him and attack northwards to his rear. He retreats to confront them, but both sides avoid battle as the Persians are nervous of the disciplined Greek infantry and the Greeks fear the Persian cavalry. A truce is agreed and the two satraps suggest that a peace could follow – Persia will guarantee the independence of the Greek cities in Asia Minor and Sparta will evacuate all her garrisons there. This is agreed, and the satraps promise to put it to the Great King but he has appointed the Athenian mercenary commander Conon as his admiral and sent him to Caunus to muster a large fleet for a campaign in 396. Pharnabazus visits Cyprus to gather ships for Conon's navy.

Conon's Persian squadron is blockaded in the harbour of Caunus as the Spartan admiral Pharax arrives by sea with 120 ships from his base at Rhodes via Sasandra, but the Spartans cannot force an entry and Dercyllidas' land-army has moved back north; the fleet has to retreat as Pharnabazus arrives on land with a relief-army.

?Conspiracy of the ambitious young 'second-class' citizen Cinadon in Sparta, aimed at rallying those excluded by strict rules from the full citizenship for a coup; he is betrayed, lured out of the city with a picked squadron of men to allegedly arrest some malefactors but then seized himself by his companions, interrogated, tried, and executed.

Winter – Sparta abandons her hope of imminent peace with Persia after a Syracusan, Herodas, reports to the city that when he was in Phoenicia recently he saw large numbers of ships mustering, apparently to go to Asia Minor for the use of Tissaphernes. Lysander leads the 'war party' and urges a bold attack on the Persian forces in southern Ionia to drive their fleet back to Phoenicia and a land-march emulating the 'Ten Thousand', who have shown up Persian vulnerability.

?Lysander, as Agesilaus' friend and possibly ex-lover, writes around the friends he made in Greek cities in Asia Minor in the 400s and asks them to send appeals to Sparta to have Agesilaus appointed to command the expedition to aid them.

397/6

Death or deposition of the boy-king Orestes of Macedon; succeeded by his uncle and regent, Aeropus.

396

Sicily

Dionysius sends his brother-in-law Polyxenus for help to Sparta, and admiral Pharacidas arrives with thirty Peloponnesian triremes; many of the citizens are by now mutinous and have taken heart from their forces managing to intercept a Carthaginian supply-ship en route to the enemy camp while Dionysius was away at sea meeting a supply-squadron, but Pharacidas ignores appeals from them at a meeting of the assembly to help against the tyrant and backs up Dionysius and his mercenaries.

Plague ravages the Carthaginian camp on the unhealthy low ground by the Great Harbour, and is blamed by the locals for their pillaging the nearby temples of Demeter and Persephone; Dionysius leads a dawn attack on them by land while his fleet crosses the harbour for a simultaneous attack on the enemy fleet, and their forts at the south-west side of the harbour at Dason and Polichna are captured. Most of the Carthaginian fleet is destroyed, though they hold onto the southern promontory of Plemmyrium; Himilco sends to negotiate for a safe retreat.

A few days later, Himilco and his Carthaginian citizen soldiers escape by night on fourteen surviving ships leaving their mercenaries and the local Sicilian tribesmen to fend for themselves; Diodorus reports a story that he paid Dionysius to let him leave. The tribesmen manage to make off back to their inland hills, but the mercenaries are forced to surrender or are captured as they try to flee; some from Spain are enlisted in his army and the rest are enslaved.

Dionysius commences war to regain control of the inland Siceliote tribes.

Greece

Agesilaus is appointed the Spartan land-commander, with 2000 Spartans/'helots' and 6000 Peloponnesian allies being sent to Asia Minor to join the c.10,000 troops already there under Dercyllidas and local Ionian volunteers – but not many cavalry. Lysander is appointed to lead the annually replaced staff corps of thirty senior Spartan citizens who assist the King.

Spring – The army musters at Geraustus in southern Euboaea; Agesilaus sacrifices to the gods at Aulis as Agamemnon legendarily did before the attack on Troy, which this expedition is to emulate as 'Greece versus Asia'. Allegedly, the sacrifice is disrupted by a group of Boeotian horsemen, sent by the Boeotian League's 'Boetarchs' who are angry at the sacrifice not being done in the local Boeotian manner and who seize the offerings and throw them in the sea; this causes bad feeling between Sparta and Thebes. Athens and Corinth do not send troops to the expedition, either.

Agesilaus lands in Ionia, goes to Ephesus where he raises 4000 local troops, and agrees a truce with Tissaphernes to cover Caria at the latter's request, urging the satrap to get the Great King to meet his terms of freedom for all of Greek Ionia; he sends Lysander, who has been throwing his weight around and is feted by the locals to Agesilaus' annoyance, to the Hellespont to collect local reinforcements. Xenophon and his troops fight with Aegisilaus' army into 395, and then in 394 accompany him back to Greece.

Tissaphernes ends the truce; Agesilaus pretends he is intending to attack Caria, and when his foe has taken the Persian army there he moves north instead to ravage Hellespontine Phrygia; he later retires to Ephesus in the autumn. He invades Lydia to head for Sardes and ravage the plain, and Tissaphernes (who expected this to be a bluff and Caria the real target) returns from his precautionary move into Caria to confront him; before all the Persian army has arrived, Agesilaus launches a surprise attack on the satrap, routs his army, and as they flee loots their camp.

395

Winter–?March – Agesilaus recruits troops from the Greek cities of Ionia and trains them in the latest mainland Greek fighting-tactics at Ephesus, holding Games so they can become fit and compete for prizes. Lysander returns home with the other senior officers whose turn of a year in office has expired, in a sulk after Agesilaus gives him no new role in the campaign following his successful recruitment of his old friend Spithridates to defect from Persia and aid Sparta.

Spring – Agesilaus defeats the Persian cavalry at the river Pactolus in Lydia, near the capital at Sardes, and takes seventy talents of loot at their camp. Satrap Tissaphernes, who was at Sardes and did not come to the rescue, is arrested and executed for incompetence by the Great King's new appointment to replace him, Tithraustes, who arrives at Colossae with the King's orders to kill him and gets the local satrap to invite Tissaphernes there then has him beheaded in the bath. Tithraustes pays Agesilaus thirty talents to attack Pharnabazus in Hellespontine Phrygia instead and give him a truce of six months. Agesilaus marches north, and near Cyme a Spartan envoy arrives to instruct him to appoint a naval commander of his choice and open a naval war too. He appoints his brother-in-law Peisander, and calls on his island and mainland allies to send ships to him. A navy of 120 triremes is created for the next campaign.

Agesilaus ravages Hellespontine Phrygia, but cannot force the Persians to a decisive battle.

Summer – Before the Spartan navy is ready, Conon arrives from the eastern Mediterranean with an enlarged Persian squadron (eighty ships), lands at Rhodes, and links up with the local democratic plotters who overthrow the pro-Spartan oligarchy in the eponymous capital and let his ships into the harbour. He sets up a base there, intercepts a convoy of supply-ships from Egypt to the Spartans who think that Sparta is still occupying the harbour, and summons more Persian ships (seventy from Phoenicia under the lord of Sidon, and ten from Cilicia). He has to go off to Tithraustes for more pay as his money runs out, and possibly goes on to Mesopotamia and the royal court too; in his absence a Cypriot squadron mutinies and sets up a rival command at Caunus.

Summer – Ismenias and Androcleides lead an anti-Spartan faction at Thebes, incite a war between Phocis and Locris, and get the latter to appeal for help to the Boeotian League; they then persuade the League to intervene. Phocis appeals to Sparta and the 'ephors' tell the Boeotians to let the Spartan alliance's council arbitrate; Ismenias persuades the Boeotians to ignore this and to invade Phocis. Sparta and her allies prepare to attack Boeotia.

The Persian agent Timocrates of Rhodes tours central Greece distributing Persian money (fifty talents) to potential allies and announcing that the Persian fleet will be coming to attack the Spartan hegemony in 394; Athens ignores him but politicians at Thebes (Ismenias), Corinth (Timolaus and Polyanthes), and Argos (Cylon) accept his bribes.

Late summer – Athens forms a defensive alliance with the Boeotian League and another with Locris.

Lysander invades Boeotia, marching from Locris with the Spartan troops at Heraclea and with aid from anti-Theban Orchomenus in Boeotia; King Pausanias is en route from the Peloponnese across Mount Cithaerron, but Lysander over-confidently does not wait for him and after securing friendly Orchomenus and plundering Lebadea attacks Haliartus. He has told Pausanias (now at Plataea) to meet him at Haliartus at dawn next day, but his messenger is captured by Thebes and the latter sends to Athens to speed their help up so some Athenians arrive at the city that night. Next morning the unaware Lysander decides not to wait for Pausanias and attacks alone, but is repulsed from the town's walls, and as a relieving Theban army arrives unexpectedly early he is killed and his men are routed. The survivors drive the Thebans back and withdraw to a defensible position outside, but that night disheartened allies desert and Pausanias arrives too late, next morning. The Athenians have now arrived too and are backing the Theban army to outnumber his cavalry, and the only way he can recover the bodies of the dead as his demoralized officers want is to agree to a truce and to promise to withdraw. Judging success in battle unlikely, he does so.

Back in Sparta Pausanias is prosecuted for cowardice and condemned to death; he flees to Tegea and is succeeded by his young son Agesipolis, who is under-age.

Autumn – The Persian defector Spithridates persuades the local Paphlagonians under king Cotys to supply 1000 cavalry and 2000 infantry to Agesilaus; Agesilaus occupies Pharnabazus' abandoned headquarters and palace at Dascylium for the winter. Spithridates and the Spartan general Herippidas finally corner the retreating Pharnabazus four or five days later, and attack and loots his camp; however, the Spartan conducts what his co-commander considers an unfair and insulting distribution of loot, forcing the Paphlagonians to hand over all they have taken for redistribution, and he and the Paphlagonians leave the army and go off on their own raids.

Autumn? – Conon returns to Rhodes, puts down a revolt there, and suppresses the mutiny at Caunus; around a hundred rebels are executed and the fleet is reunited.

Corinth, Argos, Euboaea, Leucas in the Ionian Islands, Ambracia opposite the latter, and the Chalcidian League join Thebes and they set up a common council at Corinth to run the war; the Spartan garrison at Pharsalus, Thessaly, is overrun and its soldiers enslaved by Medius, lord of Larissa, who is at war with the pro-Spartan tyrant Lycophron of Pherae. The Boeotians, having assisted Medius, secure the Spartan garrison at Heraclea by treachery, kill them, and give the town to the local Trachis tribesmen.

Sicily

After Dionysius resettles his loyalists in and garrisons war-wrecked Messina, the alarmed Rhegians attack and seize it to drive the Syracusans out; Dionysius launches war on them, but first has to deal with the inland Siceliots who are occupying Tauromenium on the east coast; he takes the town of Tauromenium by a surprise assault on the slackly guarded acropolis around mid-December.

394

Greece

Early – Agesilaus meets Pharnabazus at a truce-meeting under the auspices of their mutual friend Apollophanes of Cyzicus.

Sparta sends orders to Agesilaus to return home once it is confirmed that Persia is funding its enemies; the offensive war in Asia Minor is abandoned and he leaves Euxenus as the local commander as he heads to the Hellespont.

May/June – Before Agesilaus can return from the Hellespont, the allies muster at Corinth to attack: there are around 7000 from Argos, 6000 from Athens, 5000 from Boeotia, 3000 from Corninth, 3000 from Euboea, and around 5000 cavalry plus light infantry; the Sparta 'home army' has around 6000 Spartans under Aristodemus (regent for boy-king Agesipolis, son of Pausanias) and 14,000 allies. The Spartans move quickly up to collect the contingents of Tegea and Mantinea, and assemble at Sicyon; the allies at Corinth head for Nemea, where the Spartans manoeuvre themselves onto rough ground that the allied cavalry cannot use easily.

June/July – Battle of Nemea, near Argos: the Boeotians on the allied right and Athenians on the allied left face the Spartans; the Boeotians lead the attack, moving their line to the right as they advance so the Athenians have to move right too to avoid leaving a gap between their contingents. The Spartans move out to their own right, thus outflanking the Athenians on the allied left wing, and the Spartan right wing marches round behind them to take them in the rear; the Spartan allies on their left wing are driven back by superior Theban numbers and the unusual depth of the Theban line, but the Spartan right wing defeats the Athenians in the meantime. The Spartan left wing (its allies) breaks and flees, and the allied right wing chases it off the battlefield and then returns in separate city contingents one after another to try to tackle the Spartans but is defeated as it attacks them piecemeal – first Argos, then Corinth, and finally the Boeotians. Sparta loses around 1000 allied troops but allegedly only eight of its own men, and the enemy loses around 3000 out of around 20,000.

Agesilaus leaves 4000 men at Sestos to control the Hellespont, and marches back overland through Thrace; en route he defeats the Trallians who try to demand a bribe to let him pass, and he is given free passage by the impressed king of Macedon who sends a similar demand and is ignored; he hears of the battle of Nemea from Dercyllidas at Amphipolis. He enters Theban-allied Thessaly while Dercyllidas goes to the Hellespont to take command, and sends envoys to hostile Larissa who are arrested so he stops to negotiate their release; Agesilaus defeats the Thessalian cavalry near Mount Narthacium, then marches on to Trachis and Locris to collect reinforcements from his allies before heading into Boeotia as the 'ephor' Diphridas tells him to attack now not later as he prefers; a Spartan regiment arrives by sea from Sicyon to join him, and he takes the Spartan garrison from local Orchomenus to assist him, too.

July – Death of king Aeropus of Macedon, after a two/three-year reign; the Macedonian citizens' assembly ignores his son Pausanias and elects Amyntas II ('the Little'), son of Menelaus son of Alexander I.

August – Naval battle of Cnidus: Conon and Pharabazus with ninety ships advance from the Chersonese; they defeat the Spartan fleet under Peisander, who is killed as his left wing (his allies) crumbles and who refuses to flee; Peisander loses fifty of his eighty-five ships sunk or captured. Sparta loses control of the eastern and northern Aegean to the Athens/Persia alliance.

News of the battle of Cnidus reaches mainland Greece; 14 August. As Agesilaus is heading into Boeotia the sun is eclipsed and he hears of the battle of Cnidus and loss of the Spartan fleet. He pretends that Peisander won to keep up his men's morale, and marches on via the River Cephissus to Coronea.

Battle of Coronea: Agesilaus faces the combined forces of Thebes/Boeotia/Athens/Corinth/Argos/Euboea. The Thebans on the allied right wing rout their local enemies from rebellious Boeotian city Orchomenus, and chase them back to their camp; meanwhile, Agesilaus (on his right wing) has taken advantage of their absence to push back the rest of the allied army, led by the Argives, who break and flee for the slopes of Mount Helicon; as the Thebans return he clashes with and holds them, but cannot prevent most of them escaping past his troops to the allies' camp on Mount Helicon and is wounded in the thick of the fighting. Agesilaus allows the enemy refugees in sanctuary in the nearby temple of Athene Itonia to leave unharmed, and puts up a trophy before heading back to Sparta via Delphi where he attends the Pythian Games and sets up a trophy. His subordinate Gylis stays on to harass Thebes and raids Locris but is killed. Back in Sparta, Agesilaus uncovers Lysander's written plans to form a faction and force a reform of the Spartan constitution and covers them up for the good of public morale rather than prosecuting the late general's allies.

Autumn – Pharnabazus and Conon expel the Spartan garrisons and oligarchies from the Ionian coastal islands of Cos, Teos, Chios, and Lesbos and the city of Erythrae, and assure the inhabitants of their autonomy from now on; Pharnabazus lands at Ephesus and marches his army to Sestos on the Hellespont by land to deal with Dercyllidas' Spartan garrison there, while Conon and forty ships go by sea; they blockade Spartan-held Sestos and Abydos by land and sea but cannot take them.

As rumour has it that the pro-oligarchic faction in Corinth is using war-weariness at Spartan raiding from Sicyon to rally support for peace, the allies arrange a massacre of suspects in the city of Corinth and Iphicrates brings Athenian troops to the city to secure the harbour for the allies. Around five hundred people are exiled. Argos takes over control of the city with an effective 'union' with it under its democratic faction. Pasimelus and other surviving anti-Argives flee to seek help from the Spartans at Sicyon, and the Spartan commander Praxitas leads an attack on the city, which ends in an armed clash with the Argives there.

394/3

After a reign of under a year, Amyntas II of Macedon is murdered and replaced by his predecessor's son Pausanias. (Diodorus does not mention Amyntas and has Pausanias succeed his father Aeropus directly.)

393

Pharnabazus abandons the attempt to drive Sparta from the Hellespont, and leads a Persian-funded but Greek-manned mercenary fleet across the Aegean in consort with Conon's Athenian fleet; they raid the Cyclades and occupy Melos, and then Pharnabazus and Conon raid the Laconian coast and set up an Athenian base under Nicophemus at Cythera to harass Sparta's trade and her fleets emerging from Gytheium. They then sail to the Isthmus of Corinth where Pharnabazus addresses and offers bribes to a congress of the anti-Spartan alliance, urging them to rally to the Great King. He then returns home, and Conon sails with some of his ships to the Piraeus to use the sailors as labourers (paid by the Persians) to speed up the rebuilding of the Long Walls and so make Athens protected from blockades again. Thebes lends masons to assist in the work.

Athens forms alliances with Dionysius of Syracuse, Evagoras king of Salamis on Cyprus, and Eretria in Euboea.

Sicily

Dionysius attacks but fails to take Rhegium and extend his power into Italy, and the Southern Italian Greeks form a league to oppose him.

The Carthaginians under Mago land in Sicily to enlist more tribal support with heavy subsidies, then advance into central Sicily; Mago tries to head for Messina but is forced back.

392

Mago and up to 80,000 soldiers fight Dionysius and his ally Agyris, tyrant of Agrium, in central Sicily but runs short of food; he agrees to a treaty, which abandons the Siceliote tribes and the rebel city of Tauromenium to Syracuse; Carthage leaves the war.

Greece

Thebes issues new Persian-funded coinage with Heracles and the Boeotian shield symbol on the coins, to subsidize the war-effort; Rhodes, Cnidus, Iasos, Samos, Ephesus and Byzantium adopt this coinage and join alliance. Lampsacus, Cyzicus, Zacynthus, and Croton in Italy later adopt these coins too.

Corinth builds and launches a Persian-funded fleet, commanded by Agathinus, and contests the Gulf of Corinth with the Spartan fleet under Podamenus. The latter is defeated and killed and his deputy Pollis is wounded; Herippidas takes over command.

Proaenus, the new Corinthian admiral, has to abandon Rhium to Sparta. Teleutias, Agesilaus' brother, takes over the Spartan naval command.

Lemnos, Imbros and Scyros are occupied by Athens and colonies of 'cleruchs' established there.

Autumn – Sparta sends envoy Antalcidas to Caria to negotiate peace with satrap Tiribazus and via him the Great King, hoping the Persians will be alarmed at the revival of Athenian power; Athens hears of this and sends Conon with an embassy too, supported by Thebes, Corinth, and Argos. Antalcidas proposes that all mainland Asia Minor states be ceded to Persia and the rest of the Greek states be guaranteed autonomy as individuals – i.e. existing alliances are broken up, ending Athens' new colonies, the Boeotian League, and the Argos/Corinth alliance, all to Sparta's advantage. These are the basic terms on which peace will be agreed in 386 and Athens and Thebes are not in favour as they will lose their current dependencies; but although Tiribazus is agreeable, gives Antalcidas money to hire new allies, arrests Conon to hinder the Athens war-effort, and goes to see Artaxerxes the Great King does not proceed with the plan. Instead, Artaxerxes sends a new Persian representative, Strouthas, to take over Lydia from Tiribazus and to aid the anti-Spartan coalition with money to hire men and ships.

Conon is deported to Cyprus and interned by the Great King, probably suspected of double-dealing with his subsidies and not being a reliable conduit to Athens, and dies there later.

Winter – Sparta sends out envoys inviting the Greek states to a peace-congress and proposes Antalcidas' terms of general autonomy for the Greek states, but now with Athens keeping her three new colonies, the Boeotian League remaining in being, and Orchomenus remaining independent of Thebes. This is designed to lure Athens and Thebes away from Argos/Corinth and so isolate the latter for Spartan pressure and/or attack. Athens refuses to participate on these terms, although the wealthier citizens are mostly in favour of peace and the 'hard-liners' including Thrasyboulus (a close Theban ally from their sponsorship of him in exile in 404/3) are criticized. He and his ally Epicrates now want to use the rebuilt fleet (manned by poorer citizens as oarsmen) to regain control of the Chersonese, but Dercyllidas and his Spartan army are standing in their way.

392/1

King Pausanias of Macedon is murdered and replaced by a cousin of his, Amyntas III, who after a brief deposition within months is soon restored and goes on to rule until 370 – Diodorus says twenty-four years but this is probably an error.

391

Early? – Teleutias drives the Corinthian fleet back from the western end of the Gulf of Corinth.

Spring – Agesipolis raids the Argolid, leading the Spartan campaign in the centre/ East of the Peloponnese; Teleutias leads the Gulf of Corinth fleet to sack the Corinthian dockyards on the Gulf of Corinth shore at Lechaeum, while Agesilaus, commanding on land, is taking the city's 'Long Walls' to the port.

Sparta sends a new expedition to Ionia to push Persia back and force Tiribazus and the Great King to moderate their stance; Thibron retakes Ephesus for Sparta and then raids into Lydia to attack the new satrap Strouthas, while Teleutias and the fleet occupies Samos, isolates pro-Athenian (democratic) Rhodes, and captures ten Athenian ships en route to Evagoras of Salamis on Cyprus.

Thibron is ambushed and killed by Strouthas in person in a cavalry charge during a raid; he is succeeded by Diphridas as Spartan commander in Ionia, and Sparta sends out the refugee Rhodian oligarchs to assist the latter.

Athens' ally, king Evagoras of Salamis in Cyprus revolts against Persia in alliance with Egypt.

390

Spring – Thrasyboulus and forty ships avoids tackling Teleutias and his Rhodian allies, and overruns the northern Aegean, backed up by Eretria, Boeotia, and Thessaly, which supply him; he occupies Thasos and Samothrace, and kings Amadocus and Seuthes of Thrace ally with him.

June/July? – He approaches the Hellespont, avoids Dercyllidas at Abydos, and enters the Propontis to reach Byzantium where the pro-Athenian democrats open the gates to him. Chalcedon across the Bosphorus allies with him and Pharnabzus in Hellespontine Phrygia protects his eastern flank (and threatens Dercyllidas who cannot leave his bases to attack Thrasyboulus), but due to shortage of funds from Athens he re-imposes the taxes on shipping passing through the Hellespont, which Athens used to levy in the fifth century. The fleet remains in the Propontis for the rest of the year.

Sparta (led by Agesilaus) and Argos hold rival Isthmian Games at Corinth, one after another, by occupying their usual site at the time of the Games, as the civil war there continues; while Agesilaus is insulting some Theban ambassadors (by refusing to receive them) during his capture of the temple of Hera at Pechora on the Corinth expedition, Iphicrates' Athenians storm the nearby Spartan base at Lechaeum and kill several hundred Spartan citizens, the worst loss they have suffered for years.

Persia/Egypt
Alliance between the rebel Pharoah Hakor and the anti-Persian rebel ruler Evagoras of Citium on Cyprus, providing Egyptian naval help for the Cypriot rebels.

389

Greece
Early? – Thrasyboulus sails south-west to Lesbos, and lands to occupy various pro-Spartan towns with the aid of pro-Athenian Mytilene. He defeats and kills Therimachus, Spartan commander of Methymna. He loots the enemy to pay his troops, and with men from Mytilene and Chios to reinforce his ships he sails on south along the Ionian coast levying blackmail money from the local communities. He goes on round Caria to Aspendus in southern Asia Minor.

Thrasyboulus is killed in a skirmish on the River Eurymedon in Pisidia when locals raid his camp at night, arising from his local plundering; his fleet moves back to the Aegean to oppose the Spartan one based at Abydos. Argyrrhius takes over command.

Agesilaus is able to cross the Gulf of Corinth into Acarnania, at the appeal of his ally Achaea which is in possession of Calydon (on the northern shore) but is under attack there by Acarnania and Athens; he attacks the allies of Corinth there and ravages the countryside but cannot take any towns and in the autumn leaves via Aetolia.

Eteonicus' Spartan fleet bases itself at Aegina to harass Athenian shipping. Athens lands an army under Proxenus to blockade the eponymous capital of Aegina, but Teleutias (Spartan senior admiral for the year autumn 390– autumn 389) arrives with more ships to drive him off.

?Artaxerxes sacks Strouthas as satrap of Lydia and brings back his predecessor Tiribazus, logically out of unease at the success of the anti–Spartan alliance giving them confidence to reject Persia's terms for a Greek general peace and its plans to regain Ionia.

Autumn – Hierax takes over command at Aegina from Teleutias as the new supreme Spartan admiral for the next year. Later he sails off to Rhodes to assist Antalcidas in the Spartan command in Ionia, leaving part of his fleet at Aegina under Gorgopas.

388

Low-level naval skirmishes between Athens and Sparta in Ionia, as Anaxibius brings out Spartan reinforcements to Sestos and raids into Persian-held Aeolis and Iphicrates is sent by Athens to oppose him; based on the Chersonese, Iphicrates ambushes and kills Anaxibius as he is returning by land to Abydos from a looting expedition.

A Spartan fleet based at Aegina, commanded by Eteonicus again, harasses trade to Athens. Antalcidas sends Nicolochus to the northern Aegean; he raids Tenedos and is blockaded by the Athenian fleet at Abydos.

Athens sends its commander Chabrias to act as mercenary general to rebel king Evagoras in Cyprus, with some Athenian troops and ships despatched to help him, which is seen as a hostile act by Persia. En route to Cyprus he puts in at Aegina to help the Athenians there, and ambushes and kills the Spartan commander Gorgopas.

King Agesipolis leads the Spartan invasion of Argos.

Autumn – Teleutias assumes the next annual Spartan supreme naval command, after Hierax, and returns to Aegina. He raids the Piraeus by night from Aegina and damages shipping there.

Winter – Antalcidas, now the year's Spartan supreme naval commander, is sent to Persia to negotiate, utilizing irritation there at the Athens/Evagoras alliance; this time Great King Artaxerxes backs him.

Sicily

Dionysius besieges Rhegium for around a year (389–8 or 388–7?) for defying him; this takes place during the 388 Olympics, when he sends a magnificent embassy and racehorses to the Games. When the city falls he has the general Phyton flogged and drowned for leading opposition to him there. He also annexes and razes Caulonia at around this time, defeating an attempt to relieve it by the exile Heloris who has brought military aid from Croton, and moves its populace to Syracuse.

?(Traditional date, but only approximate) Plato visits the court of Dionysius of Syracuse at the tyrant's invitation, as part of the latter's cultural and intellectual pretensions as a patron. Possibly Plato's growing hostility to the concept of democracy (due to the catastrophes in Athens in the 400s and the execution of Socrates?) and interest in the rule of a just but despotic 'Philosopher King' make Dionysius seem a potential convert to his ideas. Allegedly, he soon changes his mind over Dionysius' viciousness and paranoia, and the angry despot has his 'ungrateful' protégé sold off as a slave; Plato's friends have to rescue him and smuggle him back to Athens.

387

Greece

Spring – Antalcidas informs Sparta that Persia will back them militarily until Athens and her allies accept the terms he proposed earlier, i.e. autonomy and the dissolution of alliances for Greek states and the return of Ionia to Persia; he is sent overland with Persian troops under Tiribazus to the Spartan base at Abydos (where Nicolochus is being blockaded) and links up with the Spartan fleet plus Persian-hired local Asia Minor reinforcements and twenty ships sent from Sicily by Dionysius. He outmanoeuvres the Athenian fleet under Iphicrates and blocks the Hellespont to hostile shipping, while in a co-ordinated move the Spartan fleet at Aegina blockades the Piraeus.

Autumn – Tiribazus summons the Greek states to send envoys to him and hear Artaxerxes' terms – autonomy for all Greek states, breaking up the alliances except Sparta's, Athens to keep Lemnos, Imbros, and Scyros, and all of mainland Ionia plus Cyprus to return to Persia. The latter will attack or fund attackers of any states which do not sign up to this. The envoys take these terms home, and the Greeks except for Thebes agree to this 'Peace of Antalcidas'.

386

Spring – As required, the Greek states take oaths to ratify and abide by the 'Peace of Antalcidas'; Agesilaus collects an army of Sparta's allies and marches into Boeotia, and Thebes gives way too; the Boeotian cities take oaths to the Peace separately to confirm that they are all now independent of Thebes' leadership. Argos gives way and breaks up her alliance with Corinth, and the oligarchs return to the latter; Corinth then rejoins the Spartan alliance.

Persia

Tiribazus of Lydia and his fellow-satrap Orontes of western Armenia, Artaxerxes' brother-in-law, collect a large fleet in Ionia, mostly crewed by Greek seamen, to launch the Great King's planned invasion of rebel Cyprus; they have up to 300,000 men (Diodorus). On the island, Evagoras of Salamis has around seventy ships and 6000 Cypriots plus a mercenary army, paid for by his secret ally King Hecatomnus of Caria, and ships from allied Phoenician rebels and from Egypt. The Persian fleet sails east to Cilicia to collect the waiting land-army and cross to Cyprus.

385

Tiribazus goes from Cyprus to Susa to report on the war; Orontes takes full control of the attack on Evagoras. During the war in Cyprus, Evagoras and his fleet nearly destroy the Persian fleet under admiral Glos off Citium near Salamis, thus cutting off the Persian army on shore, but are defeated in a major battle; the siege of Salamis follows later this year or in 384 and at some time into it Evagoras manages to escape and goes to Egypt to ask for help.

?Tithraustes and Pharnabazus lead an unsuccessful Persian attack on rebel Egypt, possibly to prevent the latter aiding the rebels on Cyprus.

Greece

Sparta orders Mantinea to raze her walls on the excuse of her failure to provide all the support she was supposed to do to Sparta in the war with Corinth. Mantinea refuses, appeals to Argos and Athens for help to no avail, and is besieged by King Agesipolis; his co-ruler Agesilaus asks successfully to be excused from the campaign as Mantinea was a close ally of his father. Possibly the future Theban leaders Epaminondas and Pelopidas serve in a volunteer Theban regiment that is sent to assist Mantinea, where Pelopidas is nearly killed in a skirmish but saved by his friend (according to Plutarch), and so learn how to counter Spartan military tactics for future use.

?Dionysius of Syracuse sends a mercenary force by sea to restore the expelled king Alcetas of Epirus, maternal great-grandfather of Alexander 'the Great', to his throne. He also agrees an alliance with the Illyrians as he expands his naval power across the Adriatic, and sets up a base at Lissus (in modern North Albania).

384

After the Spartans divert the river flowing through Mantinea to undermine and wash away the mud-brick walls, the city has to surrender; Sparta pulls down its walls and reduces it from a city into five autonomous village communities. The leading democrats are exiled but are not molested by the angry but disciplined Spartan soldiers as they leave.

Treaty of alliance between Athens and its ex-league stalwart, Chios; implicit defiance of the curtailing of Athenian naval power by the Peace of Antalcidas.

Birth of the philosopher Aristotle, as son of Nicomachus of Stagira in the Chalcidice, court doctor to King Amyntas III of Macedon.

Persia

Evagorus returns to Cyprus and reaches an agreement with the returned Tiribazus that he will restrict himself to ruling only Salamis and become the Great King's tributary vassal. The furious Orontes complains to the Great King at these lenient terms, and Artaxerxes recalls and arrests Tiribazus; Orontes takes over the war, but is unable to storm Salamis and with his men grumbling about the unfair treatment of Tiribazus he has to agree to peace on the terms that Tiribazus proposed. Back in Susa, Tiribazus is tried but acquitted and restored to favour; Orontes is sacked instead.

A campaign is led by Great King Artaxerxes against the Cadousian hillmen in the western Zagros mountains, which is unsuccessful despite his having up to 300,000 troops (Plutarch); his general Tiribazus saves the situation by sending envoys to each of the two rival chieftains of the rebels, saying that the other is negotiating with the Great King; they hasten to accept peace-terms. ?Artaxerxes' eldest son, Darius, becomes titular co-ruler as army commander on his first campaign.

After the war, ex-satrap Tiribazus of Lydia is fully restored to favour.

After the Persian fleet withdraws from Cyprus, its admiral Glos (Tiribazus' son-in-law) uses his control of the navy's funds and his Ionian Greek mercenary sailors to revolt against Persia and seize control of the southern Asia Minor seaways, allied to Egypt. He is probably afraid of sharing in Tiribazus' expected disgrace, though this does not happen.

384/3

Sicily/Italy

?Dionysius raids Pyrgi, the port of the Etruscan city of Caere, during his campaign in the Tyrrhenian Sea to suppress pirates and extend his influence.

383

Greece

Birth of the future king Philip II of Macedon, third son of the embattled King Amyntas III who is currently being hard-pressed by the Illyrians and has been forced to become an ally of the Olynthian League in Chalcidice.

382

An appeal from either King Amyntas III of Macedon (Diodorus) or from the threatened autonomous cities of Acanthus and Apollonia in the Chalcidice is made to Sparta against the Olynthian League, led by Olynthus, in the Chalcidice. (Possibly both appeal.) Amyntas has entrusted some of his lowland cities, including Pella, to the League to defend them while he was fighting off an Illyrian war recently and the League has now annexed them. The appeals are probably also that the League is threatening states guaranteed their autonomy by the Peace of Antalcidas (though Amyntas is not a signatory to that); possibly also Thebes is currently negotiating with Olynthus, which alarms Sparta, and Thebes refuses to let any of its citizens serve in the war against Olynthus.

Sparta declares war on the Olynthian League, which it feels is a local threat to Spartan power.

Summer – An expedition is sent there, led by Eudamidas; en route across Boeotia the latter's brother Pheobidas, bringing reinforcements, accepts an invitation from the oligarchic party in nearby Thebes, led by Leontiades and Archias, to march on and seize the Cadmeia citadel by surprise to assist their coup against Ismenias' faction. Some sources imply that Pheobidas did not just spontaneously accept a plan proposed by Leontiades, but that Agesilaus had already suggested the idea to him.

(During the feast of the 'Thesmophoria') A Spartan garrison is brought into the city of Thebes and installed in the Cadmeia by Leontiades, who announces it to the ruling city council as necessary to help avert a war with Sparta (over Olynthus?); a group of oligarchs occupy office as 'polemarchs', headed by Leontiades. Leading democrat Ismenias is executed and others are exiled, including the future leaders Epaminondas and Pelopidas; most of the exiled go to Athens, where Androcleides is assassinated by agents sent by the new Theban regime.

Sparta dismisses and fines (100,000 drachmas) Pheobidas for his unauthorized actions, but Agesilaus saves him from execution on the grounds that he only did what was best for their city; Sparta keeps the Cadmeia.

Teleutias, brother of Agesilaus, commands the attack on Olynthus and ravaging of its territory, based at Potidaea; Amyntas of Macedon assists him. The Thracian king Derdas aids the first Spartan attempt to assault Olynthus (autumn?) and saves the Spartans from a rout as they are driven back.

381

Sparta sends King Agesipolis to Olynthus with reinforcements as the city holds out. Agesilaus besieges the city of Phlius in the north Peloponnese for not restoring the rights of its exiles as demanded by Sparta.

Teleutias is killed in an attack on Olynthus.

381/0

The Athenian orator Isocrates' first 'Panegyric', a call for another national Greek expedition against the Persians as in 396–5 but this time led by Athens due to Sparta forfeiting its moral right to do so by its recent misbehaviour.

380

Summer – King Agesipolis of Sparta, commanding their expedition against Olynthus, dies of a fever and is succeeded by his younger brother Cleombrotus.

(or 379) After a year's siege, Agesilaus starves Phlius out and installs a garrison for six months while his new oligarchic regime conducts trials and executions of their enemies. Olynthus is forced to sign up to a treaty becoming a Spartan ally and dissolving its League.

Persia
?Rebel Persian admiral Glos, controlling the Asia Minor/Ionia seaways, is assassinated; he is succeeded by Tachos, who founds a new city near Clazomenae.

379

Greece
December – Twelve (according to Plutarch)/seven (Xenophon) Theban exiles, led by Melon and including Pelopidas and Damocleides, who are in league with the oligarchs' secretary Phillidas (who met Melon on a recent trip to Athens) merge with and borrow clothes from the rural labourers walking back into Thebes for the night. They then hide at the house of a sympathizer, Charon, for twenty-four hours. Their main group waits some miles away on the Thriaisian plain for a signal to proceed. A rumour reaches chief oligarch Archias, who sends for Charon to question him but is lulled by him into a false sense of security. That evening some of the twelve infiltrate the ruling council's feast at Archias' house to mark the end of their year in office, disguised as dancing-girls, sit on their couches with them, and stab them to death; Pelopidas and another group kill leading oligarch Leontiades by overpowering his porter and storming his bedroom, and other leading oligarchs are hunted down and killed and Phillidas kills the porter at the prison's door and leads an attack inside to release the prisoners. The attackers' allies in the city are told of the success and help to loot the weapon-manufacturers' workrooms and shops; Epaminondas and others arrive from the Attic frontier next morning to join them and the new regime elects Pelopidas as 'Boetarch' i.e. military commander; a rescue-mission of cavalry sent to the Spartans by Plataea is intercepted and destroyed.

An Athenian force under two generals follows the attackers to help the coup, not officially authorized. The Spartan garrison is blockaded in the Cadmeia, and its nervous commanders Herippidas, Arcippus, and Lysanoridas negotiate a safe evacuation

– Xenophon implies after a short siege (which means that the garrison panicked and negotiated too soon so Sparta was correct to prosecute its commanders), Diodorus says after a longer blockade. They retire to Megara to join a relief-army sent out under King Cleombrotus, which is making full speed for Thebes; their decision to retreat is thus a blunder and they are accused over it. (Agesilaus has refused to take command, alleging that he has served the traditional forty years' soldiering of a Spartan citizen but possibly disapproving of the occupation of Thebes anyway.) Chabrias' Athenians hold Eleutherae to block one line of approach to Thebes, but Cleombrotus takes the pass above Plataea and makes for Thespiae to join the Spartan garrison there. They attack Thebes but are repulsed, and he soon retires with the main army to Aegosthena but leaves Sphodrias with a force at Thespiae to harass Thebes.

A relieved Athens sentences the two generals who helped the coup to death to appease Sparta; Herippidas and Arcippus are executed and Lysanoridas is fined and exiled by Sparta.

378

Sphodrias foolishly raids the plain between Athens and Eleusis in a night attack to intimidate the so far neutral Athens – and was heading for the Piraeus to take it when he was spotted. Apparently (Plutarch) he was conned into the attack by a Theban agent, sent by Pelopidas, who urged him to take the Piraeus and thus blackmail Athens into abandoning Thebes, which Sparta would reward him for. He thus arouses public opinion in Athens, though the visiting Spartan ambassadors are arrested and assure his action was not sanctioned by Cleombrotus or the government in Sparta and he will be executed. Sphodrias is summoned home, but refuses to go and is acquitted in his absence as Agesilaus speaks up for him. Athens votes in reprisal to send 200 cavalry and 5000 infantry under Chabrias to aid Thebes.

Agesilaus reforms the system whereby Sparta's allies send troops to aid her wars in order to make greater demands and have the numbers to crush Thebes, granting them the right to pay money if they prefer so he can hire mercenaries and probably arousing discontent. (Early autumn?) He invades Boeotia with 18,000 infantry and 5000 cavalry, and confronts the Theban and Athenian armies holding a strong defensive position on a ridge near the city of Thebes, which he is too cautious to assault. His allied troops are unwilling to fight a risky battle. He raids the countryside, imposes new local garrisons to harass Thebes, and goes home.

Sicily
Carthage renews the war against Syracuse as Dionysius demands their complete withdrawal from Sicily; Dionysius' brother Leptines is killed with many of his soldiers at the battle of Cronium in western Sicily.

(or 377) Peace between Dionysius and Carthage; Dionysius pays an indemnity of 1000 talents and the river Halycus is to be the frontier, thus extending Carthage's power eastwards.

Winter 378/7

Greece
The Thebans defeat the Spartan garrison at Thespiae and kill its commander Pheobidas and many of his troops.

Athens commences re-forming her island League dissolved in 404, technically now of equal autonomous states not subjects; Thebes, Chios, and Byzantium are external allies of this alliance. The Piraeus is refortified.

A higher property-tax, at a lowered level of applicability to the citizens than before, is introduced in Athens to pay for its league and navy.

377

March – Athens announces the constitution of the League and invites all Greek states not subject to Persia to join, with equal status, autonomy, no interference in their constitutions or garrisons, and no tribute to be paid. It is aimed specifically at making Sparta accept the autonomy of all other Greek states, and thus breaking up its centralized and aggressive league/empire. The state of Athens and the, separate, 'Council of the Allies' will decide on policy between themselves and the allies' council is to meet at Athens but have equal votes for all with majority votes binding and an annually-elected president. Athens acts as leader in implementing military policy and negotiations, but as directed by the votes of the allies' council and its own government; usually it is Athens' generals that command in wartime, but they are constrained by the alliance's charter. Athens and the allies' council assess and impose their own, separate financial contributions on their own polities to pay for the alliance's actions, especially wars; both bodies have to approve admissions to the alliance and any treaties (or wars?) with states outside the alliance, and joint judicial bodies to rule on infringements of the terms are created. A religious headquarters is set up, at Delos as in the first Athenian alliance/empire; the first states to join are most of Euboea, the northern Aegean island of Sciathos, Maronea in Thrace, and Perinthus on the Propontis.

Spring–summer – Agesilaus invades Boeotia again, but cannot bring the Thebans to battle and ravages the countryside again. After two years without being able to cultivate a harvest the Thebans have to resort to buying in corn from Pagasae in Thessaly; their ships are, however, looted by the Spartan commander at Oreus, Alcetas.

On Agesilaus' return journey to Sparta, he suffers violent cramps in his leg in Megara (?a burst blood-vessel) and is incapacitated for weeks.

Greece/Egypt
Chabrias assists King Nectanebo at the head of a Greek mercenary force against a Persian attack, but is recalled to Athens to take naval command.

377/6

Greece
A board of ten new naval commissioners is set up in Athens to run the navy.

376

The fighting in Boeotia continues inconclusively as with Agesilaus recuperating Cleombrotus tries to force the passes over Mount Cithaeron in order to enter and ravage Boeotia but is driven back. Sparta's disgruntled allies request her to try a naval blockade of Athens to force her out of the war. Thebes starts to re-from the Boeotian League as more cities in the area throw off their Spartan garrisons and constitutions and become independent democracies; the League is now formed of more democratic regimes than earlier, and is again dominated by Thebes; a general assembly of all the cities elected by all male citizens meets regularly at Thebes to decide policy and elect magistrates, councils, and military commanders. Thebes represents three-sevenths of the electorate due to her size in population, and provides most of the seven annual 'Boetarchs' as the supreme leadership.

Sixty Spartan ships based at Aegina, commanded by Pollis, blockade the Saronic Gulf in a nautical challenge to Athens; September. The Athenian fleet under Chabrias defeats it off Naxos.

?Sparta sends to the Great King to ask him to mediate; a letter from him to the Greek states is subsequently sent but ignored.

Sicily

?Dionysius captures Croton in southern Italy to extend his power there, but fails to take Thurii.

375

Greece

The Spartan fleet is at Aegina again; one Athenian fleet under Chabrias moves along the Thracian coast signing up new members to the League, and a second under Timotheus goes to the Ionian Sea to win over Corcyra, Cephallonia, and Acarnania and later agrees to an alliance with King Alcetas of Epirus.

June? – Sparta sends a fleet of fifty ships under Nicolochus to the Ionian Sea to oppose Timotheus, but it is defeated at a battle off Alyra in Acarnania; Corcyra then sends ships to reinforce the Athenians.

The Theban 'Sacred Band', of 300 male lovers and led by Pelopidas, attacks the Spartan garrison at Orchomenus (two infantry squadrons) while most of the troops are away raiding Locris; he intends to take the city if it is feasible, but more Spartan troops have arrived so he retreats. As he passes the temple of Apollo at Tegyra the returning Spartan raiders under Gorgolyon and Theopompus spot him, and he attacks despite being outnumbered. The Thebans fight in an unusual compact square rather than the usual long line of infantry 'hoplites', and break though and rout the conventionally arrayed Spartans and kill both their commanders.

After this battle, the tide of pro-Theban risings in Boeotia soon leaves only Orchomenus in Spartan hands; the northern Spartan outpost at Heraclea guarding the approaches to Thermopylae is now a vital link through to Sparta's ally in Thessaly, Polydamas of Pharsalus, who is being menaced by the expanding power of pro-Theban Jason of Pherae to his north.

Thebes invades pro-Spartan Phocis; its ally Jason of Pherae threatens Polydamas with attack, and he (in person) and Phocis ask Sparta for help. King Cleombrotus is sent across the Gulf of Corinth to aid Phocis, but not to assist Polydamas as this is too far a distance; Jason invades Pharsalus and forces Polydamas to accept him as his overlord and send him his children as hostages, and is then elected as leader ('hegemon') of Thessaly.

Athens, probably over-burdened financially by her new league's expansion and annoyed at Thebes not paying its annual contribution to the alliance's treasury, negotiates with Sparta.

July – Peace is agreed in a congress at Sparta, on the basis of the 'status quo' of the Greek states as in the Peace of Antalcidas in 386 and again with the Great King as guarantor, but now with Sparta recognizing the new Athenian alliance and allowing Thebes, as a member of it, to negotiate peace with Sparta.

The news is sent to the Athenian fleet in the Ionian, where Timotheus proceeds to land his democratic exile allies from Zacynthus on that island so they can overthrow the oligarchic regime there; the latter protest to Sparta, which sends an embassy to Athens demanding that the Zacynthus democrats be stopped; Athens refuses so Sparta withdraws from the treaty.

374

Two Spartan fleets are sent out to the Ionian Sea, the first (possibly late 375) of twenty-three ships under Aristocrates and the second commanded by Mnasippus, to regain control of Zacynthus and also help Corcyra where a pro-Spartan minority invites them. Sparta also sends to Dionysius of Syracuse to urge their mutual interest in keeping Athens out of the Ionian Sea. Mnasippus blockades the eponymous capital of Corcyra.

?Civil strife and unsuccessful plots to overthrow the incumbent regimes in Corinth, Megara, Sicyon and Phlius.

373

Early – Sparta sends fleet to Zacynthus and Corcyra. Short of funds for a naval campaign, Athens sends 500 mercenaries under Ctesicles by land to Epirus to cross to and assist Corcyra, with local king Alcetas assisting them. They sneak into the eponymous capital of Corcyra unobserved by the besiegers. Iphicrates follows by sea once the fleet can be funded, but in the interim Mnasippus has been killed in a sortie from the capital of Corcyra (possibly as late as early 372).

Iphicrates reduces Cephallonia, and takes a squadron sent by Dionysius to assist Sparta at Corcyra by surprise while the crews are ashore and captures most of it.

Timotheus takes the fleet round the Aegean – possibly originally intended to go to the Ionian too but he does not have enough ships to make this safe. He signs up new members for and thus pledges of money to the alliance, lands in Thessaly, and persuades Jason of Pherae to join – Athens will now guarantee his local power though this contradicts her supposed campaign for states to be autonomous. Amyntas III of Macedon also signs up as an ally.

September – The fleet is laid up at the southern end of Attica, opposite the Spartan base at Aegina to hinder its use, as there is no money for an expedition; Callistratus and Iphicrates prosecute Timotheus for incompetent generalship in his recent naval expeditions, but he is acquitted after Jason of Pherae and Alcetas of Epirus sends a supportive embassy. Iphicrates takes over the naval command from him; new taxes are imposed to pay for the fleet's 372 campaign.

The Temple of Apollo at Delphi is destroyed in a fire. An earthquake sinks the seashore city of Helice in the Gulf of Corinth.

(or spring 372) Thebes destroys Plataea after its capture from Sparta by a sudden descent that catches most of the menfolk outside the walls in the fields, as a warning to those Boeotians who chose to support Sparta against her in recent years; the inhabitants are expelled. Thespiae is deprived of its autonomy and becomes a Theban garrison. Fears rise of Thebes dominating the Boeotian League as its subjects not its allies; the exiled Plataeans agitate for help in their refuge, Athens.

372

Iphicrates takes the fleet (seventy ships) to sea against Aegina, and the Spartan fleet withdraws. However, when he takes it on to the Ionian Sea he cannot fund his supplies for his men, and has to hire them out as labourers on the farms on Corcyra in return for food; a garrison is placed on Cephallonia.

Greece/Persia
Revolt of Datames, satrap of Cappadocia, against Great King Artaxerxes, probably due to his fearing arrest and execution as a result of a court conspiracy to discredit him.

371

(? or 372) Sparta takes over and razes Thespiae in Boeotia.

Encouraged by exiles from Plataea and Thespiae expelled by Thebes, the Athenians send a delegation led by Callias, torch-bearer of the 'Mysteries' of Eleusis and Calistratus, to Sparta to successfully propose that Sparta call a congress for peace which they will assist.

Summer – The Greek states send delegates to a congress held at Sparta, and Great King Artaxerxes II sends envoys to pressurize for peace so he can recruit mercenaries to use in his planned attack on Egypt. Sparta, backed by Athens and Persia, proposes an agreement that all states should be independent, all garrison withdrawn, and armies stood down; if any of the signatories are attacked the others are at liberty but not obliged to assist them in defence. This is approved, oaths are taken to it led by Sparta on behalf of her allies, and the congress's participants agree to send envoys round to supervise the evacuation of garrisons. Athens and her allies, and Thebes and her allies, take the oaths separately from each other. The Chersonese and Amphipolis are recognized as Athenian, and King Amyntas of Macedon is at the congress and agrees to this.

Next day Thebes, led by Epaminondas, asks for the word 'Thebes' to be replaced with 'Boeotia' so her league can be recognized in the treaty along with those of Sparta and Athens; Agesilaus refuses on the grounds that the oaths have been taken so the terminology is already agreed. The Thebans ask for their names to be removed from the treaty and walk out.

The treaty and disarmament go ahead without Thebes, and Athens recalls Iphicrates and her fleet. Spartan king Cleombrotus, however, stays on with his army in Phocis, and the Spartan assembly debates whether or not to withdraw him too; Prothous proposes withdrawing the army and making a formal dedication at the temple of Apollo at Delphi to raise the treaty to 'sacred' status, so that any who break the peace by occupying another's land can be proceeded against easily. The assembly, however, votes to order Cleombrotus to attack Thebes if she does not dissolve the Boeotian League immediately; and as Cleombrotus is close to Thebes the latter will not have time to raise a full-size Boeotian army or call in Jason of Pherae from Thessaly. Thebes defies Sparta.

Cleombrotus marches via Creusis on the Gulf of Corinth, evading a pass that the Theban army has blocked, to Boeotia, and reaches the plain of Leuctra near Thespiae, ten miles from Thebes; Thebes has an army of around 6000 infantry and 600 cavalry to 10,000 Spartan infantry and 1000 Spartan cavalry.

Battle of Leuctra – at midday Cleombrotus deploys his army on the plain after an emboldening midday drink with himself and around 2000 Spartans on their right wing, his allies in the centre and left wing, and the cavalry in front. The Thebans are persuaded to attack not await attack as usual by Epamonindas, possibly with reference to a prophecy that the Spartans will be defeated at a monument to some virgins once raped by Spartans that is nearby and is decorated with garlands to earn divine goodwill; the troops of Thespiae panic and withdraw and the Theban non-combatant food-suppliers are harassed by the Spartan light skirmishers as they leave and retreat to the Theban camp to rejoin the troops. The crack Theban regiment of the 'Sacred Band', famously made of pairs of lovers, under Pelopidas are on the Theban left wing, which is the 'deepest' part of the line and thus has the force to 'punch' through the enemy, and the centre and right are to let the left wing move ahead first with Epaminondas planning to deploy his right wing at an oblique angle to the main battle-line so they will engage first and can use their numbers and discipline to smash through the enemy left. The Boeotian cavalry attack and drive the smaller Spartan cavalry back; Pelopidas leads a Theban left wing charge against Cleombrotus' wing, which is still deploying to its right to outflank the Theban right wing and is caught unprepared. The Thebans drive the Spartans in on themselves with the force of the charge, mortally wounding Cleombrotus, though his troops recover and manage to reclaim his body before a second Theban charge drives them back again. The weight of the Theban centre under Epaminondas then drives the Spartans back across their whole left wing, and about half the Spartan army including around 400 Spartan citizens are killed; the Spartans break and flee, leaving their allies in the centre and right wings exposed; the latter withdraw to the Spartan camp without engaging the Thebans, and persuade the Spartan survivors not to renew the battle. The Spartans send envoys for a truce to collect their dead and concede defeat.

Jason of Pherae arrives with his cavalry at the battlefield ?a day or two later, refuses to assist a Theban attack, and arranges an armistice for the Spartan survivors to evacuate their camp unhindered; they retreat overnight to Creusis and thence Aegosthena.

Sparta hears the news on the final day of the 'Gymnopedae' festival, and the officials keep the news to themselves and carry on the latter as normal, informing the relatives of the dead individually and the city later and banning mourning; next day all citizens under sixty are called up and the surviving King Agesilaus's son Archidamus leads the relief army out to join up with their Peloponnesian allies; he meets the retreating survivors of Leuctra at Aegosthena, hears of the extent of the disaster, and decides to send his demoralized allies home as a sign that the campaign cannot be won, conceding control of Boeotia to Thebes. At Athens, a Theban envoy arrives to announce the victory and ask for alliance against Sparta but the 'Boule' does not respond.

Cleombrotus is succeeded as king in Sparta by his son Agesipolis II, who is probably only a youth.

Jason attacks the Hyampolitans and Heraclea in Phocis to enforce his local power, then returns home.

Winter – Athens calls a congress to uphold and implement the Great King's proposed terms of earlier 371, in the hope of using majority opinion and the argument that this treaty has already been sworn to as a means of reducing the effect of Thebes' victory. The

Athenian naval alliance will now act as chief guarantor of the peace and the other Greek states can form defensive alliances with it to assist in peace-keeping and dealing with any who try to control other states. Most of the Peloponnese sends delegates and agrees to these terms, forming alliances with Athens, but not Sparta or Elis.

Persia
?Rebel satrap Datames of Cappadocia fights off a first attack on him by loyalist army under satrap Autophradates.

Greece

Winter 371/0
Agesilaus is authorized to reform the Spartan constitution; he refuses to extend the Spartan citizenship as some wish in order to increase the size of the citizen-army and merely refuses to implement the usual legal ruling on survivors of major defeats losing their citizenship.

Tegea, Mantinea, and probably Corinth, Megara, and Sicyon break away from the Spartan alliance and evict their oligarchic governments; in Tegea the minority anti-Spartan party of Callibius and Proxenus (who want to create an Arcadian League) secretly call in help from a Mantinean military force to aid them as they attack and evict their rivals under Stasippus.

370

Early spring? – Mantinea re-forms itself as one city and rebuilds its walls, snubbing Agesilaus who is sent there by Sparta to ask them to stop this unfriendly act; it joins Tegea to set up an Arcadian League, to which others join in defiance of Sparta; they ally to Elis and Argos.

Agesilaus leads a tentative Spartan attack into Arcadian territory to punish Mantinea, avoids a major battle near the city with the Arcadians and Mantineans who are in turn held back by the Eleans, and does some ravaging to restore his men's morale.

Epamonindas leads and advises the Boeotian League as its annual 'Boeotarch' (general) with Pelopidas, and persuades its members to re-admit rather than punish Orchomenus; alliances with Phocis, Ozolian Locris, and Aetolia.

Uneasy alliance between Jason of Pherae, who now dominates Thessaly and overruns the Spartan garrison at Heraclea, which he gives to Malis and Oeta to build up his clients in Locris, and Thebes; Jason proposes to act as president of the forthcoming Pythian Games at Delphi.

July/August? – Jason of Pherae is assassinated before he can run the Pythian Games; Opuntian Locris, Malis, Heraclea, Euboaea, and Acarnania decide to seek Theban protection and join the Boeotian League after the death of their potential leader or oppressor Jason. His brothers Polydorus and Polyphron succeed him, but the former is soon killed by the latter.

Democratic revolution at Argos sees 1000 of the oligarchs' party being massacred by the democrats; it joins Elis and the new Arcadian League in challenging Sparta.

Autumn – The pro-Spartan faction exiled from Tegea appeal to Agesilaus, and he leads a Spartan army there to restore them and so pull Tegea out of the Arcadian League; the Arcadians also fight Orchomenus and Heraea, which call on Corinth and Phlius for aid.

Arcadians call in the Boeotian League to help them against their rebels and Sparta, and alliance between the two Leagues is agreed.

Late – Death of King Amyntas III of Macedon, paternal grandfather of Alexander 'the Great'; succeeded by the oldest of his three sons, Alexander II. Possibly Amyntas has also made an agreement with the family's rival Ptolemy, son of his cousin Amyntas II, who marries Amyntas III's daughter Euryone, that he will succeed Alexander.

?Death of Alexander 'the Great's' maternal great-grandfather, King Alcetas of Epirus; succeeded as joint rulers by his sons, Neoptolemus and Arybbas.

370/69

Death of the new Agid king, Agesipolis of Sparta, after a reign of one or two years; succeeded by his brother Cleomenes (II).

369

Early? The Boeotians march into the Peloponnese, led by Epaminondas and Pelopidas, to assist the Arcadians in conquering Orchomenus and Heraea; they are then asked to stay on by Arcadia, Argos and Elis and the Arcadians seize a pass into Laconia; a joint Boeotian/ Arcadian /Argive/Eleian army of around 40,000 invades Laconia and descend the east bank of the River Eurotas to Sparta.

The remaining 800 or so Spartan citizen-soldiers and 6000 (Xenophon)/1000 (Diodorus) armed 'helots' are blockaded in Sparta with their Orchomenus mercenaries; the fields and villages outside Sparta are burnt; Agesilaus refuses to march out against a vastly superior army. Agesilaus puts down a mutiny by a unit of plotters who have seized part of the defences, at the 'Issorium', by going up to them pretending ignorance of their plot and saying that they have mistaken their orders and are to be split up and assigned to different posts; they believe they are undetected and duly split up, and then he has them individually arrested and executed, illegally without trial; nevertheless large numbers of helots and 'periocoi' join the Thebans. Epaminondas marches on south, crosses the Eurotas at Amyclae to the west bank, and moves back up to the south side of Sparta; his cavalry enter the 'city' (actually four villages with remarkably little grand buildings or planning) but are driven out; he withdraws to besiege the naval base of Gytheium at the river-mouth but cannot take it. Corinth, Sicyon, Phlius, Epidaurus, Troezen, and other cities and districts in the north-east Peloponnese send help to Sparta and some of the Thebans' allies leave for home with their loot.

Messenia has its independence restored by Thebes to block Sparta's control of the southern Peloponnese, and Messene is rebuilt.

?Polyphron of Pherae, lord of Thessaly, is murdered at the instigation of his wife whose brothers do the deed – to the benefit of his nephew Alexander, son of his murdered brother Polydorus, who seizes power.

While Epaminondas is in Laconia, Pelopidas is sent to answer an appeal from Thessaly against Alexander of Pherae, who has take Pherae's rival city Larissa; Pelopidas marches there and compels him to withdraw, but the two men quarrel as Alexander resists taking instructions on moderating his harsh treatment of his subjects/allies and the tyrant leaves for home in a rage.

April – Epaminondas withdraws from Laconia; Athens agrees to an appeal from Sparta for help, with its supporters arguing that if Thebes destroys Sparta they will be next, and sends troops under Iphicrates to aid its new ally Corinth in blocking the Isthmus; Epaminondas evades them by taking an unguarded route near Cenchrae and reaches Boeotia safely.

An alliance between Athens and Sparta is formalized.

368

?Civil war between King Alexander II of Macedon and his brother-in-law Ptolemy of Alorus, son of Amyntas II; assuming that Diodorus' reference to a three-year reign by Ptolemy (to 365?) implies his time as sole ruler, Alexander is assassinated (by his rival?) later in this year.

During the civil war in Macedon between Alexander II and Ptolemy, their neighbour Alexander of Pherae attacks the Thessalian League. Thebes sends Pelopidas and Ismenias as envoys, but they have no troops; the Athenian admiral Iphicrates is backing Ptolemy, but Pelopidas goes to the Macedonian court and wins Ptolemy over to alliance and brokers a truce between him and Alexander. Ptolemy enters offensive and defensive alliance with the Boeotian League and sends Alexander's youngest brother Philip, aged sixteen, as a hostage to Thebes with thirty other prominent young Macedonians. This will enable the future conqueror of Thebes, Philip II, to study her military tactics and learn from her greatest generals Epaminondas and Pelopidas; possibly Philip stays with Epaminondas' father and learns from him personally. Some time later Alexander is assassinated and Ptolemy takes all Macedon, probably supported by the nobles as Alexander's next brother, Perdiccas, is still only in his teens and Ptolemy acts as his guardian and makes him his heir.

Pelopidas raises a force of Thessalians opposed to Alexander of Pherae to aid him as he has no military power to coerce the latter.

Iphicrates' Athenian fleet successfully intervenes in Macedon to assist Ptolemy against a pretender, Pausanias the son of the late king, Archelaus, who has invaded eastern Macedon with his brother-in-law Philip, Ptolemy's brother.

Early summer? – Epaminondas' second invasion of the Peloponnese, with 7000 infantry and 600 cavalry; he faces a joint Corinth/Athens/Sparta army of around 20,000 blocking the Isthmus around Oneum, but attacks the western end of their defence-line before dawn as the guards are changing their posts and the new rota are still half-asleep and storms it; he moves on into the north-east Peloponnese to link up with his Arcadian allies and force Sicyon and Pellene to join the Boeotian League to protect his approaches to Laconia and threaten Corinth.

He plunders the territory of Epidaurus and Corinth before going home, but an opportunistic attack on one of the gates of Corinth by the 'Sacred Band' is defeated by a sortie.

Assistance from Dionysius of Syracuse arrives in Sparta in twenty triremes with some Celtic allies from Italy; the Sicilian cavalry helps Sparta and Corinth to harass the Thebans as they leave the Isthmus, and then they attack Sicyon.

The Arcadian League builds a new federal centre at the new fortified city of Megalopolis ('great city'), blocking the route north from Sparta towards Argos and Corinth; the aggressive Lycomedes of Mantinea emerges as the Arcadian leader and urges them to rely less on doing what the Thebans want.

Alexander of Pherae arrests Pelopidas and Ismenias when they visit him at Pharsalus despite a truce, and imprisons them at Pherae; their subsequent antagonism may imply that he uses physical violence or threatens this. He allies with Athens, though Iphicrates' Aegean fleet (in the region each year to 365) is little practical help to him. Autocles and thirty ships are sent to Thessaly for the next few months by Athens to help Alexander.

Winter – The Persian envoy Philiscus of Abydos arrives in Greece and, backed by Athens which makes him a citizen, summons a peace-congress to Delphi to try to broker a treaty and end the war between Sparta and Thebes/Arcadia. Sparta refuses to give up its claim to Messenia and the congress fails, and Philiscus uses his money to hire 2000 mercenaries to supply to Sparta to aid its defence.

December? – Dionysius of Syracuse finally wins a prize for his theatrical works at a Greek festival, to his great delight – his 'Ransoming of Hector' wins first prize at the 'Lenaia' in Athens.

367

A second contingent of troops from Dionysius of Syracuse comes to the Spartan/Corinthian/Arcadian alliance's meeting at Corinth to aid Sparta, and then proceeds to Laconia; with its help Archidamus raids Arcadia and fights off the Arcadians at the drawn 'Tearless Battle' where morale is helped as not one Spartan citizen is killed.

Sicily

Early spring – Death of the tyrant Dionysius of Syracuse who has ruled the city for thirty-eight years, allegedly after celebrating his victory in the annual theatrical competition at the 'Lenaia' in Athens with a drunken party. He is succeeded by his timorous and easily influenced son Dionysius II (born around 392?), who for the moment is politically reliant on his uncle and brother-in-law Dion. The latter persuades his friend the philosopher Plato to come to Syracuse again, to tutor Dionysius II and supposedly train him in the paths of virtuous rule; Plato and Dion see the tyrant as a potential 'philosopher-king' who can be turned into an ideal ruler, but the weak-willed young man is also subject to the efforts of the wily politician Philistus who Dionysius recalls (at Dion's enemies request to counter his influence?) and who then tries to lure the tyrant into easy living and wild parties. Philistus starts to work on Dionysius with flattery to make him jealous of Dion.

Greece

Boeotia sends 8000 infantry and 600 cavalry to invade Thessaly and force the hostages' release, and it arrives before the Athenians' thirty ships and 1000 infantry does. The Boeotians cannot bring Alexander to battle on the plains of Thessaly, and are harassed by his cavalry until Epaminondas, currently only a junior officer instead of their commander, which may imply recent political criticism at home, is given command of the Boeotian force and drives them off.

Epaminondas commands a second expedition to Thessaly himself, and forces Alexander to release Pelopidas and Ismenias.

Athens allies to Dionysius II of Syracuse in her search for new allies, but gets no aid; her allies are restive at the cost of the Theban war, so she follows Sparta in sending an embassy to the Great King (Timagoras and Leon) to ask for his mediation. Antalcidas, negotiator of the 387 Sparta/Persia treaty, represents Sparta; the Boeotian League sends Pelopidas with a rival request, as do Arcadia (boxing champion Antiochus), Elis (Archidamus), and Argos.

Greece/Persia

Autumn – The Greek envoys arrive at Susa; Great King Artaxerxes II mediates, honours his old acquaintance Antalcidas but also the heroic victor of Leuctra Pelopidas, and decides in favour of the proposals made by Pelopidas on behalf of Thebes – all Greek states will be autonomous and keep the peace with each other, and no occupation of other states will be permitted; Athens will have to lay up her fleet and accept the loss of Amphipolis to Macedon, and Sparta will have to give up her claims to Messenia. The 'Peace of Pelopidas' is taken back to Greece to be put to the states, but the Spartan envoy Antalcidas, who had not expected this outcome given his earlier credit at the Persian court, kills himself. The Athenian envoy Timagoras is executed on his return home for receiving a large quantity of lavish gifts from Artaxerxes, with Leon saying that his fellow-envoy did what Pelopidas wanted.

?(or 366) Rebel satrap Datames of Cappadocia defeats a second Persian attack under Ariobarzanes of Hellespontine Phrygia; Ariobarzanes is then dismissed in favour of the late satrap Pharnabazus' son Artabazus, the future rebel, exile in Macedon, and ally of Alexander 'the Great', refuses to retire, and revolts himself.

366

Greece

Early – Epaminondas is elected 'Boetarch'.

Spring – Thebes summons a congress of the Greek city-states, and the Persian envoy unseals and reads out the Great King's mediation decisions for autonomy and liberty for all states and the independence of Messene and Amphipolis. Thebes' rivals refuse to accept it at this congress and insist that their own citizens must approve or reject it, led by Sparta and Athens, and Lycomedes of Arcadia backs them; Thebes has to send envoys round to argue their case to each city. Corinth is the first city to tell the Theban envoys who are sent round the various cities that she will not accept the terms and this emboldens others. Athens refuses to lay up her fleet and sends an army into Megara to oppose Thebes' expected attack, and Sparta sends Agesilaus off to assist rebel satrap Ariobarzanes and receive money from him, which he can then use for war against Thebes.

Epaminondas marches into the Isthmus of Corinth with the year's Boeotia expedition, and is helped by Argos to break through the enemy's defence-lines; he joins up with the Argive/Arcadian/Sicyon/Elis/Messenian forces in the north Peloponnese and invades Achaea. The Achaean League agrees to join the Boeotian League in alliance.

Epaminondas issues orders for the Achaean League to keep its present city constitutions and not exile any of the oligarchic factions, to preserve it and its new Boeotian guarantors from any political backlash and build up support; however, some of the Boeotian democrats fear that this will mean that surviving oligarchic regimes will revert to Spartan alliance once they find it safe to do so, and link up with his foes in Thebes. The Thebes assembly votes to ignore Epaminondas' decisions, install democratic regimes in all of Achaea, and exile the oligarchs with a series of Boeotian garrisons installed. This is resented, and the

Achaean democrats are forced by local resistance to a Boeotian 'dictat' to recall their exiles within months. New alliances with Sparta follow.

Arcadia and Argos garrison Sicyon to help the oligarchs who Epaminondas has left in power, but are won over by the ambitious Euphron, one of the latter, to assist him in proclaiming a democracy as a means to saving the city from its oligarchs allying with Sparta; he is elected as one of the annual generals (with Hippodamus, Acrisius, Cleander and Lysander) and his son Adeas as the commander of the city's mercenaries in place of Lycomedes by the new regime, and he seizes temple treasures and the confiscated property of victimized wealthy citizens to pay for more mercenaries with whom he deposes his fellow-generals and makes himself tyrant. Boeotia accepts this but sends a garrison to watch him.

Summer – Oropus, Athens' anti-Theban ally in Boeotia, is seized by its pro-Theban exiles aided by their host Themison, tyrant of Eretria; it is handed over to the Boeotian League, while Chares is away with troops assisting Phlius in the north Peloponnese against Argos and Arcadia. Athens sends an expedition, but the Thebans have occupied the town before they arrive so they go home. Callistratus and Chabrais are prosecuted for treason in Athens in discontent at their military failures, but are acquitted.

Athens forms an anti-Theban alliance with Arcadia, following an overture from Lycomedes of Mantinea; the latter visits Athens to conclude the treaty, but is assassinated on his way home by vengeful exiles. Athens is alarmed at her current ally Corinth expelling her troops from their strongpoints in the city's territory after Demotion carried a motion at the Athenian assembly in favour of forcing Corinth to keep in line with her; Chares is sent to occupy Corinth in case its oligarchic government turns to Thebes, and to install a pro-Athenian democracy. The plot is betrayed and as he lands his troops at Cenchrae he is met by armed Corinthians and told to leave; Corinth and her allies Phlius and Epidaurus agree to peace with Thebes instead, but Sparta refuses to negotiate as the Corinthians advise her to do as she will have to accept the loss of Messenia.

Euphron, his 2000 or so mercenaries, and the Boeotian garrison raid Phlius in alliance with an Argos/Arcadian attack, but the suspicious Arcadians under their annual general Stymphalius try to expel him and take over the city of Sicyon. He retreats to and seizes the harbour and sends Pasimelus of Cornth as his envoy to the Spartans, to whom he hands the harbour; Athens sends him mercenaries and he overruns the town, but the Boeotian garrison holds out in the citadel; he then goes to Thebes to try to restore relations, but is assassinated by his opponents from Sicyon while addressing the council of the Boeotian League in the Cadmea citadel. The murderers are tried, but are acquitted after one of them points out that they only committed tyrannicide without trial like the Thebans did to their oppressors.

The Arcadians defeat the men of Elis as the latter try to force defector town Lasion back into Elena suzerainty and out of the Arcadian League; they advance via Olympia on Elis itself but are defeated and driven out of the city; however, the Elis democrats under Charopus take heart from the military power of pro-democracy Arcadia in the region and seize the acropolis of Elis. The ruling oligarchs' cavalry drives them out, and they seize Pylos on the coast and ally to Arcadia; civil war in Elis (into 365?), and Sparta assists the oligarchs by seizing the frontier town of Cromnus; King Agesilaus' son Archidamus has to rescue his garrison in Cromnus from an Arcadian siege, and is defeated and wounded in the process though part of the Spartan garrison escapes successfully.

Athens recalls Timotheus and sends him with thirty ships and 8000 mercenaries to assist Ariobarzanes and earn his money and goodwill; Timotheus expels the pro-Persian ruler of Samos, Cyprothemis, after a six-month blockade (late 366 or early 365) and installs Athenian colonists, 'cleruchs', to keep the island loyal.

Sicily

Dion is exiled from Syracuse by Dionysius after his plans for conducting the forthcoming negotiations with Carthage personally and unsupervised are revealed to his paranoid nephew by the mischief-making Philistus; a friendly letter that Dion has written to Carthage asking their leaders to ask Dionysius to use him as negotiator is given to Dionysius by Philistus, and he is accused of wanting Carthaginian help for a coup; Plato fails to mediate and he is bundled out of Syracuse secretly on a ship (autumn?) and dumped in Italy. He is allowed to keep his revenues from his estates, as he retires to Athens to stay with his friend and later military lieutenant (and murderer) Callippus. Later the spiteful Dionysius insists that Dion's wife Arete, his sister, divorce Dion and marry a crony of his.

?Plato returns to Athens after giving up on attempts to influence the erratic Dionysius II, having been detained in the Ortygia citadel as a 'guest' for some weeks after Dion was exiled so he would not return home angry and blacken the tyrant's name; Dionysius promises to recall him after an imminent military campaign but does not do so.

366/5

Greece

Death of King Ptolemy of Macedon, according to the chronology of Diodorus who gives him a three-year reign and Perdiccas III a six-year reign to 360/59. Accession of his brother-in-law Perdiccas III, now probably around or over twenty? Return of Perdiccas' younger brother Philip, later King Philip II, from Thebes to Macedon.

365

Uneasy unofficial truce between the Theban and Spartan alliances in the Peloponnese, following the recapture of Selassia on the Arcadian border by Sparta and its Sicilian mercenaries sent by Dionysius II.

(Possibly the Cromnus incident between Arcadia and Sparta occurs in this year.)

?Timoleon of Corinth, future ruler of Syracuse, kills his would-be tyrant brother Timophanes to halt his plot, thus earning a reputation for strict democratic probity.

364

Thebes/Boeotia agrees to an appeal to send an army of c.7000 to assist the Thessalian League against Athens' local ally Alexander of Pherae, who has garrisoned towns in Phthiotis and Magnesia.

13 July – An eclipse of the sun delays the army setting out, and is declared a bad omen so the plan is abandoned; Pelopidas insists on going to fulfil Thebes' promise and collects some 300 Boeotian citizen cavalry volunteers. They join the Thessalian army, and fight Alexander at Cynoscephalae ('Dog's Head', near Pagasae; later site of 197 battle between Macedon and Rome). The Pherae infantry, outnumbering the Thessalians' infantry, is

positioned in the foothills above the plain; Pelopidas sends his infantry to attack them and his cavalry then routs the Pherae cavalry in the plain, but as he prepares a cavalry attack on the Pherae infantry in the flanks they push his Thessalian infantry back down the hill. He takes an infantry force to attack Alexander's right wing of mercenaries and win the battle by destroying the enemy leader and is successful, but he runs ahead of his men in the charge and is killed unsupported in combat as the enemy break; his cavalry routs the enemy and c.3000 are killed, but the loss of Pelopidas ruins the victory and Alexander continues the war.

Epaminondas cruises the Aegean with the new Theban fleet, which he has persuaded his city to construct, but achieves little.

July – The Arcadian army, aided by its allies Athens and Argos, occupies the sanctuary and Games precincts at Olympia and sets up a fortified position on the 'Hill of Chronus' so that its allies the Pisatans, not the Eleans, will run the Olympic Games; Elis appeals to its ally Achaea, and they attack the sanctuary during the Games (second half of August?) but are unable to storm it as the Arcadians, aided by Argos and Athenian cavalry, defend a line along the River Cladeus and have to give up after a day of fighting in the precincts with defenders pelting the attackers with tiles from the Olympia temples' roofs. Seeing the stockade that the defenders have erected with pieces of temples overnight, the attacking Eleans retreat on the second day.

The Arcadians, led by Tegea, then sacrilegiously loot some temple treasury money from Olympia to pay their troops (the regular League army of 5000, the 'Eparitoi'), and Mantinea leads complaints at this in their League council; the Tegeans secure a majority in their favour, aided by their city's democratic credentials, which attracts Theban support, and accuse the Mantineans of damaging the League's interests; the League council votes to summon the leaders of Mantinea, who refuse to come, and when troops are sent to arrest them Mantinea shuts its gates. The oligarchic regime in Mantinea turns to Sparta for help.

Autumn – Thebes is shamed into avenging Pelopidas; 7000 Boeotian infantry and 700 cavalry under Malcitas and Diogeiton attack Pherae, besiege Alexander, and force him to accept terms as an ally of the Boeotian League supplying troops when required.

?Athens installs colonists ('cleruchs') in Potidaea on the Macedonian coast.

Persia
Mithridates, son of rebel satrap Ariobarzanes, seizes the port of Heraclea in Paphlagonia.

363

Greece
The Arcadian League council votes in Mantinea's favour, condemning the looting of the treasuries at Olympia and forbidding more use of them, and abolishes pay for their League troops to save money and asks Thebes not to send any troops in future unless asked. Part of the unpaid Arcadian army deserts. A truce with Elis is negotiated, though the Arcadian leaders who agreed to loot the treasure fear they will be prosecuted and ask Thebes to help them militarily; at Tegea, as oaths are being taken by the League's various military contingents to the armistice with Elis a disgruntled Theban officer commanding the Theban contingent there talks the Tegean city leaders into rounding up their opponents,

implying Theban backing for this. He then loses his nerve and persuades the city to release the accused, alleging that it was only a defensive measure in case they admitted an approaching Spartan force, and flees to Thebes; the anti-Thebans in Tegea complain about his conduct to the League, which complains to Thebes; Epaminondas says that the Arcadians have broken the terms of their alliance with Thebes by a unilateral truce with Elis, and he threatens invasion; Tegea and Megalopolis support Thebes but Mantinea and a rival faction defies it and asks Sparta for help. Arcadia asks Athens and other allies for help against the threat of Theban conquest.

Summer – The Theban navy, reinforced by new ships built with Thessalian/Macedonian timber, sets out (100 ships) under Epaminondas for the Hellespont with envoys sent secretly to Byzantium, Rhodes and Chios to encourage them to abandon Athens. The Athenians avoid an engagement, and Epaminondas reaches Byzantium and attacks Athenian corn-ships; Ceos and possibly various Propontis cities join Thebes. The expedition returns safely but has not achieved any major victory.

Plot to betray the Theban democracy while the fleet is away, led by various Theban exiles and their allies in the Boeotian city of Orchomenus who want Thebes humbled; the plot is discovered and the Thebans call a meeting of the Boeotian League, which has Orchomenus razed to the ground for treachery and its males executed and women and children sold as slaves; Epaminondas protests at this on his return.

Persia
Aroandas/Orontes, ex-satrap of Armenia, joins the rebel Asia Minor satraps' coalition.

Clearchus, a Greek mercenary captain, seizes the Paphlagonian coastal town of Heraclea while its governor Mithridates is absent and sets up a tyranny.

362

Greece
Epaminondas invades the Peloponnese again with a mixture of Boeotians and his Thessalian allies, including a contingent sent by Alexander of Pherae but not Phocis, which complains that they should only defend Thebes, not assist aggression; he sets a trap for the Athenian army expected to be hurrying to help Sparta, but they go by sea. He joins the Arcadians and Messenians at Tegea and heads into Laconia, leaving an Arcadian/Spartan army at Mantinea behind him; when he hears that Agesilaus is marching north via Pellene and Sparta is undefended he marches on Sparta; after an overnight march through the hills avoiding Pallene he reaches and assaults the city of Sparta itself, but Agesilaus has been warned in time by a deserter and has sent some troops back. The Thebans enter the city but are held back at barricades, Agesilaus arrives with the main army (nine of the twelve infantry battalions), and the attackers are driven out in street-fighting with Agesilaus' son Archidamus distinguishing himself in driving Thebans back; that afternoon the Thebans retire towards Epaminondas' base at Tegea; they camp for the night in open country.

Epaminondas reckons that the enemy at Mantinea will have sent many of their troops back via Pellene to defend Sparta, and leaves his camp-fires burning while he leads the army off to try to surprise Mantinea; he reaches Tegea and sends his cavalry ahead, but a squadron of Athenian cavalry has just arrived from the Isthmus at Mantinea unaware of the Thebans' approach that evening and the citizens, seeing the Thebans advancing, ask them to help; they drive the Theban cavalry back in time; among the casualties is the historian Xenophon's son Gryllus. Sparta and its allies Athens, Elis, Messenia, and Achaea assemble their armies of c. 20,000 men at Mantinea; Epaminondas has to fight or leave as the time-limit for his allies' service is expiring shortly.

4 July – Battle of Mantinea: the Messenians are on the allied right, then the Spartans in the centre guarding the main road, then the Athenians on the right, all facing south. The allied cavalry are on the wings in front. Epamonindas and c. 30,000 infantry (the solid phalanx, thickest on their left wing) and 3000 cavalry, on the wings, face them with the Thebans on the left and the Argives on the right. He plans to attack the enemy right wing with his phalanx on his left, which will be reinforced on its left wing with more 'depth' than usual to smash the opposition easier but this will be hidden behind the front ranks' helmets, and drive the enemy back onto their left. He manoeuvres around the western side of the plain in the morning to lull the enemy into a false sense of security that he will not attack that day. While the Mantineans and Spartans are taking their midday meal in a wood back from their position he attacks suddenly on the enemy right, and they have to hurry back into position; the Theban phalanx in a 'bow' form attacks the enemy right and the Theban cavalry, backed up by light infantry, drives into the enemy cavalry like a wedge; the Mantineans and Spartans break and flee, and the Thebans move right onto the allied left wing from behind them, but Epaminondas is mortally wounded by a spear in his hour of victory and allegedly suggests to his officers as he dies that Thebes join a common Greek peace/league to preserve its strength; his co-commanders Iolaidas and Diophantus are also killed. As the news spreads the Thebans halt, and the retreating Athenians on the allied left break through the Theban right wing to escape; the battle is thus a political stalemate but the Thebans have the better of it militarily.

Athens compels Ceos to rejoin their League as a subject ally and enforces a democratic regime on Iulis, exiling its anti-Athenian leadership – signs that the League is becoming as one-sided as the Delian League in the fifth century.

Winter – After the death of Epaminondas halts Theban aggression, the main Greek states hold a meeting and agree a 'common peace' and mutual defensive alliance to preserve the peace, with a regular system of conferences and a joint League council probably formed. Sparta refuses to ratify the agreement as its claim to Messenia is not recognized.

362/1

Callistratus, founding political leader of the second Athenian Confederacy, is tried and sentenced to death 'in absentia' in political dispute; Aristophon is tried but wins his case by two votes.

Persia

?Orontes of Armenia invades Mesopotamia but is bought off by Artaxerxes; Datames of Cappadocia continues in rebellion but is later killed in battle.

At around this time, Artaxerxes II executes his eldest son Darius for a conspiracy to overthrow him; his second son Ariaspes becomes his heir.

361

Greece/Macedon

Timotheus fails to take Amphipolis from Macedon and retreats, burning his ships.

Alliance between Athens, Arcadia, Achaea, and Elis, and another with the Thessalian League; both are implicitly aimed against local Theban influence and so undermine the new 362/1 common alliance of mainland Greece. Thebes sends troops to protect Megalopolis against an Arcadian attack.

360

Plato returns to Athens from Syracuse after a second stay at Dionysius' court where he could not get Dion recalled and the erratic tyrant veered between affection and threats; his Pythagorean friends in southern Italy who asked him to go to Dionysius have to send a galley to Syracuse to evacuate him after he appears to be in danger.

King Cotys of Thrace takes Sestos from Athens in a war in the Chersonese.

Persia/Egypt

King Agesilaus of Sparta and the Athenian general Chares go to Egypt with a mercenary force to aid the new Pharoah Tachos in a campaign against Artaxerxes II by invading Phoenicia. Agesilaus commands the infantry mercenaries and Chares the fleet, disappointing the former. The high taxes imposed on Egypt cause a rebellion, in which Tachos' nephew Nectanebo (II) becomes involved; Tachos reportedly asks Agesilaus for help in crushing the rebellion and is told that he came to help the Egyptians, not kill them; Nectanebo also asks the two Greek generals for help, and Agesilaus sends messengers home asking Sparta to abandon its worthless ally Tachos; they send him orders to defect if he judges it best for Sparta's interests, which he does. The Phoenician campaign is called off and Chares goes home; Tachos is overthrown and flees to Sidon en route to Prince Ochus' army in Syria to get Persian help but later dies in exile. After the successful coup by Nectanebo, Agesilaus has to help him against a pretender who revolts in the province of Mendes, and when Nectanebo shirks battle and retreats to a walled city Agesilaus organizes the defence and helps him to trap and rout the attackers. After victory he sets out back for Sparta, but dies en route aged over eighty and possibly eighty-four; he is succeeded by his son Archidamus, who was a young man (late teens?) in his father's Asia Minor campaigns in the mid-390s so he is probably already well over fifty.

Philip and Alexander: 359 to June 323

359

Greece/Macedon

Cotys, Great King of Thrace, is succeeded by his son Cersobleptes; possible break-up of kingdom as local kings in the outer regions, e.g. Berisades in the west, assert themselves.

Early? (or possibly late 360) – Death of Perdiccas III of Macedon in battle against the aged king Bardelys of Illyria; his infant son Amyntas IV may succeed as king, but with Perdiccas' younger brother Philip (born 383) as regent (Roman account by Justin), or else Philip becomes king immediately by election by the Macedonian 'people-in-arms', the army assembly. The third-century BC biographer Satyrus says that Philip was king for twenty-two years (i.e. until August 336) so this would make him succeed as king only after August 358 and be regent until then; Diodorus has him reigning for twenty-four years (or his twenty-fourth year of rule?), which would suggest an accession date before August 359.

Argaeus, refugee pretender to the throne, is backed as candidate for kingship by Athens, which sends him with a mercenary force of 3000 men under Mantias to Methone, on the coast near capital of Pella; Argaeus is to hand back Amphipolis from Macedon to Athens in return. Meanwhile, a certain Pausanias, another pretender, marches on Pella from Thrace in the north-east with local help, possibly supported by local king Berisades. Philip's three half-brothers, the sons of Amyntas III and Gygaea, are ruled out by the Macedonian assembly as they make a claim so (?) two of them now flee to the Chalcidian city of Olynthus for aid as Philip kills the third, probably Archelaus.

Philip rallies the army, recalls the garrison of Amphipolis, and probably reaches an agreement with Bardelys of Illyrias as the war soon ends; now or soon he marries Bardelys' daughter or grand-daughter Audata. Philip then bribes or makes offers to the leaders of the rebel Paeonians in north-west Macedon to ally with him, and pays the Thracian king Berisades to murder his pretender Pausanias. He tells Athens that his withdrawing the garrison of Amphipolis means he is abandoning claims on it, and possibly makes it autonomous; Athens withdraws support from Argaeus, who has to pay his own mercenaries as he invades Macedon and he marches on Aegae; there is no support for him, and he has to retreat and is ambushed and either captured or killed in battle by Philip as he tries to retreat to Methone. Philip sends to Athens to agree an alliance, and surrenders any claim on Amphipolis. The alarmed Olynthians send an embassy to Athens to forestall this treaty and arrange a joint attack on Macedon, but are ignored. Philip subsequently radically reforms and extends the Macedonian army, building up a highly disciplined and manoeuvrable infantry 'phalanx' armed with long spears ('sarissas') and versatile light infantry skirmishes and cavalry, and probably founds the Macedonian siege-train of artillery.

Persia

?Great King Artaxerxes II's son Ochus gets Tiribazus' son Artepartes to kill his brother Arsames.

Ochus then leads an army south towards Egypt, preparing for an invasion next year.

358

Persia

Early? – Death of Great King Artaxerxes II after a forty-six-year reign, aged eighty-six(?); he has recently executed his latest heir, his second son Ariaspes, for an alleged plot (though this is possibly invented by his third son, Ochus, and guard-commander Tiribazus in order to remove the prince). Artaxerxes supposedly dies of grief at his sons' behaviour. He is succeeded by his third and eldest surviving son, Ochus, now commander of his army and a ruthless operator who takes the royal name of Artaxerxes III. Allegedly up to eighty royal relatives are massacred so that Ochus will have no rivals for the throne. The invasion of Egypt is postponed.

Greece/Macedon

Philip defeats the Illyrians under Bardelys, probably near Lake Lychnitis. He routs the enemy using his newly constructed infantry 'phalanx' to smash through the Illyrians' left wing then turns his cavalry on the centre; around 7000 Illyrians are killed and Bardelys is forced to surrender all the districts of western Macedon, including Orestis. Philip builds new cities to protect his western flank, and abolishes the autonomous and virtually independent tribal monarchies of Orestis, Elimeotis, Lyncestis, and Pelagonia; Macedon is virtually doubled in size as the area's nobles and infantry are enlisted in his service.

Autumn – Philip marches into Thessaly to assist his new ally, the city of Larissa, and the leaderless Thessalian League against the city of Pherae; he becomes the ally of the League and can call on its cavalry for his army. He marries Philinna of Larissa as his third(?) wife as part of the alliance; she will have a son by him. Arrhidaeus (later king as Philip III) in the mid-350s but the boy is either born or becomes mentally feeble, allegedly due to poison administered by his next wife Olympias of Epirus.

358/7

Greece/Macedon

Alliance between Philip and king Arybbas of Epirus, head of the largest tribal chieftaincy of the kingdom (the Molossians); Philip marries the King's niece Olympias, daughter of the late King Neoptolemus, who is probably in her late teens at the time; she is probably his fourth wife and supersedes his senior wife, Phila. Traditionally, he first meets her at the sanctuary on Samothrace in the northern Aegean.

357

Amphipolis, alarmed at the expansion of Macedon, sends envoys to Athens for help and invites the Athenians to take over the city; the assembly votes to send an expedition and sends two ambassadors, Antiphon and Charidemus, to Philip to negotiate his acceptance of this. He is apparently offered the Athenian-owned coastal city of Pydna in return for handing Amphipolis to Athens when he takes it, or so Demosthenes later claims. A letter from Philip to Athens promising to hand over Amphipolis is more certain.

Summer – Before the Athenian expedition arrives Philip has stormed Amphipolis. The anti-Macedonian leaders there are exiled, by the city assembly's vote so the democracy is kept in being, but Philip does not hand over the city; instead he quickly attacks and overruns Pydna too. Athens declares war on him.

Alexander of Pherae, leading tyrant in Thessaly, is murdered by his estranged wife, who summons her brothers to infiltrate his bedchamber (which he has protected by being at the top of a ladder guarded by a ferocious dog) and catch him unawares one night. Tisiphonus, one of the assassins, takes power in Pherae (to 353).

Sicily

Dion sails from Zacynthus to Sicily with his invasion-force, led by him, his brother Megacles, and Athenian mercenary Callippus; he evades Philistus and the Syracusan fleet, and lands in friendly Carthaginian territory at Minoa. Dionysius II is absent in Italy with a fleet of eighty ships, and as he hurries back Dion sets off to Syracuse and is joined by 200 cavalry from Agrigentum and others from Gela. The people of Camerina receive Dion as a liberator, and an army of peasants rallies to him; allegedly the messenger sent from Syracuse by the loyal general Timocrates to warn Dionysius in Italy has his wallet containing the letter carried off by a wolf while he is resting by the roadside and he flees to evade punishment so the tyrant does not find out for days.

Dion arrives at the city of Syracuse with 5000 men, having sent a fake message to the Leontinoi contingent in the garrison that he is to attack their city first so they hurry home; once they have left Dion is informed, at night, and advances speedily to the city gates where the populace welcome him while the tyrant's men are attacked. Timocrates cannot get back to the citadel of Ortygia and flees on horseback, and the mainland city is overrun apart from the fortified hilltop Epipolae quarter, which is soon overrun. Dion and Megacles are elected generals, with a governing board of twenty of whom ten are from Dion's exiles. Dionysius returns by sea to secure the citadel of Ortygia a week later, and Dion besieges it; Dionysius is told that he must abandon his tyranny and leave, but will have his possessions guaranteed; private communications to Dion are banned by the latter to show the people he is a democrat who does not do shady deals. During the siege, Dion's siege-engines are attacked by a sudden sally from the citadel by the mercenaries inside during a truce at the tyrant's order and drive the citizens back until Dion arrives to help them; Dion reportedly fights Dionysius in person.

357/6

Greece/Macedon

Winter – Alliance between Philip and Olynthus; Philip will retake Potidaea for Olynthus and expel the Athenians, then hand it back to the Chalcidian League.

Sicily

The exiled Heracleides sails back to Syracuse to take advantage of the amnesty; he gets himself made admiral by the Syracusans, but Dion is suspicious, protests that this encroaches on his agreed position as supreme commander, and forces him to resign. The intriguer Sosis wounds himself and claims that Dion sent his 'mercenary' attackers with swords in an attempt to murder him, but is found out by forensic examination of his wounds compared with his details of the attack and a razor is found near the scene of the alleged attack, not a sword. Sosis is executed, but Philistus and the Syracusan tyranny's main fleet arrives to back Dionysius up.

Persia

Revolt by Artabazus, satrap of Hellespontine Phrygia, against the new Great King Artaxerxes III Ochus; he enlists Greek mercenaries, including the brothers Mentor (who marries his daughter Barsine, later the alleged mistress of Alexander 'the Great') and Memnon of Rhodes.

356

Greece/Macedon

Early spring? – The new King Cetriporis of Thrace attacks the Thasian colony of Crenides in the mining district of Mout Pangaeum in south-west Thrace, on the eastern frontier of Macedon. The locals appeal to Philip for help, and he drives the Thracians out. He then annexes the region to secure the valuable gold and silver mines for himself, and later founds the city of 'Philippi' there to protect them. Grabus, king of the Illyrians, and Lyppeius of Paeonia in west Macedon come to Cersobleptes' aid, and attack Macedon; Philip deals with Cersobleptes and probably the Paeonians too and sends his general Parmenion against Grabus. Athens backs Philip's enemies, ineffectively due to the Aegean war.

Spring – At the spring Amphictyonic Council meeting, Thebes leads the way in demanding that the Phocians pay up unpaid fines for tilling 'sacred' land owned by Apollo on the plain of Cirrha near Delphi and Sparta pay up fines for illegally occupying the citadel of Thebes in 382–79. The two states refuse to co-operate.

Chios, Cos, Rhodes, and Byzantium revolt against Athens and its Confederacy; King Mausolus of Caria supports them, and they assemble a fleet off Chios; Athens sends Chares and Chabrias with a fleet; Chabrias lands on Chios but is killed in battle, and Chares is defeated at sea so the attack is abandoned; Lemnos and Samos join the revolt and the Athenian colony of 'cleruchs' is driven out of the latter.

Athens sends Iphicrates, Menestheus and Timotheus with a fleet to assist Chares; the combined force attacks Chios, but despite bad weather Chares ignores his co-commanders' advice and insists on fighting near Embata and is heavily defeated and loses many ships. Athens has to accept the independence of Chios, Cos, Rhodes, and Byzantium; the Second Athenian Confederacy is reduced in power as more allies later follow.

Late June? – Philip defeats Cetriporis' Thracians, then attacks nearby Potidaea while Parmenion deals with Grabus. Philip takes Potidaea, expels the Athenian colonists but sends them home unharmed and hands the city over to the Chalcidian League.

Mid-July? – Birth of Philip's son Alexander 'the Great', which is legendarily announced to him on the same day as he hears that Parmenion has defeated Grabus. Also, he supposedly hears at the same time that his racehorse has won a race at the Olympic Games, but this would only occur about a month later.

Persia

The Temple of Artemis at Ephesus is burnt down by a publicity-seeking arsonist, traditionally on the same day as the birth of Alexander 'the Great'. It is then rebuilt as one of the seven wonders of the ancient world.

Sicily

Early summer? The democratic Syracusans' ships defeat and capture Philistus, who is beheaded and dragged through the streets by jeering crowds.

Agreement between Dion and Dionysius II is planned to end the civil war, with Dionysius agreeing to evacuate Ortygia and leave Syracuse. Dion insists that the citizens have to see and accept these terms, and they turn the offer down as they hope to take the tyrant alive. Dionysius sails off to Locroi with most of his ships, leaving the wearying defence of Ortygia to his son Apollocrates and his mercenaries; the citizens are furious with Heracleides for not intercepting Dionysius at sea, and he has to propose a drastic agrarian distribution of land to the poor to regain their favour.

A democratic upsurge against any danger of a new tyranny is led by the ambitious Hypereides, and sees turbulence at the annual elections of new generals; eventually a board of twenty-five is elected, including Hypereides. Dion is under political attack and the new generals and democrats try to subvert his mercenaries to enter their service and so end his power, but are refused by the indignant soldiers; Dion removes himself from the turbulent city where he is now under suspicion, and as the city crowds throw missiles at his troops as they leave the city for Leontinoi Dion has to avoid a battle breaking out.

Greece/Macedon

Summer – Philomelus is elected as 'hard-line' general by the Phocians, and he sends envoys to Sparta to promise to get the Amphictyonic Council to reverse its fine of Sparta; in return King Archidamus lends him money to hire 5000 mercenaries.

Aided by his new troops, Philomelus seizes the temple of Apollo at Delphi as his headquarters and fortifies it, thus committing 'sacrilege'; the Locrians, its current custodians, send troops to evict him but these are defeated, captured, and thrown off the cliffs.

Thebes leads moves to have the Phocians punished; Sparta stands aloof.

Autumn? – Chares prosecutes his fellow-generals for allegedly accepting bribes not to fight and so foiling his chances of winning at Chios; Timotheus is convicted, fined 100 talents, which he cannot pay, and flees abroad, but the others are acquitted.

Sicily

Nypsius of Naples, a mercenary in the service of Dionysius II, arrives by surprise with a fleet at Syracuse and sails into the harbour of Ortygia to aid Apollocrates in the citadel. The citizens cannot drive him out, but their ships defeat the tyrant's ships in the harbour and they celebrate with a drunken feast; during this Nypsius attacks the siege-lines, routs the guards, and tries to overrun the city too; a panicking delegation recalls Dion as the city is set afire and sacked, and he returns from Leontinoi; as he approaches that night, the night after the feast and breakout, the Dionysian mercenaries are back in the citadel with their loot so the democrats try to refuse Dion entry, but they are taken by surprise as the mercenaries break out into the city again and Dion is able to enter the city to drive the mercenaries back into Ortygia. He is welcomed back to the city as he is able to protect it, and an uneasy truce follows.

355

Greece/Macedon

Winter – Philomelus sends envoys around Greece promising not to touch the cities' treasuries at Delphi and urging support for Phocis against aggression led by Thebes.

Sicily

Dion forces Dionysius' son Apollocrates to agree to evacuate Ortygia and sail off with the mercenaries his father hired, leaving Syracuse free but ruined by war and faction; Dion rules as effective chief magistrate.

Greece/Macedon

Autumn – The Amphictyonic Council declares a 'Sacred War' on Phocis to recover Delphi, at the motion of Thebes; Philomelus the Phocian general seizes some of the treasures of the Greek cities' treasuries at Delphi to pay his troops, and attacks the enemy, especially Locris, where he defeats an army sent by Thessaly. He drives the Thessalians back with another victory at Argolas in eastern Locris, and the Thessalian city of Pherae appeals to Athens for help but most of the region backs the Thessalian League's decision to ask Philip for help instead.

?Philip besieges Methone, the last Athenian city on his central coast; the strong walls require him to use siege-engines, and the defenders do so, too; a bolt from a catapult in the city hits Philip in the face and he loses the sight of one eye (probably the right, as seen from the body and the models found in what is probably his tomb at Verghina in 1977); his doctor Critoboulus attends to him successfully.

354

Spring? – Fall of Methone to Philip, before another relief-force sent by Athens can arrive; this secures all the Aegean coast of Macedon for Philip.

Pammenes of Thebes leads an Amphictyonic Coucnil-sanctioned army to defeat the Phocians at Neon, in the upper Cephissus valley; the Phocians are driven back up Mount Parnassus and Philomelus avoids capture by throwing himself off the mountainside, which is seen as appropriate for his sacrilege. Onomarchus is elected to succeed him as Phocian commander, and the Phocians restore their morale as the invaders fail to march on Delphi.

Demosthenes' first speech to the Athenian assembly, 'On the Symmories', on foreign policy and finance. At around this time a new treasury, the 'Theoric Fund', is created by the proposal of the leading politician Eubulus, to finance the city and its port of Piraeus and help trade as well as its official purpose of aiding the poor, with a ban on using the money for any other purposes.

Sicily

Dion kills his rival Hypereides who is suspected of planning another coup, and is increasingly isolated and feared; (June) he is assassinated in his house by a group of his Zacynthian mercenaries led by his ambitious mercenary officer and close friend Callippus the Athenian, aged around fifty-three. His pregnant widow Arete, who has been a hostage in Ortygia until Apollocrates left, is imprisoned, released later, and flees to Dion's ally Hicetas of Leontinoi.

Callippus rules Syracuse, but is soon deposed as he is attacking Catania and has to be content with ruling that smaller city; he is later deposed and ends up some time later as a mercenary commander at Rhegium, where he is murdered by some of his unpaid troops.

Persia

Death of King Mausolus of Caria; succeeded by his brother Idreius and widow Artemisia. The eponymous 'Mausoleum' tomb-shrine is built at Halicarnassus in his honour.

353

Revolt of satrap Artabazus of Hellespontine Phrygia against Artaxerxes III Ochus, aided by Orontes of Mysia; they defeat a Persian army sent against them.

Sicily

Hyparinus, Dionysius II's half-brother, takes over the leaderless Syracuse as tyrant after Callippus' expulsion.

Greece/Macedon

Philip campaigns in Thrace, to protect the eastern approaches to his new mines at Mount Pangaeum.

Onomarchus plunders to pay his extra mercenaries, bribes the Thessalians to back off, invades Locris and takes and sacks Thronium, and overruns Doris. He attacks Thebes and takes its ally Orchomenus, while the Theban general Pammenes is absent helping Artabazus' revolt in Persia; Thebes drives him back from Chaeronea, while pro-Athens ruler Lycophron of Pherae in Thessaly attacks pro-Philip city of Larissa.

Philip aids Larissa, and Lycophron appeals to Onomarchus for help and so puts himself at risk of the wrath of the Amphictyonic Council; Onomarchus sends his brother Phayllus to aid Pherae, but Philip intercepts and defeats the latter; Onomarchus takes c.20,000 infantry and 5000 cavalry into Thessaly to confront Philip, and wins two battles against him – one by apparently luring him within reach of concealed catapults behind a hill and bombarding his men who flee. Philip pulls out of Thessaly with his men's morale poor.

Summer? – While Philip is in Thessaly, Athens sends Chares to shore up its position in the Chersonese against King Cersobleptes of Thrace; he sacks Sestos, kills its male citizens and sells the women and children as slaves. Athens sets up a colony of 'cleruchs' there to protect its trade-route; Cersobleptes deserts Philip and recognizes Athens' rights in the Chersonese, except to Cardia.

352

Philip returns to Thessaly with 20,000 infantry and 3000 cavalry, wearing laurel wreaths as they are now fighting in the cause of Apollo against the despoilers of Delphi; Lycophron of Pherae appeals to Onomarchus for help, and the latter enlists Athens (supposedly by bribes so that Athens will not have to pay for an expedition) as an ally; Athens sends a force to the port of Pagasae on the eponymous Gulf to keep Philip out and land Chares and troops there.

Philip takes Pagasae before Chares can arrive; he fights Onomarchus and the Phocian army at the battle of the 'Crocus Field' and the Macedonian cavalry routs the Phocian cavalry, leaving the latter's infantry exposed to a charge by the Macedonian phalanx.

Onomarchus and over 600 men are killed, and the survivors flee to the coast nearby and try to swim out to Chares' ships offshore. Some 3000 prisoners are captured and then executed by drowning for sacrilege to Apollo.

Thessaly is left at Philip's mercy, while Phayllus is elected Phocian commander and hires new troops with the 'sacred' loot seized from Delphi. Lycophron and Peitholaus of Pherae surrender and are allowed to leave for exile with their supporters; they join the Phocians.

Philip takes over Thessaly and evicts his enemies among its rulers; he is elected as 'archon' of the Thessalian League, and at around this time marries a Thessalian woman called Philinna by whom he has a daughter, Thessalonice (who will duly marry King Cassander of Macedon). He takes Pagasae and its port-revenues for himself.

August – Philip heads on for Thermopylae, but Phayllus manages to rally enough new mercenary troops with his offers of high pay to block the pass; Athens agrees with Eubulus' suggestion to send 5000 infantry and 400 cavalry by sea to join them and protect themselves from a possible Macedonian attack. Philip returns home.

Autumn – The city of Byzantium on the Bosphorus and its western neighbour Perinthus aid Amadocus, king of central Thrace, to attack his expanding rival Cersobleptes; they besiege him in Heraion Teichos, near Perinthus, and Athens votes to send Chares and forty triremes to aid Cersobleptes but later changes its mind. Philip returns to Thrace to campaign against Cersobleptes.

Persia

Defeated rebel satrap Artabazus flees to Macedon as a refugee with his family, and lives there for some years until his pardon. He thus meets his future employer and overlord Alexander, and probably influences him in his positive attitude towards Persian culture. Also exiled to Macedon are Artabazus' daughter Barsine and son-in-law/mercenary commander Mentor of Rhodes, and Mentor's brother Memnon – who will later fight against Alexander and probably learns the new Macedonian military tactics that Philip is now using.

Assassination of tyrant Clearchus of Heraclea in coastal Paphlagonia; he is succeeded by his son Timotheus under the regency of Satyrus.

351

Greece/Macedon

Late summer? – Athens sends out a small force of ten ships, commanded by local expert Charidemus, to aid Cersobleptes on a false rumour that Philip is ill or dead.

October/November? Philip takes Heraion Teichos and hands it over to his ally Perinthus; he also probably deposes Amadocus as king of eastern Thrace in this campaign and installs his son Teres as a Macedonian ally, and kidnaps Cersobleptes' son and uses him as a hostage to force a suitable settlement.

Some time in 351, possibly en route home from his Thracian expedition, Philip also either threatens militarily or wins over Olynthus to expel its anti-Macedonian leaders, replacing them with Lasthenes and Euthycrates.

Persia/Egypt

Artaxerxes III invades rebel Egypt to attempt to overthrow Pharoah Nectanebo, who is aided by Greek mercenary forces commanded by Diophantus and Lamius.

Death of queen and co-ruler Artemisia of Caria; Idreius is sole ruler. ?Hermeias, a former slave and now a wealthy courtier, succeeds his ex-master Eubulus (who has recently made him co-ruler) as the tyrant of Atarneus in the Troad.

Sicily

Assassination of Hyparinus of Syracuse; succeeded by his brother Nisaeus.

350

Greece/Macedon

Philip attacks and defeats king Arybbas of Epirus, and takes his nephew Alexander, teenage brother of his own wife Olympias, back to Macedon as a hostage for his good behaviour. At around this time he annexes the northern Macedonian district of Paeonia, pushing back the local tribes, and the passes west into Epirus.

?Demosthenes delivers his 'First Philippic', urging Athens to persevere and make financial sacrifices to build up its resources and struggle to retake Amphipolis from the major threat of Philip rather than give up. From now on he builds his career on relentless mistrust of Macedon and increasingly personal hatred of Philip as a tyrannical threat to Greek freedom.

Persia/Egypt

Defeat of Artaxerxes III's attempt to overrun Egypt.

349

Greece/Macedon

Tension between Philip and Olynthus after the latter gives refuge to his two surviving paternal half-brothers, Arrhidaeus and ?Menelaus; (summer) he demands their handover and (late summer?) on Olynthus' refusal attacks the city, invading the Chalcidice.

September/October – Olynthus sends an embassy to Athens asking for help; the assembly is not that supportive but Demosthenes urges sending aid in his three 'Olynthiac' speeches, the first two during this mission. He wants to build up the Chalcidian League as a block to Philip's advance and alleges that defeating him will not be difficult and then the fragile Macedonian state will implode and remove this unpopular usurper; the assembly agrees to send 2000 mercenary infantry 'peltasts' and thirty ships, commanded by Chares.

Peitholaus returns to Pherae, probably while Philip is preoccupied attacking Olynthus, and Pherae seizes Pagasae and refuses to continue sending its revenues to Philip; the Thessalian League asks Philip for help against Pherae and its ally, Phocis, and Philip marches into Thessaly and postpones the attack on Olynthus. Philip defeats Pherae.

348

Spring – Philip's second attack on Olynthus; Athens sends Charidemus from the Chersonese to command a new force at Olynthus of eighteen triremes, 4000 mercenary infantry and 150 cavalry; he is sent money and supplies by Orontes, rebel satrap of Mysia who is made an Athenian citizen. He joins 1000 Chalcidian light infantry ('peltasts') and 200 heavy infantry to attack Philip's recent acquisitions in the Pallene peninsula but cannot rescue Olynthus.

Spring – Plutarchus, tyrant of Eretria, appeals to Athens for help against his aggressive neighbour Callias, tyrant of Chalcis; at Eubulus' suggestion Athens sends a force led by Phocion; Demosthenes serves on the campaign. Eretria fails to send as much help as promised as Phocion heads for Chalcis, and he is besieged at Tamynae by Callias; he and his army drive off the besiegers and take many prisoners, releasing the Greeks as a goodwill gesture, and he goes to Eretria to arrest and depose Plutarchus. He is then sent by Athens off to Lesbos, and Molossus takes over at Eretria; he is evicted by the returning Plutarchus.

Fall of Apollonia and Torone to Philip, followed by (May/June?) Mecyberna, the port of Olynthus; he tells the Olynthians that either they leave their city or he leaves Macedon, but they refuse to surrender and appeal to Athens again.

Demosthenes deliver his third 'Olynthiac' speech, in favour of intervention and (vainly) using the Theoric Funds for the war; seventeen triremes, 2000 infantry and 300 cavalry are sent out under the returned Chares. The fleet is unable to sail because of adverse winds – the Meltemnian winds, which blow from the north-east across the Aegean (usually starting in June).

July – Athens has to accept the independence of all Euboea except Carystus to extricate itself from the campaign there.

August? The Olynthian cavalry defects to Philip in a clash outside the city. Euthycares and Lasthenes, the elected 'hipparchs' of Olynthus, betray Olynthus, according to Demosthenes due to bribes; Olynthus is stormed and sacked, and the city is razed and the survivors enslaved in hard labour in the Macedonian mines and fields. The Athenians in the city are sent to Pella as hostages. Philip executes his refugee half-brothers, and annexes all of Chalcidice to use its resources; Demosthenes later claims he razes thirty-two cities but this is unlikely. A few days later the Athenian fleet arrives too late, after a forty-day delay due to the wind.

August/September – Illegal capture of Athenian citizen Phrynon of Rhamnus by Macedonian pirates during the Olympic truce; he ransoms himself and goes home to ask the city assembly to complain to Philip. An Athenian embassy led by Ctesiphon goes to Philip to complain, probably around the time of the fall of Olynthus.

Philip sends Ctesiphon back to Athens with a placatory message saying he wants peace with a formal treaty and the war was a mistake. Philocrates son of Hagnon has a vote passed (unanimously) in the assembly for a mission to Philip, but this is subsequently declared illegal – possibly as violating the terms of Athens' alliance with Olynthus over no unilateral peace-deals with Philip. Philocrates is prosecuted for putting forward an unconstitutional law, but is successfully defended – ironically, by Demosthenes. This all probably precedes the definite news of the fall of Olynthus.

Eubulus secures vote in Athens for a mission to the Peloponnese to gather support for a general alliance against and war on Philip; Demosthenes does not volunteer for it and instead it is the normally moderate Aeschines who leads it.

?Phalaecus the Phocian commander takes Coronea and Orchomenus from Thebes, showing up their inability to bring the 'Sacred War' to an early conclusion.

Autumn – Philip celebrates the annual festival of Zeus Olympios at Dium on the slopes of Mount Olympus, having left the final stages of the Chalcidice campaign to deal with the anti-Macedonian stance taken by tyrant Peitholaus of Pherae, Thessaly, who is expelled.

347

Spring/early summer – Peitholaus is sacked as Phocian commander for plundering temple treasuries; he and other past generals are prosecuted for corruption and embezzlement, and Deinocrates, Callias and Sophanes replace them; they attack Boeotia again, and Thebes appeals to Philip for help; he sends Parmenion with troops, alarming Athens.

Summer – Demosthenes, as a member of the 'Boule' for 347–6, proposes an expedition to Thrace and the Hellespont to stop Philip expanding eastwards and threatening their Black Sea trade-route. Chares is sent to the Chersonese and links up with the Thracian king Cersobleptes; garrisons are set up in the Propontis. Phocis is defeated by Thebes and Parmenion while fortifying the shrine-town of Abae; Phocis appeals to Athens and Sparta for aid and offers to surrender the towns controlling access to Thermopylae from the south, and this is agreed; Spartan king Archidamus brings 1000 men, and Athens sends fifty ships commanded by Proxenus. The fleet is also to help the anti-Macedonian town of Halus in southern Thessaly against pro-Macedonian Pagasae.

Death of the philosopher Plato, aged eighty or eighty-one, at Athens; his nephew Speusippus is appointed by him to succeed him as head of the 'Academy' school, and the disappointed Aristotle soon leaves for the city of Assos in the Troad. He soon ends up at nearby Atarnaeus, birthplace of his late guardian as a child, as he has been invited to advise the Grecophile tyrant, Hermeias. The latter is now or soon in diplomatic contact with Macedon, where Philip is considering a Macedonian expedition at the head of a Greek coalition against Persia (as promoted in Greece by the Athenian Isocrates) and Hermeias is a potential ally.

Sicily

Dionysius II regains control of Syracuse, but is soon challenged by his local rival Hicetas, tyrant of Leontinoi.

Persia

?Satraps Belasys of Syria and Mazaeus of Cilicia are commissioned by the Great King to suppress a Phoenician revolt, which is led by King Tennes of Sidon and backed by Egypt.

346

Greece/Macedon

Early? Athens sends envoys round southern and central Greece to invite states to send envoys to Athens for a council of war on whether to ask Philip for peace or attack him. Meanwhile, Parmenion attacks Halus, and Philip sends Iatrolces, one of the Athenian hostages taken at Olynthus in 348, to bring a peace offer to Athens. A second mission is undertaken by Aristodemus, an Athenian envoy sent to Philip at about this time by the assembly to ask what he proposes to do about the said prisoners and whom Philip sends back with a message asking for peace and an alliance. Aristodemus informs the Boule (and is later awarded a crown in congratulations for his peace efforts on the motion of Demosthenes), but the effect is spoilt by the simultaneous news that Phalaecus has been reinstated in command in Phocis and has sent the Athenian and Theban troops home. Possibly Phalaecus' restoration to favour is a Phocian response to an overture from Philip offering to mediate and have the harshness of the expected peace-terms for them mitigated.

Left without an ally in Phocis, the Athenian assembly votes in favour of Philocrates' proposal to send a ten-man delegation to Philip to ask his peace-terms. Demosthenes and Aeschines are on the mission.

March – The embassy arrives in Pella, via Larissa; Demosthenes 'dries up' with fear and is unable to deliver his planned speech to Philip, as stated later by (his foe so could have exaggerated?) Aeschines. Philip proposes keeping the territorial 'status quo' and a defensive alliance, binding on the allies of both sides, with no aid to any pirates; Athens attempts to have Amphipolis restored, to no avail, but their claims to the Chersonese and access to the Black Sea are accepted. Oropus will be restored and Athenian influence in Euboaea recognized; Philip will intervene to help bring Phocis to negotiate if he has Athens' backing – in fact, he is probably already involved in this. The embassy leaves for Athens around '20th day of month Anthesterion', that is, 18 March.

Early April – About a fortnight after leaving Pella, the embassy reports to the Boule in Athens. A Macedonian embassy arrives. Demosthenes proposes that the terms be discussed at the assembly one day and then voted on, with the Macedonians present, the next day; this is agreed. The debate and vote are put off for after the 'Great Dionysia' festival, which takes place on '9th to 13th day of the month Elaphebolion', that is, 9–13 April.

'18 Elaphebolion' (15/16? April) – First day of assembly meeting, with debate on peace-terms; Philocrates proposes accepting the terms offered, abandoning their allies Halus and King Cersobleptes as Philip requires; the council ('synedrion') of the Athenian Confederacy calls for a 'common/general peace' with Philip, i.e. one to which other states can then be admitted, and as this can offer a way to help Phocis and Halus escape Macedonian punishment both Demosthenes and Aeschines support it. But the ex-embassy to Philip, Demosthenes included, are all aware that Philip does not want a 'common peace' as he will be unable to punish his foes.

'19 Elaphebolion' – Macedonian envoy Antipater is asked if Philip will agree to a 'common peace'; he says not. Aeschines now backs peace with Macedon due to the gravity of situation, but Antiphon calls for no abandonment of the just cause of recovering Amphipolis from Philip, which will be abandoned if they accept the 'status quo' terms. (Demosthenes, rotating chairman of the assembly that day, cannot speak due to this role.) The assembly votes to accept Philocrates' motion and send envoys to Philip to negotiate – but with the terminology of including their allies in the treaty, so hopefully they can get Phocis and Halus on that list.

Mid-April – Philip leaves Macedon to attack and defeat Cersobleptes, who is forced to accept terms and abandon Thrace West of the River Nestus to Philip (by mid-June).

Late April – The second Athenian delegation goes to Macedon, after a delay over who is to comprise it; the original ten envoys are to go. It arrives in mid-May to find Philip absent in Thrace, and Philip returns about '23rd day of month Thargelion' (17 June?). Other Greek delegations are in Pella too; on Philip's return he receives the embassies, and a joint Theban/Thessalian embassy asks him to invade and punish Phocis (and thus bolster Thebes' power in the region by removing a rival and disconcerting Athens). Aeschines then asks Philip to carry out the Amphictyonic Coucnil's decisions and intervene, but to punish the actual temple-despoilers among the Phocians, i.e. the individuals not the whole state which will foil Thebes, and the Athenian embassy is warmly received by the king.

Demosthenes presses Philip on the release of the Athenian prisoners from Olynthus, i.e. doing so now that Athens has agreed to a peaceful resolution not waiting for the actual treaty and thus stopping their use as a blackmail-counter. Philip promises to hand them over by the feast of the 'Panathenaia', about two months ahead, as a compromise; he swears an oath to the forthcoming peace, and sets out quickly for Halus to secure it without the Athenians finding out; his allies also swear, a few days later at Pherae in Thessaly on his march south.

The 'Peace of Philocrates' comes into effect, with Halus, Phocis, and Cersobleptes all left to Philip's mercy – and due to Philip's swift move Athens is unable to send any more troops to Halus to block his acquisition of it in an angry reaction to his not handing over the Olynthus captives yet, as Demosthenes is probably planning. Philip reaches Thermopylae (early July), and is let through by his secret new ally Phalaecus and the Phocian army.

Mid-July, after envoys' arrival on '13th of month Skirophorion'/9? July – In Athens, the assembly is urged by Demosthenes to reject the sham peace and stand by Phocis, with him accusing Aeschines of being bribed to help Philip; the walls are manned in panic lest Philip march on Athens; however, three days after the envoys' arrival a second meeting of the assembly votes to accept a conciliatory letter sent by Philip calling for alliance and to confirm the peace, extending it to Philip's successors so long-term; Phocians (which of them is unclear) are to be told to hand over Delphi to the Amphictyonic Council or Athens will attack them.

The third embassy leaves to meet Philip, probably unaware he is already atThermopylae; he is joined there by a Spartan army but a Theban army approaches with possible hostile intent to him and he asks Athens to send him troops to show goodwill. The Athenian assembly debates this on '20 Skirophorion' (16? July) and with Demosthenes opposing sending any troops (or thus annoying his potential anti-Philip ally Thebes) it votes against sending any, defeating the conciliatory Aeschines. The Athenian embassy now halts at Chalcis, possibly alarmed lest the news of his not being given any troops annoys Philip; the Phocis general council surrenders personally to Philip, not to the Amphictyonic League, and (17? July) Philaecrus and his army of 8000 men are allowed to leave unmolested for the Peloponnese as Philip wants, not arrested for sacrilege.

With the 'Sacred War over, the Athenian envoys return home; the Phocians in Delphi surrender, and the Amphictyonic Council meets with Philip nearby (possibly at or near Thermopylae); Athens sends an embassy, with Aeschines but not Demosthenes. The Amphictyonic Council votes to put a curse and outlawry on all who occupied Delphi and to seize their property, and Phocis is expelled from the League and has all its weapons and horses confiscated – no horses are to be bought until the large fine that is imposed on Phocis (sixty talents a year) has been paid off; all but one of Phocis' towns are to be razed and the people are to move to undefended villages of limited size, with Philip sending troops to check that the Council is not victimizing the populace. Orchomenus and Coronea, taken by Phocis from the Boeotian League, are handed back to the latter, which razes them and enslaves the inhabitants; Halus is treated similarly by its new owner Pharsalus.

Philip gets the Phocians' two votes on the Amphictyonic Council and the presidency of the Pythian Games; he returns the Athenian prisoners from Olynthus in time for the Panathenaic Games (mid-August) and Demosthenes urges the assembly (in his speech 'On The Peace') to accept the Peace of Philocrates as the only deal on offer and necessary to avoid an attack by the Amphictyonic League for alleged impiety in resisting the 'sacred' peace.

Philip presides at the Pythian Games (September) and returns to Macedon, leaving the Thessalians in control of the town of Nicaea guarding the pass of Thermopylae.

Isocrates composes and delivers his 'Phili', an oration calling on Philip to unite the Greeks and concentrate on attacking Persia in revenge for the invasion of 480.

Persia/Egypt

By this year Mentor of Rhodes has left Macedon and is in the service of Pharoah Nectanebo II of Egypt, as he commands an army sent into Phoenicia to assist a rebellion by the king of Sidon, Tennes, against the Great King. He is defeated and captured and taken into Persian service.

346/5

Idrieus, king of Caria, is commissioned to lead a Persian naval expedition to rebel Cyprus to overthrow the rebels, and enlists four thousand mainland Greek mercenaries commanded by the Athenian general Phocion; King Evagoras II of Salamis, son of Nicocles (d. c. 360) and grandson of Evagoras II (d. 374), also aids the successful campaign.

Artaxerxes III Ochus and an army of up to 300,000 invade Phoenicia, and Idrieus of Caria commands the fleet that blockades the city (presumably after the fall of Cyprus). Outnumbered, King Tennes of Sidon negotiates his surrender and hands over 100 top citizens of his city to the Great King for execution; when the city is occupied Artaxerxes massacres the elite and burns the place to the ground as an example.

345

Greece/Macedon

Demosthenes gets his ally Timarchus to prosecute Aeschines for allegedly corrupt accepting of bribes on the second embassy to Philip in 346; in reply, Aeschines prosecutes Timarchus for immoral living as an alleged male prostitute so he will be stripped of his citizenship and cannot act in a court; Timarchus is found guilty and sacked from citizenship.

Spring – Athens has to defend its current ownership of the sacred shrine of Apollo on Delos against a case brought by its ex-owners, the Delos islanders, before the Amphictyonic Council; Aeschiens is initially chosen to appear for Athens but is replaced by Demosthenes' ally Hyperides. Athens wins the case.

345 or 344

Philip campaigns against the Ardaeoi tribe, one of the most powerful in Illyria on his north-west borders, under their ruler Pleuratus (probable ancestor of the kings of Illyria in the later third century). His campaign may be followed by the widespread transfers of population to less well-occupied areas of his kingdom testified to by the Roman historian Justin, or else this is an event of the late 350s.

?Philip enrols his wife's kinsman Leonidas, an appropriately named enthusiast for Spartan austerity and military training, to train his son Alexander as a warrior.

344

?Philip's precocious son Alexander displays his prowess on and is given the valuable but 'uncontrollable' horse Bucephalus ('Ox-Head'), who is proving difficult to mount at a Macedonian horse-fair; reportedly, Philip says that he can have the horse if he can ride him and Alexander notes that the horse is frightened of his own shadow.

Summer – After the hostile Aleudae family have been restored to power in Larissa in another factional dispute, and anti-Macedonians have taken over Pherae too, Philip invades Thessaly; he expels the two new regimes and others of his foes and installs a board of ten men in each of various captured cities. He divides Thessaly into its original four rural regions as four new Macedonian provinces under his nominees as governors, thus creating a 'tetrarchy' ('rule of four'). Demsothenes presents this as conquest and slavery.

Persia
Death of Idreius, ruler of Caria; succeeded by Pixodarus.

Sicily
Arrival of Timoleon of Corinth (born c. 411) in Syracuse to assist the city, after it sends to its founder Corinth for a general to take command and end endemic factional strife and evict Dionysius II. The assembly of Corinth votes on who to send but no important citizens volunteer; an anonymous voice then successfully proposes Timoleon. He brings seven ships and 700 mercenaries, collects three more shiploads of volunteers at Leucas, and after a voyage apparently 'celestially blessed' by the sighting of a 'torch' in the sky (a meteorite?) puts in at Metapontum in Italy. Meanwhile, a large Carthaginian army under Hanno (50,000 men?) is overwhelming western Sicily, and Carthage has formed an alliance with Hicetas, tyrant of Leontinoi, who wants Timoleon stopped so he can have Syracuse himself. The Carthaginians attack Entella, whose Campanian mercenary garrison appeals for local help but gets little and is overwhelmed; the town is sacked. A Carthaginian galley puts into Metapontum – with Syracusan power eclipsed there is not a coherent local force to challenge their fleet – and Timoleon is advised by the Carthaginian envoys to give up his plans and return to Corinth, but he goes on.

Timoleon goes on to Rhegium; meanwhile, three days before his arrival there, Hicetas of Leontinoi is besieging Syracuse from his new fortress-camp at the 'Olympeion' outside when he has to go back to his city to collect supplies and Dionysius tries to ambush him to be routed. Hicetas takes advantage to hurry back to Syracuse ahead of Dionysius and storms the unguarded gates, and Dionysius can only secure the Ortgygia citadel where Hicetas blockades him.

A Carthaginian squadron intercepts Timoleon at Rhegium and demands a meeting with him and the citizens; he sends his other ships out of the harbour quickly and stays on, apparently to attend the meeting and promising that he will go home so the Carthaginians relax their vigilance; the meeting starts at the open-air theatre, with him in the audience so the Carthaginians can see, then with local help he slips out of the theatre and leaves the city in his own ship, evading their naval patrols offshore, which are intending to stop him. He lands at Tauromenium /Taormina in Sicily with his men, rallies the locals under Andromachus who lends him 1000 more men, and defeats the intercepting Hicetas at the battle of Adranum where he advances quicker than expected and catches the enemy having dinner in camp. He goes on to Syracuse with the aid of Mamercus, tyrant of Catane, and is welcomed, and Ortygia is blockaded; Hicetas holds on to the Achradina and Neapolis quarters with his surviving men.

344/3

Greece/Macedon
Winter? After the Thessaly expedition, Philip sends Python of Byzantium on a goodwill embassy to Athens, aided by Argos and Messene envoys, to reassure that he is keeping to the peace-terms of 346 and his Peloponnesian targets are not party to that treaty, and to offer to extend the peace/defensive alliance to include new allies if Athens wants this. The assembly agrees to this on Aeschines' proposal. Demosthenes replies to Aeschines with the 'Second Philippic', accusing Philip of planning to destroy Athens and Megara and proposing an amendment to include assorted past or current Athenian colonies around the Northern Aegean (including ones occupied by Philip) in a revised treaty as explicitly Athenian possessions so Philip will have to accept this and hand them back or refuse these terms. His ally Hegesippus gets a vote passed demanding the return of Amphipolis, and the ex-Athenian island of Halonessus off Thessaly (seized by pirates then occupied by Philip) is also demanded. The assembly backs Demosthenes and Hegesippus.

Python has to report to Philip that Athens demands the lost Northern Aegean cities back as the price of extending the treaty of 346, and then Hegesippus arrives with the formal Athenian decision; Philip offers to give up Halonessus and is told that he can only 'return' it, i.e. accepting that he had no right to it in the first place, so he refuses.

343

Sicily
150 Carthaginian ships land at the Great Harbour of Syracuse to unload 5000 troops and attack the city; however, firstly Mamercus, tyrant of Catane, and then other locals bring help to Timoleon and Corinth sends him ten more ships. Some of the forts held by Hicetas and Dionysius II in Syracuse are handed over to him by their garrisons, and Corinth's relief-force evades a Carthaginian squadron waiting at Rhegium and lands successfully.

Dionysius II negotiates the surrender of Ortygia, in return for being allowed to leave for Corinth with his private wealth; he is escorted through the areas of Syracuse occupied by Timoleon's party to his camp to surrender, and is given a ship to sail to Corinth. Hicetas holds out in part of the city, but (?)disease on the unhealthy Great Harbour shores hits the Carthaginians; the latter are also unsettled by fellow-mercenaries of theirs in Timoleon's camp asking their mercenaries to desert and save Syracuse from Carthaginian tyranny, and their general Mago embarks and sail off again. Hicetas is left on his own and has to retreat.

Greece/Macedon
Phocis starts to pay its fines for the last 'Sacred War'.

In Athens, Philocates the ex-ambassador is put on trial, accused by Demosthenes' ally Hyperides of accepting bribes from Philip; in fact, the gifts he received (as did other envoys who have not been prosecuted) were in the course of normal diplomatic courtesies and his proposal of alliance with Philip can be portrayed as in the common good not the result of bribes, but with the jury expected to be hostile he flees before his trial; he is sentenced to death in absentia and his property is sold.

Late summer? – Philip expels King Arybbas of Epirus, his untrustworthy Western neighbour, and replaces him with the latter's nephew, Philip's wife Olympias' brother Alexander who has been his protégé/hostage in Macedon for a decade; Arybbas moves to Athens. He also sends an embassy to Athens proposing a 'Common Peace' and a joint naval expedition in the Aegean to put down piracy, but this is rebuffed.

September? – Demosthenes formally accuses Aeschines of misconduct on the second embassy in 346, for suspiciously lenient peace-terms and delaying the embassy to help Philip overrun part of Thrace before he had to accept a ceasefire in the agreed truce; he delivers his speech 'On the False Embassy' at the trial as prosecutor, while Phocion and Eubulus speak for the defence; Demosthenes does not have enough tangible evidence and Aeschines can point to his own participation in the embassy where he was not anti-Macedonian either, and Aeschines is acquitted by thirty votes.

Winter 343/342

Philip takes over part of Ambracia and Cassiopia, south of Epirus at the mouth of the Gulf of Corinth, and hands it to Epirus; the alarmed Ambracians send an appeal to Corinth for help, and the latter asks Athens to send expedition.

Philip summons the philosopher Aristotle (from Stagira in the north-east Chalcidice) from the court of Hermeias at Atarneus to serve as Alexander's tutor – probably as his father was physician to Philip's father, Amyntas III, and he may have met Philip as a boy there. This follows Philip's secret diplomatic contacts with Hermeias, who is intended to assist a future Macedonian/Greek invasion of Asia Minor. A group of noble young Macedonians are collected as Alexander's fellow-pupils, among whom are many of his future close friends and generals. As well as his closest companion and alleged later lover, Hephaistion (seen as 'Patroclus' to the 'Iliad' enthusiast Alexander's 'Achilles') there are Ptolemy son of Lagus, the future Phaorah of Egypt (said in some sources to be really Philip's illegitimate son, which Ptolemy himself probably played up or may have invented to gain Macedonian support post-323), Philotas son of the general Parmenion, Nearchus the Cretan, Lysimachus, and the future treasurer Harpalus. They are to live at the 'Gardens of Midas' at Mieza, west of Pella and away from the court.

Also in 343/2 (probably), the expelled ex-citizen Antiphon sneaks back secretly into Athens for an attempt to set fire to the Piraeus dockyard, which would destroy the Athenian fleet; he is arrested and prosecuted, defended successfully by Aeschines, but then tried again before the Areopagus with Demosthenes prosecuting; Demosthenes has him convicted and executed and claims Philip was behind the plot.

Persia

Artaxerxes III Ochus invades Egypt with a huge army, reportedly of 300,000 men including 14,000 Greek Ionian vassals, a force of 4000 Greek mercenaries under his generals Mentor and Memnon of Rhodes, 3000 Argives under Nicostratus, and 1000 Thebans under Lactanes; they defeat Nectanbeo II, who is outnumbered by about three to one, and take the cities of the Nile delta with Ochus' Greek mercenaries encouraging their fellow-Greeks in Nectanbeo's besieged garrisons to surrender in return for pardon. The last native ruler, Nectanebo II, flees up the Nile to 'Ethiopia'/Nubia and Memphis falls and has its walls levelled; the elite is massacred, the city is subdued by a reign of terror, and the local religious shrines are pillaged, which turns the priesthoods definitively against Persia as will be seen in 332; the sacred bull of the god Apis is killed and served up for dinner in a deliberate act of contempt for the local religion.

After the expedition, Mentor takes command of the Great King's Western army in Asia Minor, probably based at Sardes, and probably at this time secures the pardon of his father-in-law Artabazus who returns to the Persian court.

342

Callias, tyrant of Chalcis in Euboaea, goes to Macedon to interest Philip in helping him to set up an Euboean League, led by himself and Chalcis, but is sent home without any promises.

May/June? – Philip commences the systematic conquest of the Thracian kingdom after king Cersobleptes starts to attack the Greek cities on the Hellespont.

Summer/autumn? – Athens sends troops to assist Ambracia against the new pro-Macedonian king, Alexander of Epirus; they are successful and envoys are sent to Corinth (at its own request), Argos, Megaloplis, Achaea and Aetolia who agree to an anti-Philip alliance.

Sicily

Timoleon rules Syracuse unchallenged and restores order with a new law-code, a political truce if not harmony, and mercantile trade and prosperity. He razes the fortress of Ortygia and its walls as a symbol of his expulsion of the tyranny. His army bottles up but cannot evict Hicetas of Leontinoi, and he goes on to defeat Letpines of Engyum and Apollonia. While he is busy with Engyus, Hicetas attacks Syracuse, but he is driven off.

Timoleon compels Hicetas to abdicate and Leptines of Engyum/Apollonia to leave for Corinth; Demeretus and Deinarchus campaign on his behalf in western Sicily to help the local cities throw out their Carthaginian garrisons, and Entella is recovered from Carthage. The latter commences to prepare a new army of its best men to attack Sicily.

Greece/Macedon

During Philip's Thracian campaign, the tyrant Plutarchus of Eretria is overthrown and the new regime takes neighbouring Porthmus and appeals to Macedon for help; Philip sends Hipponicus and 1000 mercenaries to aid them, followed by an expedition led by Parmenion and Eurylochus. Hipponicus installs Cleitarchus as ruler of Eretria and drives a pro-Athenian faction out of Porthmus, installing a pro-Macedonian triumvirate who face several revolts; Parmenion installs Philistides as pro-Macedonian tyrant of Oreus, alarmingly close to the Attic coast for the nervous Athenians.

Autumn – Philip completes the conquest of the Thracian kingdom, forces the tribes to recognize him as ruler and send tribute and troops, sets up a new local military command to be aided by loyal regional chieftains, and founds new cities including 'Philippopolis' (Plovdiv) in the Hebrus valley and Berroea (Stara Zagora). He then goes on to attack the 'Getae', in the Danube valley beyond the main Balkan range, and King Cothelas surrenders and sends rich gifts plus his daughter Meda to marry Philip (his sixth wife). His senior general Antipater represents him at the Pythian Games in Delphi.

Persia

?Artaxerxes Ochus has Hermeias of Atarneus summoned to his court on campaign in Asia Minor, arrested, sent to Susa for interrogation, and executed for treasonable contacts with Macedon.

?Pixodarus of Caria expels his sister and co-ruler, Queen Ada.

341

Greece/Macedon

Spring – Dispute between pro-Macedonian city of Cardia, in the Chersonese at the mouth of the Hellespont, and its neighbours who are Athenian settlers ('cleruchs'); the Athenian mercenary commander Diopeithes is aiding the latter and committing piracy on passing Macedonian ships, and has arrested and tortured Philip's envoy Amphilochus. Cardia appeals to Philip; he sends a small force, plus an ambassador to Athens to complain about Diopeithes. Demosthenes backs up Diopeithes in his speech 'On the Chersonese', saying the region is outside Philip's agreed sphere of influence so he has no right to interfere there and his attitude implies aggression so Diopeithes should be sent help and his enemies killed as Macedonian agents, and Hegesippus also urges defiance of Macedon.

May? – Demosthenes' 'Third Philippic' and 'Fourth Philippic', calling for Philip's allies to be killed and money and troops raised for an expedition to deal with him and assistance sought from Persia. The assembly backs him, and Diopeithes is sent assistance and Ephialtes is sent as envoy to Great King Artaxerxes Ochus and apparently returns with money to hire allies.

Diopeithes dies some months later.

Callias, anti-Macedonian tyrant of Chalcis in Euboae, sends to Athens proposing anti-Philip alliance if they will support him in creating a new Euboean League dominated by Chalcis; Demosthenes persuades Athens to back him.

Summer – Cephisophoron and Phocion lead an Athenian army to attack Oreus (aided by Megara) and Eretria in alliance with Callias; Athens loans Calais ships to overrun pro-Macedonian towns on the Gulf of Pagasae opposite north Euboea, and he attacks Macedonian shipping as well; after the campaign Callias is voted an Athenian citizen and Athens agrees to his formation of an Euboean League.

Chares is sent with a fleet of forty ships to the Chersonese to bolster resistance to Philip.

Autumn – Callias of Chalcis sends envoys with Athenian ones to tour the Peloponnese to stir up anti-Macedonian feeling and sign up new allies for an Athenian war with Philip in defence of Greek liberty. He and Demosthens address the Athenian assembly afterwards and claim that all the Peloponnese and Megara will support them; Demosthenes is sent as envoy to Byzantium, at the eastern end of the Propontis, to arrange alliance to block threat by Philip to the trade-route there, and Hyperides is sent to Cos, Chios and Rhodes to acquire votes for sending ships.

340

Greece/Macedon

Spring – Philip sets out with c. 30,000 troops to overrun the pro-Athenian cities on the Propontis, and leaves the sixteen-year-old Alexander in Pella as his regent, assisted by his generals Antipater and Parmenion. This marks the end of Alexander's education at Mieza; now, or in a couple of years, Aristotle leaves the Macedonian court to return to Stagira, which Philip has rebuilt as promised.

April – Demosthenes is voted an honorary crown during the annual festival of Dionysus in Athens, and receives it at a ceremony in the theatre.

Philip's fleet enters the Propontis, and he besieges Perinthus on the nothern shore, around thirty miles west of Byzantium; his siege-engines smash breaches in the walls, but the city is built on a steep hill with close-set houses so when the outer wall is damaged the defenders retreat inside and barricade the gaps between the houses to good effect. Troops and supplies are sent across the Propontis by Arsites, satrap of Hellespontine Phrygia, on Great King Artaxerxes Ochus' orders to help the defence, Byzantium loans some catapults to attack Philip's siege-engines and troops, and the Athenian navy is nearby at Elaius commanded by Chares, ready to help if asked.

The Maedoi in the upper Strymon valley revolt in Philip's absence; Alexander mounts his first, successful campaign to defeat them in the forests and hills with a swift attack, calling on his friend the ex-hostage son of the local tribal Agrianoi to assist him. He routs the rebels and founds a city of 'Alexandropolis' to emulate Philip, settled by Macedonians, and Antipater and Parmenion follow up to overrun the Tetrachoritae/Bessoi on the River Hebrus, the Dantheletai at the head of the Strymon, and the Melinophagi north-west of Byzantium.

August/September? – Philip leaves the siege of Perinthus to part of his army, and takes the rest on to attack the rebels' ally Byzantium, on the triangular promontory at the east end of the Propontis at the mouth of the Bosphorus; Cos, Rhodes, and the Persians send the city assistance. Possibly Philip is hoping to incite Athens into showing its hand openly; if so this is successful, as the threat to the city's trade-lifeline through the Bosphorus leads to the assembly voting to smash the stone recording the Peace of Philocrates and so to declare war on him. (Demosthenes later times the declaration of war as after the corn-fleet's seizure, below, but this is unlikely.) Phocion and Cephisophon are put in command of a second fleet and sent to help Chares and Byzantium.

Philip succeeds in getting his men inside the walls of Byzantium one night, but is betrayed by the sound of barking dogs and driven out again – possibly this is also the occasion when the crescent moon, adopted as the city's symbol (and hence taken for the Turkish flag?), lit up his men and so alerted the defence.

The second Athenian fleet heads for the Propontis (after the harvest, so September?); Chares is called off to a meeting of the local Persian satraps to arrange help for the two besieged cities, and in his absence Philip's admiral Demetrius attacks the annual Athenian corn-supply fleet (230 ships?), which is assembling at Hieron; Philip confiscates the corn and all the Athenian ships (180), but allows the others to leave; he uses the timber of the Athenian ships for his siege-engines and returns the captured Byzantine, Cos, and Rhodian ships to their owners as a goodwill gesture, thus indicating his desire to end the sieges.

The second Athenian fleet blocks the Hellespont to Philip, but he sends a fake letter to Antipater saying that he is returning home due to a rebellion in Thrace and arranges for the Athenians to capture it; they sail off to look for and assist the rebels and Philip's fleet can slip past them, as he marches back on a parallel course on land into Thrace and abandons the sieges.

Sicily

Mamercus of Catane and Hicetas invite Gisgo the Carthaginian general to invade Sicily as their ally against Syracuse. Timoleon attacks them, and subsequently captures and executes Hicetas.

Persia

Mentor, mercenary commander of the Persian army in Asia Minor, dies and is succeeded by his brother Memnon who marries his widow, Barsine, daughter of Artabazus.

339

Greece/Macedon

Spring? – After having to lift the siege of Byzantium, Philip decides on war against the 'Scythians' on the lower Danube, who are ruled by aged king Atheas and are expanding southwards into lands that he now claims. The occasion of dispute is Atheas' asking him to send military help against the Histrianoi during the war against Byzantium, Atheas' foe, in 340/39 and promising to make Philip his heir in return but then changing his mind and sending the troops home without pay. Philip asks for unhindered passage to the mouth of the Danube to erect a statue to his 'ancestor' Heracles, but Atheas refuses and tells him to send the statue, which he will erect – if the Macedonians invade he will resist and turn the bronze statue into arrow-heads. Philip attacks the Scythians and defeats them in battle near the Danube, where Atheas is killed; his leaderless people submit as Philip's vassals, possibly after or before he crosses the Danube into Wallachia.

Spring – The seasonal meeting of the Amphictyonic Council at Delphi, presided over by anti-Athenian Cottyphus of Pharsalus, sees Thebes' local ally Amphissa accuse Athens of impiety in using the re-dedication of their trophy shields from the battle of Plataea (479) at the rebuilt (after 373 fire) Temple of Apollo at Delphi to change the inscription so that it insults the Thebans by pointing out that the shields were taken from the Persians and Thebans – reminding all of Thebes' 'Medizing'. The probable intention is to provoke Athens into refusing to pay a huge fine so the Theban-inspired allies can declare war on them – Macedon's involvement is unclear. The leading Athenian delegate Aeschines is left to reply by his colleagues, and turns the tables by saying that Amphissa is guilty of sacrilege by cultivating sacred fields dedicated to Apollo on the nearby plain of Cirrha and has built a harbour on sacred land. The Council agrees with him, and next day orders Amphissa to do restitution or face a 'Scared War' declared at the next Council meeting; when the Athenians get home Demosthenes accuses Aeschines of being bribed by Philip.

Summer? – On his way home across Thrace, Philip's way is barred by the local Triballoi tribe who demand a share of the loot; he refuses and they attack. In the battle he is seriously wounded in the leg by a spear (?accidentally by one of his men) and faints from loss of blood, and his men panic and retreat taking him with them, leaving the baggage-train, which the Triballoi loot. Philip is lamed, and takes months to recover.

June? – Before the next Amphictyonic Council meeting, Thebes seizes the Thessalian-held town of Nicaea on the road north of Thermopylae, evicts its Macedonian garrison, and installs its own troops in an act of challenge to Philip. The Council meets at Thermopylae, but neither Thebes nor Athens attends in protest at the alleged victimization of Amphissa – Demosthenes has persuaded the Athenians to stand by Thebes (and thus support its seizure of Nicaea), not by the Council. The Council declares a 'Sacred War' (the fourth) on Amphissa; Cottyphus, presiding, is to command the expeditionary force sent if the Amphissans do not pay a large fine, and Philip will be invited to succeed him.

Sicily

70,000 Carthaginian infantry and 10,000 cavalry land at Lilybaeum and march east towards Syracuse. Timoleon and a much smaller army (12,000?) head to intercept them, but en route Thrasius the Phocian (one of those exiled for his part in occupying Delphi) declares that they will be overwhelmed and it is folly to go on, leading a mutiny; Timoleon has to allow him and his supporters to leave the army.

(Midsummer; end of month 'Thargelion' according to Plutarch.) At the river Crimessus near Silenus Timoleon intends to block the invaders' path, but he arrives to find that their advance-guard has already crossed; these are smaller than his army so he attacks at once and drives them back, but the rest of the enemy crosses to help their compatriots. The Greeks are driven back, but a violent storm hits the battle and blows wind and rain in the Carthaginians' faces and they are defeated; they flee to the river and many are drowned while crossing. Timoleon pursues them to storm their camp, securing a major victory. The Carthaginians retreat west and all of Greek Sicily allies with Syracuse; later, Timoleon catches up with and expels the refugee Thrasius and his mercenaries.

338

Persia

Great King Artaxerxes III Ochus is poisoned by his chief eunuch, Bagoas; his son Arses succeeds, probably in his twenties at most as he is inexperienced, but Bagoas wields the real power.

Sicily

Peace between Carthage and the Greek states; the River Halycus is confirmed as the frontier.

Corinth sends 10,000 new settlers to repopulate Syracuse.

Italy

The Eurypontid king of Sparta, Archidamus (III) son of Agesilaus, is killed at Manduria in Apulia on an expedition to deal with tribal attackers of the coastal towns; from his age at the time of his youthful service in Asia Minor under his father in the mid-390s, he is probably over seventy. He is succeeded by his son Agis (III).

Greece/Macedon

Early – Philip joins in the 'Fourth Sacred War' as leader of the Sacred League and commander of its army, along with his own Thessalian, Dolopian, Phthiotian, and Aetolian allies, the last two presumably as long-term enemies of the Locrians; he marches round Mounts Oeta and Callidromous to the region of Doris, and fortifies Cytinium near the Gravia Pass to his target Amphissa. The locals block his route; he swings round south-east down the upper Cephissus valley into Phocis and seizes Elatia, on the road from Nicaea to Thebes, so he cuts Nicaea off from help and can strike at Thebes and Athens. At the news that Philip is in Elatia with an open road ahead of him there is panic in Athens, and the fearful assembly looks to Demosthenes for advice; he delivers one of his great orations, as he boasts later in 'On The Crown', advising resistance with the help of Thebes as the only way to deal with tyrants. He calls for all men of military age to muster at Eleusis and envoys to go to Thebes to negotiate an alliance against Philip; this is agreed.

Philip sends his own officers Amyntas and Clearchus and representatives of the Sacred League states to Thebes asking the Thebans to either join with him or stand aside as he marches on Athens, resisting at their peril, with the right to loot Attica if they join him and hand over Nicaea to its legal owners, Locris. Demosthenes arrives at Thebes too with the Athenian embassy, and the Theban assembly votes to back Athens and stand up to Philip; however, they require Athens to accept their hegemony of the Boeotian League and to pay two-thirds of the land war costs and all the naval war costs; the land army will be under Theban command, at Thebes.

Thebes sends troops to the Gravia Pass to block Philips' route to Amphissa, with 10,000 Athenians headed by Chares and Proxenus. Another joint force occupies Parapotamii on the Boeotian/Phocis border; Athens and Thebes send envoys round Greece for help, but only Megara, Corinth, and Achaea sign up. Phocis backs Philip, but the Peloponnesians stand aloof.

Late spring – Philip calls on all allies of the Amphictyonic League to send troops to him; he and the Theban/Athenian/Locris forces manoeuvre against each other in the upper Cephissus valley; there are minor clashes with the anti-Macedonian forces holding Philip back. He returns to the Gravia Pass and allows a fake letter to be captured with information that he is about to abandon Cytinium; the enemy relaxes, and at night Parmenion advances suddenly on their lines and storms them; most are killed and by morning the Macedonians are in Amphissa. The Amphictyonic Council meets and banishes those held guilty of 'sacrilege', and Parmenion occupies Amphissa and then takes Naupactus on the Gulf of Corinth beyond to execute its Achaean garrison and hand it to Aetolia as promised earlier by Philip.

The enemies of Macedon evacuate Parapotamii and move back onto the plain of the lower Cephissus in Boeotia to await Philip's attack; he advances from Elatia to Parapotamii.

Probably 2 or 4 August – Battle of Chaeronea: Around 30,000 Macedonian infantry (c.6000 of them allies, mainly Thessalians) and 2000 cavalry face around 30,000 infantry and 3800 cavalry; Chares, Lysicles and Stratocles command the Athenians and Theagenes the Thebans, the latter with around 12,000 infantry, including the 'Sacred Band' of 300 male lovers; Athens sends around 6000 natives and 2000 mercenaries and Achaea sends 2000 infantry. Battle is joined on a line approximately south-west to north-east, stretching across a plain between two ridges, with the town of Chaeronea on the hill above the south-west edge of the battlefield. The Athenians are on their left wing, nearest to Chaeronea, by the River Haemon, with the light infantry beyond them up the hill; the Thebans are on their right wing at the north-east end of the line, by the Cephissus. Philip is on his right wing, nearest the Athenians; his phalanx is on the centre and right, and Alexander commands the cavalry on their left wing near the Cephissus and opposite the Thebans. Philip moves his troops forward at an angle so his right wing clashes with the Athenians while his left wing is still some distance away from the Thebans; after the initial clash he pulls back in a feigned retreat, and the Athenians charge after him, leaving a gap between them and the allied centre. The Thebans have to move towards their centre to plug the gap, but the 'Sacred Band' stays put to guard their right flank by the Cephissus; then Alexander leads the Macedonian cavalry into the gap between the allied centre and right wing, and part of the cavalry turns right, onto the allied centre, while Alexander turns left to encircle the 'Sacred Band'. The latter is annihilated to a man after a fierce struggle, and the Macedonian right wing stops retreating and turns on the allied left wing; the Athenians are smashed and driven back to the river behind them, with around 2000 killed and 1000 captured; Demosthenes is said to have dropped his shield and run away from his first major battle.

Philip holds a victory feast with a torchlit 'comus' (drunken Dionysiac procession), and is allegedly rebuked by an Athenian prisoner called Demades, a moderate opponent of Demosthenes, for behaving like the loutish Thersites not the lordly national coalition leader Agamemnon in the 'Iliad'; he subsequently sends Demades to Athens to deliver his terms. The 'Sacred Band' are given a state funeral and their own burial-mound, still extant, with the 'Lion of Chaeronea' monument; nearby the Macedonian dead have another mound.

Philip requires Thebes to pay a ransom for their dead at Chaeronea, sells his Theban captives as slaves, and orders a recall of their exiles from whom an oligarchy of 300 serves as the new regime; a garrison is put in the Cadmea citadel and all the local towns that Thebes has demolished in the past for resisting it are rebuilt; the Boeotian League survives but as a confederation of equals with Thebes only having one vote.

Charidemus the mercenary takes command of the Athenain army as Lysicles is condemned to death for incompetence/treachery, all males under 60 are called up and those deprived of citizenship restored to it, 'metics' are enrolled in the army, and the women and children and treasure are evacuated to the Piraeus; imminent sack by Philip is expected, but he sends Demades as his envoy followed by Alexander and Antipater to return the ashes of the dead. Athens is required to agree to peace and send an embassy to Philip for this, but when these men (Demades, Aeshcines and Phocion) arrive at the Macedonian camp their city is not punished apart from losing its naval Confederacy and the 'cleruchs' settled in the Chersonese are to be recalled. Athens agrees with relief, and Demosthenes goes off on an overseas mission to collect grain-supplies out of the way of any reprisals; Philip and Alexander are granted citizenship and statues of them are set up in the Agora.

Autumn – Philip campaigns in the Peloponnese, having received the surrender of Megara and Corinth and garrisoned at least the latter. He visits his dynasty's alleged home-town of Argos, and invades and burns the crops in Laconia but is defied by Sparta and does not attack the city. King Archidamus is probably absent campaigning in Italy at the time.

Winter 338/337

Philip summons representatives of all the Greek states to a meeting at Corinth, his military headquarters; Phocion tries to persuade Athens to stand aloof but is voted down, and only Sparta does not turn up. There, Philip announces the formation of what is generally known as the 'Hellenic League' or 'League of Corinth', officially the 'Community of the Greeks', with a common peace and elected delegates ('synedroi') sent by each state (the number probably proportionate to their military capacity) meeting regularly at a council ('synedron') with himself as leader, 'hegemon'. All disputes between states are to be sorted out by the League, not by unilateral action; no state is to carry out any action that would undermine the current political order in its own or other states, interfere in another state's affairs, or ally with a foe of the League; all are to swear allegiance to each other and to Philip and his descendants. There is to be a common military, financial, domestic, and foreign policy for League matters decided by majority vote and binding on all members.

?Philip meets the dispossessed ex-tyrant Dionysius II in Corinth.

337

The delegates go home, and their states duly ratify the League and elect the 'synedroi' for the second meeting of the League, which occurs at Corinth in the spring. There, the League is inaugurated and arrangements are made for an army to be collected for the invasion of the Persian empire, with Philip as leader.

Summer? – Back in Macedon, Philip makes his ?seventh marriage – to the young Cleopatra (renamed 'Eurydice'), daughter of his general Attalus. Olympias is furious and probably plays on Alexander's insecurities about his being superseded as heir. At the wedding feast, Attalus calls a toast to a 'true-born' new Macedonian heir, presumably a reference to Alexander's Epirot mother, and Alexander throws a goblet at him; the drunk Philip tries to attack his son with a sword, but falls over as he jumps off his couch and Alexander sneers that he cannot get from one couch to another let alone to Asia. Alexander walks out and takes Olympias back to Epirus, where she tries in vain to get her brother King Alexander to invade. Alexander goes on to Illyria, presumably to arrange a tribal invasion, but is persuaded to come home by Philips' envoy, the Athenian Demaratus. He returns, and possibly Olympias does so later or in 336 if she is present at her husband's murder that summer.

336

Persia
The eunuch chief minister Bagoas murders Great King Arses, probably over fears that the latter is seeking to break away from his authority; he installs the ruler's distant cousin Darius (III) Codomannus as the new ruler. Darius, possibly in his forties, is best-known according to one story for defeating a giant Cadousian swordsman in taking up his challenge to single combat while fighting in Artaxerxes Ochus' army. The new ruler speedily poisons Bagoas and asserts his own authority.

Sicily
?Death of Timoleon at Syracuse (or 336).

Greece/Macedon
Early (or late 337) As part of his plans for invading Ionia, Philip arranges an alliance with or is approached first by Pixodarus, Persian vassal-king of Caria and son of the late Mausolus, who offers him the hand of his daughter Ada for Philip's second but illegitimate son, Arrhidaeus (who is mentally unfit and incapable of ruling unaided in 323). Alexander gets to hear of this, and sends the actor Thessalus as his personal ambassador to Pixodarus to offer himself as husband instead – probably out of panic that Philip is thinking of making Arrhidaeus his heir. Philip finds out, and has Thessalus arrested and sent to him in chains

for questioning; he arrests and questions his son in private (apart from Parmenion's son Philotas, who Alexander will later kill), abuses him for meddling, and exiles his friends Ptolemy, Harpalus, Nearchus the Cretan, and the brothers Erigyius and Lysimachus.

Attalus, Parmenion, and the princely dynast Amyntas of Lyncestis lead 10,000 troops across the Hellespont to secure the Troad ahead of Philip's invasion; some local north Ionian towns throw out their oligarchs/tyrants and Persian garrisons and join them, as do Tenedos, Lesbos, and Chios.

July/August – Philip arranges the marriage of his daughter by Olympias, Cleopatra, aged around fifteen, to her maternal uncle King Alexander of Epirus to keep him loyal while Philip is in Asia; at the wedding at Aegae, games and a theatrical festival are held. A parade is held in the open-air theatre in front of the envoys of the allied Greek cities. Philip's image is carried in procession with those of the twelve Olympian gods – seen by some as blasphemy? As the King enters the theatre alone without bodyguards to impress the visitors that he is not a tyrant, he is stabbed fatally in the chest by an attendant officer called Pausanias, a noble from the Orestis district – possibly paid by Persia, and possibly arranged by a vengeful Olympias. According to the 'back story' of the assassin which reached Aristotle and the later historian Diodorus, Pausanias was an ex-lover of Philip's who became jealous of his young successor, a kinsman of Attalus, and provoked the youth into proving his bravery on an Illyrian campaign by getting killed (344 or 337?); Attalus lured Pausanias to dinner, got him drunk, and had his stablemen rape him. In addition, Philip denied him justice out of partisanship for Attalus, or else gave him promotion but no personal vengeance so when Attalus became Philip's father-in-law he decided on revenge. (It is the Roman historian Justin who is the first to explicitly mention Olympias as behind the killing.) Philip is aged around forty-seven. Pausanias tried to flee to waiting horses, but is caught as he trips over a vine-root and killed by Alexander's friends – Alexander's denigrators claim that he was 'silenced' to shield Alexander or Olympias. Demosthenes announces the regicide suspiciously early, claiming divine information, and calls for a vote of thanks to Pausanias; did he know in advance? He puts a garland on his house, although his daughter has just died, and is accused of tastelessness.

Alexander's Empire

Accession of Alexander; purge of his rivals, in which Philip II's nephew the 'rightful king' Amyntas IV is executed along with Amyntas of Lyncestis, an ex-royal princedom on the western borders of Macedon, and one of his two brothers – Alexander of Lyncestis is the survivor. (Was one of them the intended beneficiary of the assassination, or Amyntas IV?) Assassins are sent to the Macedonian force in the Troad to assassinate Attalus and take over his army; Parmenion, already to the south in Aeolis, hears of the murders and returns to the main base where he probably takes over the army. In Macedon, Olympias allegedly crowns Pausanias' exhibited body with a garland to celebrate her husband's murder. Alexander's friends are recalled from exile.

October? – Thessaly revolts against Macedon, and a force blocks the pass up the Vale of Tempe into Thessaly from the coast; Alexander marches south to find this, and cuts a new route across the slopes of Mount Ossa to the south of the pass to circumvent it. The Thessalians surrender and confirm their alliance with Macedon and Alexander's succession to Philip as their overlord, and he reminds them of his descent from the local hero Achilles. The 'Sacred League' has called a military force together and camped at

Thermopylae, but now surrenders and he calls their League to meet at Delphi and elect him as leader. Thebes and Athens decide against resistance, and Athens votes him as an honorary citizen and sends him gifts. Alexander marches on to Corinth and is elected 'hegemon' by the Hellenic League to succeed Philip; Sparta refuses to send envoys to the meeting and claims that it leads and does not follow others, and is left alone. Probably the (apocryphal?) meeting between Alexander and the unimpressed philosopher Diogenes, founder of the ' Cynic' school at Corinth and an ascetic who lives in a barrel, takes place during this visit.

November? – Alexander returns to Macedon via a visit to Delphi to ask questions of the oracle of Apollo there.

335

Spring – Alexander invades Thrace to secure his rear from the restive tribes before his Asian campaign, sending ships up the Black Sea coast to the Danube in anticipation of crossing the river; a new unit of the tribal Agrianoi in north Macedon is added to the army, as light skirmishers and archers/javelineers. Antipater is regent in Macedon and probably Parmenion is by now commanding the 'advance-force' sent across the Hellespont by Philip. Alexander leaves Olympias in Macedon; she murders Philip II's last wife, Eurydice, and her child in his absence.

Alexander faces a Thracian army drawn up behind wagon-barricades at the Shipka Pass, and organizes his men to either scatter to one side or lie down behind their shields as 'ramps' as the wagons are rolled downhill onto them so nobody is killed; the Thracians retreat into the forests, but in the following days of clashes are lured out by a hail of arrows and then charged by the infantry and the cavalry attack from the flanks where possible. The Triballoi tribe are overrun to the line of the Danube, and their king, Syrmus, flees to an island in the river; Alexander joins his (small) fleet at the Danube and crosses, using sewn-together and inflated tent-skins as rafts to take more troops over the river at one movement than his ships can manage – in the dark, some distance from the tribes waiting on the far bank. The latter are caught out as the Macedonians cross a field of corn under cover of the high stalks to emerge onto the open plain and charge them at dawn, and they are routed by a disciplined charge and flee to a small fortress and thence onto the open plains by horse. The Getae tribe and others beyond the river are awed into agreeing peace and sending gifts, and the Triballoi survivors on their island do so too; volunteers are enrolled to join the Macedonian army. Possibly also tribal envoys arrive from the upper Danube and modern Croatia/Austria to ask for alliance.

The Illyrians, led by their king Bardelys's son Cleitus, have attacked western Macedon in his absence and taken Pelion; Alexander marches swiftly south to intercept the attackers and besieges Pelion, in a narrow valley. Another king called Glaucias brings a second Illyrian force to attack Alexander and blockades the pass out of the valley to Macedon; Alexander uses a 'parade' of his army's infantry in the narrow pass in front of the Illyrian lines to suddenly charge Glaucias' men and rout them; the cavalry and light skirmishers then head uphill to deal with the abandoned Illyrian guards there, who are driven back too. While this is going on, the rest of the army fords the river in the pass to secure the far bank under cover of catapults; Alexander then joins them. The Illyrians pull back to their main camp, and three nights later Alexander storms it in a surprise attack; the tribes flee and Pelion is captured.

On a rumour of Alexander's death, Thebes revolts and besieges the Macedonian garrison in the Cadmeia citadel, killing some of them who are caught by surprise in the city; they are encouraged (and sent weapons?) by Demosthenes who urges Athens to send help; probably he has been sent money by Persia to pay for a revolt. Alexander is told and marches quickly south before it is known that he is alive let alone on the march. He reaches Thebes in fourteen days from Pelion, startling the rebels who initially assume it must be Antipater or his senior officer Alexander of Lyncestis in command; Alexander demands the handover of the rebel leaders and is refused this. Athens hastens to send envoys to make terms and abandons Thebes to its fate.

Three days into the siege, Perdiccas leads troops into the city hard on the heels of a retreating sortie (against orders according to Ptolemy's account, but Ptolemy was a personal rival of his after 323) and is wounded; Alexander follows with the main army; Thebes is ruthlessly sacked, though this is mostly carried out by the allied Greek army from Thebes' neighbours rather than as a deliberate Macedonian act of terror, and Alexander orders the city to be razed to the ground as a warning, leaving only the temples and the house of the early fifth century poet Pindar. The Thebans are enslaved.

Alexander sends to Athens to demand the exile of Demosthenes and seven of his fellow-anti-Macedonians Charidemus and Lycurgus with others; the alarmed assembly sends the moderate leader Phocion on an embassy to persuade him to pardon them, which he does (except for Charidemus). Also mediating is Demades, who takes over the leading role in the city from the discredited Demosthenes.

October? – Alexander returns to Macedon and holds the annual festival in honour of Zeus and the Muses at Dium near Mount Olympus, with games and a theatrical festival; Antipater is named as regent for when he leaves Macedon for Asia but Alexander does not marry to beget an heir before he leaves.

334

May – Alexander leaves Pella, and marches with an army of c. 35–36,000 men (32,000 infantry – 6000 Foot Companions in six regiments, 3000 'Shield Bearers', 1000 skirmishers, 7000 Greeks, and 7000 Thracian/'Celt' infantry – plus 1800 Companion Cavalry and 1800 Thessalian cavalry and possibly 2500 Mounted Scouts and auxiliary cavalry – to the Hellespont. A total of 150 Greek allied warships are waiting at Sestos; he crosses to join Parmenion, taking the tiller of his ship and sacrificing a bull to Poseidon in midstream. He lands the first of his men in full armour in the manner of the Greeks landing for the Trojan War, which is supposed to occur at the chosen site of his landing (the 'Bay of the Achaeans'), throwing his spear into the ground to claim the soil of the Persian empire.

He detours for a sightseeing tour of the site of Troy/Ilium, where he visits the then village on the site and is crowned by his helmsman (who is named after his 'ancestor' Achilles' companion Patroclus' father), and honours his 'ancestor' and exemplar Achilles by then racing around the walls of Troy, to place a garland on his tomb while Hephaistion does so at the tomb of Patroclus, his mythical exemplar. Alexander receives the 'Shield of Achilles' and a suit of armour from the temple of Athene nearby (the shield is, however, first heard of with him in 326/5) and leaves his own armour there as a gift; he sacrifices to the legendary king of Troy, Priam, so he will not hinder his conquerors' descendants.

Alexander rejoins his troops at Arisbe, and advances east along the Propontis to the banks of the River Granicus where satraps Spithridates of Lydia and Asistes of Phrygia have arrived from Dascylium in Phrygia via Zeleia with the Greek mercenary commander Memnon to contest their crossing. Memnon has advised the satraps to burn the crops and retreat inland to make the invaders run out of supplies, but was ignored by the over-confident Persian nobles.

The Persians probably have 35,000–40,000 men, and Alexander over 45,000 due to his joining with Parmenion's advance-guard.

Battle of the River Granicus (six days into the Greek march from the Hellespont): the Persians station their heavy cavalry on the high river-bank to contest the crossing, with their 20,000 Greek mercenary infantry behind. Possibly Parmenion advises camping overnight and attacking next day and is over-ruled, but this is not found in all sources and may be an apocryphal account featuring him as the 'voice of caution' as on later occasions. The Greeks do camp, and next day cross the river unopposed at dawn while the Persians are probably still forming up in their camp a mile or two back. The Persian cavalry charges ahead of the infantry at the Greeks, and Alexander leads a charge in reply; a cavalry clash follows and Alexander is nearly cut down from behind in the melee but his life is saved by senior officer Cleitus 'the Black', brother of his nurse, who cuts down his attacker. The Persians are routed, with several of their generals including satrap Mithrobarzanes of Cappadocia being killed; as their cavalry flees Alexander surrounds their Greek mercenaries, who refuse to surrender and are massacred; perhaps 2000 of them are captured and enslaved as traitors to the national Greek cause. Memnon escapes south into Ionia; Asistes kills himself; Alexander orders ceremonial funerals for the twenty-five dead Companion Cavalry and tax-remission for their families; the high-ranking Persian dead are also honoured.

Alexander orders that his troops are not to plunder the region, as they are liberating it; he makes the Macedonian Calas governor of local Hellespontine Phrygia, thus keeping on the Persian system of government, and makes the local tribes pay tribute at the same rate as they did to Persia; Parmenion is sent ahead to Dascylium; Alexander pardons the Persian headquarters town of Zeleia and advances to Ephesus, whose garrison has fled on news of the Granicus battle, entering it four days after the battle and evicting the Persian-allied oligarchy in favour of the democratic party.

Alexander marches on inland to Sardes, the Persian western capital and home of their regional treasury, where governor Mithrines surrenders; he appoints Asander, Parmenion's brother, as governor of Lydia. The refugee Persian mercenary general Memnon heads for Caria with his fleet.

Parmenion conquers nearby Aeolia; Alexander announces that he supports the removal of all the pro-Persian oligarchies and tyrannies in Aeolis and Ionia in favour of democracy, which boosts his local support. He also refuses to impose tribute.

Alexander marches on across southern Ionia to Caria, where Orontobates the satrap holds out. He besieges Miletus, where the commander has changed his mind about surrendering on hearing that Memnon and the Persian fleet are on their way, and the main city is occupied but the citadel holds out; the Macedonian/Greek fleet under Nicanor arrives and occupies the outer harbour. 400 Phoenician ships of the Persian navy arrive to bolster the defence, but Alexander refuses to risk a naval battle; the rest of the city is stormed and the survivors of the garrison and oligarchy flee to an offshore island but have to surrender as Alexander pursues them there; the locals are pardoned and the 300 mercenary troops are enrolled in the Macedonian army. Miletus becomes a democracy.

The Persian fleet has to retreat, short of water as Alexander has sent troops under Parmenion's son Philotas to harass their landing-parties from collecting any; it heads off into the Mediterranean and Alexander dismisses the Macedonian fleet as he prepares to head on by land alone.

Alexander enters Caria; exiled queen Ada, sister of the current pro-Persian king Pixodarus, joins him at her citadel of Alinda and adopts him as her 'son'.

Alexander besieges Orontobates and Memnon in Halicarnasssus; his siege-engines are attacked in a major sally, but the latter is repulsed, its commander Ephialtes is killed, and some of his men are cut off retreating as the gates are closed before they can get back inside; the city surrenders before the damaged walls are stormed, and Memnon flees but Orontobates holds out in the citadel. Ada is restored as ruler, and there is no talk of democracy in Caria.

Alexander sends Parmenion on the inland route from Sardes directly east into Phrygia, heading for Gordium and receiving the reinforcements who are due to arrive for the 333 campaign en route. He allows his married troops to return home for the winter.

Alexander marches into Lycia, where the garrison of Hyparna surrenders; he rounds coastal Mount Climax, taking a path along the beach at low tide and so avoiding a detour and according to Callisthenes receiving divine assistance via the sudden lull in the southerly winds, which were blowing the sea across his route. He receives the surrender of and an honorary crown from Pisidia. At around this time there is apparently some revelation of a suspect message sent to Alexander of Lyncestis, commander of the Thessalian cavalry and princeling of a defunct ex-royal dynasty of a western Macedonian principality, from Darius via a Persian noble called Sisines who Parmenion arrests and sends to Alexander, but details are confused as to dates and import. Apparently, Alexander of Lyncestis is offered the Macedonian throne with Persian help.

Aspendus surrenders; Sagalassus is taken by storm; Alexander heads on north into Phrygia.

Midwinter 334/3

Alexander reaches Celenae, capital of the satrapy of Phrygia, which surrenders; he enters the two of Gordium on the Royal Road from Sarrdes to Susa, which is the designated rendezvous for Parmenion and reinforcements from Thrace /Macedon/Greek allies who are due shortly. While there, legend has it that Alexander inspects the 'Gordian Knot', the complicated tether that attaches the chariot of the founder-king Gordius of Phrygia to a pillar in the temple and which only the 'King of Asia' is supposed to be able to undo, and cuts it with his sword.

Alexander's uncle and brother-in-law, King Alexander of Epirus, accepts an invitation from Greek cities in southern Italy, led by Tarentum, to aid them against local tribes and possibly also the Romans and Samnites to the west of these as ultimate threats to their security.

333

May? – Parmenion arrives with c.3000 Macedonians and 1000 Greeks and others; an Athenian embassy arrives to ask for the release of Athenians captured fighting for Darius at the Granicus, but is told that it must wait for the end of the war.

Alexander's troops take Ancyra (Ankara), which surrenders, and overruns Paphlagonia; he leaves Gordium to march on to the Taurus mountains, with the general Antigonus 'Monopthalmus' ('One-Eye'), aged around sixty and later a leading 'Successor', left in command at Celenae to subdue the central Anatolian tribes. Sabictus is installed as governor of Cappadocia.

Memnon campaigns with 300 ships in the eastern Aegean from his headquarters on Cos and takes Chios; Alexander is informed and sends 500 talents from seized Persian treasury at Sardes' home to Antipater to pay for a fleet and 600 more with two officers to raise an allied Greek fleet.

Nearchus the Cretan, later Alexander's admiral, becomes governor of Lycia on the south-west coast of Asia Minor.

June – Memnon dies at the siege of Mytilene; his widow, Barsine, the daughter of senior Persian satrap Artabazus who was once an exile at Philip II's court, is apparently in Syria as she is later captured by Alexander there. The Persian fleet, now commanded by his nephew Pharnabazus, take Mytilene and forces it to become a subject ally (August) and so secures Lesbos, then goes on into the Cyclades, installing or restoring pro-Persian tyrants.

Late June/early July? – Hearing of the death of Memnon, Darius holds an emergency council-of-war of his generals in Susa as they await Alexander. Darius executes his mercenary general Charidemus the Athenian for alleged insolence in asking that he be placed in command of an army, dominated by 30,000 Greeks, to face Alexander. The court moves to Babylon and Darius decides to take command himself; a massive army is collected and moves on Syria.

The Persians send orders to Pharnabazus to take c.200 ships and deliver a force of hired mainland Greek mercenaries to Darius, landing them at Tripoli in Phoenicia; this delays the campaign and only about half the fleet returns to the Aegean to join the squadron that has been left there.

Datames and a northern section of this, ?ten ships, flees Antipater's Macedonian admiral Proteas in an encounter after taking Tenedos.

July – Alexander crosses the Taurus through the 'Cilician Gates' pass into Cilicia; on arrival he plunges into the icy River Cydnus at Tarsus for a swim and gets a severe chill, and is about to drink some medicine given by his doctor Philip when a letter from Parmenion arrives alleging that Darius has bribed Philip to poison him. He hands the doctor the letter to read while he drinks.

Ptolemy and Parmenion's son Asander defeat Orontobates, governor of part of Caria, and complete the conquest of the Ionian coast with Halicarnassus while allied ships take the Persian naval base at Cos; Alexander halts in Cilicia for around a month (possibly due to his illness), holds Games at Soli, and (early September?) advances via Mallus and Myriandros/Iskenderun.

Early October? – Alexander's friend Harpalus leaves for Megara to rally Greek resistance to the Persian fleet; Alexander of Lyncestis is deprived of his cavalry command amidst suspicion of contacts with Persia, and may be arrested.

Parmenion sends word that Darius is nearing the 'Persian Gates' pass across the Amanus range from the Euphrates; Alexander advances to Myriandrus to meet Parmenion and they cross the Amanus into the Orontes valley in northern Syria looking for Darius' army, which is somewhere to his east, inland.

Darius comes down to the coast to Alexander's rear, capturing his 'base camp' hospital at Issus on the coast and mutilating the sick and wounded; Alexander is informed, sends scouts back along the coast who see the Persian camp-fires, and moves back through the pass to confront him. As a result Darius is fighting facing south-east on the Issus plain, Alexander facing north-west; the river 'Pinarus' is between the two armies.

?Early November – Battle of Issus: Alexander, possibly with 25–30,000 troops (5000 cavalry) and outnumbered, advances around ten miles from his overnight camp to the Persian position in the plain of Issus near a river (probably the Payas). Alexander commands his right wing with his Companion cavalry, with the 'Shield-Bearers' regiment on the right of the main infantry in the centre, the Foot Companions in the centre of the infantry, and the Greek mercenaries on the left of the infantry; on the left wing are the other Macedonian infantry and some cavalry with Parmenion in charge. The sea is to the left of Parmenion on the left wing; the hills are to the right (east) of Alexander's right wing. The battlefield is fairly narrow so the Persians cannot overwhelm the Macedonians by outflanking on the plain; however, Darius sends some light infantry into the hills on Alexander's right to outflank him and the Agrianoi are sent to drive them back.

Darius moves some cavalry to his right, on the west side of the battle by the shore; Alexander sends some Thessalian cavalry from his right to his left to confront them, out of sight behind the front line. Two Companion Cavalry squadrons plug the gap. Alexander's cavalry on his right wing charges; the opposing Persian cavalry then charges onto Alexander's advancing force but is repulsed; the Companion Cavalry pushes the Persian left wing back, then moves in on their infantry in the centre. Darius' Greek mercenaries cross the river to attack the Macedonian infantry but are driven back by the Companion Cavalry taking them in the rear and retreat; on the Macedonian left Parmenion drives the Persian right wing back onto their centre. The Thessalians on Alexander's left wing now charge on round the retreating Persian right wing to join the attack on their centre, and Darius is threatened with encirclement and turns his chariot to retreat; his brother Oxathres and other Royal Guards protect his flight as he has to abandon his chariot on rough ground and flees on horseback. 2000 of his Greek mercenaries also escape to join him, while another force heads for Tripoli to embark on the Phoenician fleet there.

The Persians lose supposedly 100,000 and the Macedonians around 300, according probably to Callisthenes, but this is unlikely; Alexander pursues Darius into the Amanus foothills but he escapes in the dark. Alexander returns to camp, and next morning inspects the high-ranking captives who include the Royal Family womenfolk. Traditionally, when he enters the royal tent with his officers the Great King's wife, Stateira, does homage to Hephaistion by mistake (as he is taller?), and Alexander promises the family his protection and forms a friendship with Darius' mother Sisygambis. The Great King's son, aged around six, and two daughters are kept as hostages with his wife and mother, and the boy probably dies later as he is never heard of again. Letters are found in the Great King's camp retailing his contacts with dissident Greeks, including possibly Demosthenes.

The Hellenic League sends Alexander a gold crown on news of the victory.

Italy
Alexander of Epirus forms the cities of southern Italy into a league and leads them in successful battles against the inland Lucanians, sending prisoners and hostages to Epirus.

332

Alexander's Empire

January? – Alexander invades Phoenicia; Strato, son of the absent king who is in the Phoenician fleet at sea, surrenders the walled island city of Aradus, avoiding a long siege; Alexander is encamped there when Darius sends an embassy, apparently offering friendship and alliance (and a ransom of 10,000 talents?) in return for his family. Traditionally (but apocryphally?), Alexander writes back to Darius accusing him of murdering his predecessor, being involved in Philip II's killing, and bribing the Greeks to rebel against Macedon and bringing up the sack of Athens with its temples in 480 and other blasphemies committed by Persia; he says that the gods are clearly on his side and in future Darius should address him as lord of Asia.

Sidon surrenders, and Alexander allows Hephaistion to choose the new king – Abdalonymus, the modestly living local descendant of the old royal family who is working in a (his own?) garden when the Macedonians come to interview him.

Chios returns to allegiance to the Greek cause; Cleander brings reinforcements from the Peloponnese to Alexander.

?Greek envoys sent to Darius before Issus, including Iphicrates of Athens, are arrested at Damascus and interned; so is Memnon's widow Barsine, who apparently becomes Alexander's mistress if her son 'Heracles' is indeed by him (he only appears in 323 as a candidate for the succession).

Tyre refuses to let Alexander enter their island city and sacrifice to 'Heracles' at his temple (that is, equivalent local god Melkart) there, and tells him to sacrifice in the mainland suburb's temple instead. He besieges the island, and demolishes the mainland district's buildings to build a 'mole' out to the walls (about half a mile away from land) for his siege-engines to use. Before the work gets underway, he sends an embassy for surrender; the defenders kill his envoys and throw their bodies off the walls. The causeway is protected from bombardment from the walls by two siege-towers erected at the seaward end, but the defenders send out ships towing a loaded fireship, which crashes into and burns the towers; Alexander has the mole widened and more towers constructed, and goes off via Sidon to collect timber for this from the forest of Mount Lebanon; after he leaves a storm damages the mole and holds up work.

Most of the Phoenician fleet in Persian service in the eastern Aegean deserts to Alexander now its homeland is under threat; Rhodes sends him ships, and the Cypriot kings arrive to pledge allegiance and give him 120 ships; he now has around three times the size of the Tyrian fleet, and can bottle the latter up in the island's harbours and starve the city. Some 4000 hired Greek mercenaries arrive, as does a ship from Antipater in Macedon with news of plots by King Agis of Sparta and his Cretan allies.

On Alexander's return, his engineers devise a plan to hang battering-rams from platforms at the mastheads of his ships, sail these up to the walls, and swing them at the top of the walls to breach the latter before men swarm across on 'bridges'; this is tried out to add to bombardment at sea from ships and from the mole but the Tyrians drive the ship-board equipment back from the seaward walls with grappling-hooks and flame-throwers. Ships are harassed by divers and having their anchor-cables cut.

Darius' wife Stateira dies while in Macedonian captivity, probably during childbirth. A second embassy arrives from Darius, offering the hand of his elder daughter as a Persian ally and all the lands west of the Euphrates; the siege is bogged down into a stalemate and most of the Companions have backed abandoning it at a recent council, and Parmenion traditionally advises Alexander to accept the Great King's offer. He says he would accept it if he were Alexander; his king replies that he would accept if he were Parmenion and turns it down.

Alexander's new fleet clears the eastern Aegean of Persian allies, and overthrows Chares the Athenian mercenary who has seized Miletus but who now flees. However, Pharnabazus ships 8000? refugee Greek mercenaries from Darius' army from Phoenicia to Crete to be used for the planned revolt by his ally, Agis of Sparta.

Late July/early August? (seven months into siege) – Thirteen Tyrian warships emerge from the island harbour during 'lunch-break' for the Greek naval patrols to attack Alexander's Cypriot allies' ships while these are beached in the harbour on the northern side of the mainland, but Alexander is informed and leads a quick sally by sea from the southern mainland harbour to take the enemy attackers in the rear and destroy them. After two days' rest Tyre is attacked by land and sea and attackers climb up siege-towers on the mole and on ships placed by the walls to storm the damaged walls while the Greek ships attack the island's harbours, and the 'Shield-Bearers' lead the first breach of the walls, although their commander, Admetus, is killed. Alexander follows, and the city is stormed and sacked; 8000 of the populace are slaughtered and the rest (30,000?) who have not fled by sea earlier are enslaved, with the exception of those who manage to get to sanctuary in the temples, which Alexander has announced will be preserved. Envoys from their African colony of Carthage, which has lent the defence ships, are also spared. The city is handed over to a Greek garrison and settlers, but refugee king Azemilk is allowed back to rule nominally.

Alexander heads south for Egypt; the Jews are traditionally granted autonomy as Alexander passes their lands.

Batis, governor of Gaza, and his Arab garrison refuse to surrender; he believes the huge walls are too high for Alexander's siege-towers, so Alexander constructs a massive 'ramp' to the walls to enable his engines to reach the top. The walls are also undermined by sappers, and when breaches are opened the Greeks attack. Alexander is wounded in the shoulder by a catapult-bolt on one of the early attempts to storm the walls, but (October? – two months into the siege) at the fourth attempt the city is taken; the men are killed and the women and children are enslaved, and according to some versions Alexander has Batis tied behind his chariot and drags him round the walls (if true, presumably as an echo of Achilles doing this to Hector at Troy).

Alexander enters Egypt unopposed as satrap Maxaces surrenders at Pelusium; possibly the garrison has been weakened by the recent plundering incursion of Amyntas, a refugee Macedonian exile in the Great King's army, and his mercenaries after they fled from Issus in 333. The fleet sails up the Nile to Memphis, the ancient capital, while the army marches parallel.

14 November – Alexander is crowned as Pharoah at Memphis with Egyptian rites; he honours the local gods, especially Apis the sacred bull whose worship was profaned by past Great Kings, and goes down the western branch of the Nile to its mouth where he decides to found a new port and capital for the province, an exclusively Greco-Macedonian settlement.

Italy

?Revolt of Tarentum against the authority of Alexander of Epirus; he has to move his headquarters for campaigns to loyal Thurii.

331

Alexander's Empire

Alexander's Aegean fleet delivers prisoners from their round-up of rebels to him in Egypt; he sends the arrested Greeks home to be judged in their home cities and sends the leaders of the rebel garrison of Chios to serve as convicts at a fortress by the First Cataract.

January–February? – Alexander leads a picked force across the desert, south-west from Alexandria to the oracle of the god 'Ammon' /Amun-Ra (identified with Zeus) at the distant oasis of Siwah. The mission is later written about (e.g. by Arrian in the second century AD) as a quest to discover his true identity and whether he is the son of a god, as well as (or instead of?) Philip II; he will adopt the two horns of the god Ammon on his coins. He has also been invited by the local Greek colony at Cyrene to visit them in return for an alliance and aid (a detail left out by Ptolemy, who conquered Cyrene and so reversed the initial 'alliance' policy), and possibly Greeks from Cyrene either tell him of the oracle or are among his guides. He goes along the coast to Paraetonium halfway to Cyrene, then south inland, travelling by night – with or without supernatural 'help' (crows or snakes) to assist him on the right route as some (Callisthenes? and Ptolemy) later write of the eight-day journey. Some of his senior officers are with him, probably Ptolemy, the later ruler of Egypt in 322–283, and at the shrine he is greeted as the 'son of Zeus/Ammon' (the normal nomenclature of the Pharoah) according to Callisthenes. Possibly his personal interpretation of this affects his increasingly bold view of his own exalted rank as a living 'hero' like Achilles or Heracles.

Alexander returns to Memphis where he holds Games; he appoints two Persians (one is Doloapsis the Egyptian) and two Greeks (one is Cleomenes of Naucratis, in charge of finances) as governors of Egypt.

7 April – Traditional date of the foundation of Alexandria, which Alexander lays out plans for with his architect Aristoboulus and others – though he may have planned the site on a visit in late 332 and this date be the start of construction months later.

Probably after 11,000 reinforcements leave Macedon for Alexander, King Agis of Sparta launches a revolt in the Peloponnese, aided by the force of mercenaries that he has brought back from Crete.

May – Alexander bridges the Nile at Memphis and sets out for Syria and Mesopotamia to confront Darius; Parmenion's younger son Hector is accidentally drowned in the Nile, and possibly his elder brother Philotas comes under suspicion of a plot but is cleared. Alexander of Lyncestis, eldest of the three brothers of that western Macedonian ex-principality's royal family, is imprisoned over this or another conspiracy. Meanwhile, the new Alexandrian (Persian) governor of the Palestinian province of Samaria, married to the daughter of the Jewish 'High Priest' at Jerusalem, has died and his Macedonian successor has been murdered in a native revolt; Alexander suppresses the Samaritans and hands part of their territory to the neighbouring Jews, hence possibly the later legend of his meeting and doing obeisance to the Jewish 'High Priest'.

May–July – Alexander prepares his army at Tyre, and holds Games; he receives reports on the Spartan-led revolt in the Peloponnese, and sends a squadron of ships commanded by Amphoterus to the Aegean to keep the islands from joining in and then land in the Peloponnese to recruit allies, and 100 Cypriot and Phoenician ships are sent to Crete to overrun towns loyal to their recent ally Agis of Sparta. Chios and Rhodes send envoys to have their garrison removed, which Alexander accepts to win them over; Athens sends an embassy headed by the usefully named Achilles to flatter Alexander into releasing his Athenian prisoners from Darius' navy, and he agrees but keeps the sailors in his service so they do not return home and defect to Agis.

Coeranus becomes his tribute-collector for Phoenicia, and Philoxenus for Western Asia Minor. Menander becomes governor of Lydia; Asclepiodotus replaces Arimnas in Syria. Harpalus becomes senior treasurer.

Memnon, governor of Thrace, revolts against Antipater but is defeated and is forced to surrender in return for keeping his post.

July – Hephaistion is sent ahead to bridge the Euphrates. Having trained his army back to war-readiness after a year without combat, Alexander follows a few weeks later; the bridging-work, at Thapsacus, is delayed by the arrival of Darius' advance-guard on the opposite bank to block it, led by Mazaeus the evicted governor of Syria and Cilicia. These retreat when Alexander arrives and the river is bridged, with iron chains holding the wooden structure in place; Alexander avoids the direct route east to Babylon down the Euphrates valley as Mazaeus is burning the crops ahead of him to deny him fodder. He moves north-east across the hills to the Tigris, and crosses the river unopposed to find the land unburnt so his horses can feed.

20 September – Eclipse of the moon; Alexander offers sacrifices to the relevant gods ahead of battle. Darius is in the city of Arbela down the Tigris valley, while his troops prepare a battlefield at Gaugamela seventy miles away by levelling the plain for his scythed chariots.

21 September – Alexander advances on Gaugamela; he has around 47,000 troops, and estimates vary of Darius' army with many exaggerations but it is clearly far larger, possibly 200,000 as they include levies from all the eastern satrapies to the Indus (plus 4000 Greek mercenaries).

29–30 September – Alexander orders his army to march on the Persian camp at night, ready for a surprise attack; they arrive at the final ridge before the camp to find that the Persians are all drawn up in battle array. On Parmenion's advice (assuming that this is not apocryphal as Parmenion is always portrayed in the sources as the voice of caution), Alexander decides not to attack in case of traps and orders his men to camp; a delay will also cause the Persians to have to stand to arms for another day and so unnerve them.

30 September – Alexander and his officers investigate the battlefield on horseback, and note the pits and stakes ready to deal with his cavalry. He makes sacrifices at dusk, including (uniquely) to the goddess of Fear, and a Macedonian council-of-war is held; the officers urge a night-time attack but Alexander refuses.

1 October, Battle of Gaugamela – Alexander places the Foot Companions in his centre, with the 3000 of the 'Shield-Bearers' regiment on their right extremity; then himself and his cavalry Companions on the right wing, with 2000 archers and Agrianoi tribal light infantry in front. On the left wing are Parmenion and the allied Greek cavalry. Squadrons of mixed infantry and cavalry are on the flanks to protect against an enveloping movement

by the far larger Persian army on the main wings' rear, and 20,000 Greek and allied ex-Persian infantry make up the reserves behind the main wings. Opposite the Greeks, Darius is in the centre in his royal chariot behind a screen of fifteen Indian elephants, with Mazaeus in command of the right wing and Bessus, satrap of Bactria, and the troops from the Eastern provinces on the left wing. The content of Alexander's speech is probably less rhetorical than the long-winded version in Curtius Rufus, but the reminder that they are fighting for all Asia and the command to raise a loud war-cry (in Arrian) are likely enough.

Alexander advances on the Persians, moving his right wing and centre at an angle rightwards to stop the Persians opposite overlapping them and thus opening a gap between his right-centre and his left. He moves onto stony ground beyond the levelled area that the chariots will not find easy to use; the Persian right wing light cavalry (especially 'Scythians' from the Central Asian steppes) moves out to his right to outflank him, and then charge; this attack is held and repulsed with an initial retreat to lure them forward against a smaller-sized foe, which reserves to the rear then reinforce. The remainder of the Persian left wing moves up to help the Scythians against Alexander's right wing; the Persian scythed chariots charge in the centre, but the Greek archers and javelineers (especially the Agrainoi) pick their drivers off then attack the horses from close range so they career out of control, the Greek ranks opening up to let them pass by. With the Persian left wing having moved away from the centre to support the Scythians, there is a gap between their left and centre and Alexander now leads a Companion cavalry charge (4000 men?) into this. The cavalry crashes into the Persian centre infantry in front of Darius, and the Foot Companions (7000 men?) follow them; traditionally Alexander kills Darius' charioteer, and the Great King soon retreats out of range onto the road to Arbela.

The Persian cavalry on their left wing attacks the Greek infantry, but is held by a smaller force in a phalanx; on the Persian right Mazaeus is pushing Parmenion back, and 3000 Persian cavalry apparently ride round the side of the Greek army to their baggage-train to rescue Darius' family but ?his mother, Sisygambis, refuses to be rescued; Greek reinforcements drive the attackers off. Similarly, a Persian and Indian force slips through the gap beyond Alexander's Foot Companions' advance and breaks into the Greek camp to loot the baggage and is driven off by the Greek reserves. (Or is this two versions of one rescue-attempt?)

Alexander leads 2000 cavalry after the fleeing Darius, but? (not agreed among sources as to timing or content of message) receives a messenger from Parmenion saying he is in serious danger and ?turns back to charge the latter's attackers in the rear. This may be the clash where sixty Companions are killed and Hephaistion wounded – or else that refers to the attack on Darius' rearguard in the pursuit later. Possibly the 'message from Parmenion' was exaggerated (though unlikely to have been invented) in accounts written after the general's execution in 330 to play up his poor generalship. With or without Alexander's assistance, Parmenion repulses the Persians largely due to his Thessalian cavalry. Alexander returns to the hunt and arrives at the empty Persian headquarters at Arbela, at the River Great Zab at dusk; he has to call off the pursuit as Darius is too far ahead; Darius gets away to Ecbatana, capital of Media, across the Zagros Mountains to the north-east. The battle ends with unknown but massive casualties.

Autumn – Antipater defeats and kills King Agis of Sparta in battle at Megalopolis; the revolt in the Peloponnese collapses. Eudamidas succeeds his brother Agis as the Eurypontid king.

Italy
Alexander, king of Epirus, is killed in battle by the Lucanians in southern Italy on his expedition to assist the local cities against inland tribes; succeeded by his infant son by Philip II's daughter Cleopatra, Neoptolemus II.

Alexander's Empire
Alexander arrives at Babylon, which its governor Mazaeus (a senior commander at Gaugamela) has surrendered; Mazaeus and his sons come out to meet him a few miles away, and escort him to the city; he draws his army up in battle array before the walls in case of trouble, but a procession of the inhabitants emerges to welcome him with officials and priests; he enters the city in the Great King's chariot for a ceremonial welcome and occupies the main palace. He orders the restoration of temples damaged by Xerxes and makes sacrifices to the god Bel-Marduk, thus allying with the priestly orders against the Persian monarchy. Mazaeus is made satrap of the province, with two Macedonan generals to guard him; Mithrines, ex-governor of Sardes, is given the satrapy of Armenia.

September–October? – Alexander spends five weeks celebrating and recuperating in Babylon.

Alexander sets out for Susa and Persepolis, leaving Darius untouched in Ecbatana rather than tackle the Zagros mountains in midwinter; around 15,000 Greek, Macedonian and Thessalian reinforcements arrive to join the army, which is now around 45,000 strong.

Alexander enters Susa, and occupies the royal palace. The local governor is retained; the statues of Harmodius and Aristogeiton the 'tyrannicides' looted by Xerxes from Athens in 480 are sent back to Athens in a highly symbolic gesture.

Late December? – Alexander marches on towards Persepolis; a local tribe who are usually given heavy bribes by the Great Kings not to interfere with traffic on the Royal Road are denied their money and resist, so they are suppressed and their chieftain intercedes with his aunt, Darius' mother Sisygambis, who secures their pardon in return for paying tribute to Alexander.

The main army and baggage is sent on along the coastal road under Parmenion via Kazarun into the Persian homeland, while Alexander and a picked force of fast-moving Companion Cavalry, Foot Companions, and light infantry head inland for the pass of the 'Persian Gates' that block the direct route to Persepolis; four days later they arrive at the narrow pass to be bombarded with stones from catapults by a large force of Persians (40,000?) behind a wall blocking it. Alexander has to retreat out of range, and he has to contemplate leaving this route blocked until a local shepherd shows him a path round the mountains to the rear of the pass. He leaves most of his men (4000?) in camp with fires lit overnight to lull the Persians into security, and leads a smaller force along this narrow track over another pass in the snow; once they are over into the plain four brigades of heavier infantry are sent ahead to the bridge over the river before Persepolis, while Alexander and the others run back across the foothills to take the Persian Gates guard-force in the rear. The enemy are caught unawares, and a trumpet is sounded to alert the main Greek army to attack them too; most Persians are killed.

330

January – The governor of Persepolis surrenders; Alexander enters the Persian capital and tells the descendants of deported Greeks settled nearby the previous century that they can go home. The city is sacked, but the palace is retained temporarily as his residence; he sits on the Great King's throne and allegedly (here or at Susa?) it is too short for his legs to reach the ground so he has to use a table as a footstool, to the distress of attendant court servants who Parmenion's son Philotas jeers at.

Pasargadae surrenders; the royal treasure stored across the Persian homeland is collected and readied for movement west.

Demosthenes defends his past conduct to the assembly of Athens in his speech 'On the Crown', after attack by Aeschines.

?Olympias leaves Macedon, to Antipater's relief, to assist her daughter Cleopatra in Epirus as regent for the latter's young son Neoptolemus II.

?April – Alexander decides to move into Media after Darius; before he leaves he burns the royal palace to the ground. One version (derived from Ptolemy, via Plutarch) has it that this is arranged as a calculated act of symbolic revenge for the sacks of Athens and other cities in Greece in 480 and Parmenion advised him not to do it as it all now belongs to him; another version famously has it that it was decided upon at a final banquet in the palace, at the suggestion of Ptolemy's Athenian courtesan mistress Thais, and Alexander drunkenly agreed and let her throw the first torch into the buildings before a general move to emulate her.

May – Alexander moves north from Persepolis on Ecbatana/Hamadan, and is joined by 6000 reinforcements; Darius retreats towards the Caspian Sea with a small mixed force of Persians and Greek mercenaries, and fails to hold the 'Caspian Gates' pass into Hyrcania; he plans to head for Bactria, but (early June?) is arrested in his camp by a group of nobles led by his cousin Bessus and the satrap Nabarzanes.

June – Alexander enters Ecbatana, and establishes his treasury and a rearguard garrison of 6000 troops there led by Parmenion. He dismisses his Greek and Thessalian troops who were enrolled for the war with Persia, implying that this is now over; Parmenion is to defeat the Cadousians to the south-west and Harpalus to be treasurer in Ecbatana.

Alexander sets out for a swift cavalry pursuit of Darius; he misses the disintegrating royal escort on the side-roads in an eleven-day search, and arrives in Ragae/Rayy to be told by two loyalists of where Darius is being held prisoner in his camp by Bessus and Nabarzanes. He gallops there, and in the desert near Damghan he and c.60 light infantry on fast horses reach the enemy camp where the rebel leaders stab Darius, leave him dying in a wagon, and ride off.

Darius is apparently discovered by a Macedonian searching the wagons, and is either dead or (later sources) dies minutes later; his body is sent to Persepolis for burial and his brother Oxathres joins Alexander's 'Companions' as Bessus is hunted for rebellion and regicide.

Alexander marches through the forests of Hyrcania, on the south shore of the Caspian Sea; Nabarzanes the regicide, encamped nearby, negotiates his pardon (surprisingly) and surrenders to be sent home; according to some accounts his intermediary was Bagoas, Darius' favoured court eunuch, who now goes into Alexander's service and becomes his lover (and probably acts as a crucial agent in introducing him to Persian court manners).

Bessus flees east into Bactria. Alexander pardons the last 1500 loyal Greek mercenaries of Darius, commanded by Paron, and those who entered his service before the Philip/Persia war opened are allowed to go home and the rest are enrolled in the Macedonian army at the same rates of pay. The local tribesmen are put down for raiding, and Alexander's kidnapped horse Bucephalus is recovered.

Alexander camps at Zadracarta, at the south-east corner of the Caspian; more eminent Persians surrender and are enrolled in his army, and the ?octogenarian satrap Artabazus, mother of Alexander's alleged mistress Barsine widow of Memnon, and his seven sons arrives.

Alexander reaches Mashad, as Bessus arrives in Bactria and claims to be the new Great King, assuming the upright ceremonial cap/tiara of state. He avoids heading straight, north-east, for Bactria, as satrap Satibarzanes of Areia to the south-east, a former commander at Gaugamela and in Bessus' conspiracy, offers to surrender and comes to the frontier to do so. Alexander keeps him in office, and enters his province en route to Bactria and its capital of Zariaspa/Balkh; he burns the excess baggage in his camp so the army can move faster.

Satibarzanes raises revolt at his capital, Saticoana/Herat, kills his new Greek officers, and besieges the loyalists in the citadel there; Alexander hastens his army to the town, and the rebel army takes refuge on a wooded hill outside but Alexander fires the scrub and kills those who do not emerge to face his troops. He then batters down the town's walls and kills or enslaves the inhabitants; 'Alexandria', now Herat, is founded on the site and garrisoned. Satibarzanes escapes into the mountains and flees to join Bessus.

?Alexander starts to wear Persian court dress and use their court etiquette, at least with Persian courtiers; this arouses disquiet among some of his more nationalist officers, possibly including Philotas, last surviving son of Parmenion (see below).

Late August? – Alexander is joined by 6000 reinforcements from Macedon; he marches south into Seistan, not east into Bactria, as its rebel governor, another assassin of Darius, flees to the Indus valley but is arrested there by the locals and sent back to Alexander to be executed. Alexander camps at Farah in the north of the province, where a story allegedly emerges of a plot to kill him known to or headed by his close aide and boyhood friend Philotas, commander of the Companion Cavalry ('Hipparch') and son of Parmenion who now commands the rearguard and supply-route to the west at Ecbatana. According to the version derived from Ptolemy, a junior officer called Ceballinus finds out from his brother that the latter's lover, Dymnus, has told him that he is involved in a plot to kill Alexander; Ceballinus goes to the royal tent to report it to the senior officer on duty, Philotas, but the accused are not arrested so next day he tries again and is told that Philotas had no time to approach his busy sovereign. After another day without action, Ceballinus reports the matter to one of Alexander's 'Royal Pages', his aristocratic teenage attendants; the latter tells Alexander at once in his bath, and the accused are arrested except for Dymnus who kills himself; however, the extent of the plot is unclear, and Philotas is at least suspected over his not reporting it earlier. The anti-Alexander accounts (mostly connected to Athens tradition, influenced by his treatment of their historian Callisthenes in 327, below) imply that Philotas was innocent and was 'set up' for opposing Alexander's recruitment of Persian officers and governors and move towards adopting Persian court etiquette. Others imply that Philotas was guilty and planned to murder Alexander as charged, with or without the support of his father Parmenion. The Ptolemy-derived versions have it that Philotas has already aroused disquiet for an alleged plot back in Egypt in 332 but been exonerated, and that his boasts about he and his father doing everything for which Alexander has taken the credit have been betrayed by his mistress Antigone (?to Craterus).

Philotas is questioned casually by Alexander but denies everything, and is arrested on the advice of the King's other senior commanders led by Craterus (Arrian and other Roman history versions); he is questioned, and (Ptolemy's version) brought before the army for a traditional Macedonian trial where Alexander accuses him of plotting regicide; he cannot deny that he ignored information about a plot, and he is sentenced to death with the other plotters; the army kills them with javelins. Three officers (including the later 'Successor' general Polemon), brothers of an officer who fled as soon as Philotas was arrested, are tried before the army but are acquitted and their brother is asked to come back and is acquitted too; probably Alexander of Lyncestis, kept a prisoner since earlier plots, is executed too. More dubiously, a messenger, Philotas' friend Polydamas, is sent speedily on a fast camel to Parmenion at Ecbatana; he arrives eleven days later, delivers Alexander's instructions to some of Parmenion's officers, and next morning lures Parmenion away from his officers into the palace garden. Polydamas gives him a 'letter from Philotas' to read, and he and the loyal officers stab Parmenion to death – possibly just as a precaution lest he revolt in Alexander's rear, possibly as he has been implicated in Philotas' alleged plans. (Was the letter from Philotas significant and did it refer to the plot, so as Parmenion seemed pleased at it this implies that he knew the plan to kill Alexander?) His other officers accept the King's verdict that he was guilty and obey Alexander's letter, sent with Polydamas, to let the latter take over at Ecbatana; the troops remain loyal.

September – Alexander and c.35,000 men head from Farah across Areia towards Arachosia (Helmand and the region west of Kandahar), with Cleitus and his 4000 men rejoining them en route.

November – Kandahar is occupied and renamed 'Alexandria' with a garrison of 4000 installed; Alexander crosses the 'Paropamisadae' /Hindu Kush mountains north into the lowlands of Bactria, heading for Bessus' headquarters at Balkh. Satibarzanes moves south from Bactria to invade Areia behind Alexander, who has to send 6000 troops back to deal with him. The army crosses the Hindu Kush in snowstorms, heads north-east to the Kabul region, and secures the passes into Bactria, which Bessus has left open as he did not expect an attack this year; Alexander winters at Kapisa, which is renamed 'Alexandria-in-the Caucasus' and given a Greek urban settlement.

329

May? – After seven months encamped around Kapisa, Alexander crosses the Khaiwak pass (11,000 feet) across the northern end of the Hindu Kush into the Oxus river-valley plains of Bactria. Meanwhile, the rebellion in Areia is put down by a mixed Greco-Persian force and Artabazus reportedly kills Satibarzanes in personal combat in battle near Herat; Bessus burns the crops around Balkh as Alexander approaches and flees to cross the Oxus; 6000 of his cavalry desert.

Early June? – Alexander occupies Balkh, and Artabazus arrives to report on the victory and is made the new satrap of Bactria. Alexander chases Bessus across the desert to the Oxus, having to travel by night due to the heat and reportedly refusing a drink of water from a helmet as all his men cannot drink (a similar story is told of him in the Makran desert in 325). He camps near Kilif on the south side of the river, and sends a force of veterans and invalids who will find the hard campaigning ahead difficult home with orders to father children for his future army. Bessus has burnt the boats in the river, so Alexander has the leather tent-skins blown up into inflatable rafts and the army crosses on those.

Alexander advances into Sogdia/Sogdiana, around modern Samarcand (Maracanda), and Bessus' henchmen arrest him and send to Alexander to offer to hand him over to gain time for their own plans. Alexander agrees, and Ptolemy collects the prisoner from a village rendezvous and brings him in a 'yoke' like a Persian convict to the new ruler. Alexander arrives to find Bessus standing beside the road and asks why he betrayed and murdered his lord, and Bessus blames his subordinates for talking him into it; he is flogged and sent back to Balkh and on to Persia under escort of Darius' brother Oxathres, to be executed and exhibited on a cross as a regicide according to Persian law.

Alexander crosses Sogdiana to the River Jaxartes (Amur Darya) at the furthest north-eastern boundary of the Persian empire and 'civilization', and punishes the locals for attacking his patrols; he is wounded in the ankle by an arrow during a skirmish and has to be carried in a litter. The infantry and cavalry quarrel over who is to have the honour of escorting him so they take it in turns.

July – Alexander occupies Maracanda/Samarcand, the provincial capital, and reaches the Jaxartes; Alexander founds a new Alexandria (now Khojend) to replace the Persian fortress there. The nomad 'Scythians' on the far bank defy him. Meanwhile, a group of Bessus' lieutenants, led by Spitamenes, have risen in revolt behind Alexander and their agents have encouraged local villagers to attack his garrisons so he burns assorted villages. The walled ex-Persian fortress of Kurkath (founded by Cyrsu 'the Great') is a more serious proposition than the poorly walled villages as it has high walls and Alexander does not have stones for his siege-train to use in bombardment, but the summer has dried up the river-bed passing through the town and exposed a gap under the walls at its exit so he leads his men inside that way; the town is destroyed as an example.

August? – The new 'Alexandria' is founded and built by the army; as Spitamenes attacks the garrison in Maracanda the Scythians north of the Jaxartes are emboldened to gather on the river-bank and defy Alexander, so he sends 2000 mercenaries off to relieve Maracanda and prepares his rafts to cross the river. The omens are deemed unfavourable, so he sets up his catapults on the bank and fires missiles across the river to break up the nomads; once they are demoralized he crosses the river on the rafts, their horses swimming alongside and archers firing at the Scythians to keep them back from the bank. The Macedonians land and their cavalry repels the enemy; as the Scythians move in for battle he leaves a smallish advance-guard in front of his main force to lure them on, then once the enemy are within reach his main cavalry and their new local mounted archers charge them. The Scythians lose 1000 men and flee to the safety of the hills; Alexander pursues them but catches dysentery from the poor water and has to give up the chase.

Spitamenes and his local cavalry archers attack, defeat, and later destroy the relief-force sent to Maracanda en route, at the Zarafshan River; Alexander takes 7000 Companion cavalry and light infantry in a quick dash to Maracanda, arriving within three days; Spitamenes abandons his attack and flees out of reach into the desert to the west. Alexander pursues him to the Oxus, but has to give up the search and retires to Balkh for the winter.

Some 21,600 reinforcements ordered from the west arrive, led by Asander and Nearchus the Cretan, later Alexander's admiral.

328

Alexander winters at Balkh; the new satrap/governor of Ariea, Stasanor, brings his predecessor Arasces and Barzanes, ex-satrap of Parthia, there for ?execution. Scythian tribal envoys and Pharasmanes of the Chorasmians (south of the Aral Sea) submit.

Alexander marches back to the Oxus, and discovers some gushing oil-wells there; three army divisions cross the Oxus to tackle Spitamenes while two remain to garrison Bactria and the fifth, led by Craterus, founds an 'Alexandria' at the oasis of Merv.

Alexander campaigns in Sogdiana to suppress the local tribes while Craterus and Cenus pursue the fugitive Spitamenes.

Early autumn – Based at Maracanda/Samarcand, Alexander murders his veteran senior officer Cleitus 'the Black', co-'Hipparch' of the Companion Cavalry with Hephaistion and just appointed governor of Bactria to replace the aged Artabazus, in a drunken brawl. Boasting at a party about the respective merits of Philip II and Alexander as creators of Macedonian triumphs gets out of hand – due to the poor quality water and an epidemic of dysentery the Macedonians are drinking unwatered wine. Cleitus tries to insist that Alexander owes it all to Philip and has just used his creations, and reminds him about how he had to save the rash King's life at the battle of the Granicus. (One account, not others.) He is hustled out of the room as Alexander looks for a weapon and hits a guard for not sounding the alarm as he demands. ?Later when Cleitus returns, or in the same brawl, he hurls another insult and Alexander snatches a guard's spear and runs him through. Alexander sobers up and falls into a deep depression, starving himself for three days, and has to be talked round by his officers, while a priest obligingly says that the god Dionysus is to blame out of anger that Alexander forgot the day's due sacrifice to him; the army condemns Cleitus to death so his murder was technically legal. ?Was Cleitus resentful at being sent off active service to be a governor as a form of punishment for his attitude to adopting Persian court ritual?

Most of the Sogdians surrender; Spitamenes manages to launch a raid on the town of Balkh while the army is away and mauls its garrison, but has to retreat to the desert and en route runs into Craterus who routs him and destroys most of his Scythian nomad cavalry; he is forced into hiding and killed by his followers who send his head to Alexander.

Alexander plans to introduce the Persian 'kow-tow' prostration, the 'proskynesis', to his court and to have Macedonians as well as Persians do it to make them equal, but this is fiercely resisted by a substantial section of the officers; he tries it out on his senior commanders and other friends at a private party (to avoid humiliation?), with those who do it then given the Persian royal kiss of admission into the ranks of 'Royal Kin' where they will be exempt from doing it in future. The historian Callisthenes, Aristotle's nephew, objects to the practice as un-Greek and only fitting for the gods, and has already clashed with Alexander's ally, the Thracian 'sophist' Anarxarchus, about it at a recent dinner-party – where Anaxarchus argued that Alexander would surely be given divine honours once he was dead so it was only anticipating this to treat him like a god for his divine achievements now. Callistenes apparently tries to acquire the royal kiss without having to prostrate himself first, but his omission is pointed out by a witness on the spot so he is denied one; Callisthenes encourages resistance.

Alexander winters at Nautaca.

327

Early – Final campaign opens to overrun the rebels in the mountains of eastern Sogdiana.

The veteran Sogdian chieftain Oxyartes centres resistance to Alexander on his 'Sogdian Rock' fortress, allegedly impregnable at the top of a cliff. Alexander arrives and launches a siege, and is told by Oxyartes' envoys that he will only get up the rock if he can find flying men. He selects a group of picked volunteer mountaineers, with a promise of twelve talents to the first to the summit and less for the others; 300 men climb up the adjacent cliff in the dark to a point overlooking the fortress; then they signal their arrival and Alexander's herald shouts up to announce to Oxyartes that Alexander has found his fliers. The chieftain has fled but his son surrenders the rock, and a banquet is held; it is arranged for the chieftain's daughter Roxane ('Little Star') to marry Alexander, and Oxyartes is summoned to the camp to give his consent and assist Alexander in getting others to surrender too; after the wedding Oxyartes becomes governor of the surrounding province.

Alexander besieges the nearby 'Rock of Chorienes' (Koh-i-Noor mountains), where the deep ravine ahead of the main wall is filled in by soldiers with mud and earth once pegs and a series of hurdles have been put in place to prevent this cascading down sideways. Catapults are moved up to bombard the fortress, and the commander (Sisimithres) is persuaded to surrender by Oxyartes and is allowed to keep his stronghold as an ally; Alexander spends the summer at Balkh preparing for his invasion of India.

Some 30,000 Persian boys are enrolled as a new army to be trained in Persia in the Macedonian manner, ready for Alexander to use on his return from India; Hephaistion receives the Persian rank of 'Grand Vizier' as chief minister, 'Chiliarch' in Greek.

There is a conspiracy of some of the 'Royal Pages', high-born Macedonian youths serving as Alexander's personal attendants, to murder him; they are tutored by Callisthenes and allegedly he has been inveighing about the King as a tyrant and bemoaning his autocratic behaviour and Persianized court etiquette. The leading plotter, Hermolaus, has recently been flogged and disgraced for illegally spearing the king's designated boar on a hunt and his officer father has been sent home involuntarily to Macedon. The conspirators arrange for them to take over the roster in Alexander's tent one night, but he is late back from a party and apparently is waylaid by a local woman fortune-teller camp-follower who says it will be unlucky for him to go straight to bed so he goes off to another party. The loyal pages are on guard by the time Alexander returns, and the plot leaks out; the youths are sentenced to death by the army and executed, with Hermolaus abusing Alexander as a tyrant according to Roman sources (possibly using anachronisms based on how a pupil of Aristotle's nephew would be expected to treat a tyrant). Callisthenes is investigated and probably tortured over allegations that he inspired the plot, and is variously said to have been killed or kept in chains and died later in India. Possibly his correspondence reveals that Aristotle was 'in on' the plot too, given his poor views on the Persians.

Autumn – Alexander crosses the Paropamisadae/Hindu Kush to the Kabul region, aiming for India, and sends ahead to summon the local kings around the upper Indus (as part of the old Persian empire) to submit and bring him elephants at the Indus. Alexander marches down the passes on the north side of the Khyber Pass to subdue the local tribes, while Hephaistion takes the main army down the Khyber to the Indus crossing to build ships. Alexander subdues the tribes of Swat, and one of the latter's town is identified as the legendary town of 'Nysa' once ruled over by the god Dionysus.

326

January? – Alexander is wounded in the ankle in a failed attempt to storm the walls of a hilltop fortress in the Kargala pass, 'Massaga'; a mound is built across the valley before the fortress' main entrance so catapults can be wheeled there and bombard the walls, but the earth collapses during another attack due to the number of men pressing across it and many soldiers are killed; the bombardment, however, kills the fortress' commander and his men surrender. Their 7000 Indian mercenaries take service with Alexander, but next night are spotted trying to sneak out of the camp and desert so they are massacred.

March? – At the rock of 'Aornus' by the Indus (identified as Pir-Sar by Sir Aurel Stein in 1926), the locals are holding out on a rocky summit above the river, which allegedly even Heracles could not storm. Alexander fails to progress far in a day and a half of skirmishes in the woods on the river-bank below it, and sends out a force under Ptolemy and Eumenes with a local guide to take a prominent spur of the main ridge, which they do. He then sets out to join them with the rest of the army, but their smoke-signals have alerted the enemy and two days of skirmishes follow until the army is reunited. Then they climb up the ridge to the hilltop across a ravine from the summit of Aornus, but it is too difficult to bring up earth or stones to fill in the ravine so Alexander has trees felled and piled up in a platform that he can cross. This takes four days. A first attack across the ravine and up the rock is repulsed, but after a two-day halt Alexander leads a picked force up ropes to the top of the rock at night to find only a few guards around who are killed – the majority of the Indians are preparing to withdraw down the far side of the rock and are taken by surprise. The rock is taken and an altar is built to celebrate with a sacrifice to Athene as goddess of victory.

Alexander marches to Taxila just beyond the upper Indus, capital of main local Indian kingdom, and allies with its King 'Taxiles'/Ambhi, who draws his army up on the bank of the Indus to greet him and escorts him into his capital. He has a Greek's first encounter with Hindu holy men, the 'gymnosophists' ('nude wisdom-seekers') at Taxila, and the ascetic 'Calanus' leaves them to join his entourage. Alexander gives Taxiles 1000 talents worth of loot, and agrees to help him against his enemy to the east, the king 'Porus' of the Pauruvas, who rules on the far side of the River Jhelum, and marches to the Jhelum. Philip son of Machatas becomes governor of the new province west of the upper Indus, ruling in alliance with Taxiles.

May – Porus refuses to accept Alexander as his lord and bring tribute as ordered, and encamps on the far side of the Jhelum (probably near Haranpur) with a huge army including possibly 30,000 infantry and 5000 cavalry plus a large force of elephants ready to trample on anyone who attempts a crossing; spikes are driven into the ground at the landing-places. The river is fast-flowing, and rafts cannot cross easily or unnoticed. Alexander unnerves and exhausts the Indians by sending cavalry patrols upstream constantly as if they are about to cross so the latter have to follow with elephants, has constant noise in his camp at night to keep the Indians alert lest he is about to cross the river, and builds up supplies in his camp in view of the enemy as if he is intending to wait and will thus be caught out by the monsoon swelling the river.

One night Alexander leaves a third of his army under Craterus in camp opposite Porus with instructions to cross the river next morning if Porus withdraws his elephants as then Porus will be fighting his army. Meanwhile, he goes off on a cavalry mission to 'forage' and once he is out of sight of the enemy heads for the best located upriver-crossing; he takes the rest of the army upriver to join a force of mercenaries sent up to a ford seventeen miles upstream, taking boats and rafts with them. Some 6000 infantry and 5000 cavalry led by the King's own cavalry regiment of the Royal Squadron (i.e. a force that Porus will outnumber by around five to one in infantry) cross, fording the river in a storm, which hides the noise of crossing, first to an island and then on to the east bank; the necessity to hurry and the swiftness of the current in the unexpectedly deep second part of the river causes Alexander to lead the cavalry in swimming across to secure the bank, himself on Bucephalus. Hephaistion, Perdiccas, Lysimachus, Seleucus, and possibly Ptolemy participate. Porus' scouts arrive too late, and alert their king; he sends a force of 120 chariots and several thousand cavalry to attack Alexander but it is repulsed and its commander killed. Alexander marches on down the bank to Porus' camp; the enemy now has only around 2000 cavalry left to his 5000.

Battle of the River Hydaspes (Jhelum) – Alexander commands his right wing with the main Companion cavalry in two squadrons, and sends out his light Thracian cavalry archers to harass before he attacks the Indian left wing. He avoids their elephants in the centre where the infantry are; his left wing under veteran 'Hipparch' Coenus is ordered to wheel round behind the Indian right wing, which it does taking them by surprise as they have just moved their main cavalry to repulse Alexander. Then the Greek infantry moves forward onto the Indian infantry, and the archers and Agrianoi javelineers aim at the elephants' mahouts while the 3000-strong 'Shield-Bearers' regiment attacks the elephants' legs and trunks with axes. Fifty elephants are put out of action and the others panic, and the Macedonian cavalry charges the exposed Indian infantry; Craterus can now cross the river, and the mercenaries left behind at the upriver ford arrive to join in. The enemy are pushed back, and Porus is wounded in the shoulder and withdraws on his wounded elephant; Alexander sends Taxiles to ask him to surrender, but Porus tries to attack his old enemy; he surrenders to a more acceptable envoy, and tells the arriving Alexander that he would like to be 'treated as a king'. Alexander obliges. He is pardoned and enrolled as Alexander's ally to rule the east bank of the Indus, aided by a Maedonian governor and garrison.

Alexander's aged horse Bucephalus, wounded in the battle, dies soon afterwards; Alexander founds the city of 'Bucephala' at the upriver crossing, the site of his final exploit. He founds 'Nicaea' ('victory city') at the site of the battle.

Alexander marches on across the Punjab towards the upper Ganges, apparently intending to attack a rumoured kingdom there (the kingdom of Magadha at Pataliputra) whose alleged army of 200,000 plus thousands of elephants unnerve his army. He will then reach the 'World's End' (according to vague Greek cartography of India) at the mouth of the Ganges to erect an altar commemorating his journey. Hephaistion is sent on a more northerly route, towards Kashmir. The lands to the Chenab, with thirty-seven cities, are conquered to be added to Porus' province; at the river Ravi the local tribes surrender and inform on their neighbours' war-readiness and potential.

Alexander's army encounters the monsoon at the River Chenab, and overruns the 'Cathaioi' near Lahore – their principal town is Sangala, which holds out so he undermines the walls with tunnels. Porus is sent back to collect elephants and the siege-train, but before his arrival the tunnels are complete and the wall collapses; the breaches are stormed and the inhabitants massacred. Weeks of heavy rain bogs down the troops, rots their clothes, and undermines morale as does the size of the expected next enemy (probably Magadha, and ruled by king 'Ksandrames' who Porus knows about) and the distance to the mouth of the Ganges. Alexander takes no notice.

At the River Beas, the army mutinies and the officers refuse to march any further as Alexander addresses them on his plans; Coenus, as a senior 'Hipparch' of the cavalry, is their spokesman. Alexander is furious and after a night to reflect he calls another meeting but meets the same response. He tells them to go home and tell their families that they deserted him; he will go on with volunteers. They do not respond. He withdraws to his tent in a rage and stays there for two days refusing to see anyone, hoping to win the troops round, but they refuse to change their minds. He has to give in, and consults the omens at sacrifice to be told by the priests that they are unfavourable so he can say that the gods want him to turn back; he agrees to return to Mesopotamia to great jubilations. He erects twelve altars at his camp to the Olympian gods to mark his furthest penetration of India and founds the city of 'Alexandria-the-Furthest' there.

November – Alexander returns to the new town site of 'Nicaea' on the Jhelum, where 35,000 new troops have arrived from the west, and constructs a fleet to sail down it into the Indus and so on to the sea whence his fleet will sail west to the mouth of the Euphrates. He is probably intending to open up a trade-route from Babylon to India and link the Persian heartland to the upper Indus; he is told that there are seven kingdoms to cross to the Indus-mouth. Hephaistion, as 'Chiliarch' /Grand Vizier, and Craterus lead the land-forces, the main army, along the banks (the left and right banks respectively) while Alexander sails on the fleet as far as the junction of the Chenab and Jhelum where he will land to campaign against the locals if they resist; Porus tells him that the 'Malloi', who have fought him, will resist. Ptolemy brings up the rearguard with the baggage. Alexander insists on all the small local Indian kingdoms and independent towns he passes through accepting him as their lord.

Coenus dies at Nicaea and is given an honourable funeral to show he is forgiven.

325

January? – Near the junction with the lower Indus, the 'Malloi' refuse to accept Alexander as their ruler so he besieges and storms their towns one by one and massacres inhabitants. The town of Aturi is stormed with Alexander leading the way onto the ramparts, and a large enemy force waiting at the nearby ford over the Ravi withdraws outnumbered into Multan. At Multan, the main town in the region, Alexander attacks one side of the town while Perdiccas is sent round to the far side. The town walls are breached, but the defenders flee into the citadel. The grumbling soldiers hang back from climbing up siege-ladders to the top of the wall so Alexander leads the way in person, fights on the ramparts amid risk of being hit by missiles, and drops down the far side into the citadel to avoid being hit by missiles, without adequate support. Then a ladder breaks so more men cannot get up the wall and through to him. He is cut off with three officers and is severely wounded by an arrow in the lung; Peucestas, the future governor of Persia, holds the 'Shield of Achilles' from Troy over him to protect him while Leonnatus and Abreas (the latter being killed) hold off the Indians until the other soldiers can put up more ladders and rescue him. He is carried back unconscious to the camp, and the army slaughters the entire town. After he has not been seen for a week the main army downstream panics believing he is dead, and refuses to accept his letter to Hephaistion reassuring them as it could be forged; he has to put in a personal appearance and is taken down-river in a barge to the main camp to show himself to the soldiers who roar with relief as he waves to them. He then lands and mounts a horse to show that he is alright, before a prolonged recuperation.

Alexander sails on down the Indus, and the other local towns surrender after what happened at the Mallian citadel. Local governor Musicanus surrenders, Oxycanus resists and is killed, and Sambus of Sind submits but his people revolt led by their Brahmins and are massacred. Musicanus then rebels too; his people are dealt with similarly. The veterans and infirm, with the baggage-train, leave for an easier march across northern Baluchistan to Persia with Craterus commanding, but Alexander will take the main army west across coastal Baluchistan and then the Makran desert near the sea, within reach of the fleet, which will sail parallel along the coast to the Persian Gulf and map the route for a trade-link from Mesopotamia to the lower Indus. A major new 'Alexandria' is founded on the lower Indus near Sirkot as a port, with a garrison of 10,000 and a dockyard, and a second is founded near Pattala at the river-mouth.

There is a revolt by some of the despairing Greek/Macedonian settlers 'dumped' in towns in remote Bactria, who want to go home; they elect an Athenian as their leader, but their army breaks up amidst quarrels over what to do and they are put down later.

A local rising in the province of the Hindu Kush/Paropamisadae is put down by Alexander's father-in-law Oxyartes; he is appointed the new governor, to combine it with his existing province. Another local rising is in the Helmand valley north-west of Baluchistan, so Alexander instructs his veterans /invalids sent back that way under Craterus to deal with it; this is duly done and the prisoners delivered to him later in Carmania. In the meantime there has been a native revolt under Baraxis, a pretender to the Persian throne in Media, who is suppressed and arrested.

July? – Alexander sails out into the Indian Ocean to sacrifice to Ammon and Poseidon, and then commences his march west. The fleet under Nearchus will sail parallel to him and deliver supplies if needed, but it is held up on the lower Indus for three months (until the second week of October) by the monsoon winds and then at the river-mouth for a further five weeks. Unaware of this, Alexander marches on – he has some idea of the hazards, as according to the account of Nearchus he has been told that Cyrus 'the Great' crossed the Makran desert but only seven of his army survived. The new local governor of the lower Indus has been told to bring supplies to the first nominated coastal supply-base for the fleet and then go off to subdue the local Oxeians, but on his homewards march after their submission they revolt and defeat and kill him.

August? – Alexander crosses coastal Baluchistan and founds a new Alexandria there; September?–November – Alexander runs short of food and water in the desert, and has to kill the baggage-animals; there is no sign of the fleet whenever they approach the coast. In the intense heat the army can only march at night; he insists on avoiding riding and on marching with his men, and famously on one occasion is brought a helmet filled with water but pours it away rather than drink while his men go thirsty. It rains inland of his route, but this causes a flash-flood to sweep down a dried-up river-bed and inundate his camp and many people are drowned.

Early December – Sailing along the coast and encountering whales and the savage 'Fish-Eaters' tribe, Nearchus arrives safely but short of supplies at the Bandar Abbas region and lands men to explore; they find fruit to eat. Nearchus leads scouts out to find the scouts expected from Alexander's army, and they do so but the latter think these few bedraggled men are the only survivors of some disaster. They reassure Alexander's men that the fleet is safe, and are taken to Alexander. The news that the fleet is safe is brought to Alexander and the others, and there is much rejoicing; what is left of the army replenishes its supplies and arrives safely in fertile Carmania/Kerman. Games are held to celebrate, and Alexander reportedly travels in a carriage in emulation of the legendary arrival there of Dionysus (but this may be due to exhaustion). Peucestas joins the seven Royal Bodyguards, headed by Hephaistion, in honour of his saving Alexander's life.

The fleet goes on to the mouth of the Persian Gulf; Alexander arrives in Persia to find that in his absence many of his governors have been looting and ill-treating the locals, and he summons and executes four of them as an example. His generals in charge in Media (including Coenus' brother) and their mercenaries are accused of looting temples and ill-treating the locals and summoned too, and 600 of them and two of the generals are executed. Alexander also sentences and executes the prisoners who have arrived from risings in Bactria and Media, including Baraxis the pretender, and divides up the province of the upper Indus (where governor Philip as been murdered in a mutiny) between a Thracian officer and the local king 'Taxiles'.

The Indian guru 'Calanus' falls seriously ill, and insists on commuting suicide by means of a funeral pyre when the army arrives at Persepolis; he allegedly says he will see Alexander in Babylon.

Sicily/Italy

?The future tyrant Agathocles of Syacuse, illegitimate son of an expatriate potter from Croton in southern Italy and a Carthaginian woman, launches a successful career as a soldier by serving as a mercenary in the army of his father's home-city against local tribes; a year or two later he returns to Syracuse to start his political career with fellow-soldiers' backing but is soon exiled by the democratic faction led by Sosistratus.

324

Alexander's Empire

January – Alexander reaches Pasargadae, and finds that the tomb of Cyrus 'the Great' has been despoiled; the architect Aristoboulus is ordered to restore it as a gesture by Alexander to the Persians (influenced by his own reading of the largely fictional 'Life of Cyrus' by Xenophon so he regards Cyrus as a model for himself?). Later the venal self-appointed satrap of Persia province, Orxines, is arrested for peculation and misrule and executed, and replaced by Alexander's trusted aide Peucestas.

Alexander's embezzling and extravagant treasurer Harpalus, who has reportedly made his deceased concubine Pythonice the subject of a cult as a goddess, is currently in command of the treasury in Cilicia; he fears prosecution, loots the treasury of 6000 talents, and flees by ship to Greece (spring?).

March – Alexander marches to Susa to link up with Nearchus and the fleet; he receives and imprisons the local, Persian governor who he accuses of failing to send supplies to his army, and executes his son. He holds mass-marriages of Macedonians and Persians, both officially recognizing the many liaisons his soldiers have with local women and a series of political marriages by his elite. He marries Darius III's elder daughter Barsine/

Stateira, and Hephaistion marries her sister Dryeptis; ninety leading Macedonians marry too, including Ptolemy to Artakama the daughter of aged satrap Artabazus of Bactria, Eumenes to her sister Artonis, Seleucus to Apame the daughter of late satrap Spitamenes, and Craterus to Amastrine daughter of Oxathres. The new consort and her family are installed at Susa, but Roxane as senior wife continues to travel with the court.

Alexander reviews the army of 30,000 young Persians trained in Macedonian military style, the 'Successors'; he cancels all debts owed by his troops, and issues a decree requiring the Greek city-states to accept back all their exiles, which is to be read out at the Olympic Games by his envoy Nicanor (late August?).

May/June – The refugee Harpalus leaves his mercenaries encamped at Cape Sunion in Attica, and goes to Athens to seek support; he fails to win military backing despite lavish promises of aid from him and is asked to leave, but is persuaded to leave some of his looted treasure on the Acropolis under the city's guard. He goes off to seek support elsewhere, and his mercenaries are stationed at Cape Taenarum in Laconia. The homes of people who spoke in his favour are searched for signs of bribes, and Demosthenes comes under suspicion for stopping his initial anti-Harpalus attitude and is supposed to have been given a valuable cup by him.

Alarm at Athens over the 'Exiles Decree' as Alexander has announced in Mesopotamia in response to an appeal from refugee Samians expelled by Athens that the restoration will include giving Samos back to its original inhabitants and removing the Athenian colony – which supplies many oarsmen and ships to the Athenian navy. There is a debate in the Athenian Assembly over whether to try to avert the decree by an embassy to Alexander and flattering him, e.g. by granting him divine honours as other Greek cities are planning, or to revolt with little hope of prevailing over Antipater or in 323 the returned Craterus. Even Demosthenes agrees that granting Alexander divine honours is necessary to help save their Samos project, and an embassy duly sets out to him; but Leosthenes, one of the new generals for the year 324–3 and a 'hard-liner', is not stopped from a private plan to tour Ionia collecting dismissed mercenary troops from the private armies, which Alexander has ordered his governors to dismiss. These troops are shipped to Cape Taenarum in case a war against Macedon is necessary.

Alexander leaves his new wife and the rest of the Persian royal family at Susa, and marches into Mesopotamia; at Opis his Macedonian troops mutiny as he announces at a rally that he is sending the aged and infirm home, including some of the veteran regiments such as the 'Silver Shields'. He is heckled and told that if he wishes to discharge part of his army he should discharge it all and go campaigning with just the Persians, and pointed references may be made to his supposed father the god Ammon. He jumps down from the rostrum to arrest thirteen ringleaders for execution and is not resisted, then shuts himself in his quarters and refuses to see any but a few advisers (including the Bodyguards) and Persian officers. He announces that he plans to remould his army with Persians staffing the traditional regiments, and the mutinous soldiers panic and rush to his residence to clamour to see him and promise to arrest the agitators. As he emerges a veteran cavalry officer complains that only Persians have been given the rank of 'Royal Kin' and so allowed the honour of kissing him, and Alexander says he will make them all his kin to loud cheers. A feast of reconciliation is held, with a guest-list of 9000 for an outdoor celebration centred on religious ceremonies by both Greek and Persian priests performing religious rites; all drink libations and Alexander leads the way with a prayer that Greeks and Persians will share the rule of the empire.

Around 10,000 troops, led by the 'Silver Shields', duly leave for Macedon, commanded by Craterus, who may be sent to replace Antipater as regent there and is possibly antagonistic to the 'dual rule'/fusion of ruling class of Greeks and Persians, with veteran Polyperchon (who criticized Greeks having to do the 'proskynesis' to Alexander) as his deputy. The homeward-bound veterans are replaced in the royal camp by the traditional Persian royal bodyguard, the 10,000-strong 'Immortals'.

Late summer? – Quarrel between Hephaistion and the royal secretary, Eumenes of Cardia, on the court's way to cooler Ecbatana in Media, allegedly over Eumenes' parsimony and a joke that if the archives tent was on fire he would rescue the money inside ahead of the documents; Eumenes blames a subsequent fire there on Hephaistion. The two men abuse each other in front of their officers and are ordered to apologize.

The court celebrates games and a theatrical festival at Ecbatana, with a play mocking Harpalus' pretensions and lifestyle; during the celebrations Hephaistion is ill with a fever (typhoid?) and restricted to his room, and after a temporary improvement orders a chicken and wine to celebrate but deteriorates and dies within hours. Poison is a possibility, but food-poisoning more likely. Alexander is devastated, shuts himself up refusing food for three days, and has an apparent nervous breakdown – the loss of 'Patroclus' to his 'Achilles'? Messengers are sent to the oracle of Ammon at Siwah to ask if Hephaistion can be honoured as a god, and giving him the honours of a semi-divine 'hero' is approved as a compromise.

Alexander executes the deceased's doctor Glaucias, and arranges an extravagant funeral, which will be held at Babylon once the Siwah verdict on divine rites for the ceremony is known. A sculpture of a lion is built at the city of Ecbatana, the 'Lion of Hamadan', which still survives. Hephaistion's office of 'Chiliarch'/Grand Vizier goes to Perdiccas. There is some possibility that Ptolemy arranges for Cleomenes, the allegedly venal governor of Egypt, to have immunity for prosecution for various offences in return for promising to set up a priesthood of Hephaistion (possibly at Siwah), but this may be a later story.

October? – Harpalus is murdered in Crete by one of his officers, Thibron the Spartan.

(Later 324/early 323) The treasure of Harpalus on the Acropolis at Athens is depleted by mysterious thefts from 700 to 350 talents, and Demosthenes is accused of stealing it by his rival, the orator Demades. Demosthenes is fined fifty talents and is exiled.

Alexander sends Hephaistion's cortege to Babylon with Perdiccas in charge, while he campaigns against the mountain nomad Cossaeans in Luristan (?Kurds) who have not been paid the usual Persian royal tribute as a bribe to keep from attacking travellers on the Royal Road; the six-week campaign is marked by atrocities, possibly seen as sacrifices to the spirit of Hephaistion as Achilles killed Trojans in Patroclus' memory.

323

Early – Alexander descends to the Mesopotamian plain and receives embassies from the Libyans, Carthaginians (?afraid of being his next target), 'Ethiopians' (Nubia?), Celts from the central European tribes, and from the Greek southern Italian cities asking for help against the inland tribes such as the Samnites, and from the latter. This is probably the context of the alleged Roman embassy to Alexander, Rome being at odds with the Samnites over their conquest of Campania and anxious to avoid attack.

A naval survey down the Persan Gulf conducted by Nearchus returns, after going as far as ?Bahrain; Alexander plans a march south-east along the southern shores of the Persian Gulf to Oman and a co-ordinated naval expedition alongside it as far as possible, allegedly as far as Aden, followed by the circumnavigation of Arabia to open up a route to the Red Sea. A new harbour is to be built on the lower Euphrates for the fleet that Nearchus is to command again. The shores of the Persian Gulf are to be settled by colonists to stimulate trade. The possibilities for the 'future plans of Alexander' revealed after his death and cancelled by Perdiccas are unclear due to propaganda possibilities, but a Sicilian/southern Italian expedition and attack on Carthage (from Sicily or via a march from Egypt?) are later quoted along with a 'Suez' Canal from the Mediterranean to the Red Sea and a canal through the peninsula of Mount Athos to avoid navigation round its rocky tip. An expedition by Alexander to the Caspian Sea and a sponsored attempt to circumnavigate Africa (as previously ordered by Xerxes) are also possible.

Pregnancy of Roxane is announced; the baby is to be born in ?late summer.

Alexander is advised against entering Babylon by its western gate as unlucky by the city's Chaldean astrologers, and decides to use the eastern suburbs instead but cannot march across the marshes round the city so he enters by the Western route; later seen as an omen.

Spring – Alexander ventures down the lower Euphrates by boat, and orders the repair of the neglected canal-system and better drainage. Allegedly, his royal hat blows off on one journey and a sailor sent to retrieve it puts it on his head, which is seen as a bad omen; he is flogged or executed, as later is a madman who wanders into the palace in Babylon and sits on Alexander's throne. The Greek cites' envoys are received, agreeing to worship him as a god.

?Cassander arrives as an envoy from Antipater, possibly to check whether Alexander wants his father to leave Macedon in 323 and if so to try to halt this; according to Plutarch, he sneers at the Persian manners of Alexander's court and is assaulted by him.

Alexander extends the army to make up for the loss of the departed veterans, with new Persian regiments kitted out and fighting as Macedonians in their style.

May? – The embassy from Siwah returns; Hephaistion is given a grandiose funeral with a massive pyre 200 feet high, a ceremony reported to have cost 10,000 talents and probably modelled on the funeral of Patroclus in the 'Iliad'. Alexander has the sacred Persian 'Royal Fire' put out during the ceremonies, as is normally only done for a king or his heir.

The Persian Gulf expedition is due to leave on 4 June.

29 May – A late-night dinner-party given by one of the Companions, the Thessalian Medius of Larissa, sees Alexander (?who has been drinking heavily since Hephaistion's death) turning up unexpectedly, after leaving an evening banquet already drunk. During the course of a series of toasts between himself and Proteas, nephew of the murdered Cleitus, Alexander apparently experiences some discomfort while drinking from a 'cup of Heracles' given him by Proteas and falls, complaining of a sudden pain in his side like an arrow – and some subsequent accounts go into detail about a alleged plot to poison him launched by Antipater and his family, possibly to pre-empt their removal from Macedon and feared disgrace, which Olympias has been urging on her son. According to this version, Cassander brought a vial of poison (in a mule's hoof) from the River Styx in Arcadia when he arrived in Babylon and handed it over to Alexander's personal attendant/cupbearer, his younger brother Iollas (Medius' lover), who mixed it with the wine in his cup at

Medius' feast; among the twenty attending Ptolemy, Perdiccas, Eumenes and three others knew nothing of the plan but fourteen others did, including Nearchus and Alexander's doctor Philip. The extant accounts of this version are part of a largely fabulous collection of apocryphal Roman-era legends, the 'Alexander Romance', but some details may come from a genuine contemporary diary of events from the very exact account. The probably partly genuine 'Diaries' of Alexander's last weeks (allegedly by Eumenes) do not mention poison at all, but do refer to heavy drinking for weeks. If poison was used, it was slow to work as Alexander's decline was gradual. The 'Diaries' account was probably the 'official' version of events put out, either by Perdiccas in 323-2 (but their version's details are not known to contemporary historians c.312 so this is debateable) or by another 'Successor', possibly Cassander exonerating himself from accusations of poison. The 'poison' story was current by 317, when Olympias smashed up Iollas' tomb.

Other suspects named by various theories for killing Alexander are Aristotle (over his pro-Persian policy or in revenge for killing Callisthenes?), probably advising Antipater rather than acting alone – he was later accused by Antigonus 'Monopthalmus'; in modern times suggestions have been made about various senior officers alarmed at Alexander's impractical and dangerous future plans. But infected rather than poisoned drink acting on a constitution weakened by alcoholic excess is as likely.

29–30 May – Alexander sleeps off his drinking in his bathroom following a bath after the feast – already feverish according to one account, not by below account.

30 May (Diaries version) – Alexander is physically normal at first, with a late 'lie-in' followed by a second evening with Medius. This time he falls asleep after the party in his bathroom, already feverish.

31 May (Diaries) – Unable to walk and still feverish, Alexander is carried on a litter to the planned sacrifice to the gods; back at his apartments he discusses the Persian Gulf expedition plans with his senior officers (Plutarch). He lies down in his bathroom and listens to Nearchus' account of his voyage in the Red Sea. Later on, he is moved over the Euphrates into the royal gardens, where he continues to plan, baths, and sacrifices and plays dice with Medius.

1 June (Diaries) – Alexander is too ill to attend the daily sacrifice, and has a high fever; he is moved to a palace near the royal swimming-pool.

2–3 June – He is still able to transact business about the expedition; when he becomes too ill the departure is postponed.

6 June (Plutarch) – He orders his officers to remain on call in the palace courtyard.

7 June (Diaries) – Alexander is moved back to the main royal palace; he is too ill to speak to his officers.

9 June (All accounts) – The soldiers riot and demand to see their king, and the guards (who have not seen him for several days) support them. They are allowed into the palace in a procession and troop past his bed. Alexander is too ill to speak to them but conscious. At some point after this he is asked who he wants to leave the throne to, and he says 'to the strongest' ('kratistos') unless this is a mistake for 'Craterus'. He gives his signet-ring to Perdiccas.

(Diaries) Some of Alexander's senior officers, led by Peithon and Seleucus, go to a prestigious temple to ask whether he should be moved there, and are told not to do so – this is stated as the 'Temple of Serapis' but worship of that god had not yet commenced, so this is either a mistake for another god or incorrect.

10 June – Death of Alexander, aged thirty-two and probably ten or eleven months.

The Hellenistic Era 1 –
the Successor States 323 to 200

323

'Diadochi' – Successor States

1 June – The late King's seven official 'Bodyguards' – Ptolemy, Perdiccas, Peucestas, Peithon, Leonnatus, Lysimachus, and Aristonous – and the 'Companions' lead an assembly of the senior officers, among whom are crucial figures such as Seleucus, commander of the 'Silver Shields' regiment and the admiral Nearchus; also present in the palace but probably not at the meeting is the royal secretary and archivist Eumenes. Perdiccas probably takes charge in the decision not to wait for Craterus or his deputy Polyperchon to arrive from his army of returning veterans en route to Macedonia, now in Cilicia. The meeting is held in front of Alexander's empty throne, on which the royal emblems are placed. Perdiccas wants no nomination of a new king until Roxane gives birth to a child, expected to be in six to eight weeks, but apparently Nearchus speaks up for Alexander's alleged illegitimate son by Memnon's widow Barsine, Heracles, probably aged around seven, as someone who can take over immediately but also as a relative of his wife. He is voted down by Perdiccas' faction, (?) as the boy was not acknowledged by Alexander, and Ptolemy proposes a temporary ruling council of the senior officers with no decision on any new king to put off a clash. Aristonous proposes Perdiccas as king, as a competent adult even if from the Macedonian provincial ex-royal house of Lyncestis not the Argead dynasty, but Perdiccas is hesitant about doing this and arousing antagonism; Meleager proposes a shared regency; Peithon warns against selecting the adult but mentally deficient Arrhidaeus, Philip II's illegitimate son, and proposes Perdiccas and Leonnatus as regents of Asia and Antipater and Craterus as regents of Europe for Roxane's child if it is a boy. This is agreed.

The senior officers send delegates to tell the Macedonian infantry and cavalry the decisions; the cavalry agree but Meleager and Attalus tell the infantry and face hostility to the idea of a half-Persian ruler and noisy demands that the popular and wholly Macedonian Arrhidaeus be sole king. The two officers, possibly hoping to become the regents for Arrhidaeus and get rid of Perdiccas, accept this and lead them and their candidate on their march to the palace, with Arrhidaeus being given the name of 'Philip III' and dressed up as Alexander. The cavalry object, and the Bodyguards and Companions retreat out of the way into the palace, while the two rival factions of soldiers 'face off' noisily in the palace, apparently with some fighting in the royal bedchamber around Alexander's body.

12/13 June? – Perdiccas negotiates an agreement that the leadership will accept Arrhidaeus to buy time, and Leonnatus leads the cavalry out of the city to the main army camp with the elephants – i.e. abandoning Perdiccas? Later Perdiccas slips out to join him, probably in fear of Meleager as 'kingmaker' killing him. The cavalry then blockades the infantry in the city.

c. 15 June? – Eumenes proposes a compromise – Arrhidaeus and Roxane's child (if he is a son) as co-kings, with Meleager as deputy to Perdiccas in Asia, Antipater regent in Europe, and Craterus 'protector of the kingdom' and ?treasurer. Meleager agrees; Perdiccas agrees and ends the blockade, and the agreement is ratified in the presence of Alexander's body.

Around this time, Roxane murders Alexander's and Hephaistion's Persian wives, Barsine and Dryeptis the daughters of Darius III, to ensure that she bears the only heir of the Achaemenid dynasty; traditionally she has Barsine summoned to Babylon in Alexander's name before the news of his death reaches the princesses in Susa and throws her down a well.

Perdiccas offers his daughter to Meleager's friend Attalus to win him over, and at the subsequent military review parade to acknowledge King Philip III Perdiccas proposes the execution of some leading mutineers, which is accepted, then reads out the names of 300 of Meleager's supporters who are trampled to death by the elephants. A few days later, Meleager is summoned to meet Perdiccas and is killed trying to escape (official version).

The senior officers meet again and ratify Perdiccas as sole regent in Asia and 'Protector of the Kings'; Seleucus is to be his deputy and commander of the Companion Cavalry; Antipater is to be regent in Europe and Perdiccas suggests that he marry Antipater's daughter Nicaea, and Antipater's eldest son, Cassander, is offered the command of the 'Shield-Bearers' regiment. The satrapies/governorships are rearranged – Leonnatus is to have Hellespontine Phrygia, Eumenes is to have Paphlagonia (which would normally go with H. Phrygia) plus Cappadocia, Ptolemy gets Egypt with current governor Cleomenes as his deputy, Antigonus retains Phrygia, Lycia, Pamphylia, and Lycaonia and to command in war on northern Asia Minor independent ex-Persian states with Leonnatus. Menander retains Lydia and Peucestas retains Persia; Sibyrtius gets Arachosia; Archon gets Babylonia; Stasanor gets Areia and Drangiana; Philip gets Bactria and Sogdiana; Lysimachus gets Thrace. Craterus is left without a province, and as Alexander's planned naval expedition round Arabia is cancelled the fleet is redundant and commander Nearchus joins Antigonus' staff. Alexander is to be buried in Aegae, Macedon, with his ancestors.

August? – Birth of Roxane's son, who is named King Alexander IV.

Early autumn? – Revolt of most of Greece, except for Sparta and Boeotia and led by Athens; annoyance at having to receive political exiles home as per Alexander's 324 degree is a major factor. Athens decides on revolt as soon as Alexander's death is rumoured, and confiscates Harpalus' treasure stored in their city to hire 8000 of his former mercenaries who are stationed at Cape Taenarum awaiting Macedonian orders. The Athenian mercenary Leosthenes is sent to become their commander and hires recruits. Once the news of Alexander's death is definite this becomes open, and Leosthenes wins over Locris and Phocis to supply troops; Aetolia sends 7000 men. The Athenian assembly votes to enrol all men under 40 as soldiers and send envoys around inviting all Greek states to fight for liberty under their leadership as in 480; they supply 5000 infantry and 500 cavalry to the allied army. Around 25,000 men march north towards Thessaly, while in Epirus Olympias organizes an invasion of Macedon to try to overthrow Antipater.

Antipater summons Craterus from eastern Asia Minor to help him, along with Leonnatus from the north-west, as potential allies against Perdiccas as well as the Greeks, and offers them his daughters – Craterus to marry Phila. Perdiccas sends to Athens and Aetolia for alliance in retaliation.

Late autumn? – Revolt of 20,000 infantry and 3000 cavalry among Alexander's mercenary garrisons in Bactria, who want to leave for home in Greece; they elect Philon of Athens as leader and start to march for Mesopotamia. Perdiccas sends Peithon, as the new governor of Media, with 3000 troops to put them down and wants them killed but after defeating them thanks to his secret agreement with one of their senior officers, Letodorus, who withdraws from battle, Peithon decides to send them home as requested. His annoyed Macedonian troops, however, slaughter them as Perdiccas wanted, amid suspicion of why Peithon was being so lenient, i.e. recruiting the rebels against Perdiccas later.

Ptolemy arrives in Egypt and (323/2) sacks and kills Cleomenes despite Perdiccas' orders; Lysimachus arrives in Thrace and defeats local tribal king Seuthes but for the moment is unable to secure full control to the Danube as the Thracians hold out.

In Cyrene, Harpalus' ex-officer Thibron and some of his mercenaries arrive from Greece to seize the city; it is retaken on Ptolemy's behalf by his general Ophellas, who becomes governor.

Leosthenes occupies the pass of Thermopylae to hold up Antipater's advance across Thessaly; Antipater has only 13,000 infantry and 600 cavalry as so many Macedonians are in Asia. Leosthenes surprisingly defeats Antipater in an opening skirmish north of the pass, and Antipater finds his Thessalian troops deserting; he retires into the town of Lamia and is besieged (midwinter?).

Pytheas and Callimedon, pro-Macedonian Athenians, join a pro-Macedonian delegation travelling around Greece urging the states to stay loyal to Macedon; the rebel envoys who try to win support for their cause are led by Demosthenes, with the result that the democracy votes to recall him.

322

Leosthenes is killed in a skirmish outside Lamia; this demoralizes his army but the siege continues.

As Perdiccas marches for Cilicia with the kings and court, en route to an expedition against northern Asia Minor dynasts but implicitly Antipater too, Craterus avoids him and accepts Antipater's request; he and c.6000 veterans march for Macedon while Perdiccas sends Cleitus with the royal Mediterranean fleet into the Aegean to assist Athens. Leonnatus, now in Cappadocia with Eumenes awaiting the Perdiccan Asia Minor expedition, turns against Perdiccas too – Olympias has informed her ally Eumenes that her daughter Cleopatra will marry him, so although he officially goes to help Antipater in Macedon he has his own ambitions there as a potential regent and when he arrives refuses to marry any of Antipater's daughters. Eumenes rejects Leonnatus' appeal to come with him, and instead goes to warn Perdiccas that Leonnatus is intending to usurp the regency in Macedon.

June? Leonnatus arrives via Macedon with a large army to rescue Antipater, and attacks the besiegers under Antiphilus (infantry); however, the rebel Thessalian cavalry, led by Menon, gets the batter of his cavalry and he is unhorsed and killed. Both sides have heavy losses, the Macedonian infantry escapes to a secure hill that the enemy dare not attack, and the rebels hesitate. Next day, the Macedonian infantry joins up with Antipater's army outside Lamia, and Antipater withdraws to Macedon.

June – Cleitus's royal fleet defeats the Athenian-led allied rebel fleet off Abydos in the Hellespont, and as they withdraw south defeats them again off the island of Amorgos; Craterus is able to cross to Europe with 10,000 Macedonian and 1000 Persian infantry 1500 cavalry and arrives in Macedon to join Antipater as his deputy. They now have over 40,000 infantry and 5000 cavalry (Diodorus) as they camp together at the River Peneius in Thessaly.

Perdiccas invades Cappadocia; he defeats, captures, and executes the local ex-Persian governor and king, Ariathares, wipes out his dynasty, and installs Eumenes as governor. He then invades and ravages Lycaonia.

August – Antipater, with superiority of numbers to the c.25,000 rebel Greek infantry and 3500 rebel cavalry, advances across Thessaly and bribes some of Athens' mercenaries to desert and offers easy terms to allied cities if they withdraw their contingents which some do; he wins the battle of Crannon, where his larger infantry pushes back and crushes the enemy phalanx but the latter manage to break off and retreat to safer high ground, protected by the cavalry, so they are not wiped out. The rebels are able to withdraw unmolested, and Antiphilus sends to Antipater for negotiations but is told that each city must negotiate separately; he and Craterus start to reduce the remaining Thessalian rebel cities, and the majority of the rebel allies panic and send to Antipater for peace; they are granted easy terms and the Athenians are abandoned.

Death in exile of Aristotle, who has been forced to leave Athens as a Macedonain collaborator, aged sixty-two.

Antipater reconquers Thessaly and marches on Athens; the panicking citizens vote for Demosthenes to be put to death, as proposed by his rival Demades, to appease Antipater but he has already fled the city. Phocion leads a delegation to Antipater, who is occupying the Cadmeia citadel at the ruins of Thebes, and is told that Athens must accept his 'dictat' not negotiate but he will refrain from immediate invasion to give them time to accept. Athens has to surrender (Athenian month 'Boedromion') and Antipater takes no chances despite Phocion's request for mercy and no garrison. They are to abandon democracy for a Macedonian-allied oligarchy, accept a garrison in the Piraeus, keep a reduced fleet, and pay a large indemnity. Several of the anti-Macedonians named by Antipater are to be executed, led by Demosthenes and his ally Hyperides. The new garrison, led by Phocion's friend Menyllus, enters Athens on the day of the annual procession to the Eleusinian Mysteries (20th of Boedromion), which emphasizes the humiliation. Demosthenes is cornered in sanctuary at the temple of Poseidon on the island of Calauria near Troezen by the 'bounty-hunter' Archias from Thurii and takes poison, aged sixty-two, despite an 'invitation' to come to Antipater. Hyperides is caught and killed at Cleonae. Demades and Phocion retain prominence under the new regime.

?Philip II's illegitimate daughter Cynnane, widow of the executed (336) Amyntas IV, Alexander's and her cousin, decides to take her daughter Adea to Asia Minor to join the court and marry her off to Philip III Arrhidaeus with Olympias' encouragement, possibly as planned in Alexander's lifetime; Antipater fails to stop them embarking. Perdiccas is, however, unwilling to see another powerful Argead woman and Olympias ally prominent at Court, and when she lands sends his brother Alcetas to stop her. Their escorts clash and Cynnane is killed; however, the Macedonian troops are angry at the killing and demonstrate loudly demanding that Adea be allowed to marry Arrhidaeus, and Perdiccas has to agree. The marriage is carried out, and Adea is renamed 'Eurydice'.

Perdiccas overruns Isauria, in south-east Asia Minor; the clearing of autonomist local lords and cities that Alexander failed to do protects the main 'Royal Road' from Sardes to Syria and Babylon, but the amount of killings increases Perdiccas' reputation for ruthlessness.

Sicily/Italy
?Attack on Rhegium by the oligarchic regime of Syracuse, headed by Sosistratus; it is driven off by the city's mercenary commander, the future Syracusan tyrant Agathocles (born 361), son of exiled Rhegium citizen Carcinus (who settled in Syracuse under and was granted citizenship by Timoleon, and was a potter) by a Carthaginian woman, raised by his maternal uncle Heraclides after his father abandoned him then by his father and trained as a mercenary. Followng this, Sosistratus and his colleagues are impeached and exiled and the democracy is restored; Agathocles returns to Syracuse.

Winter 322–1

Diadochi
Antipater sends out his own daughter Nicaea to Asia Minor to marry Perdiccas as arranged in their alliance, plus Alexander's sister Cleopatra. Perdiccas goes ahead, but intends to abandon Nicaea later and marry only Cleopatra in order to secure supreme power as regent for the kings as Alexander's brother-in-law. Antigonus, who is on bad terms with him and fears arrest, finds out this plan and, with his son Demetrius, secretly leaves the court and sails on an Athenian ship to Greece to warn Antipater.

Antipater and Craterus are blockading the Aetolians in their mountains in midwinter weather when Antigonus arrives to warn them; they return to Macedon to plan invasion of Asia Minor, with Craterus to command there as royal general of all Asia and replace Perdiccas once he wins while Antipater commands in Greece. They send to Ptolemy for an alliance.

321

Perdiccas decides to attack Ptolemy next rather than attack Antipater in Macedon, and sends Eumenes to guard the Hellespont against Antipater and Craterus.

The funeral cortege of Alexander leaves Babylon for Macedon after long delays to enable the preparations of a grand carriage/chariot under the supervision of the officer Arrhidaeus; when it reaches Syria Ptolemy arrives and hijacks it to Egypt, claiming that Alexander wanted to be buried at the shrine of Ammon at Siwah. He installs the cortege temporarily at Memphis pending the completion of a tomb at a focal point of the new city of Alexandria, where it is later installed.

Perdiccas regards this as a challenge to his authority and is determined to invade Egypt.

320

Perdiccas sends Cleitus with fleet to block the Hellespont and Bosphorus to Antigonus and Craterus; Eumenes is given an army of 20,000 for Asia Minor, and Perdiccas' brother Alcetas and Neoptolemus, as governor of Cappadocia and in charge of the army that has occupied Armenia, are to assist him.

Antigonus lands in Asia Minor and is joined by Asander, governor of Caria, and Menander, governor of Lydia (presumably in revenge for Perdiccas backing Cleopatra against him); Antigonus advances quickly to attack Eumenes at Sardes but Cleopatra warns him to escape inland in time. Cleitus defects to Antipater's side with his fleet on request, and Neoptolemus opens negotiations while Alcetas refuses to fight Craterus for fear the latter's popularity will cause his men to mutiny.

Eumenes retreats into Cappadocia; Perdiccas, meanwhile, marches with the court into Cilicia, to depose the suspected governor, and on to Syria en route to tackle Ptolemy and sends an officer to depose the pro-Ptolemy governor of Babylonia. The royal fleet is divided, with Attalus to take half alongside Perdiccas' army for the attack on Egypt and Aristonous with the rest to wait on Cyprus and keep the local princes and towns from supporting Ptolemy with men and supplies.

Antipater and Craterus cross the Hellespont; Antipater heads for Cilicia and the royal treasure-depots, while Craterus confronts Eumenes. Neoptolemus plots in favour of the army going over to Craterus and on being discovered by Eumenes sets out to join Craterus, but (May) is intercepted and defeated by Eumenes. Eumenes seizes his baggage-train and uses it as a means to persuade Neoptolemus' army to surrender and join him, but 300 cavalry flee with Neoptoelmus to Craterus.

Craterus, with 20,000 infantry and 2000 cavalry, fights Eumenes somewhere in Cappadocia, and Eumenes (20,000 infantry and 5000 cavalry) tells his men that Neoptolemus is commanding the enemy to reassure him as he is a poorer general; Eumenes' cavalry on his left wing opens battle as the enemy phalanx is still forming up and charges Craterus on his right wing, and it quickly breaks up the enemy cavalry as Craterus is unexpectedly trampled underfoot in fall from horse and killed. Eumenes then turns on Neoptolemus' wing (the enemy left wing) and kills him in person, and the cavalry survivors retreat to the protection of the infantry phalanx. Eumenes' offer to them of peace in return for their joining his army is accepted, but they slip away later to reinforce Antipater.

With Antipater heaving left Greece, the Aetolians revolt by arrangement with Perdiccas and invade Thessaly; they defeat and kill Antipater's general Polycles but retreat as the Acarnanians attack them in the rear. They leave Menon and part of their army in Thessaly, but these are defeated and expelled by Antipater's deputy Polyperchon.

May/June? – Perdiccas reaches the eastern mouth of the Nile at Pelusium with his huge army unchallenged, and marches upstream towards Memphis. He finds a ford to cross the river, possibly a branch formerly a canal (Diodorus), but the dam that has held back the canal-waters breaks and hundreds are drowned. The rest of the army refuses to cross. Perdiccas bribes his men to keep on and they march up-river to cross at the 'Fords of the Camel' and attack a nearby fortress before Ptolemy arrives, but the advance-guard that arrives at the fortress first cannot storm the walls and the rest of the army are still crossing the river when Ptolemy brings reinforcements; those already across are repelled and are thrown back into the river.

Perdiccas heads on at night up the East bank of the Nile to Memphis, and starts to cross the river near the city at a ford to an island halfway across with the elephants placed upstream of the main army to break the force of the water. But the army is halfway across when the sandy river-bed shifts and the river increases force, and around 2000 men are drowned; the others refuse to cross and the men already across have to be recalled and swim back. As Ptolemy continues to keep his distance the royal army is stuck in camp unable to cross the river, and growing discontent ends with officers Peithon and Antigenes surprising Perdiccas in his tent and stabbing him to death, possibly bribed by Ptolemy and with his foreknowledge.

The murder of the regent leaves the army leaderless, and next day Ptolemy is allowed into the camp by senior officers for talks as the men prefer the Alexandrian generals to ally with not kill each other. They call an army assembly and Ptolemy explains his innocence of Perdiccas' charges and is believed; he promises to supply them as they leave Egypt. The officers offer the regency for Alexander IV and Philip III Arrhidaeus to Ptolemy, but he refuses and prefers to keep Egypt. Peithon and an officer called Arrhidaeus are made temporary regents, and when news of Craterus' death arrives Eumenes is tried 'in absentia' and sentenced to death as is Perdiccas' brother Alcetas. Some of Perdiccas' allies, including his sister, wife of the fleet-commander Attalus, are executed in a typical Macedonian purge of the close kin of a traitor to prevent revenge-killings by them later; Attalus, now with the fleet at Pelusium, is sentenced to death but deserts with the fleet and secures Perdiccas' treasure at Tyre with the support of governor Archelaus. Perdiccan refugees join him there. Aristonous is sacked as commander in Cyprus.

Late summer. The army marches back to Phoenicia, commanded by Seleucus, and the leadership holds a conference at Triparadeisus (?Baalbek), a former Persian royal hunting-park, where Antipater arrives from Cilicia and Antigonus from Cyprus. Eurydice, Philip Arrhidaeus' wife, attempts to secure equal status with the regents as representing her husband before Antipater arrives, and manages to have Attalus invited from Tyre to address the soldiers (and to enter and leave the meeting unchallenged) despite the wishes of Perdiccas' killers. The current regents resign, and Antipater is voted in by the army to take over as the senior surviving officer of Philip II's and as Alexander's regent of Macedon in 334–23. Eurydice opposes this but is defeated. Antipater arrives and accepts the regency, has to be rescued from an angry crowd of Perdiccas' soldiers by Seleucus and Antigenes (according to Arrian), successfully addresses the army assembly to counter Eurydice's intrigues, and tells Eurydice to keep out of politics; some of his daughters are married off to secure his position with new allies – Eurydice to Ptolemy, Nicaea to Lysimachus, and Phila (widow of Craterus) to Antigonus' son Demetrius.

Peithon is confirmed as governor of Media and gains senior rank in the eastern provinces; Laomedon of Mytilene is confirmed in Syria and Phloxenus gains Cilicia; Seleucus gains Babylonia once he evicts its incumbent, Arrhidaeus gets Hellespontine Phrygia; Cleitus replaces Menander in Lydia; Antigenes gets Susa; Roxane's local Sogdian warlord father Oxyartes gets the Paropamisadae/Hindu Kush; Nicanor replaces Eumenes in Cappadocia; and Asander retains Caria. Antigonus retains Phrygia and becomes senior general in Asia, with most of the royal army and with Antipater's son Cassander as his deputy; 3000 unruly veterans are sent off to Susa with Antigenes to collect the royal treasure there and take it to Cylinda in Cilicia. Porus is confirmed as ruler of the eastern half of the upper Indus valley (the River Jaxartes area) and 'Taxiles' of the western half, based on Taxila.

The new regime still faces a threat from Attalus, who now leaves Tyre for Rhodes but fails to take the eponymous capital there and joins Eumenes' brother Alcetas in Pisidia, central southern Asia Minor.

Autumn – Ptolemy's general Nicanor overruns the coastal cities of Palestine and Phoenicia to capture Laomedon, the ex-Perdiccan governor of Syria who the recent conference has left in place.

Antipater returns to Macedon with the two kings, via a failed attempt by his nominee Asander to drive Alcetas out of Pisidia and a tense meeting with Cleopatra at Sardes over her contacts with Eumenes. Eumenes holds out in Cappadocia against Antigonus in Phrygia, but no major fighting occurs; Eumenes successfully sends his officer Phoenix to overtake a force of deserters in camp at night and kill the ringleaders, forcing the rest to come back.

Sicily
War between the new democratic regime in Syracuse and its exiled oligarchic predecessors, who are now in the Carthaginian part of Sicily and are being backed in their attacks by Carthage.

The future tyrant Agathocles rises to prominence as a charismatic, ingenious and ruthless military commander with a substantial following; he apparently owes his financial resources to marrying the widow of his patron and ex-lover.

India
(or 319) ?Eudamus, Macedonian governor of the upper Indus valley province, kills King Porus in order to confiscate his elephants for use in wars against his rivals.

319

Diadochi
Spring – Antipater arrives in Macedon, falls ill, and recalls Cassander who is quarrelling with Antigonus.

Demades the Athenian oligarchic leader, visiting Macedon during Antipater's illness to request the removal of the garrison from Munychia, is seized and executed by Cassander for past alleged contact with Perdiccas and plan to revolt with the latter's help.

Antigonus drives Eumenes back into the mountains of east Cappadocia, defeating him in a clash despite inferior numbers (c. 10,000 to 20,000) thanks to his secret agreement with Eumenes' cavalry commander Apollonides who deserts during the battle; most of Eumenes' troops desert and he takes refuge in the impregnable fortress of Nora, which is small so he only has room for his most trusted followers and he dismisses most of the army. Antigonus has it blockaded and goes to Pisidia to confront Alcetas; he defeats Alcetas' army near Cretopolis and the loser kills himself.

Summer – Death of Antipater, aged around eighty; he appoints Polyperchon, probably in his sixties, as the next regent in Europe, with Cassander as his deputy; Antigonus is to keep seniority in Asia. Cassander is furious and after failing to stir up discontent he leaves Macedon a few months later to join Antigonus and encourage him to attack Polyperchon.

Arrhidaeus, informed that Antigonus plans to replace him as too loyal to Polyperchon ahead of a revolt, tries to relieve the siege of Nora but is driven off by Antigonus' troops; he attempts to secure the city of Cyzicus as a secure stronghold for his rebellion but the inhabitants refuse to admit a garrison from him, withstand a siege, and send for help to Byzantium so he gives up. Antigonus orders him to come and explain himself for attacking an allied free city, and on his refusal sacks him. He flees to the city of Cius on the Propontis, pursued there by Antigonus who leaves him under siege and marches to Lydia to replace Cleitus; Cleitus leaves garrisons in his main cities and goes to Macedon to warn Polyperchon.

Antigonus opens negotiations with Eumenes; Hieronymus, later historian of the wars, is Eumenes' negotiator.

318

Diadochi

?Nicanor, younger son of Antipater and brother of Cassander, flees to Macedon, fearing his removal from governorship of Cappadocia by Antigonus and replacement by Eumenes in an alliance between the two against Polyperchon; Antigonus and Eumenes negotiate at Nora and come to agreement as Nicanor had feared. Antigonus agrees to restore Eumenes to Cappadocia and the latter swears allegiance to him.

Antigonus besieges and captures Ephesus; shortly afterwards a naval contingent arrives from Cilicia, bringing 600 talents of the royal treasure from Cilicia en route to Polyperchon as regent, and Antigonus confiscates it.

As war between Polyperchon and Antigonus looms, Polyperchon writes to Olympias in Epirus to invite her to return and assume the regency; she does not agree for the moment and consults Eumenes who tells her to stay put for the moment, but this invitation is her justification for her later invasion.

Polyperchon gets Philip III Arrhidaeus to write to and offer Eumenes a commission to take command of all Asia on behalf of the regency for Alexander IV and replace Antigonus, with 500 talents from the royal treasure at Quinda/Cyinda in Cilicia for his campaigns and command of the veteran 'Silver Shields' regiment there; he agrees and Polyperchon tells Antigenes, in command of the troops and treasure at Susa, to obey him.

Eumenes goes to Cilicia to take command of the 'Silver Shields' regiment and the royal treasure, meeting Antigenes who arrives from Susa; the troops accept him as commander despite letters from Ptokemy (at Zephyrium in Cilicia) telling them to ignore him; he raises a mercenary force and with around 10,000 extra infantry and 2000 cavalry he marches into Phoenicia to raise a fleet.

Cassander writes to the Macedonian garrisons across Greece, saying that he, not Polyperchon, is his father's real heir and asking them to obey him instead; Polyperchon writes in reply to all the Greek cities announcing his support for their independence and asking them to expel their garrisons, who he fears will soon desert to Cassander. This starts the 'anti-oligarchic' and 'liberator' appeal of the Macedonian regime's foes in appeals to Greek cities, later used by Ptolemy and Antigonus.

Cassander's friend Nicanor, appointed by him as commander of the Macedonian garrison of Munychia at the Piraeus after Antipater's death, seizes the Piraeus too on Cassander's behalf; Olympias writes to him to counter this on the alleged wishes of the kings but is ignored.

Polyperchon offers the Athenians the return of Samos if they expel the oligarchs installed by Antipater in 322 and turn to him; the city's democrats agree and ask him for help.

March – Polyperchon's son Alexander is sent to Athens to assist the democrats against Cassander and his garrison; he backs the extreme democrats in a purge of oligarchic supporters with executions, and Phocion is among those who flee to Alexander asking for his intercession with his father Polyperchon; the latter hands them over to the democrats to be executed to make himself more popular so he can be supported in garrisoning the Piraeus.

Cassander arrives in Greece with thirty-five warships and 4000 soldiers lent by Antigonus.

Cassander's friend Nicanor is in command at the Piraeus, and admits him there; he takes over the Piraeus and blockades Athens. Polyperchon arrives from Phocis with 20,000 Macedonian and 4000 allied infantry, 1000 cavalry, and 65 elephants, but cannot storm the Piraeus; he leaves Alexander to watch Cassander while he marches on to the Peloponnese to evict Antipater's garrisons and allied oligarchs. Most of the peninsula revolts for him, but Megalopolis refuses so he besieges it. The defenders are aided by Damis, a veteran of Alexander's army who knows elephants and so places sharp spikes at the breaches they make in the walls so they tread on them and flee.

Polyperchon sends his admiral Cleitus to relieve Antigonus' siege of local governor Arrhidaeus in Cius on the Propontis.

Cleitus relieves Arrhidaeus, and when Cassander's friend Nicanor brings Antigonus c.100 ships from the Piraeus to help (as Cassander and Antigonus are both foes of Polyperchon) Cleitus defeats him at sea off Byzantium. But that night Nicanor returns unexpectedly and destroys Cleitus' beached ships while Antigonus attacks his and Arrhidaeus' camp on land. Their forces are destroyed, and Arrhidaeus is probably killed; Cleitus escapes on his flagship to Thrace where he is killed by Lysimachus' troops. Nicanor returns in triumph to Athens to resume command of Munychia but Cassander is dubious of his loyalty.

With Eumenes at large in the Levant Antigonus cannot attack Macedon yet, and he goes east after Eumenes. Polyperchon abandons the siege of Megalopolis and returns to Macedon.

Peithon, governor of Media, tries to take over all of the Eastern governorships and executes Philotas, governor of Parthia, who he replaces with his own brother Eudamas; he is defeated and expelled by a coalition led by Peucestas, governor of Persia (the Persian 'homeland' around Persepolis and Pasargadae). He flees to Mesopotamia, where he and Seleucus (governor of Babylon) are asked for support by letter by Eumenes but insist that he is still a rebel as covered by the decisions of the 'high command' in 320; they try to win over his army to desert him but fail and then negotiate.

Sicily
?Acestorides the Corinthian ends period of generalship at and leaves Syracuse; the exiled oligarchs led by Sosistratus are allowed to return in amnesty.

317

Diadochi
Eumenes, pursued by Antigonus, retires into lower Mesopotamia to rally support, but Peithon and Seleucus avoid fighting him openly and ask Antigenes to use the 'Silver Shields' to arrest him as legally required by the Triparadeisus decisions. He refuses, and as Eumenes camps on the Tigris up-river from Babylon, Seleucus and Peithon sail down to address the soldiers from their ships and try to provoke a mutiny but fail. Seleucus floods Eumenes' camp by opening the dykes up-river; with 15,000 infantry and 3,300 cavalry Eumenes moves on into Persia while Peithon and Seleucus go west to meet Antigonus.

May – They send to Antigonus in Asia Minor, who advances to join them – they are to be his subordinates on his insistence. The trio then march into Mesopotamia. Eumenes summons a meeting of the governors of the eastern provinces, led by Peucestas; Eudamas comes from the Indus with Porus' confiscated elephants, and Stasander of Areia brings troops from Bactria. Some 18,700 infantry and 4600 cavalry are assembled (Diadorus). They gather in Alexander's campaign-tent at Susa in front of his empty throne. They agree to alliance, but the governors are wary of accepting Eumenes as their superior so he has to hold daily councils in Alexander's tent with the pretence that the late king is their joint, divine superior and all are equal.

Macedonian military prisoners from Alcetas' overrun governorship held by Antigonus, led by officers Attalus, Polemon, and Docimus, revolt in their mountain-top prison fortress and throw governor Xenopeithes off the cliffs; they seize the fortress but cannot agree about holding out or fleeing to Eumenes and are besieged by Antigonus' men.

Antigonus takes the abandoned Susa, where he leaves Seleucus to besiege the citadel while he marches after Eumenes; his army is ambushed as it crosses the River Cophrates (modern Dez) and 4000 killed. Antigonus occupies Ecbatana (late August?) and Eumenes retires further into Media and thence to Persepolis; he holds a grand rally of the Eastern provinces' troops at the site of the burnt Achaemenid palace's parade-ground to drum up support but is suspicious of the prominent role given by Peucestas to himself and the latter's acclaim from the crowds. He produces a forged letter from Macedon saying that Cassander is dead and Olympias in control of Macedon with Polyperchon already marching into Asia to catch Antigonus, to reassure his grumbling commanders that the war is going their way and avert a mutiny. He has Sibyrtius, governor of Arachosia and friend of Peucestas, accused of a 'plot' to intimidate the other officers, but his victim escapes. Antigonus offers money, a place in his army, or free passage home to settle in Macedon to Eumenes' soldiers to win them over but fails.

The armies confront each other warily.

October – Drawn battle of Paratacene, in Gabene (near Isfahan) between Antigonus and Eumenes: Eumenes sends fake deserters to Antigonus' camp saying that he will attack that night so Antigonus will stay on guard and he can have extra time to get a 'head start' on the march to fertile grazing-land and supplies at Gabene. Antigonus dashes after him with his cavalry in advance of Peithon with the infantry and is spotted moving onto hilly ground, and Eumenes thinks Antigonus has the entire army there and draws his men up for fight. He fails to attack so Peithon can join Antigonus and even the numbers; battle follows and Peithon's light cavalry on Antigonus' left wing are routed, but his right wing heavy cavalry, commanded by son Demetrius (in first battle aged nineteen/twenty) and elephants rout Eumenes' opposing wing. Both armies fail to secure victory and withdraw, but Antigonus has lost four times as many men and he leaves Gabene to Eumenes.

Eurydice, wife of king Philip III Arrhidaeus, persuades her husband to announce Polyperchon's dismissal while he is in Epirus with Alexander IV to arrange Olympias' return.

She (using Arrhidaeus) appoints Cassander as regent instead; he arrives from his current campaign in the Peloponnese to retake Polperchon's garrisons there.

Athens signs terms with Cassander, who is allowed to retain Munychia as its ally. Cassander installs the philosopher Demetrius of Phalerum at the head of new oligarchic regime under his control in Athens.

When Cassander returns to campaigning in the Peloponnese and is held up attacking Tegea, Olympias invades from Epirus with Polyperchon and the boy-king Alexander IV.

The army of Philip III Arrhidaeus and Eurydice surrenders to them on the battlefield at Euia in Dassaretia, and Olympias persuades Eurydice, in flight for Amphipolis, to return with fake promises.

Olympias imprisons them in a small cell at Pydna, but faces criticism for her harshness so she decides on murder. She kills the captive Arrhidaeus (who she probably hates as her late husband's bastard) after a reign of six years and four months (Diodorus), aged probably in late thirties, and Eurydice too, ordering Eurydice to commit suicide and offering her a noose, and massacres her enemies. She kills Cassander's brother Nicanor, and disinters the ashes of another brother, Iollas, Alexander 'the Great's late cupbearer – probably implying that he poisoned Alexander at Antipater or Cassander's request. Around 100 of Cassander's friends are slaughtered too.

Cassander abandons the siege of Tegea and marches back to Macedon, leaving Alexander son of Polyperchon in command in the Peloponnese.

Sicily

Agathocles leads a force of exiles on Syracuse and besieges the city until the regime agrees to admit him and his allies in supposed political truce. He swears allegiance to the city's democracy and is elected as their general, but then enrols assorted ruthless personal dependants from his exiles' force and his impoverished Syracusan supporters to the army so it answers only to him.

317/316 Winter

Diadochi

The Aetolians try to hold up Cassander at Thermopylae, but he transports his troops round the pass by sea.

Cassander sends one army under Attarhias to block the passes from Epirus to prevent aid from King Aecidas to his cousin Olympias and a second under Callas to hold up Polyperchon while he marches against a third, led by Antinuous and with the royal family, who is probably affected by resentment after Olympias' executions and faces desertions so he retreats to Amphipolis. Cassander besieges Olympias and her faction, including Alexander IV, Roxane, and Aecidas' daughter Deidamia (later married to Demetrius), in Pydna.

Aecidas, king of Epirus, is deposed by his countrymen who are unhappy at being forced to take part in his private family war on Olympias' behalf; they send to Cassander to arrange alliance and he agrees and sends Lyciscus as his representative to govern them and arrange for a new ruler.

Cassander marries one of Philip II's illegitimate daughters, Thessalonice (after whom he named new city of Thessalonica), to boost his legitimacy.

Mid-late December 317 – Antigonus attempts a complicated march round the salt desert between him and Eumenes to march at night without fires and attack him by surprise, letting it be known that he is attacking Armenia and leaving Eumenes alone to confuse the latter. But his army is spotted after his freezing men disobey orders to light fires; his army is only four days away from Eumenes as the latter hears and some of Eumenes' detachments are six days away so Eumenes cannot collect all his troops in time, but he refuses Peucestas' suggestions to retreat and lights a lot of his own fires to alarm Antigonus into thinking he has more men than in reality. Antigonus takes a less direct and dangerous route to attack Eumenes, allowing him to assemble his army in time; another stalemate follows.

316

January? – Antigonus defeats Eumenes at battle in Media: he has 22,000 infantry, 9000 cavalry, and 65 elephants (Diodorus). Eumenes' general Antigenes, commander of the 'Silver Shields', sends a representative out to hail the enemy soldiers and ask if they are wicked enough to fight against their fellow-veterans of the world-conquering army of Alexander, which has some effect on the Antigonid phalanx. Antigonus' main infantry force in phalanx is routed, but part of his cavalry, sent off at a distance to fall on the enemy baggage-train by surprise, is undetected in the dust raised by battle on the sandy terrain and captures it. Some of Eumenes' men disobey his orders and hasten to try to rescue their captured families and possessions which they fail to do; Peucestas in particular defies orders to join an attack on Antigonus' retreating infantry. The battle ends for the night, and the Eastern governors want to retreat but Eumenes refuses. Eumenes' troops insist on negotiations to release the captives. Antigonus promises their safety in return for handing over Eumenes, which is agreed.

Eumenes is captured and executed, along with leading ani-Antigonid officers who have joined him such as Antigenes (who is burnt alive), and Eudamas of the upper Indus province; the enemy's most prestigious regiments are broken up. Antigonus secures control of the eastern governorships. Peithon is promised security and continuation in Media in return for surrender, but plans a revolt; he is summoned to a meeting at Ecbatana and executed, and his officers led by Meleager revolt but are defeated and killed.

Antigonus is accepted as ruler of the East by a meeting of its leading nobles in Persia; Peucestas is deposed as governor of Persia but Tlepolemus keeps Carmania and Sibyrtius keeps Arachoisia; Oxyartes is kept on in the Paropamisadae/Hindu Kush as it would be too difficult to remove him; the 'Silver Shields' are dispersed and sent off in small groups to remote areas to be put on active duties with orders to their governors to see that they get killed. Antigonus loots Eumenes' treasure and that remaining at Susa (25,000 talents) for his own regime, which now controls all of the Asian part of Alexander's empire apart from Phoenicia and Palestine, which Ptolemy has seized during the Antigonus vs Eumenes war.

After wintering at Ecbatana, Antigonus holds court at Persepolis (its final appearance in active history) and then at Susa; he spends the summer in Mesopotamia and Seleucus is received at court.

Early spring? – Cassander forces Olympias and her faction to surrender, on promise of safety, after they run out of supplies, the elephants die, and she has to send some troops away from Pydna to find supplies; her governor Monimus surrenders Pella on the news, and Olympias has to write to order Antinuous at Amphipolis to surrender too. Cassander has Olympias tried by the Macedonian army, which includes relatives of her victims, and they sentence her to death; a 'hit squad' of 200 soldiers sent by Cassander to kill her refuses to obey, so she is executed by relatives of her victims, aged probably in late fifties. Alexander IV and Roxane fall into Cassander's hands and are interned as his powerless prisoners, now or later sent to Amphipolis under the control of the new ruler's henchman Glaucias; Cassander refuses to let the young king have the usual attendance of noble 'royal pages'. Antinuous is murdered too. The fiction that Cassander is only regent for Alexander IV is maintained, but in effect he is sole ruler.

State funerals for Philip III Arrhidaeus and Eurydice, probably at the tomb discovered in 1977 at Verghina (Aegae); Polyperchon flees to Epirus. Cassander founds new city of Cassandreia on the peninsula east of Pella, near the site of his later city of Thessalonica.

Polyperchon withdraws to Aetolia.

Antigonus' troops manage to end the siege of the prisoners from Alcetus' army after a year, when a convict who has been sent out secretly to appeal to Antigonus' wife Stratonice is arrested and shows the besiegers the secret path he used from the mountain-top; the rebels are overpowered by surprise and executed.

Cassander marches into Boeotia and refounds Thebes to secure the alliance of the Boeotians and so add to his security in central Greece. Alexander son of Polyperchon blocks the Isthmus of Corinth to him, so he sails to land at Epidaurus and secures the alliance of Argos and then most of Messenia by campaign.

Sicily

(probably 316 rather than 317; first half of year) Agathocles massacres his enemies, principally the oligarchic faction of the 'Six Hundred', with claims to a suddenly called assembly of the city's soldiers who he commands that he is the victim of a murder-plot by forty of the oligarchs so they sentence the plotters to death and he sends out killers to destroy all his foes under cover of the legal killings; he becomes 'Plenipotentiary of Syracuse', in effect sole ruler.

315

Diadochi
Ziboetes of Bithynia allies with Antigonus and is not deposed.

Spring? – Seleucus is ordered to produce his accounts, and claims he is immune from this as granted by Alexander; fearing the same fate as Peithon, he flees to Egypt to seek help from Ptolemy; Antigonus replaces him, and according to Diodorus hears a prediction by the Chaldaean astrologers that if Seleucus is replaced and flees abroad he will return successfully and kill Antigonus in battle so he sends envoys to recall him but fails. Antigonus goes on to Cilicia.

Lysimachus, Cassander and Ptolemy send a joint delegation to Antigonus to demand a share of the royal treasure and the reinstatement of Seleucus; Ptolemy wants recognition of the rule of Phoenicia and Palestine plus control of Syria and Cassander wants Cappadocia and Lycia. These terms are refused; a coalition is arranged against Antigonus by his three rivals, and he sends his nephew Polemaus to drive Cassander's representatives out of Cappadocia and envoys to Rhodes to secure naval aid. Polemaus relieves Amisus on the Black Sea from a siege by Cassander's officer Asclepiodorus and forces King Ziboetes of Bithynia into an alliance.

Antigonus founds the 'Cycladic League' to unite the central Aegean islands in his favour, centred on Delos; he sends Aristodemus of Miletus to the Peloponnese with money (1000 talents) and troops to join the refugee Polyperchon and to raise mercenaries to aid the latter against Cassander.

Antigonus invades Phoenicia, besieges Tyre, and founds a new fleet to challenge Ptolemy in the Eastern Mediterranean and assist his planned invasion of Egypt; the Rhodians send him timber for building ships. Ptolemy, however, occupies Cyprus via a fleet sent (with Seleucus on board) to assist King Nicocreon of Salamis and his allies.

Antigonus retakes Joppa and Gaza from Ptolemy's troops; Seleucus with the Ptolemaic fleet attacks Erythrae, in central Ionia near Chios, but withdraws as Polemaus arrives.

Antigonus is joined by Polyperchon's son and envoy Alexander during the siege of Tyre, and agrees to Polyperchon becoming his commander in Greece but insists that he, not Polyperchon, is now the legitimate regent of all the empire of Alexander IV; in that capacity he holds an assembly of all the Macedonians in his army, i.e. representing the nation, to try and condemn Cassander for the killing of Olympias and detention of Alexander IV and Roxane. He declares that the Greek states should be allowed autonomy and kept free of garrisons.

Cassander is thus portrayed as the friend of oligarchic tyranny, which his troops' massacre of 500 'rebels' at Argos assists; Ptolemy issues his own declaration supporting the autonomy and freedom of Greece too. Ptolemy sends his brother Menelaus, general Myrmidon the Athenian with 10,000 troops, and Polycleitus with 100 ships to Cyprus.

Asander, governor of Caria, defects from Antigonus to the alliance of Ptolemy, Lysimachus and Cassander; Antigonus sends his nephew Polemaus to deal with him and a long war follows.

Late summer? – Cassander lands from Macedon at Cenchrae, port of Corinth, with fifty ships lent to him by Ptolemy and retakes much of the Peloponnese, including Orchomenus, but not Messene; he attends the Nemean Games. After he has returned home his general Prepelaus continues the war, and succeeds in persuading Polyperchon's son Alexander, now commanding for his father at Corinth, to defect; Alexander is appointed Cassander's titular commander in the Peloponnese and Polyperchon withdraws south-west to Messene.

314

Sicily

Many Sicilian Greek cities, such as Messina, Akragas, and Gela, revolt against Agathocles' tyranny at Syracuse; Agathocles campaigns against Messina, which summons help from Sparta; Prince Acrotatus successfully asks to be allowed to command this force, and turns into a despot at Rhegium so he is deposed and flees for his life back to Sparta.

Autumn – The Carthaginian statesman Hamilcar negotiates a truce between the outnumbered rebels and Agathocles, whereby the latter is recognized as titular overlord by the rebel cities but they are in practice still autonomous. Back in Carthage, his foes prosecute him for giving away an advantage to the Greeks but he dies during the trial.

Diadochi

Aristodemus, as Antigonus' envoy, persuades the Aetolians to defect from Cassander to him.

Cassander invades Illyria against King Glaucias; he reaches the Adriatic coast and annexes the towns of Apollonia and Epidamnus there.

Autumn – Antigonus secures Lemnos and Imbros to control the trade-route to Greece from the Black Sea.

Assassination of Alexander, son of Polyperchon; his garrisons of Corinth and Sicyon are taken over by his widow Cratesipolis, independent of all the rival rulers.

Fall of Tyre gives Antigonus control of all Phoenicia; Polemaus defeats Asander and his new reinforcements from Macedon under Prepelaus, sent by Cassander.

Leaving Demetrius with a small army to face Ptolemy in southern Phoenicia, Antigonus takes his main army into Asia Minor en route for Caria while his fleet sails round by sea; he winters at Celenae.

?Zeno of Citium in Cyprus, later founder of the Stoic school of philosophy, goes to Athens as a student at the Academy.

313

Greece

King Aecidas is driven out of Epirus by Cassander's agents, along with his son Pyrrhus (the later king); he plans a counter-invasion but is defeated and killed by Cassander's brother Philip. Neoptolemus, the son of Alexander the Great's uncle Alexander and sister Cleopatra, probably in his late teens, becomes sole ruler as Cassander's nominee.

Diadochi

Early spring – Antigonus attacks Caria and forces Asander to surrender in return for keeping the province. But Asander soon changes his mind, rescues his hostage brother, and sends to Ptolemy and the other allies for help; Antigonus invades and either drives him out or kills him.

Antigonus sends an army by sea to the Peloponnese, led by his nephew Telesphorus, and drives out many of Cassander's garrisons; they secure all the north except Cratesipolis' Sicyon and Corinth, and then Polemaus lands on and conquers Euboea too after Telesphorus fails to take it.

Antigonus persuades Ophellas, Ptolemy's governor of Cyrene, to revolt to keep him occupied so he cannot send his fleet to help Lysimachus or Cassander.

Antigonus stirs up tribal revolt in Thrace, led by King Seuthes, against Lysimachus, planning to send troops across the Hellespont to assist it; however, Lysimachus holds him back at the straits and defeats the rebellion except for the city of Calatis (conquered 309), and then marches against Antigonus' troops; Seuthes defects again and blocks a crucial pass but Lysimachus defeats him again, forces him into an alliance, and defeats Antigonus' invaders.

Antigonus heads for the Propontis to invade Lysimachus' realm as his fleet moves up the coast; Byzantium, dominating the Bosphorus, remains neutral at Lysimachus' request to deny Antigonus a landing-point so invasion delayed.

Cassander sends a request for talks to Antigonus to gain time for his Greek dependencies to hold on against Telesphorus.

Cassander calls off negotiations with Antigonus as Lysimachus and Ptolemy sends more help.

Sicily

War between Agathocles and the Greek Sicilian rebels.

312

Greece

Alcetas, brother of Aecidas, becomes co-ruler of Epirus with Neoptolemus to win over disaffected factions within the ruling dynasty and pre-empt revolt.

Glaucias of Illyria retakes Apollonia and Epidamnus from Macedon to restore his position on the Adriatic coast.

Diadochi

Ptolemy concludes conquest of Cyprus, aided by Seleucus, and then raids Cilicia; Demetrius moves north to defeat them but they have sailed off.

Telesphorus, annoyed at Antigonus appointing Polemaus to supersede him as supreme commander in the Peloponnese, leaves his army and withdraws in a sulk to Elis; his looting mercenaries cause local disaffection and Polemaus loses valuable time forcing his submission in return for pardon.

Autumn – Ptolemy invades Palestine and decisively defeats Demetrius at the Battle of Gaza; Alexander's admiral Nearchus, now working for Antigonus, serves as Demetrius' lieutenant at the battle and may be killed there.

Sicily

Agathocles defeats the rebels and takes Messina, but a Carthaginian force lands in western Sicily to assist Akragas and Gela against him.

311

Diadochi

Spring – Ptolemy withdraws from northern Phoenica. Seleucus is given 1000 troops by Ptolemy and crosses the fringes of Antigonus' territory undetected to Mesopotamia; April ('1 Nisan' in local Persian calendar). He re-enters Babylon and expels Antiogonus' governor, and is welcomed by the populace. The Antigonid garrison holds the citadels briefly but have to negotiate their safe exits. The date of return of Seleucus is reckoned as the commencement of the new 'Seleucid era' in the Babylon calendar.

Demetrius invades but is driven out of Nabatea, across the Jordan and Gulf of Aqaba from Palestine, by local Arab tribal chieftains.

Autumn – General peace-conference between Antigonus, Ptolemy, Lysimachus, and Cassander at unknown site leads to 'Peace of the Dynasts'. All the above are recognized as the local viceroys /'generals' of King Alexander IV until his majority, with Cassander controlling Macedon and Greece, Lysimachus controlling Thrace but not Hellespontine Phrygia which he has to return to Antigonus, Ptolemy controlling Egypt/Cyrene/nearer Arabia/part of the Aegean but returning Phoenicia and Palestine to Antigonus. Seleucus is not invited or mentioned but Antigonus is recognized as 'Lord of Asia' so it is implicitly up to Seleucus to try to hold onto Babylonia by his own efforts. Polyperchon in the Peloponnese is abandoned to Cassander. The allies agree to allow the Greek city-states to become independent, but do not usually allow this in practice.

While the talks are concluding, Demetrius makes an attempt to drive Seleucus out of Babylon and enters the city while Seleucus is away campaigning to take over the Iranian plateau. He succeeds in occupying the half of the city west of the Euphrates while the Seleucid governor holds the citadels, but after he leaves for Syria Seleucus returns and harasses his supply-lines to Babylon. Eventually, Demetrius has to evacuate the city.

Greece

?Pyrrhus, son of Aecidas, invades Epirus with Illyrian help from King Glaucias to kill his pro-Cassander uncle, King Alcetas; he becomes co-ruler with Neoptolemus II.

Sicily

There is war between Agathocles and Carthage; Agathocles advances on Gela to offer them a garrison if they hold out against Carthage, but is afraid he will be refused a full garrison lest he seize power so he offers a few men to help them and smuggles extra in a few at a time;

once he has enough men inside they admit his army and he massacres his enemies there. He confronts the Carthaginian general Hamilcar son of Gisgo at the nearby river Himera, and the two armies each hold one bank with neither risking an attack so stalemate follows.

Battle of the River Himera: a Sicilian force crosses the river to drive off Carthaginian cattle for food, and is ambushed on their way back to the river but drives the enemy off and chases them back to their camp. Agathocles brings his main army up as he sees that the enemy camp is not guarded alertly, and takes the Carthaginians by surprise; the Sicilians are getting the better of the battle when enemy reinforcements from Libya land nearby and hurry to assist them. Agathocles loses around 7000 men to the Carthaginians' 500, and retires into Gela; Hamilcar marches east to besiege Syracuse and Agathocles has to return there.

310

Diadochi

?Now or within a year or so Cassander secretly kills Alexander IV, aged around fourteen, and his mother Roxane in custody at Amphipolis, probably by poison. They are probably buried at Aegae, where Alexander's tomb may have been discovered (1977); notably none of the other major dynasts ruling in Alexander's name bothers to enquire about his fate.

Antigonus' nephew Polemaeus rebels in the Peloponnese, incited by Cassander.

Summer – Antigonus invades Mesopotamia with a large army and retakes Babylon after street-fighting; possibly the destruction and the famine accompanying this war hastens the decline of the city. Seleucus manoeuvres to keep him at bay in a long campaign, and they finally meet for a pitched battle but the first day of this is indecisive. Seleucus mounts a successful dawn attack on the enemy camp. After this Antigonus has to retreat to Syria, and probably makes a treaty with Seleucus – at any rate, he abandons the Iranian satrapies, Bactria, Sogdiana and the upper Indus to Seleucus who secures them over the next few years.

Ptolemy recovers Cyprus; his brother Menelaus is appointed governor.

Sicily

August – Agathocles leaves Syracuse blockaded by Carthage but with enough grain to stop famine, while he sails to North Africa with his army to mount an attack on the Carthaginian homeland. He is joined by Ophellas, governor of Cyrene, who is planning a revolt against Ptolemy and conquest of Egypt; they allegedly plan alliance.

310/09

Crimea

Death of long-ruling king (since 349?), Paerisades, of the Bosporan Kingdom; war between sons Satyrus, Eumelus and Prytanis, which Eumelus wins.

309

Diadochi

Antigonus sends Polyperchon against Cassander in revenge for his support of Polemaus, assisted by a supposed son of Alexander 'the Great' by Barsine, widow of Darius III's

Greek mercenary general Memnon, called Heracles. (If genuine, he would probably have been born c.330 in Syria.) Polyperchon is defeated by Cassander in Boeotia and is unable to march on to the Peloponnese to co-ordinate his army with Ptolemy's when they land.

Ptolemy prepares for naval war in the Aegean versus Cassander and occupies Cos as his headquarters.

Death of long-ruling Agid king of Sparta (since 370), Cleomenes II; he is succeeded by his grandson, Areus son of Acrotatus.

Sicily

Agathocles' brother Antanger defeats the Carthaginians in Sicily.

309/8

Diadochi

Winter – Ptolemy based with his fleet on Cos. Birth of Ptolemy's eponymous second son, his eventual successor as Ptolemy II, on Cos – the baby's mother is Ptolemy's mistress Berenice, niece of his first wife, Eurydice, who she has by now supplanted. For the moment his son by Eurydice, Ptolemy later known as 'Ceraunus' ('the Thunderbolt'), remains his heir.

308

Ptolemy puts Polemaus to death on Cos; meanwhile, Antigonus has Cleopatra the younger full sister of Alexander 'the Great' murdered for allegedly planning to escape from internment in Asia Minor to join and marry Ptolemy, but claims it was an assassination by private individuals and executes the assassins.

Summer – Ophellas of Cyrene leads an army of 10,000 infantry and 600 cavalry, plus 10,000 non-combatants, from Cyrene along the African coast to Tunisia to aid Agathocles; the two armies join forces against Carthage, but within weeks Agathocles has Ophellas murdered on suspicion of trying to take over his army and enrols the Cyrene forces under his command.

Ptolemy conquers the Cyclades, taking Andros, and lands in Greece at Corinth; he garrisons that city and Sicyon, which Cratisopolis surrenders, and possibly plans to restore the 'Hellenic League' of 338 led by himself but with all of the Greek cities technically independent. But he is soon forced to evacuate his forces, possibly due to nervousness about an attack from Ophellas on Egypt.

Antigonus fights Seleucus.

Ptolemy sends troops to reoccupy Cyrene after he hears of Ophellas' death.

Polyperchon abandons his alliance with Ptolemy and goes over to Cassander, obligingly killing his pretender Heracles to remove a threat to him.

Lysimachus founds new capital of Lysimacheia in the Chersonese, Thrace.

Death of Cleomenes, king of Sparta; he is succeeded by Areus.

Sicily

Agathocles conquers Utica and other Carthaginian towns, including Hippo Acra/Bizerta.

307

Diadochi

Antigonus' son Demetrius sails across the Aegean from Ephesus to Attica with 250 ships and a fund of 5000 talents to win support, as part of a new plan by his father to win over the Greeks by proclaiming he intends to liberate them.

June? – He lands with a small squadron of twenty ships at the Piraeus where he catches Cassander's men by surprise, forces the Macedonian garrison of Munychia fortress to surrender, and is received by the Athenians who surrender the city. He deposes Demetrius of Phalerum, who is allowed to go into exile in Thebes – whence he goes to Egypt (c. 300?) and takes up a post at the emerging institution of the Great Library of Alexandria, which Ptolemy founds around this time.

Demetrius restores democracy to Athens and leaves it ungarrisoned, after a decade of oligarchy and a Macedonian garrison; he is proclaimed 'Saviour God' along with his father, probably the first deification of a living person on the Greek mainland except for the forced deification of Alexander in 324; two new civic tribes are named after Demetrius and Antigonus.

Stratocles leads the new pro-Antigonid regime in Athens; Demetrius besieges Megara.

Sicily

Agathocles takes 2000 troops off to Sicily as Xenodocus of Akragas is leading a successful rebellion against his authority there. His son Agatharchus is left in command in North Africa. Just before he lands at Selinus his generals Leptines and Demophilus defeat the rebels and kill 1500 of them, sending Xenodocus fleeing back into Akragas; Agathocles then forces Heraclea to submit, agrees to let the Carthaginians in Therma leave and the residents to sign up as his allies, and installs Leptines at Cephaloedium; he fails to take Centoripa by storm, and sacks Apollonia despite heavy losses; meanwhile, Deinocrates has taken over the rebel command as Xenodocus is eclipsed and raises around 20,000 infantry and 1500 cavalry for an inland campaign. This outnumbers Agathocles, who has to evade battle.

In his absence from Africa Archagathas' general Eumachus has successes in plundering attacks on inland cities, but the Carthaginians send out three separate armies from their blockaded capital to fight the Sicilians (and reduce the numbers of mouths to feed in the city) and Hanno defeats Aeschrion's army and Himilco ambushes Eudamus with a fake retreat into a city then surrounds and slaughters almost all his troops. Archagathus has to retreat to Tunis as his losses are severe, and sends to Agathocles warning of need for help; their allies desert the Sicilian army in Africa and Agathocles manages to sail back there after receiving unexpected naval help from Etruria in Italy, which aids him in breaking the Carthaginian sea blockade. Leptines, left in charge in Sicily, routs Xenodocus who is exiled from Akragas by angry citizens. Agathocles thinks the tide has turned in his favour, and attacks the Carthaginians but suffers a heavy defeat. He is saved from disaster as the enemy is sacrificing some of their captives after the battle when a strong wind causes the sacred fire to set their camp ablaze and his defecting Libyan mercenaries approach at the Carthaginian camp to be assumed to be attackers and are set upon; chaos follows. The Libyans flee back to the Greek camp, where they are assumed to be attacking and another clash follows. The casualties add to Greek despondency, and Agathocles plans to abandon his army and sail back to Sicily in secret with his intimates and his favourite son Heraclides; Archagathus finds out he is to be left behind as his father does not trust him, and tells assorted officers who start a mutiny. Agathocles is seized and bound, is released in subsequent chaos by sympathetic soldiers, and flees on board ship whereupon mutinous troops turn on and kill his sons.

Agathocles returns to Sicily, summons loyal troops, and plunders and massacres at Segesta to raise funds; he sells off the citizens' children in Italy as slaves and tells his brother Asander at Syracuse to execute the relatives of the mutineers who killed his sons, which is done.

306

Diadochi

Antigonus sends Demetrius with his fleet to Cyprus to tackle Ptolemy; with 15,000 men he besieges Ptolemy's brother Menelaus and his fleet in Salamis. Ptolemy arrives from Egypt with a relief-fleet and 25,000 men, and Demetrius defeats this in epic naval battle. Forty of Ptolemy's warships and 100 supply-ships are taken, and eighty warships are wrecked; a sally by Menelaus' fleet in Salamis is routed, and after the battle he flees and Salamis surrenders. Demetrius enrols the Cypriots in an army of 16,000 infantry and 6000 cavalry (Diodorus) to aid his father.

After the victory of Salamis, Antigonus assumes the title of 'King', followed by Demetrius, thus affirming their independence of the by now mythical kingship of Alexander IV who is accepted to be dead with no legitimate heirs, though this is not specifically stated. The timing may indicate that the late king's eighteenth birthday, i.e. coming-of-age, in August 305 would have been approaching so the 'regency' of the generals must end.

November – Ptolemy assumes the title of 'King'; he is followed by Cassander, Lysimachus, and Seleucus. This marks the formal end of Alexander's technically unified empire, though it has been defunct in effect since 317/16 and certainly since the unknown date of Alexander IV's death.

Death of Philip, younger son of Antigonus.

Antigonus marches on Egypt via Palestine, with 90,000 troops and 83 elephants; Demetrius brings his fleet of 150 ships to help him, but it is damaged by storms.

November? – Demetrius is left with too few ships to attack the well-defended Nile delta in Ptolemy's rear, and Ptolemy can hold onto his positions near Pelusium; Antigonus has to withdraw.

Sicily

Carthage makes peace with Agathocles, on the basis of the 'status quo'; he fights the democratic rebellion led by Deinocrates, but his general Pasiphilus deserts to the latter with assorted garrisons.

Winter 306/5?

Agathocles offers to resign the tyranny of Syracuse and leave and let democracy be restored to the city with an amnesty for Deinocrates and his exiles, but Deinocrates refuses to ratify the treaty as he hopes one more push will enable his faction to take over Syracuse on their terms; the war continues.

305

Diadochi

Demetrius brings 270 warships to besiege the eastern Aegean maritime city-state of Rhodes, for refusing to break off its grain-trade with Ptolemy and sending help to Ptolemy's grain-ships to drive off Antigonid ships during the Egyptian war.

June? – On his arrival the Rhodians offer to break off alliance with Ptolemy and sign up to his father instead, but he demands 1000 prominent hostages and the admission of his ships to the city harbour, which is refused. The citizens send to Antigonus' enemies, and Ptolemy sends ships to run the blockade of the city and bring supplies. Demetrius' siege of the capital sees him inventing many ingenious siege-artillery machines, and a battle of wits between him and the defenders. He earns the resultant nickname of 'Poliorcetes', 'The Besieger', but he cannot take the city.

Cassander advances into Attica and besieges Athens; Demochares leads the defence and the Antigonid general Olympiodorus launches an attack on Cassander's supply-route by land from Aetolia, taking Elatia.

?Death of the Eurypontid king Eudamidas of Sparta (or as late as 300); he is succeeded by his son Archidamus (IV).

Sicily

Battle near Torgium: Agathocles and his c.5000 infantry and 800 cavalry are outnumbered by around four to one by Deinocrates (Diodorus), but put up a stronger fight and around 2000 of the democrats who are at odds with Deinocrates desert him. Deinocrates is unexpectedly defeated, and Agathocles pursues the retreating enemy and lures a body of 4000 infantry into laying down their arms on promise of pardon and massacres them. Eventually, assorted pardons win over significant numbers of the rebels, including Deinocrates himself who is given a military command in return for killing the ex-Agathoclean 'traitor' Pasiphilus at Gela.

Agathocles secures control of all Greek Sicily.

304

Diadochi

Demetrius wheels a massive, 120-foot high siege-tower, the 'helepolis' ('taker of cities'), up to the land wall of Rhodes city, and batters the wall down, but finds that the inhabitants have demolished buildings including a theatre and temples inside to construct a new wall behind the original; he turns down assorted attempts at mediation with the city authorities by neutrals. Ptolemy's relief-fleet sails into the harbour with a large quantity of corn, with the aid of a wind that holds up Demetrius' intercepting squadron.

Rhodes – Demetrius has to negotiate peace on the basis of the status quo as Antigonus sends urgent messages for his help from his fleet; the Aetolians mediate and the Rhodians agree to send help to Antigonus for all campaigns except those against Ptolemy, in return for their autonomy. The Rhodians proclaim Ptolemy as 'Saviour God' for helping them, and subsequently commission the great harbourside statue of Apollo, the 'Colossus of Rhodes', to commemorate the siege.

Cassander returns to besiege Athens again, and takes Salamis; he sends troops into the Peloponnese.

Autumn – Demetrius returns to Greece, and the Aetolians and Boeotians soon agree terms with him. Demetrius relieves Athens, and Cassander withdraws from Attica; he goes on to retake the Macedonian base of Phyle in northern Attica and marches into the Peloponnese to expel Cassander's garrisons.

Crimea
Spartocus succeeds his father Eumelus in the Bosporan kingdom.

India
?Seleucus makes peace with Chandragupta, ruler of the new 'Maurya' dynastic state in the Ganges valley, who is rapidly expanding his new empire into Northern India and may have already overthrown the Alexandrian ally-state of 'Porus' and invaded the upper Indus valley. The Indus states are ceded to Chandragupta, with the Paropamisadae/ Hindu Kush as the new frontier; Chandragupta sends elephants to Seleucus' army.

Sicily
Agathocles assumes the title of 'King' like the Alexandrian ex-empire rulers. He levies a heavy fine on the Liparae Islands.

303

Diadochi
Spring – Based in Athens, Demetrius recaptures Sicyon from Ptolemy's garrison under Philip and the citadel garrison surrenders in return for a safe exit; he then expels Cassander's garrison under Prepelaus from Corinth and agrees to citizens' request to restrict his garrison to the Acrocorinth citadel. He invades and secures the adherence of most of the northern and central Peloponnese, capturing Bura, Scyrus, and Orchomenus where he crucifies Polyperchon's commander Strombichus and his supporters as an example.

?Demetrius moves the location of Sicyon and founds a new city.

Polyperchon is restricted to Messenia, and is rendered militarily harmless to his rivals; he dies within a year or so, aged ?in his late seventies.

Demetrius apparently installs his mistress Lamia in the Parthenon at Athens, which he makes his new official residence as he is a 'god'. (303/2) He marries Deidamia, sister of his new ally King Pyrrhus of Epirus – their father, Aecidas (d. 313), was first cousin to Olympias, mother of Alexander 'the Great'.

?Exile of Demochares from Athens for intrigues against Demetrius and Stratocles.

303–2

Italy
Cleonymus of Sparta, uncle of King Areus, is sent to southern Italy with Spartan troops to answer a local appeal for aid from Tarentum against the Lucanians and Bruttians.

302

Diadochi
?Pyrrhus is exiled from Epirus by a coup on behalf of his young cousin and rival, Neoptolemus II (the son of King Alexander, d. 331, and his niece and wife Cleopatra, sister of Alexander 'the Great'), while he is campaigning in Illyria. He joins Demetrius.

Lysimachus allies to Cassander, who invites him to a 'summit' to discuss war on Antigonus; they send envoys to Ptolemy and Seleucus for a planned joint attack on Antigonus, the most dangerous foe of all three.

May/June? – Lysimachus crosses the Hellespont and invades northern Ionia; governors Phoenix and Docimus desert to him. Antigonus, at his new capital of 'Antigoneia' in northern Syria, to hold Games, is apparently unaware of the extent of the danger; Lysimachus campaigns in Hellespontine Phrygia and the Macedonian troops and general (Prepelaus) loaned to him by Cassander move south to take Adramyttium, Ephesus, and the Antigonid Ionian headquarters, Sardes (except the citadel).

Demetrius refounds the 'Hellenic Confederation' at Corinth with himself as leader and invades Thessaly with c.55,000 men; Cassander, with around 30,000 men, avoids battle and manoeuvres to hold him up in a defensive action; there is stalemate until Demetrius is summoned back to Asia Minor by his father as the latter arrives in Ionia to fight Lysimachus.

Antigonus sends a force to Babylon to hold Seleucus back; he leads his main army to Phrygia to fight Lysimachus who is joined by the retreating Prepelaus, outmanovures them but cannot bring them to battle, and besieges them at Dorylaeum.

Demetrius concludes a truce with Cassander and sails to Asia Minor.

Seleucus and his main army arrive in central/eastern Asia Minor (Cappadocia), ignoring a feint by Antigonus' Syrian army into Mesopotamia by marching north via Armenia; Lysimachus retires north-west out of Antigonus' reach for the winter; Antigonus bases himself at Celenae.

Cassander recovers Thessaly after Demetrius leaves and sends his brother Pleistarchus by land to join Lysimachus and Prepilaus.

Demetrius arrives by sea at Ephesus and recovers it from Lysimachus' garrison; he sails up the coast, recapturing the local towns, to the Chersonese and takes Lampsacus. He bases himself at Chalcedon, so when Pleistarchus arrives the latter cannot cross the Bosphorus or Hellespont for Demetrius' blockade. Pleistarchus moves north up the Black Sea coast to Odessus, acquires ships, and sails his men across to Heraclea in Bithynia in groups; one contingent is destroyed by a storm, and another is caught and destroyed by Demetrius. Pleistarchus arrives safely with around 14,000 of original 20,000 troops.

Ptolemy besieges Sidon, but makes a truce and retires to Egypt on a false rumour that Seleucus and Lysimachus have been defeated by Antigonus.

?Mithridates, who is to found the kingdom of Pontus, inherits the rule of the city of Cius and the province of Paphlagonia from his uncle (?) Mithridates II, son of Ariobarzanes, who is killed when about to defect from Antigonus to Cassander.

301

Seleucus and Lysimachus join forces and advance against Antigonus and Demetrius in Phrygia; Ptolemy, meanwhile, invades Syria but contents himself with occupying Palestine and Phoenicia but cannot take Tyre or Sidon.

Battle of Ipsus in Phrygia: Antigonus and Demetrius versus Seleucus, his son Antiochus, and Lysimachus; both armies have around 80,000 men.

Demetrius with his cavalry on the Antigonid right wing defeats the opposing Seleucid cavalry, but charges off after Antiochus and leaves the Antigonid infantry phalanx exposed.

The latter are ground down by the rest of the allies, and Demetrius returns to be blocked from rescuing the infantry by Seleucus' elephants, which terrify his horses. Antigonus is killed, aged around eighty, and the Antigonid army is destroyed.

Demetrius retires to Ephesus with the remnants of the army; on news of the battle Athens expels his wife Deidamia and his garrison and proclaims its independence.

301–300

Diadochi
Demetrius returns to Greece to base himself at Corinth; Pyrrhus is one of his commanders and builds up a force ready to attack Epirus. Seleucus and Lysimachus divide Asia Minor; Seleucus, Lysimachus, Ptolemy, and Casander meet to divide up the conquered realm of Antigonus Monopthalmus.

Lysimachus gets Ionia and the western coast with the lands west of the River Halys (including Lydia and Phrygia), Seleucus the centre and east. Cassander's younger brother Pleistarchus gains a small realm in Lycia and Cilicia.

?Cassander apparently allows his brother Alexarchus to launch utopian claims with his newly built city on the Mount Athos peninsula as 'Ouranopoulis', 'realm of the Heavens'. All Cassander gets at the conference is official recognition as king of Macedon.

300

Diadochi
Demetrius' family and remaining troops in Attica are based at Megara. The Athenians send a delegation to Demetrius, at Delos, to explain their action and he requests the return of some warships from the Piraeus; he sets up his Greek headquarters at Corinth. He and Deidamia go to Ephesus to rally his Ionian port garrisons against Lysimachus. His fleet holds Tyre and Sidon in Phoenicia.

(or 299) Demetrius overruns the Chersonese while Lysimachus is busy in Ionia; he humiliates Lysimachus' army by ambushing and looting its baggage, and the troops mutiny against Lysimachus but are slaughtered by him.

May – Seleucus founds Antioch, named after his father Antiochus, on the lower reaches of the River Orontes as his new capital in Syria, within reach of the sea, Egypt, Asia Minor, and Mesopotamia – thus stressing his imperial intentions holding the central lands of Alexander's empire. Its port down-river on the coast is Seleucia Pieria.

?Ptolemy marries off his daughter by his second wife Berenice, Arsinoe II, to the widower Lysimachus who wants his fleet to help in conquering Ionia; he marries one of his daughters by his first wife Euydice, Lysandra, to Cassander's younger son Alexander.

Asia Minor
Mithridates, a Persian-Anatolian dynast claiming Achaemenid descent who possibly fought at Ipsus, founds an independent realm in Pontus on the south coast of the Black Sea, north-east Asia Minor, out of easy reach of the rival Successor realms; the capital is Amisus.

299

Diadochi

Seleucus and Demetrius arrange a marriage-alliance, with Demetrius' daughter by Phila, Stratonice, to marry the much older Seleucus; Demetrius sails to Cyprus to collect his daughter for her wedding, and collects his late father's abandoned treasure at Quinda/ Cyinda. This is part of Pleistarchus' realm, but its king's rights to it are ignored. Cassander wanted the treasure for himself and protests, and Demetrius later sends his wife Phila to her brother to calm him. Demetrius and Phila escort Stratonice to Rhosus, where Seleucus is waiting and the wedding takes place on his flagship.

Demetrius then lands troops in Cilicia and Lycia to overrun them and expel Pleistarchus, who flees to Lysimachus and then on to Macedon.

298

Diadochi

Demetrius refuses to hand over Cilicia to Seleucus, who plans to attack his isolated stronghold at Tyre (main last remnant of Antigonid Phoenicia) in retaliation.

Death of Cassander, probably of tuberculosis and after a lingering illness, aged around sixty. He is succeeded by his eldest son Philip IV, who is already in poor health and may have the same illness.

(or 299) Pyrrhus goes to Egypt at Demetrius' suggestion as his representative, and tries to get Ptolemy's aid for an attack on Epirus, his hopes probably aided by the death of Cassander and illness of Philip; he marries Antigone, Ptolemy's stepdaughter (daughter of his current wife, Berenice, by her previous husband Philip).

Deidamia, Pyrrhus' sister, joins her husband Demetrius in Cilicia and dies; Seleucus approaches Ptolemy to arrange for Demetrius to marry Ptolemais, one of his daughters by Eurydice. The marriage has to wait as the bride is under-age.

297

Diadochi

Death of Philip IV of Macedon; his mother, Cassander's widow Thessalonice, the daughter of Philip II and half-sister of Alexander, organizes the division of the kingdom between her remaining sons, Antipater (east) and Alexander V (west). Antipater is backed by his father-in-law, Lysimachus.

Ptolemy sends an expedition to Epirus while Macedon is distracted to install Pyrrhus as king; they, however, have to accept Pyrrhus' rival Neoptolemus continuing as co-ruler.

Lysimachus sends his son by Phila's and Cassander's sister Nicaea, Agathocles, to invade the tribal lands of the Getae north of the Danube after raiding; King Dromicheites defeats and captures Agathocles, and Lysimachus is forced to sign a non-aggression treaty and marry his daughter off to the king.

Asia Minor

Ziboetes, local-born governor of Bithynia, proclaims himself king to found an independent state.

296

Diadochi

The demagogue Lachares takes over the government of Athens; his foes withdraw to the Piraeus and the city is split as in 403.

Demetrius sails from Cilicia to Greece, hoping for an invitation from Demochares' opponents in the Piraeus; this does not occur so he invades Peloponnese.

With Demetrius preoccupied in Greece, Seleucus and Lysimachus overrun and divide up his dominions on the south coast of Asia Minor; Seleucus gains Cilicia; Lysimachus gains the west; Ptolemy overruns Cyprus – where he allows Demetrius' family (wife Phila and children) to go to him in Athens-Lycia, and Pamphylia.

295

Diadochi

Demetrius campaigns in the Peloponnese, and is seriously wounded by a catapult-bolt in the jaw while besieging Messene; while he is absent Ptolemy lands in Attica, and Athens surrenders to him; Demetrius returns to besiege it and drives Ptolemy's fleet out of Piraeus so he can starve the city out.

Pyrrhus murders Neoptolemus II at a meeting at Passaron and seizes sole rule of Epirus.

Spring – Demetrius starves Athens into surrender, and Lachares loots the city's temple treasures and melts down the gold robe of the statue of Athena in the Parthenon to pay his troops. Ptolemy sends a fleet of 150 ships to relieve Athens; it arrives offshore but withdraws as a larger fleet of Demetrius appears. Lachares flees and Athens surrenders; Demetrius occupies it. This time his regime is more harsh and he installs a permanent garrison.

Antipater murders his mother, Thessalonice, to seize sole rule of his half of Macedon, and prepares war against his brother Alexander V who appeals to Pyrrhus (his wife Lysandra's step-sister's husband) for aid.

294

Diadochi

Pyrrhus aids Alexander V to drive Antipater back, but then takes the western frontier districts of Macedon for himself as the price of his aid. Alexander agrees to peace with Antipater, as he is pressurized by Lysimachus to keep Pyrrhus out of Macedon as his price for not intervening either.

Demetrius continues his planned campaign in the Peloponnese, defeating King Archidamus of Sparta at the battle of Mantinea and advancing to the outskirts of Sparta itself where he kills 200 Spartiates in a skirmish. He blockades Sparta, but at this point receives an urgent request from Alexander and heads back to Athens and on to Macedon.

Alexander changes his mind about Demetrius' aid before Demetrius arrives; he meets Demetrius at the border-town of Dium, where at a banquet Alexander either plans to murder Demetrius or the latter pretends that he was warned of this plot as an excuse. In any event, Demetrius hurries from the room telling his guards at the door to kill Alexander who is following him; the Macedonian army believes Demetrius' explanations, and hails

Demetrius as king, his wife Phila being their late king Cassander's daughter. Antipater flees to Lysimachus, who refuses to help him and agrees a treaty that recognizes Lysimachus' rights to west Asia Minor and mainland Ionia in return for his not attacking Macedon.

293

Diadochi
Demetrius conquers Thessaly.

292

Diadochi
Seleucus appoints his son (by Apame the Persian, married in 324 at the Opis feast) Antiochus, aged around twenty, as his co-ruler. At about this time Seleucus apparently divorces Stratonice after discovering that Antiochus is in love with her and hands her to his son.

Demetrius double-crosses Lysimachus by invading north-west Asia Minor from the Chersonese, but has to evacuate it as revolt breaks out in mainland Greece.

Boeotians rebel against Demetrius, led by Pisis of Thespiae and assisted by King Cleonymus of Sparta; they are attacked and Thebes is besieged by Demetrius' son Antigonus Gonatas. Demetrius arrives and marches into Boeotia, and the rebels submit. Once he has left the district, Thebes revolts against him.

Lysimachus is defeated and captured by the tribal Getae under King Dromicheites north of the Danube, when he crosses the river to punish them for the earlier humiliation of 297 and is lured into the plains and surrounded and has to surrender after defeat. He has to promise to leave their lands alone before he is released.

291

Diadochi
Demetrius successfully besieges and forces Thebes to surrender despite receiving a neck-wound; he spares the city but has thirteen of his leading opponents executed.

290

Diadochi
?Pyrrhus' wife Lanassa breaks with him and declares herself head of an independent state on Corcyra; she asks Demetrius for help and he sails to Corcyra to lend her assistance and marry her, humiliating Pyrrhus. Possibly his polygamy, though in line with Philip II's practice, increases rising dislike of his luxurious and un-Macedonian lifestyle and autocracy in Macedon as an insult to the popular Phila.

Demetrius invades Aetolia but is repulsed as Pyrrhus comes to the aid of the Aetolians and defeats his general Pantouches; however, he is able to found a new port-city headquarters of Demetrias in Thessaly around this date to control the region. He plans to build a new navy to restore his rule of the south-eastern Mediterranean and evict Ptolemy.

Demetrius is snubbed by the Aetolians, who run the Pythian Games at Delphi, as they do not invite him or his allies to attend; he holds alternative Games a few weeks later at Athens, with a grand reception for him and Lanassa, which is subsequently seen as hubristic with its hymns to them as divine beings.

289

Diadochi/Asia Minor
?Amestris, divorced local ex-wife of Lysimachus and ruler of the eponymous town in north Asia Minor, is overthrown and murdered by her sons; Lysimachus expels them and conquers the town.

Autumn – While Demetrius is ill, Pyrrhus invades western Macedonia; he recovers and drives Pyrrhus out. He prepares an expensive and unpopular expedition to attack Ptolemy in southern Asia Minor, then possibly Seleucus too to restore his father's Asian realm .

Sicily
Death of Agathocles, as ruler of all the region based at Syracuse, aged seventy-three; his realm breaks up as no heir.

288

Diadochi
Pyrrhus invades the west of Macedon while Lysimachus invades the east and Ptolemy's fleet cruises the eastern Mediterranean and threatens to aid a Peloponnesian revolt; Demetrius sends Antigonus south and marches against Lysimachus, but the latter mounts a defensive campaign behind trenches and Demetrius cannot bring him to battle.

Discovering that the allies' plan is to keep him occupied while Pyrrhus invades his heartland, he abandons his eastern front and hurries back to Edessa to confront Pyrrhus. His army mutinies, with his harsh and imperious rule and financial extortion alienating the citizen-soldiers, and he has to flee Macedon to his fleet. Phila refuses to accompany him and commits suicide at Cassandreia.

Pyrrhus takes western Macedon and Lysimachus the east; Demetrius bases his remaining troops and his fleet at Corinth.

286

Diadochi
Ptolemy's fleet lands in the Piraeus and Athens revolts, blockading Demetrius' garrison until they agree to leave.

Demetrius besieges Athens again, but this time it holds out and envoy Crates persuades him to give up and leave. His garrison in the Piraeus fortress, Munychia, remains, to keep Ptolemy's forces out of the harbour.

285

Diadochi
Demetrius sails to Ionia and conquers much of it, based at Sardes; his son Antigonus Gonatas remains in Greece in charge of his forces there. Ptolemy's ex-wife Eurydice joins him, bringing her daughter, his fiancée Ptolemais, who he belatedly marries at Miletus. (They later have a son, Demetrius 'the Fair'.)

Athenians attack Antigonus' garrison of the Piraeus and are heavily defeated.

Agathocles, Lysimachus' son by his first wife Nicaea (sister of Demetrius' late wife Phila and of Eurydice), campaigns against Demetrius in Ionia and holds his forces back as he withdraws inland and lures Demetrius away from his headquarters and reinforcements. He then marches quickly to Demetrius' rear to take Sardes, cutting him off from the sea.

Pyrrhus invades Thessaly to drive Antigonus' troops back.

Demetrius abandons the campaign in Ionia and decides to challenge Seleucus for the rule of eastern Asia Minor, including his own ex-lands in Cilicia, then Syria. He marches east, shadowed by Agathocles at first and then by Seleucus' larger army, which both avoid battle, and heads to Cilicia. The strain of the march causes some of his mercenaries to desert, but he reaches the plains and enters Tarsus.

Pyrrhus overruns Thessaly. The Athenians expel Antigonus' garrison from the Piraeus.

Ptolemy associates his son by Berenice, Ptolemy, as co-ruler, possibly due to illness as he is around eighty.

284

Diadochi

Demetrius heads off into the Amanus mountains to avoid the blocked main passes into Syria and take Seleucus by surprise; the harsh weather and lack of supplies causes many of his men to desert and the rest are demoralized as he reaches the plain to confront Seleucus.

On the battlefield, Demetrius' men refuse to fight as they are confronted by Seleucus' larger army and elephants; they respond to a personal appeal from Seleucus to defect to him, and Demetrius slips away to avoid capture. He is soon captured and is interned in a palace near Antioch, while his army takes service with Seleucus and Philocles hands over his fleet to Ptolemy.

Seleucus takes Demetrius' territory in Cilicia and southern Asia Minor; Lysimachus secures all of Ionia and asks Seleucus to execute Demetrius, which he refuses to do. Antigonus Gonatas rules the remaining garrisons in Greece, minus Athens.

Lysimachus defeats Pyrrhus at the battle of Edessa and overruns western Macedon, followed by Thessaly.

Ptolemy Ceraunus, Ptolemy's superseded son by Eurydice, flees from his father's court to Thrace and joins Lysimachus.

Lysimachus overruns Paeonia, thus driving Pyrrhus back to the old borders of Epirus.

Arsinoe II apparently makes her husband Lysimachus kill his popular son Agathocles on suspicion of an alleged plot after failing to poison him, possibly to secure the succession for herself or a relative. Alternatively, Lysimachus and his wife pre-empt a coup by Agathocles who is afraid of being superseded by Arsinoe's sons in the succession. Ptolemy Ceraunus aids Agathocles' widow Lysandra, also his half-sister, and Agathocles' half-brother Alexander in fleeing to Seleucus' court (284/3?) to turn him against Lysimachus.

283

Diadochi

Demetrius dies of alcoholic poisoning in internment in Syria, aged fifty-three or -four; his body is returned to Antigonus Gonatas by Seleucus.

Lysimachus unsuccessfully invades Epirus.

Death of Ptolemy in Egypt, aged probably around eighty-two; he is succeeded by his son by Berenice, Ptolemy II 'Philadelphus' ('Brother Lover'), aged twenty-six.

282

Italy
Rome sets up a garrison at Rhegium, and assists Thurii against local inland tribes but then sets up a garrison there too. The alarmed Tarentines decide to resist and sink a Roman naval squadron that enters their harbour; they then evict the Romans from Thurii and prepare for war.

Sicily
Phintias of Acragas destroys and levels Gela.

Diadochi
Seleucus invades western Asia Minor to deal with Lysimachus; he moves on to Ionia and Lysimachus' treasurer Philetaerus surrenders the Lysimachid treasury at Pergamum, apparently having been in touch with Seleucus earlier to arrange this in return for a promise of governorship of the city. Philetaerus becomes or remains governor of Pergamum; it is the foundation of the dynasty that will rule there to 133. Apparently, Lysandra and Ptolemy Ceraunus accompany Seleucus, probably to remind the late Agathocles' local admirers of his father's tyranny.

281

Diadochi
Seleucus invades Lysimachus' western Asia Minor lands, and kills him in battle at Corupedium (aged about seventy-five). Lysimachus is apparently killed by a javelin in combat. Seleucus overruns the rest of western Anatolia except for Bithynia, and lays claim to Thrace and Macedon. Ptolemy Ceraunus seizes control of Thrace and Macedon, officially for Seleucus, and sends envoys to Pyrrhus to negotiate an alliance.

Antigonus Gonatas recovers control of Athens to complete his rule of central-southern Greece.

Italy
Appeal for help from Tarentum to Pyrrhus against the encroachment of Rome; he decides to accept and take his army to Italy, and so recognizes Ceraunus as king of Macedon and Thrace.

280

Greece/Seleucids
Seleucus crosses from the Troad to Chersonese and marches on Macedonia, but Ptolemy Ceraunus comes to met him at Lysimacheia and assassinates him.

Death of Seleucus, aged around eighty, leaves his kingdom to his son Antiochus I, probably in his late thirties; Ptolemy Ceraunus seizes control of Macedon and fights off a naval attack by Antigonus Gonatas. The latter secures the Chersonese.

Antiochus I has to return to Syria to deal with an invasion of Palestine and Phoenicia by Ptolemy II; Antigonus survives between the two large kingdoms of Antiochus and Ceraunus but his main power is in Greece.

Ceraunus marries Lysimachus' widow Arsinoe II, his half-sister, to secure control of her late husband's kingdom of Thrace but soon faces tribal uprisings.

Italy
Pyrrhus sends his envoy Cineas the Thessalian with 3000 men to Tarentum to promise help, and follows himself with a large army of 25,000 men and 20 elephants, which have not been seen in Italy before.

May – Pyrrhrus sails, but is shipwrecked off the south-east cape of Italy by a storm en route as his royal galley hits the rocks. Some of his accompanying ships are sunk with most of his elephants so he has to struggle to Tarentum by land to meet Cineas' force there; reinforcements arrive later. He drills the locals into competent troops fighting in Macedonian style.

Pyrrhus invades Apulia, and confronts Roman consul/general Valerius Laevinus near Heraclea; he sends a herald saying that he can mediate between Rome and the Italian Greeks if the Romans are willing, but is rebuffed. The Romans cross the river to attack before Epirot reinforcements arrive, and Pyrrhus leads a cavalry attack to try to catch them midstream but has to fight on land. He defeats Laevinus at the Battle of Heraclea by wearing down Roman infantry with his phalanx, luring them to attack a friend wearing his armour who is killed while he lurks among his infantry ready to counter-attack when the Romans think they have won, then sending in his elephants to tear holes in their line before a cavalry charge. But his losses are proportionately severe – 15,000 Romans and 13,000 Greeks according to Dionysius of Halicarnassus; 7000 Romans and 4000 Greeks according to Hieronymus.

Pyrrhus marches on into Latium, joined by local Lucanians and Samnites; he sends Cineas to Rome to demand the independence of the cities of southern Italy and withdrawal of Romans from that region as his price for peace. This is refused despite his offers of gifts.

Pyrrhus returns to southern Italy for the winter; his troops at Rhegium mutiny and the locals send to Rome for help; they send a mercenary force, which seizes the town as pirates and evicts the inhabitants.

Greece
Areus the Spartan king leads a Peloponnesian revolt against Antigonus Gonatas; Argos, Patras, Achaean and Arcadian cities, Elis, and Boeotia expel Macedonian garrisons.

Seleucids
?Ziboetes, kin of Bithynia, repels a Seleucid attack.

?Defeat of general Diodorus, entrusted by Seleucus to defeat independent ruler Mithridates I of Pontus; seen as start of Pontus' independent role beyond Seleucid control.

279

Greece
A horde of 'Gauls' (culturally what was later known as 'Celts', a term not used by contemporaries, kin to the tribes of northern Italy and Switzerland and Gaul) under Boius

invade Macedon in the chaos after Seleucus' death. They defeat and kill King Ptolemy 'Ceraunus', aged probably in thirties; his army is destroyed and the countryside, towns, and cities are plundered. His brother Meleager succeeds to a precarious kingship but is unsuccessful against the Gauls and is later deposed by the general Sosthenes, who rallies the army.

Antipater, nephew of Cassander, briefly reigns in Macedonia but is helpless as a military leader against the Gauls and is deposed too.

Some of the Gauls under 'Brennus' (Gallic term for 'King') move south to outflank a blocking central Greek force at Thermopylae; they cross Aetolia and sack the sanctuary at Delphi, but are driven out and their loot recovered by an Aetolian force.

Seleucids/Egypt

Antiochus is distracted by a threat to Asia Minor by Antigonus Gonatas, based in the Chersonese, and his ally Nicomedes the new king of Bithynia. They invade Ionia and fight Antiochus, but later agree to a treaty. While Antiochus is preoccupied, Ptolemy II invades and overruns Palestine and Phoenicia.

Italy

Pyrrhus invades Apulia, besieges Venusia, and defeats the Romans at the battle of Asculum; either on one or two days. The casualties amount to either 6000 Romans and 3505 Greeks (Hieronymus) or to 15,000 on the two sides (Dionysius). The high Greek losses allegedly lead to Pyrrhus saying that one more such victory would ruin him, hence 'Pyrrhic victory'.

Pyrrhus sends Cineas to Rome again and offers friendship and alliance in return for recognizing the independence of just Tarentum; this is rejected. According to tradition this is due to the advice to the Senate of the aged ex-consul Appius Claudius 'Caecus' ('the Blind'), builder of Rome's main road to southern Italy the 'Via Appia': alternatively, the incident may occur on Cineas' first embassy.

Consul Caius Fabricius visits Pyrrhus to discuss prisoner-exchange; according to Plutarch, Pyrrhus' doctor offers to poison him to help Rome but the latter refuses and warns Pyrrhus.

278

Greece

One horde of Gauls ravage Macedon and Thrace; another crosses the Hellespont into north-west Asia Minor at the request of King Nicomedes of Bithynia, who wants mercenaries against the Seleucids ?to conquer Phrygia, but he cannot control or satisfy them with money and they start ravaging the region.

Sosthenes, a general, holds out in central/coastal Macedon. ?Antigonus Gonatas, based in the Chersonese, marries Phila II, the daughter of Seleucus and his own sister Stratonice, in a Seleucid alliance with Antiochus I (Phila's mother's current husband) to gain him Seleucid help to retake Macedon.

Egypt

Ptolemy II is in Palestine at the start of a campaign to overrun the east shores of the Red Sea and control local trade-routes.

Sicily

Threat of Carthaginian conquest causes Sostratus of Acragas to call in Pyrrhus for aid, backed by Syracuse and Leontinoi. Pyrrhus is offered possession of the three cities for a campaign. He leaves Roman war to cross to Sicily (autumn) and march west, turning down the chance to make another attempt on Macedon instead.

277

Greece

Gauls ravage Epirus and sack the Oracle at Dodona; there is chaos in Macedon.

Seleucids

Western and central Asia Minor are plundered by Gauls who have crossed from Thrace; at around this time they coalesce into a new tribal settlement in 'Galatia', east of Ionia. There is no immediate response from Antiochus due to Ptolemaic threat to Syria. Philetaerus of Pergamum holds out against the Gauls, starting his city's rise to local power.

Egypt

Ptolemy II completes his conquest of modern Jordan and north-west Arabia, to control the east shore of the Red Sea.

Sicily

Pyrrhus defeats the 'Mamertine' mercenary brigands who are based at Messina and are ravaging across eastern Sicily, forcing them to return loot and agree to peace. He overruns most of Carthaginian western Sicily, capturing the citadel on Mount Eryx; he besieges the main Carthaginian west coast fortress/port at Lilybaeum. Carthage offers him terms of abandoning all of Sicily but Lilybaeum, which he refuses. He plans to invade North Africa as Agathocles of Syracuse did and orders his allies to construct a fleet, but his high-handed behaviour and demands for men and money causes resistance and his main local ally Sosistratus flees after a quarrel with him.

Carthaginian envoys are sent to Rome and an alliance is arranged.

276

Seleucids/Egypt

Antiochus fights a prolonged campaign against the Galatians in central Asia Minor. During his absence Ptolemy II lands in Syria and attacks Seleucia, but it holds out; Antiochus returns home to relieve it and he returns to Egypt.

Greece

Ptolemy 'the Son', son of Lysimachus and Arsinoe II, flees Macedon to join his mother in Egypt.

Antigonus Gonatas returns from the Chersonese with an army to reconquer Macedon and drive out the Gauls, many of whom probably flee to Asia Minor to join their compatriots there. He storms Cassandreia, which resists him.

Italy/Sicily

Pyrrhus abandons his Carthaginian war and leaves Sicily, his fleet being attacked and defeated by Carthaginians in the Straits of Messina as he crosses. He attacks Rhegium and loots the treasures of temples at Locroi to pay his troops. His march northwards (20,000 infantry and 300 cavalry) to Tarentum is severely harassed en route by the 'Mamertines' who pursue him, but he reaches safety.

275

Italy
Pyrrhus crosses Apulia and invades Samnium, which is now lukewarm towards him after he abandoned them for Sicily; he heads for Roman general Manius Curius Dentatus' army at Beneventum while a second force goes to Lucania. Pyrrhus tries to take the Roman camp by surprise in a night march across hills, but loses his way in the forests and is spotted emerging onto the hillside above the Romans at dawn. The Romans attack and rout the advance guard as it comes downhill, and a long struggle down on level ground ends with Romans driving the remaining elephants into panic with javelins. The Romans win this battle, and the second Epirot force is defeated by Lentulus in Lucania.

Pyrrhus abandons the Italian campaign and his local city-state allies, and sails back to Epirus with 8000 infantry and 500 cavalry; his son Helenus holds out in Tarentum.

Egypt
Arsinoe II induces her full brother Ptolemy II to divorce his wife Arsinoe I and marry her; however, her rival's son Ptolemy (III) remains heir.

Seleucids
Antiochus defeats the plundering Gauls of Galatia in central Asia Minor, and regains control of the local cities; he marches west to reclaim Ionia and besieges rebel Miletus.

275/4

Greece
Aegium rejoins the new (286?) but still small 'Achaean League', to join Dyme, Patras, Pharae, and Tritaea; the commencement of the rise to power of Achaea.

274

Pyrrhus overruns western Macedon as far as the Axius river, defeating Antigonus in battle as most of the latter's infantry deserts on a personal appeal by the attacker. Pyrrhus takes Pella and Aegae to be acclaimed as king, and Antigonus flees east and only holds the coastal towns; however, Pyrrhus fails to press on and his plundering Gallic mercenaries alienated the locals, including looting some of the king's tombs at Aegae. (As shown by 1970s excavations, they miss Philip II's and probably Philip III's and Eurydice's tombs.)

Seleucids/Egypt
Ptolemy II defeats Gaul mercenary revolt in his army; Antiochus is defeated by Egyptian army in Syria.

Ptolemy drives back Magas, governor of Cyrene, who defects to Antiochus and invades Egypt to threaten Alexandria; his fleet retakes Miletus.

273

Ptolemy attacks Syria.

Embassy of Ogulnius from Rome to Egypt, possibly aimed at anti-Pyrrhus alliance.

Greece

Antigonus Gonatas drives Pyrrhus out of Macedon; he retires to Epirus where he receives Cleonymus, exiled uncle of King Areus of Sparta, and decides to use him for a Peloponnesian campaign to destroy Antigonus' allies there.

272

Greece

Pyrrhus invades the Peloponnese, claiming that he has come to 'liberate' Greece. He attacks Sparta by surprise on behalf of King Areus' anti-Macedonian uncle Cleonymus while Areus is absent in Crete, but he decides not to attack at once in darkness despite panic there. The citizens rally to hold out behind hastily-erected trenches and barricades (having no walls) with the women leading the digging, and in the two days' assaults he cannot penetrate city.

Antigonus sends Amenias with mercenaries to assist Sparta against siege, and then Areus returns with 2000 men; Pyrrhus moves off to ravage the countryside, but loses heart after his son Ptolemy is killed in a skirmish. He moves north to attack Argos on behalf of rebel Aristeas, against ruler Aristippus. Antigonus leads help from Corinth as the Argives resist, and defies Pyrrhus from the heights above the plain and refuses challenge to battle. Pyrrhus is let into Argos through a gate by Aristeas, but his elephants cannot get through the gate quickly and the citizens are alerted to the attack; the melee in the streets turns to disaster and Pyrrhus attempts to withdraw but is fatally injured by a tile thrown from a rooftop by an old woman. He is aged probably around forty-seven. His son Helenus and the Epirot army are allowed to leave for Epirus unmolested by Antigonus, and Pyrrhus' eldest surviving son Alexander succeeds to his kingdom.

271

Greece

Athens honours its leader Demochares as saviour of democracy and condemns 'oligarchy', aimed at pro-Macedonians.

Birth of Aratus of Sicyon, the Achaean leader in mid-third century, as son of the leading magistrate Cleinias.

270

Egypt

Death and deification of Arsinoe II, sister-wife of Ptolemy II and widow of Lysimachus, probably in her early forties.

Greece

Antigonus Gonatas recovers Euboea, probably with Chalcis and Eretria; he later marches into the Megarid to regain Megara.

Death of Epicurus.

Italy/Sicily

Rome recaptures Reggium and kills or deports the pirates there for execution. The 'Mamertines' at Messina hold out but are restricted to Sicily.

269

Sicily

The Syracusans vote general Hiero into power to take command against the plundering Mamertine mercenaries at Messina; he seizes power as 'tyrant'.

267

Greece

Ptolemy II inspires and pays the Athenians, led by orator Chremonides, to revolt against Macedon; outbreak of the 'Chremonidean War'.

Areus leads Sparta to join in revolt along with the small Achaean League, other Achaean cities, and most of Arcadia; a general 'league of liberation' is formed backed and paid for by Egypt.

266

Greece

Antigonus Gonatas invades Attica and besieges Athens while another army blockades the Isthmus of Corinth to Peloponnesian foes; the Egyptian fleet under Patrocles fails to come to the defenders' aid and Athens calls on Sparta for help.

265

Greece

Areus of Sparta attempts to storm the Macedonian lines across the Isthmus of Corinth but is defeated and killed; Athens is thus cut off to face Macedon alone.

Sicily

Hiero of Syracuse defeats a probe south from Messina by the Mamertine mercenaries, assumes the title of king, and besieges the invaders in Messina.

264

Sicily

A Carthaginian naval force under Hannibal arrives at Messina, installs a garrison, and forces Hiero of Syracuse to withdraw from the siege; they keep their garrison there to control the Straits.

The Roman Senate decides to respond to appeals for assistance against Carthage from the 'Mamertine' mercenaries in Reggium. The advance-force under Caius Claudius evades Carthaginian ships and drives Carthaginians out of Messina.

Appius Claudius informs Carthage and Hiero that he is only keeping faith with Mamertine allies not invading their territory, but Carthage and Hiero combine forces to besiege the Romans in Messina.

Claudius sallies from Messina to defeat Hiero, who withdraws from siege, and then defeats Carthaginians; the siege is abandoned but full war between Rome and Carthage follows.

Greece

Alexander of Epirus joins the coalition against Antigonus and invades Macedon to overrun the upper Aous valley; he faces invasion from Antigonus' son Demetrius.

Coup in Sicyon, led by the ambitious Abantidas who assassinates leading magistrate Cleinias to paralyse resistance, along with many of his family and friends; the victim's son Aratus, aged seven, escapes by hiding in the house of his uncle's wife Soso who is coincidentally Abantidas' sister. She arranges his escape to Argos, where he is educated and becomes a leading opponent of local pro-Macedonian despots and a proponent of liberation and democracy.

263

Seleucids

Death of Philetaerus, first ruler of Pergamum; as a eunuch he has no sons and his nephew Attalus succeeds him.

Antiochus I executes his eldest son, Seleucus, for treason; his younger son Antiochus (II) is now heir.

262

Sicily

Marcus Valerius Maximus and Manius Otacilius Crassus are elected as consuls, and are both sent to Sicily; Valerius marches into Hiero's territory to besiege Syracuse, while the presence of both Roman armies leads many Carthaginian- or Syracusan-allied towns to defect to Rome; the siege fails, but Hiero is overawed into joining Rome against Carthage, returning all prisoners and paying 100 talents to Rome; Syracuse retains independence but is now used as Roman base for an advance into southern Sicily.

262

Seleucids/Egypt

Ptolemy II sends an expedition to Ionia to install his stepson Ptolemy 'the Son', son of his late wife Arsinoe I and Lysimachus, as governor at Ephesus to fight Antiochus II and take over western Asia Minor.

Attalus of Pergamum defeats Antiochus as the latter's regional power crumbles.

Sicily

Summer – The new consuls, Lucius Postumius Magellus and Quintus Mamilius Vitulus, cross Sicily to the southern coast to besiege Agrigentum, the principal Carthaginian base in area, which is defended by Hannibal son of Gisgo.

262 or early 261

Sicily
Agrigentum surrenders; ?according to Polybius, the Senate decides to extend the campaign to take all of Sicily and orders building of a fleet to end dependence on smaller force of local Greek shipping.

261

Seleucids
Death of Antiochus I, aged probably sixty-two/three; he is succeeded by his son by Stratonice, Antiochus II.

Greece
Antigonus Gonatas forces Athens to surrender and installs a garrison on the Hill of Muses.

There is peace between Antigonus and Ptolemy II, also with Alexander of Epirus who surrenders the upper Aous valley to Antigonus.

?Death of Zeno of Citium, founder of the 'Stoic' school at Athens; Cleanthes succeeds him as principal Stoic teacher in Athens.

Sicily
As the main struggle in Sicily becomes bogged down in a series of minor sieges, there is a failed seven-month Roman siege of Mytistratus.

260

Greece/Egypt
Ptolemy 'the Son' rebels against his stepfather Ptolemy II and seizes southern Ionia, based on Miletus whose Ptolemaic governor, Timarchus, joins him.

Seleucids
?Persian-descended local dynast Ariathares, governor of Cappadocia for the Seleucids, successfully revolts against new ruler Antiochus II.

Sicily
Cnaeus Scipio Asina, Caius Duillius are elected as consuls.

Scipio Asina leads the first Roman naval expedition into Sicilian waters to complement a land-advance on the Carthaginian bases in western Sicily, while 'novus homo' consul Duillius campaigns on land. Scipio is over-confident of his untested fleet and, sailing to the Liparae Islands to secure their main harbour after local offer of help as an 'offshore' base to watch Panormus, is trapped by an arriving Carthaginian fleet from Panormus under Boodes. Scipio is defeated and captured.

Duillius with the main Roman fleet defeats Hannibal's 130/200 Carthaginian ships at the Battle of Mylae, using the tactic of 'Corvus' ('raven') boarding-bridges that attach themselves to Carthaginian ships in order to 'hook' and board them; thirty-three or fifty Carthaginian ships are taken but most escape.

Duillius relieves Hamilcar's siege of Segesta, and at end of campaign celebrates Rome's first naval triumph with captured ships' prows placed on the new 'rostra' at the Forum.

Carthaginian general Hamilcar Barca, father of the famous Hannibal, inflicts major defeat on Syracusans at Thermae.

259

Seleucids/Egypt
Ptolemy 'the Son' is killed by his troops; his general Timarchus rules southern Ionia as an independent warlord. Antiochus II recaptures Ephesus with the aid of a Rhodian squadron under Agathostratus, and the Seleucid/Rhodian fleet then defeats the belated Egyptian relief-squadron under the Athenian exile Chremonides.

258

Seleucids
Antiochus II expels tyrannical usurper Timarchus from Miletus and is given divine honours by the grateful citizens.

Greece
Antigonus Gonatas declares war on Ptolemy II and expands his fleet to retake Aegean.
  Aristodemus seizes control from Megalopolis as a pro–Macedonian tyrant.

257

Egypt
?Death of Magas of Cyrene, semi-autonomous Ptolemaic governor; it is planned for him to be succeeded by his daughter Berenice, who is betrothed to Ptolemy II's son and heir Ptolemy, but Antigonus Gonatas sends out his half-brother Demetrius 'the Fair' (son of Demetrius I by Ptolemy II's sister Ptolemais) to marry Magas' widow, Apamea, and take control. Ptolemy II temporarily accepts this sooner than face an additional war.

Sicily
 Caius Atilius Regulus, Cnaeus Cornelius Blaesio are elected as consuls. Regulus leads naval expedition to raid the island of Melita (Malta).

256

Greece
?Antigonus Gonatas defeats the Ptolemaic navy at the battle of Cos and regains control of the eastern Aegean.
  ?Death of Craterus, Antigonus Gonatas' half-brother (son of mother, Phila, by first marriage) and governor of Corinth; he is succeeded by his son Alexander.

Sicily
 Marcus Atilius Regulus (Caius' brother) and Lucius Manlius Vulso are elected as consuls. The consuls lead a large Roman fleet, allegedly 330 vessels, to invade Africa and attack Carthage, following the tactics used by Agathocles of Syracuse in 310, to force the enemy to withdraw from Sicily. A Carthaginian fleet of ?350 ships, based at Heraclea Minoa and led by Hamilcar, is defeated in battle of Cape Ecnomus where Hamilcar arranges for his

'centre' to withdraw from the Roman attack in order to lure the enemy forward so that his 'wings' can close in from the sides but the Romans break through.

The Romans land in Africa and take Aspis as their base; Carthaginian territory is ravaged, and Manlius leads part of forces back to Sicily for winter while Regulus commands the rest; Hasdrubal and Bostar command Carthage, and Hamilcar is recalled to assist them. Regulus advances, defeats Carthaginians outside Adys, and winters at Tunis.

255

Sicily
Regulus refuses Carthaginian peace-proposals; Carthaginians are reinforced by Spartan mercenary-commander Xanthippus who organizes the defence of the capital and re-trains the army.

Regulus is defeated at the Battle of the River Bagradas or Tunis, the enemy elephants and cavalry proving decisive, and is taken prisoner while survivors flee to Adys.

Summer – New consuls, Servius Fulvius Paetinus Nobilor and Marcus Aemilius Paullus, lead the relief-fleet of ?350 ships, which defeats Carthaginians' smaller fleet at the battle of Cape Hermaeum and evacuates their retreating army from the coast at Aspis, but is severely damaged in a storm off Camerina as it cruises along the south-western coast of Sicily.

Greece
The Achaean League reforms its constitution to have one rather than two generals in command each year. Margus of Carynia/Cerynia is the first 'strategos'.

Areus II succeeds his father, Acrotatus, as king of Sparta.

Seleucids/Egypt
Peace-treaty between Antiochus II and Ptolemy II; Egypt gives up Northern Phoenicia.

?Berenice, heiress of Cyrene, murders her stepfather Demetrius 'the Fair', half-brother of Antigonus Gonatas and Egyptian governor of Cyrene, and takes over the city.

Greece
Phocis joins the Aetolian League.

Sicily
Cnaeus Cornelius Scipio and Aulus Atilius Catalinus are elected as comsuls. Atilius and the ransomed Scipio Asina besiege and take Panormus (Palermo) on the northern coast of Sicily.

254

Seleucids
Death of Stratonice, widow of Antiochus I (and his father Seleucus) and mother of Antiochus II, and Phila II, also sister of Antigonus Gonatas.

253

Greece

?Ptolemy II induces Alexander son of Craterus, Macedonian governor of Corinth and half-nephew of Antigonus Gonatas, to revolt against Macedon with the assistance of a Cretan pirate flotilla, which defends Corinth from attack. The Cretans help Alexander to take the main central Greece Macedon garrison at Chalcis.

?Aetolian League defeats the Boeotians.

?Antigonus Gonatas' son and heir Demetrius marries Stratonice, younger sister of Antiochus II, in Macedon–Seleucid alliance.

Egypt

Berenice, heiress of Cyrene, is married to Ptolemy II's son and heir Ptolemy in a Ptolemaic alliance.

252

Greece

Birth of Achaean leader Philopoemen, son of Craugis of Megalopolis.

Abantidas, ruler of Sicyon, is succeeded by his father, Paneas, who is murdered (252/1) by usurping new tyrant Nicocles, a protégé of the Macedonian regime at Corinth. Nicocles exiles around eighty suspected citizens.

Sicily

Caius Aurelius Cotta and Caius Furius Pacilus are elected as consuls.

Romans capture the Liparae Islands.

251

Greece

(Four months into Nicocles' rule.) Sicyon exiled republican patriot leader Aratus, aged twenty, leads fellow-exiles to start a rebellion against Nicocles in his native city. They climb over the walls at night, despatch the guards, and at dawn call a citizens' assembly in the market-place to announce the revolt. The crowds join the liberators to besiege and set fire to Nicocles' palace, and he flees via a secret passage to make his way to his patron Alexander, Macedonian governor of Corinth.

Aratus persuades Sicyon to join the Achaean League for its protection from Macedonian reprisals, as the Achaeans will guarantee its safety; this means that the traditional status of Sicyon as a 'Doric' state, placed with other such at pan-Greek occasions, will be abrogated as it joins the non-'Doric' Achaeans.

Aratus uses his autonomist anti-Macedonian reputation to help arrange approaches to Ptolemy II for financial backing to boost Sicyon's armed power via mercenaries and keep Macedonians at bay.

Aratus joins the Achaean cavalry for military service, loyally serving as a junior ranker as befits his social status, not flaunting his credentials as a political leader of his city and winning admirers; he soon starts to become an influential figure in the League's councils. Probably soon after Aratus' coup in Sicyon, his friends Ecdemus and Demophilus of Megalopolis liberate their native city by assassinating its tyrant, Aristodamus; it becomes a democracy.

250

Sicily

Caius Atilius Regulus and Marcus Valerius Longus are elected as consuls.

After one consular army ends the campaign for winter, Hasdrubal besieges the other under Lucius Caecilius Metellus in Panormus; Metellus keeps most of the army within the walls, lures his opponents up to the city with bombardment of missiles as they cross intervening river, and then sallies; the Carthaginians suffer severe losses, including 60 to 140 elephants, which amounts to most of their strength in Sicily, and Hasdrubal retreats.

Carthage destroys Selinus.

Egypt

?Berenice is driven out of Cyrene by a mixture of local city republicans and their Greek mainland republican allies; she flees to her fiancé, Prince Ptolemy, and his father in Egypt for help.

249

Sicily

Rome plans to attack Drepana and Lilybaeum, Carthaginian bases controlling western Sicily, and huge combined consular force sent by land and sea (110,000 men according to Diodorus); Hannibal brings 10,000 mercenaries by sea to aid defence, evading Roman fleet; the towns are closely invested and Himilco at Lilybaeum mounts a particularly vigorous defence; Hannibal the Rhodian brings men and supplies by sea in daring manoeuvres that outwit Roman ships.

Consul Publius Claudius Pulcher, arriving for a campaign, decides to tackle the Carthaginian fleet at Drepana, but is a poor commander and is heavily defeated by Abherbal and loses ?93 ships out of 123.

Carthage sends the hostage Regulus to Rome with peace-proposals, but the Senate rejects them; according to Roman legend, Regulus persuades them to fight on and then returns to Carthage as he promised to do if unsuccessful, despite the resulting execution.

Greece

?Ptolemy II's son Ptolemy (III) reconquers Cyrene as husband to its heiress Berenice and incorporates it into the Ptolemaic realm.

248

Seleucids

?Arsaces of the Parni tribe overruns the province of Parthia south-east of the Caspian Sea with his tribesmen and expels Seleucid governor Andragoras; he founds the Parthian monarchy.

Sicily

The treaty between Rome and Hiero of Syracuse is renewed; Hanno 'the Great', Hamilcar's political rival in Carthage, leads a successful expedition into Numidia to defeat the rebel chieftains.

246

Greece
The Macedonian navy defeats Egyptians under Sophron at battle of Andros and secures control of most of Aegean; Thera and Crete remain Ptolemaic.

Alexander dies and Antigonus regains control of Corinth.

Seleucids
Death of Antiochus II, aged around forty, at Sardes; accession of elder son Seleucus II, who is with him at the time, along with ex-wife Laodice. One account has it that Laodice poisons Antiochus to secure her son's succession and forestall Berenice and the latter's infant son's chances.

Antiochus' second wife, Berenice, daughter of Ptolemy II, is at Antioch and challenges her stepson's accession, seizing the city in the name of her small son and appealing for help to Egypt.

Death of Ptolemy II 'Philadelphus', aged sixty-three; his son by Arsinoe I, Ptolemy III 'Euergetes', succeeds aged around thirty and prepares a fleet for Syria to aid his sister. She and her son are killed by loyal Seleucid troops and Antiochus II's men regain Antioch before Ptolemy arrives. Ptolemy III invades in person and overruns Syria, pretending that he has rescued his sister and nephew and proclaiming them rulers; his troops block Cilicia to the forces of Antiochus II and Ptolemy goes on into Mesopotamia to seize Seleucia.

Eratosthenes of Cyrene is chief librarian of the Great Library of Alexandria after the death of the poet Apollonius Rhodius.

245

Greece
Aratus, a foe of Macedonian control of Greece, commences his virtually unbroken annual election as the commanding general ('strategos') of the Achaean League. He joins the Boeotian league's troops for a joint campaign against Phocis and Calydon.

244

Greece
Accession of Agis IV, radical young king, in Sparta.

?The Aetolian League assists Elis against the Arcadians; Aetolia becomes protector of Elis, Tegea and Mantinea to restrict Achaean power.

Seleucids/Egypt

?Seleucus II reconquers Antioch and north-western Syria while Ptolemy is hampered by the threat by Antigonus Gonatas to the Ptolemaic positions in the south of Ionia; a Macedonian invasion is expected but does not occur. His younger brother Antiochus Hierax, probably in his teens, is his representative back in Asia Minor at Sardes, apparently backed in his ambitions by their mother, Laodice.

243

Italy
Autumn – Rome starts to construct a large new fleet of 'quinqueremes' to face the Carthaginians at sea, using the design of the captured ship belonging to Hannibal the Rhodian.

Seleucids/Egypt
Seleucus II plans a counter-offensive in Syria, but his new fleet is destroyed in a storm; his army is routed by the Ptolemaic army. An Egyptian fleet invades the Aegean and retakes Ephesus, where governor Sophron defects, then Samos, Miletus, and Priene; they land Ptolemaic troops at Aenus and Maronea in Thrace and on the Chersonese to control the western end of the Hellespont.

Greece
Agis proposes radical reforms in Sparta to rebuild the declining citizen-army, which is down to around 700 families of full citizens, partly due to the difficulty in an era of rising debt of affording to keep up the necessary qualification in land. He is supported by the new 'ephor' Lysander (a descendant of the general who defeated Athens in 404); he wants a cancellation of debts and a re-division of the land – 4500 units are to be reserved for Spartan citizens, and divided equally among them, with the richer 'periocoi' invited to take part and thus assume the citizenship; the other 15,000 units will be equally divided among the new, extended class of 'periocoi'. This is applauded by the poor and his own faction of mostly young supporters, but is controversial to conservatives and all the 'ephors' cannot agree to it; the 'Gerousia' council is divided, so Agis gets Lysander to call a meeting of the general assembly where the reformist 'ephor' offers to give up his own land first for redivision as an example and the people back him. Agis's co-king, Leonidas, tries to block his measures and the 'Gerousia' turns them down by one vote, but Lysander has Leonidas deposed on the excuse that he has violated the law by marrying a foreign woman while he was at the court of Seleucid king Seleucus II. Leonidas' son-in-law Cleombrotus succeeds him and backs Agis; the reforms are agreed.

Aratus is 'strategos' of Achaea again; he secures the allegiance of a Syrian soldier in the Macedonian army at Corinth, Erginus, who has been secretly stealing money from the King's treasury in the Acrocorinth citadel and hiding it at Sicyon. Erginus' brother Diocles is in the Acrocorinth garrison, and knows that the wall is low at a certain point and a secret path leads up the rock to it, which the Macedonians have not guarded. Aratus leads 400 Achaean troops secretly to Corinth, where he and 100 picked men climb the path to the wall at night and climb over it to overpower the guards and seize the walls before tackling the remaining soldiers. The alarm is given and part of the garrison in the city hurried up to the citadel via the main route to rescue the garrison, but are spotted and ambushed successfully by the rear of Aratus' column who are not yet at the top of the secret path. The citadel falls. Next day the Achaeans appear at the Corinth city assembly to appeal for support, and are greeted with enthusiasm. The besieged Macedonian garrison has to leave, and the city abandons Antigonus' cause, and agrees to join the Achaean League.

Megara joins the Achaeans, and Sparta and Ptolemy III become their allies; Athens refuses to desert Macedon.

Aetolians institute the 'Soteria' festival at Delphi to commemorate the repulse of the Gauls in 279, with themselves as the heroes of the latter.

242

Greece
Agis' reforms are delayed by the new 'ephors' elected for that year, so he replaces them; his uncle Agesilaus is the new chief 'ephor' but is opposed to the redistribution of land and secretly opposes his nephew; his allies accuse Lysander of breaking the laws. Agesilaus persuades Agis to cancel the debts first and postpone the redistribution of land; the records of the debts are burnt in the public market-place amidst great celebrations. Agis has the returned Leonidas driven out of Sparta again for alleged plotting; he flees to Tegea.

Aratus leads Achaean army in unsuccessful invasion of Attica; he fails to have pro-Macedonian tyrant Aristomachus of Argos, his personal target as ruling the town which harboured him as an exile, assassinated.

Seleucids/Egypt
Ptolemy III besieges Damascus.

241

Sicily
Hanno leads around 250 Carthaginian ships to bring supplies to Mount Eryx and then take on Hamilcar's men to assist in battle; 10 March – as they sail a Roman fleet under Catulus arrives.

Battle of the Aegates Islands: around 117 Carthaginian and 30 Roman ships (Diodorus) are sunk in a Roman victory, and Carthaginian survivors flee; Catulus is awarded the triumph.

Hamilcar's army is stranded short of supplies, and Carthage instructs him to open negotiations.

Terms agreed: Carthage to evacuate all Sicily, and pay indemnity of 2200 Euboean 'talents' over twenty years; neither side is to make war on or subvert the other's allies, or recruit soldiers or raise money for public buildings in the other's lands; Carthage to ransom its own prisoners but freely release its Roman prisoners.

There is a senatorial commission in Sicily for new negotiations; the indemnity is raised to 3200 'talents', 1000 payable immediately and the rest over ten years, and islands between Sicily and Africa are to be evacuated. Carthage agrees to the terms.

Seleucids
Antiochus Hierax leads Anatolian reinforcements to Seleucus in Syria in return for recognition as co-ruler; Seleucus makes peace with Ptolemy III, recognizing the loss of most of the Syrian coast.

Greece
Aratus is 'strategos' of the Achaean League (year to 240).

Ptolemy III is elected commander-in-chief of the Achaean forces as an inducement to send major financial and military support against the Aetolian attack, but fails to do so.

The Aetolians, supporting Macedon, march on Corinth; Agis of Sparta joins the Achaeans' expedition there and in his absence ex-king Leonidas returns and is voted back into his kingship by his allies, with Cleombrotus dismissed but saved from execution by his wife, the restored ruler's daughter Chilonis, and flees to the temple of Poseidon at Cape Taenarum; Leonidas carries out a purge of Agis' supporters and cancels his legislation.

Agis abandons his camp on the Isthmus and returns home too late, and is faced with prosecution; he takes sanctuary at the temple of Athene and is later lured out and thrown into prison; he is still popular, so Leonidas sends the 'ephors' to conduct a quick show-trial there and kill Agis (aged in his twenties); his supporters are killed or flee. Agis' wife Agiatis is remarried by Leonidas to his own son, Cleomenes (later another reforming king). Agis' retreat from the Isthmus of Corinth enables the Aetolians to cross, but they only sack Pallene and then return home.

Death of Arcesilas, head of the 'Academy' at Athens.

240

Greece
Aratus invades Attica but fails to take the Piraeus, and has to withdraw his army from Attica; he then fails to overthrow Aristippus the new tyrant of Argos, son of the recently murdered Aristomachus, in a botched attack and Aristippus complains to the Achaean League council; they appoint a panel of Arcadians to adjudicate, and Aratus is fined for aggression as a goodwill gesture to the Aetolians.

Aetolians invade and loot Laconia on behalf of Agis' exiled friends.

239

Greece
Death of Antigonus 'Gonatas' of Macedon, aged eighty; he is succeeded by his son Demetrius II, probably in his thirties. The Aetolians and Achaeans combine to attack Macedonian power in Greece, the former in central Greece and the latter in the Peloponnese.

(239/8) Following the death of King Alexander of Epirus, son of Pyrrhus, his son Pyrrhus II succeeds as boy under the regency of Queen Olympias; the Aetolians demand the return of the northern half of Acarnania and Olympias appeals to Demetrius II.

Demetrius allies with Epirus, and assists them against an Aetolian invasion; he marries Phthia (or Chryseis), sister of king Pyrrhus II. The Aetolians agree an alliance with the Achaeans in retaliation.

Aratus of Sucyon is 'strategos' of the Achaean League for 239–8.

238

Birth of Demetrius II and Phthia's son Philip (V) of Macedon.

237

Greece
Demetrius II defeats an Aetolian attack on Epirus.

Aratus is 'strategos' of the Achaean League for 237–6.

Seleucids

Seleucus II invades Asia Minor to fight his rebel brother Antiochus Hierax; the latter allies with the Galatians to secure tribal mercenaries; Seleucus wins two victories but cannot take Sardes. Seleucus invades Galatia but is decisively defeated by them near Ancrya (237/6), opening the region to their marauding.

Hierax also calls on Mithridates II of Pontus for aid.

236

Greece

Demetrius II defeats the Aetolians and lands an army at Demetrias in Thessaly to march south and conquer Boeotia and Phocis from them.

Seleucids

Parthians overrun Media and Hyrcania; in order to concentrate his army on campaign on the Iranian plateau Seleucus II has to recognize his brother Antiochus Hierax as ruler of Asia Minor. Hierax enrols more Galatians in his army, but lacks money and has to allow them to plunder at will outside Galatia, which causes resentment.

235

Greece

Cleomenes II succeeds his father, Leonidas, in one of the Spartan kingships; he is an admirer of the late king Agis and determined to restore Spartan power, more ruthlessly than his predecessor did.

Aratus of Achaea fails to defeat Aristippus' Argive army in battle, but later manages to ambush and kill him near Cleonae.

Andromachus II succeeds his brother Aristippus in Argos and holds off Aratus.

234

Greece

Lydiadis, tyrant of Megalopolis, fearing overthrow by Achaea on behalf of his exiled pro-Achaean democrat opponents, abdicates and leads his city into the Achaean League; he arranges in return to alternate the annual command of the League's army with their current 'strategos' Aratus. He becomes 'strategos' of the League for the year 234–3.

233

Greece

Demetrius II fights a Dardanian invasion; he has to recall his general Bithys from the Peloponnese.

Aratus of Sicyon is 'strategos' of the Achaean League (to 232).

?Death of Pyrrhus II, co-king of Epirus; his brother Ptolemy rules alone.

232

Greece
Lydiadas of Megalopolois is 'strategos' of the Achaean League for the year 232–1.

Adriatic
King Agron of the Illyrians (Ardiaei) invades Acarnania by sea; he wins battle over the Aetolians, who are besieging the town of Medeon for refusing to join the Aetolian League, by landing from his ships and taking them by surprise at night.

232/1

Greece
?Assassination of Ptolemy, last ruler of Epirus; his niece Deidamia, daughter of Pyrrhus II, claims power and seizes Ambracia with a force of 800 Gallic mercenaries sent by her sister, wife of Sicilian ruler Gelon. A republic is proclaimed and Deidamia flees to the sanctuary of the temple of Artemis but is lynched in a riot.

India
?Death of Asoka the Maurya, greatest of his dynasty and ruler from the upper Indus valley to the Tamil regions in the south; his state starts to split up, which will give the Greeks of Bactria a chance to invade.

231

Greece
Aratus of Sicyon is 'strategos' of the Achaean League for the year 231–0.

Demetrius hires the main Illyrian tribal king, Agron of the Ardiaei, to relieve the city of Medeon in Acarnania from an Aetolian siege while he is preoccupied. The Illyrians rout the Aetolians.

230

Greece
Aratus succeeded by Lydiadas as 'strategos' of the Achaean League for 230–29.

Dardanians invade Macedon and inflict a heavy defeat on king Demetrius II, opening the Strymon valley to ravaging.

(Early) Death of Agron, king of the Illyrian tribal kingdom of the Ardiaei, and accession of young son Pinnes, baby, under regency of latter's stepmother Queen Teuta. Pinnes' mother Triteuta, recently divorced by Agron, is superseded; Teuta assumes militant expansionist policy against Adriatic tribal kingdoms and ports that brings her into conflict with Roman allies. She is backed by Agron's brother and admiral Scerdilaidas.

Queen Teuta sends out her fleet to raid Epirus coast; they link up with the Epirots' underpaid and mutinous Gallic mercenaries at the town of Phoenice and bribe the latter to let them into and plunder the town. Her ally Scerdilaidas raids into Epirus by land and reaches the nearby pass of Antigoneia. The Epirots besiege and try to retake Phoenice, but their careless blockade enables the Illyrians to slip out and link up with the advancing

Scerdilaidas; at eponymous Battle of Phoenice the Epirots are defeated; they appeal to Aetolia and Achaea for help.

Seleucids
Seleucus II fights Tigranes of Parthia. Revolt of Arsames, governor of Armenia, to his rear.

Attalus, ruler of Pergamum, drives off a major plundering Gallic (Toloistoagi) attack on western Asia Minor cities from tribal Galatia, winning battle at the head of the Caicus valley. Hierax allies with the Toloistoagi and the Tectosages for a joint invasion, but Attalus defeats them all; this is used as a centrepiece of his regime's statuary/frieze propaganda on public buildings as Attalid defence of Ionian civilization from raiding Gauls. He assumes the title of 'King' as saviour of the region and becomes effectively independent as he starts to overrun Hierax's dominions.

Greece
Aetolians and Achaeans send troops to Epirus to help retake Phoenice; they advance on Helicranum (near modern Ioannina) to try to retake Phoenice from its Illyrian garrison. Teuta sends Scerdilaidas and 5000 men to the rescue; they reach the pass of Antigoneia and are joined by the garrison of Phoenice to attack Helicranum and confront the Greeks. However, a battle is avoided as the Dardanians under King Longarus have invaded troop-denuded Illyria (at the allies' behest?) and a revolt has broken out against Teuta. Teuta recalls Scerdilaidas' army and the Phoenice troops; Phoenice is evacuated and prisoners are ransomed as the Illyrians retreat with their loot, and the shaken Epirots temporarily abandon alliance with the Aetolian and Achaean Leagues and send a mission for alliance to Teuta so the latter will guarantee their security.

(230/29) Argos joins Achaean League as tyrant Aristomachus despairs of receiving any Macedonian help due to the Dardanian war; Aristomachus abdicates in favour of pro-Achaean republicans.

Adriatic
Queen Teuta of the Illyrians attacks the port of Issa, and insults and murders a Roman embassy sent to warn her to withdraw.

229

Greece
Death of the defeated Demetrius II of Macedon, probably aged around fifty; his son Philip is only nine so their cousin Antigonus 'Doson', son of Demetrius 'the Fair' of Cyrene (younger son of Demetrius I), assumes the kingship (or just regency at first) until Philip is an adult and marries his mother.

Doson defeats the invading Dardanians and drives them back up the Axius valley, then is elected to assume the crown (probably on the precedent of Philip II in 359) but as he has no son Philip rather than his brother Execrates is his heir.

With Macedon preoccupied, Aratus of Sicyon tries to bribe the pro-Macdonian 'tyrants' of the Peloponnese into deserting their paymaster and joining the Achaean League with promises of money and office. Xenon of Hermione (near Troezen) and Cleonymus of Phlius are among those who accept over the next year or so.

Adriatic

Queen Teuta of Illyria besieges coastal stronghold of Issa, alarming neighbours and Rome.

The Illyrian fleet sailing south takes Epidamnus by surprise, some sailors in civilian tunics going into the town to 'collect supplies' by agreement and then pulling daggers out of their clothes to murder the gate-guards; they occupy Corcyra, which sends an appeal for help to Achaea, and with extra ships from the Acarnanians defeat the intervening Achaean fleet at battle of Paxos.

Demetrius of Pharos, pirate admiral from the eponymous Adriatic island and Teuta's ally, becomes the Illyrian governor of Corcyra but when a Roman fleet of 200 ships under consul Cnaeus Fulvius Centumalus arrives surrenders the island to him.

Greece

With Macedon preoccupied at home, the Athenians persuade its local commander Diogenes to evacuate the Piraeus garrison and leave them independent; he has to be paid off, but Thebes, Thespiae, and Aratus loan Athens the balance of the sum required.

Aratus is back as 'strategos' of the Achaean League for 229–8. Meanwhile, the alarmed Aetolians ally with Antigonus Doson and King Cleomenes of Sparta against Achaea; Cleomenes militarily takes over Tegea, Mantinea and Orchomenus from pro-Achaean regimes and is backed by Aetolia, the towns' ally, rather than them defending right to independence.

?(or early 228) Andromachus, tyrant of Argos, comes to agreement with Aratus and the Achaeans and abdicates his sole rule; from the outcome, he is promised a share of the annual Achaean League generalship in return.

Seleucids

Attalus of Pergamum expels Antiochus Hierax from Ionia, driving him back inland after major victory in Caria, and overruns Hellespontine Phrygia too. Now or in 228 Attalus takes Hierax's capital, Sardes.

Spain

Hamilcar, as Carthaginian commander, is killed in battle with the Oretani tribe; his army entrusts the leadership to his second-in-command and son-in-law Hasdrubal, and over the next two years his mixture of campaigning and treaties with tribes brings Carthaginian power north-eastwards to the River Ebro to the alarm of Rome. Hamilcar's son Hannibal probably assists him and so learns his military skills.

Adriatic

Second Roman expedition under other consul, Aulus Postumius Albinus, is sent to cross from Brundisium to the Illyrian coast and islands to drive out local pirates at the request of Italian traders whose ships in the Adriatic are being preyed upon, having failed to secure action from the kingdom of Illyria under Queen Teuta. Commander Fulvius Centumalus sails from Corcyra to Rome's ally Apollonia to confirm its treaty with Rome, and Postumius' squadron arrives to join him and disembark 20,000 troops. The Illyrians are expelled from Epidamnus, and the latter signs up to Roman alliance as do the inland tribes of the Parthini and Atintanes (probably fearing Teuta's expanding power). Facing the Roman fleet attacking, Teuta abandons the siege of Issa, flees to the impregnable fortress of

Rhizon up the coast (in modern Montenegro), and opens negotiations; some of her troops flee to Pharos where its lord Demetrius protects them.

A permanent Roman naval base is established at Corcyra with other garrisons on the Illyrian coast such as Apollonia; Postumius winters with part of the fleet at Epidamnus while Demetrius organizes a pro-Roman tribal alliance to keep Teuta's power restricted. Fulvius sails back to Italy.

Postumius negotiates with Teuta.

228

Greece
Spring – Queen Teuta of Illyria agrees a treaty with Rome and recognizes the latter's new allies as lost to her sphere of influence; the kingdom of the Ardiaei is recognized as an ally of Rome, with Teuta deposed and her late husband Agron's ex-wife Triteuta as queen-mother/regent for her young son Pinnes. Roman envoys led by Postumius are sent to the Greek 'Isthmian Games' to announce that the Adriatic is free of pirates.

Andromachus of Argos succeeds Aratus as 'strategos' of the Achaean League for 228–7.

Megalopolis deserts its Spartan alliance to join the Achaean League; alarmed Spartan king Cleomenes invades Megalopolis to reassert his rights there and fortifies the 'Athenaeum' at Megalopolis. The Achaeans declare war on him, and he fights an inconclusive battle with the Achaean general Aristomachus of Argos at Pallantium.

With the strain of war and Spartan ravaging hitting Megalopolis, Aratus gets his local friends Nicophanes and Cercidas to ask the Achaean assembly if they can go to Macedon for help; this is agreed and the two visit Antigonus Doson to warn him of the threat of Sparta and Aetolia to his interests in Greece. Doson agrees to help Megalopolis and Achaea.

Seleucids
Seleucus III's new ally Attalus of Pergamum takes over western Asia Minor; Hierax retreats to Armenia to get military assistance from King Arsames after Attalus takes Sardes.

227

Seleucids
Seleucus III is distracted by a Parthian war, and fights in Hyrcania near the Caspian Sea; in his absence his rebel brother Hierax invades Mesopotamia from Armenia, but is defeated by Seleucus' local commander, their cousin Andromachus (probably son of a younger brother of Antiochus I) and his son Achaeus. They drive Hierax in a headlong retreat into Asia Minor.

While the King and his generals are preoccupied, Princess Stratonice seizes Antioch in rebellion but is forced by advancing loyal troops to flee to the port of Seleucia Pieria where she is killed.

Greece
Ptolemy III abandons the Achaean alliance for one with Sparta as a more secure foe of his target, Macedon.

Aratus is 'strategos' of the Achaean League for 227–6.

Achaeans under Aratus invade Elis, which appeals to Sparta for help.

Backed by Egyptian troops, Cleomenes intercepts the Achaeans en route home at Mount Lycaeum and secures a comprehensive victory; having secured full control of Sparta and with his Egyptian troops as his bodyguard, he abolishes the 'ephorate' to make the kingship an absolute monarchy.

Aratus attacks and takes Mantinea; Cleomenes wins a second victory over Achaeans at Ladocea where Lydiadas is killed. The Achaeans send Aratus' son with embassy to Doson, but the King wants them to agree to return Corinth and its citadel to him, which will not fit with the Achaean stand for the city's independence.

226

Seleucids

Hierax flees the advancing Seleucid army under Andromachus and Achaeus to Thrace, where he is murdered by his underpaid mercenaries. Restoration of Seleucid control of inland western Asia Minor; Attalus rules Ionia. Meanwhile, Antigonus Doson sails with a fleet across the Aegean and campaigns in Caria to secure it from Egyptian garrisons before the Seleucids can take it over.

Death of Seleucus II in a fall from his horse, aged probably in his early forties; he is succeeded by his elder son, Alexander, who takes name of 'Seleucus II', probably in his twenties.

Seleucus II assumes title of 'Callinicus', 'The Triumphant', now or later.

Greece

Hyperbatas is 'strategos' of the Achaean League for 226–5.

Mantinea revolts against Achaea and massacres the Achaean garrison. Cleomenes defeats the Achaeans near Hecatomberon and takes a number of Achaean cities, including Sicyon. The Achaeans are forced to agree to Cleomenes' terms of him becoming formal leader of a new league of the Peloponnese, including them, but the installation-ceremony is postponed as he falls ill at Sparta and cannot go to the event.

225

Greece

Timoxenos elected Achaean 'strategos' for 225–4.

Spring – Cleomenes meets the Achaean League leadership again at Argos to be accepted and installed formally as leader of the Peloponnesian states' new league; he insists on bringing his entire army along to camp at Lerna near Argos to intimidate the League, playing into the hands of his enemies led by Aratus; Aratus leads alarmed delegates to ask him to bring only 300 men into the city. He refuses, and as they hold out the angry Cleomenes declares war on them.

War breaks out. Aratus is elected special supreme commander ('strategos autocrator') of the Achaean League for 225–4. Cleomenes takes Argos, which Aristomachus surrenders, and ravages across eastern Achaea driving Aratus back and winning various towns. He arranges for allied Corinthians to try to kidnap Aratus, which is prevented. He advances to Corinth to take the city and besiege the Acrocorinth citadel, and forces various new enforced Achaean allies of Sparta's to leave the Achaean League to reduce its power.

Cleomenes demands control of Corinth as terms for peace, and Aratus offers it to Macedon to tempt Doson into intervening on Achaea's side. Aristotle leads an anti-Spartan coup at Argos, and Timoxenus leads the Achaean army to assist the city in driving off an attack by Cleomenes.

At some time around now, ex-ruler Aristomachus of Argos is captured by Achaeans at Cenchrae, the port of Corinth, and executed as a traitor for his defection to Cleomenes.

224

Greece

Cleomenes, assisted by Corinth, besieges Aratus' home-city of Sicyon for three months and demands that it exit the Achaean League and become his ally in return for being spared. Aratus persuades the League council at Aegium to accept this as he is too weak to rescue the city.

His military strength ebbing and Achaeans demoralized, he goes to Pegae to meet Antigonus Doson and enlist him to intervene, and Antigonus and his army swear to alliance with the Achaeans.

Aratus is elected 'strategos' of Achaean League for 224–3.

Spring – Antigonus Doson leads his army via Boeotia, which joins him, into central Greece; Cleomenes makes a successful stand at the Isthmus of Corinth, but Argos revolts in his rear and he leaves to try to recover it. He fails, and Corinth falls too; many of Cleomenes' allies desert and Doson links up with the Achaeans.

Autumn – Doson holds an assembly of the southern Greeks at Aegium to supplement the planned Achaean League meeting there. Epirus, Phocis, Thessaly, Boeotia and Acarnania send delegates. He is elected 'hegemon' of the allies' new pan-Greek league (against mainly Aetolia and Sparta), probably inspired by Philip II's league of 338. He creates a new 'symmachia' or 'league of leagues', i.e. combining the existing leagues rather than breaking them up into individual city-states.

Seleucids

?Seleucus sends his kinsman Andromachus with an army to western Asia Minor to fight Attalus of Pergamum; Attalus defeats and captures him, and later sends him to his ally Ptolemy III of Egypt to be used as a bargaining-counter.

223

Seleucids

Seleucus II is murdered by officers Nicanor and Apatrurius the Gaul, and is succeeded by his brother Antiochus III, who is aged probably sixteen/seventeen; Seleucus' infant son Antipater is superseded. Their cousin Achaeus is the new ruler's chief lieutenant and probably his heir, and venal and scheming Hermeias is the chief minister.

Greece

Timoxenus elected 'strategos' of Achaea for 223–2.

Antigonus Doson and his Achaean allies attack Arcadia, and take Tegea as the Macedonian siege-experts mine under the walls; Doson takes Orchomenus while its troops are absent in their ally Cleomenes' army defending Spartan frontier, and Aratus takes and razes

Mantinea. Heraea and Thelpousa are taken by Doson. Protests to the Achaean League council at the treatment of Mantinea are ignored; Cleomenes resorts to freeing and enrolling 'helots' in his army.

Autumn – After the Macedonian army returns home for the winter and Doson goes to his Gulf of Corinth base at Aegium Cleomenes attacks Achaea and takes and sacks Megalopolis with the aid of some Messenian exile resident in the town who let him in, razing it in retaliation for Mantinea; Philopoemen evacuates the refugees to Messene where they will form the bedrock for an anti-Spartan faction in southern Elis to block Cleomones' attacks.

Doson winters at Argos.

223/2

Illyria

By or at this date Queen Triteuta marries her admiral Demetrius of Pharos; he becomes co-ruler and supersedes (deposes?) her stepson Pinnes.

222

Seleucids

Governor Molon of Babylon revolts, seizes nearby Seleucia, and assumes the royal diadem as king of the Seleucid realm to challenge Antiochus and seize Mesopotamia. Antiochus sends Achaeus west to Sardes to control western central Asia Minor while he fights Molon.

Achaeus is entrusted with restricting Pergamene power.

Greece

Aratus is elected 'strategos' of Achaea for 222–1.

Cleomenes calls out the full strength of Spartan citizens to fight (6000?) and fortifies the hilly north-east frontier of Laconia into the Argolid with fences and earthworks to aid defence by his forces.

Summer? – Doson and the Achaeans invade Laconia from the north-east with around 30,000 infantry – up to 10,000 Macedonian heavily armed infantry plus 3000 skirmishers (peltasts), 300 cavalry, 3000 from allied tribal Agrianoi, and 1600 infantry from Illyria led by Demetrius of Pharos. Also, 3000 Achaeans, 2000 Boeotians, and 1000 Epirots and 100 Acarnanians (Polybius).

Cleomenes and the Spartan army meet them at the frontier village of Sellasia, the Spartan line along a 'saddle' between two hills (Olympus and Evas) facing the Macedonians in the valley of the river Oenus below.

Battle of Sellasia: Cleomenes commands his right wing on Mount Olympus and his brother and fellow-king Eucleidas the left wing on Mount Evas. The Spartans and their allies amount to around 20,000, dominated by 6000 Spartans (citizens alone or citizens and 'periocoi'?) (Polybius). The attacking Macedonians have to fight uphill. The struggle is particularly intense on the Spartan left wing as their light infantry ambushes the advancing Macedonians, who are trying to get round their left flank on hillside in the rear, and the Macedonian phalanx is pushed back. The rising Achaean officer Philopoemen breaks ranks to lead their cavalry in a surprise attack on the advancing Spartans and throws them back, plugging the gap between the Macedonian light infantry and the main army before it can be used against them. Eucleidas and his men wait for the attackers to reach them rather than charging downhill, and are overwhelmed by Philopoemen leading a charge; Cleomenes launches his right wing in an infantry attack but cannot push the phalanx back far and is routed in a charge.

All but c. 200 of the Spartan citizen infantry are killed; this is a catastrophe for their military strength.

Doson occupies Sparta as Cleomenes and his allies flee to Egypt, and refuses to sack it as his quarrel is a personal one with Cleomenes; he abolishes or suspends the Spartan kingship. The traditional Spartan constitution and militarized society are retained under the 'ephors', and Sparta has to join Doson's league but Elis and Messene do not.

Philopoemen goes to Crete to fight in the local 'War of Luttus' for the pro-Macedonian faction.

Autumn – With the Illyrian tribes invading Macedon again, Doson leaves the Peloponnese for home; he calls in at the Nemean Games near Argos en route.

221

Egypt
Death of Ptolemy III, aged probably in his late fifties; succeeded by his son Ptolemy IV 'Philopator', a weak teenager under the influence of his chief minister/regent Sosibius.

Seleucids
Antiochus III resumes the 'Fourth Syrian War' as Ptolemaic governor Theodotus of Coele-Syria offers to defect to him, duped by his cunning minister Hermeias who produces a fake letter by Achaeus 'corresponding' with Ptolemy IV to overthrow him; Antiochus marries Laodice, daughter of Mithradates/Mithridates II of Pontus, and attacks Gerrha and Brochi in the Beqaa valley.

Molon, rebel governor of Babylon, is joined by Ariobarzanes of Atropatene (Azerbaijan); Antiochus sends his general Xenoelas, an Achaean expatriate, against Babylon while he continues with his planned Egyptian war to wrest Phoenicia and Palestine from the weak new regency government on Hermeias' advice. Xenoelas sends to governor Diogenes of Susiana for help and crosses the Tigris downstream of where Molon, on the east bank, is expecting, and sets up camp; Molon attacks the camp but is defeated, and later destroys his attackers in a second battle, as he lures the over-confident Xenoelas with a feigned retreat; the latter's army is caught sleeping off alcoholic celebrations of their forthcoming victory in a night-attack on the camp and is cut to pieces with their general killed. The survivors are evacuated by Zeuxis, Xenoelas' cautious rival who was left behind in the 'rear base' camp. Molon takes over Seleucia-on-Tigris, drives Diogenes of Susiana out of his provincial capital, and advances to Dura-Europus on the Euphrates.

Antiochus has to abandon the Egyptian war and head to Mesopotamia; as he is short of money and the troops are unruly over this, Hermeias offers successfully to pay the army out of his own funds if the king will sack his rival Epigenes (who opposed the Syrian war).

Achaeus, officially as viceroy to his cousin Antiochus III, invades Pergamum to drive Attalus back into his capital and seize outlying towns from him.

Greece

Early? (or late 222) – Antigonus 'Doson' defeats the tribes in Macedon, but falls ill with a burst blood-vessel received in battle injury, possibly exacerbating an existing tubercular condition. He dies weeks? later, aged forty-eight; Philip V succeeds to Macedon aged seventeen and has to fight invasion by the Aetolians who now seek to dominate central-southern Greece while he is new to warfare. His chief advisers include Apelles.

Spain

Hasdrubal is assassinated in Spain; his troops elect Hannibal to succeed him; Hannibal initially campaigns in western Spain to reach the Salamanca area, but soon starts to plan invasion of Italy to cause Rome's allies to revolt and cripple her military power.

Adriatic

Demetrius of Pharos allies with the Histri of Istria, at the northern end of the Adriatic, against Rome; they are subsequently attacked by Rome and the alliance increases Roman unease about Demetrius and desire to restrain him.

221/0

Seleucids

Achaeus turns on Antiochus III and sets out to invade Syria and claim the throne.

Early – Antiochus III relieves the siege of Dura-Europos, and advances to the lower Tigris. He crosses the Tigris to attack Molon on Zeuxis' advice, despite Hermeias urging him to stay on the safer south bank. He defeats Molon, commanding his own right wing in battle while Hermeias and Zeuxis are on his left wing and being aided by many on the enemy left wing deserting to him quickly. Molon flees to and is besieged in Seleucia, and on its surrender commits suicide and is impaled.

En route from Sardes across Asia Minor Achaeus' troops mutiny in Lycaonia. He has to restrict his plans to western-central Asia Minor, ruling from Sardes.

220

Antiochus forces Artobarzanes of Atropatene to submit, but has to leave Achaeus alone to take over central-western Asia Minor for the moment. Antiochus accepts his doctor Apollophanes' warning about Hermeias, who is lured away from the royal camp on the return march from Atropatene by the king's loyalists and stabbed to death.

Greece

Co-ordinated complaints are made by Aratus and the Achaeans to the 'Hellenic League' symmachy about a long list of past aggression by the Aetolians, as part of a plan by Philip and Achaean 'war-party' to create belligerent mood for an attack on Aetolia. Philip wants to complete his leadership of the Greek states by coercing Aetolians and to boost his reputation as Greek military leader. Not many non-Achaean states are interested in war.

Spring – Aetolians send a force under Dorimachus of Trichonium to march round Achaea and base themselves at their allied town of Phigaleia on its south-west border with Arcadia as a base, cutting anti-Achaean Sparta and Arcadia off from Elis; he hires assorted freebooters and they live off raiding infuriated neighbouring Messenians. He has to go to Messene to deal with complaints of pillaging, and after one raid takes place during his visit he is threatened by their council, loses his temper, and promises Aetolian vengeance for the insults; later on a visit to Aetolia he inflames local opinion against the Messenians. The current deputy commander of the Aetolian League, and acting commander, is his sympathetic relative Scopas.

Aetolians declare war on Achaea and Messenia, and send out a fleet to the southern Ionian Sea and another to plunder Epirot coast; they send a force to Clarium near Megalopolis to plunder local Achaeans; the latter's general Timoxenus recaptures it with help from Taurion, the Macedonian commander of the Peloponnese. As the Achaeans delay campaigning while their annual changeover of generals takes place (i.e. Timoxenus to Aratus), an Aetolian army quickly enters the Peloponnese to reinforce Phigalia then attack Messenia. Messenians complain to the Achaean assembly, and despite Timarchus urging caution Aratus is appointed 'strategos' five days earlier than planned to speed up their military response. Messene asks to join the Macedonian-led 'symmachy' League of 224 so all its members will have to aid them, but is told that this must be done with the agreement of all members so not yet.

Aetolians agree to evacuate Messenia and Phigalia to satisfy Achaea until they are ready for direct clash of main armies, but as Dorimachus withdraws his garrison towards the northern coast of Peloponnese he decides to take on Aratus before the latter suspects his intentions; the Aetolians have the better of a clash at the pass of Olygyrtus and then loot the Achaean countryside as they march back to the Isthmus and Aetolia. The Achaean assembly is annoyed with Aratus for taking on the Aetolians at all as he had a smaller army and rushing into conflict early, but agrees to send to Philip of Macedon, Epirus, Boeotia, Phocis, and Acarnania to help, pointing out that the Aetolians have blatantly attacked their territory twice, violating the peace, and that the terms of their league mean mutual assistance against attackers.

Illyria/Greece
Demetrius of Pharos (fifty ships) and Scerdilaidaas (forty ships) breach the terms of the Rome/Illyria peace by sailing south of Lissus, en route to plundering attack on western Greek coasts in alliance with Aetolia against Achaea. They split up; Scerdilaidas attacks Pylos in Messenia, then allies with an Aetolian force operating in Elis to assist them in attacking Cynaethae in western Achaea, on the northern side of the Aroanian mountains. A faction of pro-Aetolian returned exiles recently allowed back into Cynaethae admits the invaders, hoping to get their help to plunder their enemies there, but everyone is indiscriminately robbed and killed, including them. The invaders then fail to take Cleitor; meanwhile Aratus sends to Philip for military help.

In the Aegean, Demetrius' squadron plunders and extorts money from the Cyclades before being chased off by a Rhodian squadron; he sails to Cenchrae, the port of Corinth, here Macedonian governor Taurion agrees to portage his ships over the Isthmus into the safety of the Gulf of Corinth if he will aid Macedon /Achaea against Aetolians.

Demetrius agrees to these terms, but campaigns ineffectively in the Gulf as the Aetolian army has by now left Achaea for home; he sails back to Illyria.

Autumn – After the Aetolians ally with Illyria to produce a threat of land-invasion to distract Philip, he wins them and their fleet back by bribes and marches to Corinth to hold a congress of the 'symmachy'. In Sparta, the majority of the ruling 'ephors' plan to abandon their Macedonian alliance and ally with Aetolia, murder the dissenting 'ephor'

Adeimantus lest he warn Philip, and assure Philip that they are loyal; he decides to believe them and not to attack Sparta as some of his advisers want. The meeting of the congress at Corinth agrees to go to war with Aetolia and demands that Aetolia hands over control of the sanctuary at Delphi. Philip agrees to meet Aetolian delegates at Rhium, but when he arrives they fail to turn up; instead, they elect the warmonger Scopas as 'strategos' for the next year. Philip sends troops to Crete to defeat the Aetolians' allied leadership (the league led by Cnossus) there, aiding anti-Cnossus rebel town of Polyrrenia, which has seceded from their league; this force defeats Cnossus and brings Crete into Philip's Greek alliance.

Meeting and alliance between Philip and Scerdilaidas, uncle and chief military support/ minister of young King Pinnes of the Illyrians (Ardiaei); he abandons his Aetolian allies as they did not give him a share of the loot of the 220 Peloponnesian campaign as promised. Epirus backs Philip and asks Ptolemy IV's regency to abandon its Aetolian alliance. Machatas visits Sparta as Aetolian envoy to try to get military help, and fails but stirs up a plot. Agesipolis III, grandson of Cleombrotus II, and the dynastically obscure but rich Lycurgus are restored as kings of Sparta, along with the old constitution, after all five of the 'ephors' are murdered during an official sacrifice-ceremony at temple of Athena by a pro-Aetolian conspiracy. The coup-leaders then appoint their own 'ephors' and arrange the restoration; Machatas returns and alliance agreed. He goes on to secure Elis for Aetolia, while Lycurgus raids Achaea.

Asia Minor/Seleucids
War between Rhodes/Prusias of Bithynia and Byzantium; the latter try to employ Prusias' exiled uncle Tiboetes, who is in Macedon, to take over Bithynia but he dies, and Rhodes persuades the Egyptian government to hand over Andromachus, father of regional Seleucid governor prince Achaeus, to them so they can send him to his son to arrange for Achaeus to back them, not his current ally Byzantium. The Galatians mediate peace.

Spain
Dispute between Saguntum and a raiding Spanish tribe, allies to Carthage, leads to Hannibal supporting the latter; Saguntum appeals for Roman support.

Egypt
Chief minister Sosibius kills his political rivals, including the boy-king Ptolemy IV's uncle Lysimachus.

219

Spain
?Spring – Hannibal marches to support of his tribal allies and besieges Saguntum; Lucius Aemilius Paullus and Marcus Livius Salvinator are elected as consuls, and are sent with a second naval expedition to Illyria, presumably before news of the siege reaches Rome.

Egypt /Seleucids
Exiled King Cleomenes of Sparta tries to launch a popular revolution in Alexandria against the Ptolemaic government after he fails to win Sosibius' assistance for a new expedition to Greece and he is put under house-arrest; he gets his guards drunk while the King is away at Canopus, breaks out of his house aided by his friends, intercepts and arrests the city

governor and leads a rally in the city square, calling for a fight for liberty, but fails to attract support; ignored by the populace and failing to get access to the citadel as the guard are now alert, he and his followers kill themselves.

Antochus III reconquers the coastal port of Seleucia Pieria by siege while his admiral Diognetus blockades it; he marches on south as Ptolemy's governor Theodotus deserts to him but the latter is quickly besieged in Ptolmais/Acra by loyal general Nicolaus; Antiochus forces him to retreat and is joined by Theodotus, securing Tyre and Ptolemais.

Egyptian chief minister Sosibius launches a radical overhaul of the army to add to its numbers, logically to face the new threat of Antiochus III's numerical superiority after he reconquered Mesopotamia; Sosibius enrols up to 30,000 native Egyptians to train as infantry in the Macedonian-style 'phalanx'. Meanwhile, he sends to Rhodes, Byzantium, Cyzicus and Aetolia to get them to send mediation missions to Antiochus to delay his attack on Egypt, and the Egyptian court moves to Memphis to flood the Nile canals in case of invasion.

Four-month truce arranged for the winter, as Antiochus is nervous of Achaeus' intentions.

Adriatic

Second Roman naval expedition to the Illyrian coast, following attacks on their local allies by Scerdilaidas and Demetrius of Pharos; consul Aemilius Paullus leads expedition to attack the town of Dimallum near Apollonia, which Demetrius has fortified with strong garrison. The town is unexpectedly stormed on seventh day of siege, and the Romans move on to Demetrius' home island of Pharos. Demetrius awaits attack in the fortified town, but Paullus lands his main force secretly in the cover of some forest and they advance on the town under cover while a smaller, decoy force sails into view. The latter lands outside the town, and Demetrius emerges confidently to attack them; the ambushers charge out to attack him in the flanks, and he is routed and loses many men. The town has to surrender, and Demetrius is exiled as Pharos and all his other possessions enter treaties with Rome as dependant allies. The inland kingdom of Pinnes, Demetrius' ward, is maintained as ally of Rome; Demetrius goes to Macedon to become anti-Roman adviser to Philip.

Greece

Philip purges anti-Achaean Macedonians, and allies with Achaea; Sparta under new king, Lycurgus, backs Aetolia.

Dorimachus and an Aetolian force attack Aegera, on southern side of Gulf of Corinth, to force it out of Achaean League; they crawl in through an aqueduct to kill guards and open the gates, but as they are busy looting, not securing all the strongpoints, the townsfolk rally and fight back and they are driven out. Euripidas, however, has more success in Elis, allied to Lycurgus of Sparta who takes the 'Athenaeum' fortress at Megalopolis.

Autumn – Philip invades Ambracia via Epirus; Scopas and the Aetolians attack Macedon in his absence and sack Dium; Philip crosses the Ambracian Gulf to attack Phoeitiae, then Stratus (where Achaean envoys arrive asking for aid), Metropolis, and Conope; he crosses the River Achelous and occupies Oeniadae, which becomes his base, and ravages into Calydon lands.

At Calydon, he hears of an imminent Dardanian invasion and returns home, but the attack does not materialize as his march has given the enemy second thoughts.

Mid-December – Philip marches south again via Thessaly with 3000 infantry ('Bronze Shields' regiment), 2000 'peltasts', 300 Cretans, and c. 400 cavalry (Polybius).

Spain
?Winter – Fall of Saguntum to Hannibal.

218

Italy/Carthage
?Early spring – Paullus and Livius are sent to Carthage in embassy; they denounce Hannibal, demand his arrest and handover, and demand to know whether he is acting with the approval of the Carthaginian Senate; despite efforts of a peace-party led by Hanno the Carthaginians resist and claim that Saguntum is none of Rome's business.

March – New consuls, Publius Cornelius Scipio and Tiberius Sempronius Longus; Scipio is sent to Spain to confront Hannibal, and Sempronius is sent to Sicily to prepare for invasion of Africa.

Hannibal raises and receives new troops, and plans to march to Italy.

?Late summer – Hannibal crosses the Pyrenees.

Greece
Midwinter – Philip marches his army quickly to Corinth and on into the Peloponnese to camp at the sanctuary of Castor and Pollux near Phlius; Philip takes the raiding Eleans and Euripidas by surprise and the latter flees into hilly country as he hears that the Macedonians have arrived; the abandoned Eleans are not even sure who the new army in view is, and are attacked and destroyed. Philip crosses the Arcadian mountains despite snow and storms Psophis, where Euripidas has taken refuge; the Aetolian general and his Elean allies are trapped in the acropolis and negotiate a safe retreat. Psophis is handed back to Achaea, and Lasion and Stratus are abandoned; Philip reaches Olympia.

Philip overruns south Elis and Triphylia, retaking Phigaleia.

Agesipolis of Sparta is exiled in new faction-feuding, and pretender Chilon, offering a redistribution of land to the people, murders the 'ephors' and gets co-king Lycurgus exiled too; Lycurgus is soon restored but is later exiled again on suspicion of wanting to set up a tyranny.

Philip ends the winter based at Argos. ?Spring – He marches across north Elis to shore up the north-west of Achaea and evict an Elean garrison from a strongpoint near allied Dyme.

May – Epiratus of Pharae elected 'strategos' of Achaea at Philip's wishes instead of the usual Aratus, after the latter is undermined by his rivals and the Macedonian minister Apelles for supposed lack of loyalty to Macedon; Apelles wants to provoke Achaeans into annoying Philip so he will reduce their autonomy to dependant status and Aratus is a major obstacle to that.

But Aratus is later cleared and reinstated in Philip's favour, while Apelles tries to get Taurion sacked instead; after the Achaean general assembly at Aegium proves niggardly in giving money to Philip for the war (which Apelles encouraged so Philip would blame Aratus) Philip calls a second assembly at Sicyon where he secures fifty talents plus a promise of another seventeen each month.

Dorimachus is chosen as Aetolian 'strategos'.

Philip prepares his fleet at Corinth and then sails to Patras; he uses his fleet to cross the Gulf of Corinth and then take over the island of Cephallonia from its alliance to Aetolia as its ships transport Aetolian troops to the western Peloponnese; he is joined by his ally Scerdilaidas' Illyrian ships and aid from Acarnania and Messenia. The Aetolians send Scopas to support Elis and Dorimachus invades Thessaly; Lycurgus of Sparta attacks Messenia. Philip attacks the town of Pale, on the south-west borders of Aetolia, but his siege has to be called off after his troops are repulsed crossing the walls and lose heart – apparently the general Leontius held back deliberately (as part of his friend Apelles' plan to undermine Philip's growing confidence and independence of his senior advisers), and he comes under his master's suspicion as a result. Leontius' advice to attack the Elis/ Aetolian army in Messenia as the Messenians want is rejected in favour of Aratus' to attack Aetolian home territory.

With most of the Aetolian army campaigning away from home, Philip attacks their south coast on the Gulf of Corinth and advances quickly to sack Thermum; his troops damage the Aetolians' religious trophies, valuable artworks, in breach of normal standards of warfare. He continues to his 219 garrisons at the north-west end of the Gulf, sacking various towns en route, including Pamphea, Metapa, and Stratus and defeating an Aetolian attack on his rearguard as they cross the River Achelous near Stratus. He arrests and imprisons his senior officer Megaleas, ally of Apelles, for attacking and abusing Aratus during the aftermath of a drunken royal feast in camp. Leontius, who joined in the confrontation but was not caught, goes bail for Megaleas. Philip returns by sea to Corinth.

Autumn – Philip retakes Tegea from Sparta and raids Laconia from Corinth; he occupies Amyclae near the city and plunders the region, and as he is leaving for Corinth he is intercepted by but routs Lycurgus; at the end of the fighting season his army at Corinth is dissatisfied with the minimal loot from the war and has been stirred up by some officers, including the ambitious minister Apelles' ally Leontius (who also clashed with and abused Aratus on the recent Macedonian/Achaean campaign to Thermum). Philip calms the soldiers and arrests and kills Apelles, now in command at Chalcis, and tries Megaleas who kills himself. He attempts negotiations with Aetolia following an offer from Rhodes to mediate, but the Aetolians' terms for attending a peace-conference are too high; he marches home to Macedon for the winter.

Seleucids

Antiochus III' s generals, including now the defector Theodotus, defeat Nicolaus in battle on the Lebanese coast and take Sidon, while at sea Diognetus' fleet meets Egyptians under Perigenes indecisively but the latter have to retreat after land-defeats; the king conquers Palestine and inland towns across the Jordan, e.g. Scythopolis, from the Ptolemies.

Attalus of Pergamum reconquers the rebel Achaeus' acquisitions in Aeolis and Mysia, north Ionia, while Achaeus is busy campaigning in Pamphylia (southern Asia Minor) after appeals for help against the city of Selge.

Italy

?November – Hannibal crosses the Alps, with c. 20,000 infantry and 6,000 cavalry. Hannibal storms the chief fortification of the Taurini tribe (Turin area) who are fighting his allies and block his advance.

?Late November – Scipio is defeated by Hannibal at the River Ticinus. The Senate recalls Sempronius from Sicily to aid Scipio; he returns swiftly, while his lieutenant Pomponius remains defending Tyrrhenian coast.

December – Hannibal wins the Battle of the River Trebbia.

217

Italy

Hannibal marches on Arretium, and starts devastating Etruria to lure consul Flaminius after him onto a battle-site of his choosing.

21 June – The Battle of Lake Trasimene is won by Hannibal. In Rome, left without effective defence, Quintus Fabius Maximus is appointed dictator with Marcus Minucius Rufus as 'Master of the Horse'; Marcus Atilius Regulus (son of the consul of 256) is the replacement consul. Hannibal fails to take Spoletium (Spoleto) and marches through Picenum into Marsi territory and thence Apulia to raise Rome's allies in revolt.

Greece

Aratus is elected 'strategos' of Achaea again for 217–16, after the restoration of good terms with Philip.

After Lake Trasimene, Philip considers alliance with Hannibal and is urged to this course by Demetrius of Pharos who is the only councillor he shows a letter he received detailing the battle.

Adriatic

Death of young king Pinnes of the main Illyrian kingdom, of the Ardiaei; succession of his paternal uncle Scerdilaidas who is now or later assisted by his son Pleuratus (III).

Adriatic/Greece

Scerdilaidas complains that Philip is late in paying his annual subsidy to him, and sends a force of warships south into the Ionian Sea to 'collect' it – and loot Philip's allies as a warning. At Leucas in the Ionian Islands they kill some Corinthian friends of Philip's and seize their four ships. They then sail on round Cape Malea to plunder the Peloponnesian coast, and Philip sends out a naval force too late to catch them; they return home with loot.

Late summer (harvest) Agetas' Aetolian army raids Acarnania and Epirus; Aratus reforms the Achaean army and helps to defend demoralized and faction-ridden Megalopolis from Spartan attack, but is kept on the defensive and has to guard the Argive harvest from Spartan attack; Lycus' Achaeans and locals defeats an Elean/Euripidas' Aetolians attack on Tritea.

Scerdilaidas raids into western Macedon, over-running Dassaretia and sacking Pissaeum in Pelagonia. Philip then campaigns across western Macedon to restore his frontier and takes Bylazora to keep the Dardanians at bay. He takes Pthiotid Thebes in Thessaly, an Aetolian base for attacks on nearby Demetrias, to force the Aetolians out of Thessaly.

Now or earlier Scerdilaidas becomes an ally of Rome.

Seleucids/Egypt

Ptolemy IV and an army of around 70,000 infantry, 5000 cavalry, and 75 elephants (Polybius) march from Pelusium on Palestine; Antiochus is waiting at Gaza with around

62,000 infantry, 6000 cavalry, and 62 elephants (Polybius). Theodotus the Egyptian defector sneaks back into their camp and penetrates the royal tent to try to assassinate Ptolemy, but misses his target as the king is not in his official bedchamber.

July? – Antiochus III is defeated by the Egyptian army at the battle of Raphia near Gaza with their larger army containing newly trained native Egyptians in a Macedonian-style phalanx. The Egyptian 'Libyan' elephants are more nervous of battle than Antiochus' Indian elephants, and they fall back onto the Egyptian left wing whereupon Antiochus and his cavalry follow them to attack Polycrates' Egyptian cavalry and the light infantry 'peltasts'. Echecrates on the Egyptian right wing cannot get his elephants even to approach the enemy elephants, but is successful in a cavalry attack on the Seleucid left wing; Phoxidas and the Egyptian mercenaries also drive back their (infantry) opponents, and with the Seleucid phalanx left exposed Ptolemy rallies his phalanx in person to advance – the one brave action of an undistinguished reign. Antiochus is too inexperienced to turn on the enemy quickly after his success and cannot see properly in the dust, and the battle is lost; he has to retreat to Gaza. Around 10,000 Seleucid infantry and 300 cavalry are killed and 4000 men captured; Ptolemy loses around 1500 infantry and 700 cavalry (Polybius).

Antiochus sends his nephew Antipater to Ptolemy to negotiate. Ptolemy IV agrees to peace, regaining rule of Palestine and Phoenicia; Andromachus is appointed governor.

Greece
Philip sets up base at Panormus, on the southern side of the Gulf of Corinth opposite Naupactus.

Autumn – Aetolians accept an offer to come to peace-conference with Macedon and Achaea at Naupactus; once they have assembled there Philip sends Aratus and his general Taurion to preliminary discussions to check that they are serious; they report favourably, so talks proceed.

Philip comes with his army to camp a few miles from the town.

'Conference of Naupactus' – Philip's decision for talks, not an invasion of Aetolia, is stimulated by concern over what is going on in Italy and possibly a plan to link up with Hannibal to destroy Roman power in the Adriatic. Also, the Aetolian delegate Agelaus urges him to help create a general peace and alliance in Greece before the winner of the titanic Rome vs Carthage struggle turns on them next. The conference of Naupactus restores a 'general peace' but with himself as guarantor and as leader of the Greeks, effectively bringing Aetolia into his power-system with the latter recognizing the need to accept his interests.

Once peace is agreed, Philip returns to Macedon; suspicious of Scerdilaidas, he overruns the frontier territory of Dassaretia to protect his western border and aid a safe passage for his forces to the Adriatic ready to take on Rome.

Egypt
Native revolt in the Nile valley against the harsh demands for men and money for the Syrian war.

216

Italy/Greece
Winter – Philip builds a large fleet of 100 warships, the first powerful Macedonian fleet since the wars of the Diadochi and the first intended for Adriatic. He plans to replace Illyria as the regional power to keep Rome out, and uses model of light, fast Illyrian galleys for his ships. Scerdilaidas is warned of the plan and asks Rome for naval help.

Caius Terentius Varro and Lucius Aemilius Paullus are elected consuls, and envoys are sent to Ligurian tribes to protest at their aid to Hannibal and to Macedonia to protest at King Philip V giving sanctuary to refugee Illyrian pirate Demetrius of Pharos.

Timoxenus elected 'strategos' of Achaea for 216–15, resuming his 220s alternation of command with Aratus.

Philip leads expedition from Macedon, round Cape Malea, into the Ionian, and up the Adriatic to Illyria to evict Roman and local pirate garrisons while the main Roman fleet is expected to be at Lilybaeum in Sicily watching Carthage. However, at Saso island near Cape Vlore, nearing Apollonia, he hears that a Roman fleet is nearby and orders a precipitate retreat, finding out later that it was only ten ships.

Sicily
Hiero of Syracuse sends grain and other aid to Rome, and unsuccessfully advises an invasion of Africa to force Hannibal's recall.

Italy
May? – Hannibal leaves Gerunium to march south and loot the ripening crops en route, followed at a safe distance by ex-consuls/proconsuls Geminus and Regulus; he captures the Roman supply-base at Cannae, on the River Aufidus in Apulia.

2 August – Battle of Cannae: the Romans are surrounded and ground down in hours of fighting, and (Livy) Romans lose c. 45,000 infantry and 12,000 cavalry killed (29 out of 48 military tribunes and 40 other senators) (Polybius puts the total of casualties at 70,000); consul Paullus is killed but Varro escapes with cavalry survivors to Venusia as c. 3000 infantry and 1500 cavalry are captured; most of Apulia, Bruttia, Samnium, and Campania, led by Capua, joins Hannibal – Campania revolts against Rome after failure to extort harsh terms from it for an alliance including a Campanian as consul. Hannibal secures Capua but he fails to take loyal Neapolis (Naples).

215

Sicily
?Early – Death of the aged Hiero of Syracuse, after a fifty-four-year reign; he is succeeded by his inexperienced fifteen-year-old grandson Hieronymus; as political faction-disputes revive, the latter seeks to auction his services to Carthage and sends envoys demanding increasingly high terms including acceptance of his rule of all Sicily once Romans evicted. Thraso, the most pro-Roman of his ministers, is executed after false implication in a plot and praetor Appius Claudius' Roman envoys to renew treaty are ignored.

Greece /Italy
Aratus is elected 'strategos' of Achaea again, for 215-14.

Philip sends orator Xenophanes of Athens with a mission to Hannibal to secure alliance and promises to attack Roman allies in Illyria; on the return journey they and Carthaginian envoys Gisgo, Bostar and Mago are intercepted by Roman ships near Cumae and captured, and Xenophanes claims to be en route from Philip to Rome but his Punic escorts are identified and his letters between Hannibal and Philip are taken and opened; later, a second Macedonian embassy reaches Hannibal and returns unhindered, and Aut. praetor Marcus Valerius Laevinus is sent with two legions from Sicily to Brundisum to guard the crossing to Italy from Epirus.

Hanno leads a force to Bruttium to aid the locals in attacking pro-Roman Greek cities; the town of Locroi is besieged but negotiates an alliance with Hannibal and the right to control neighbouring territory as his ally in return for surrender, annoying the Bruttians who looked forward to looting it.

Hannibal winters near Arpi in Apulia, while Fabius ravages Campania.

On campaign in the Peloponnese, Philip arrives with his Achaean allies at Messene the day after the populace have massacred their leaders; he is advised in favour of reprisals and keeping his garrison in the city by ruthless Demetrius of Pharos and in favour of evacuation as winning more respect by Aratus; he follows Aratus' advice. This is cited by Polybius as the point at which Philip began to turn tyrannical as overlord of and lose respect in Greece.

214

Italy/Sicily

March – Fabius Maximus and Marcellus are consuls; Otacilius is sent with an enlarged fleet to Sicily as war is expected with Syracuse; pro-praetor Quintus Mucius is sent to Sardinia, and Gracchus at Luceria and Varro in Picenum have their commands from 215 extended.

Marcellus relieves Hannibal's attack on Nola, and covers Fabius' army while he besieges and takes Casilinum; Gracchus destroys c. 15,000 of Hanno's army of c. 17,000 Carthaginians and Bruttians in battle at Beneventum.

Sicily

Early spring – Hieronymus of Syracuse is murdered by a faction at the vassal-city of Leontinoi, and the republic is restored as plotters Theodotus and Sosis arrive in Syracuse to rally support; Hieronymus' uncle Adranodorus holds the citadel but agrees to accept the republic and is among the newly elected magistrates; he and ally Themistus are assassinated as they plan to regain power in subsequent political conflict, and their royally related wives and other relatives are murdered in a political massacre; the new ruling faction includes anti-Roman brothers Hippocrates and Epicydes, two of the Syracusan envoys to Carthage in 215, and when Hippocrates is sent to command at Leontinoi he proclaims its independence of Syracuse, kills Roman residents, and starts to raid the Roman province, aided by deserters.

Marcellus is sent to Sicily; he agrees to let the disgraced Cannae survivors join his army, though the Senate insists that these 'cowards' receive no honours after the war however successful they are, and advances on Leontinoi as the Syracusan government insist its garrison's depredations are nothing to do with them. He storms Leontinoi and executes deserters, but Hippocrates and Epicydes escape, win over a Syracusan contingent sent to assist Marcellus in return for his promise of Leontinoi's return, and lead them back to seize Syracuse; Marcellus prepares to attack Syracuse and retakes revolted Helorus and Megara.

Seleucids
Antiochus invades and overruns western Asia Minor, driving Achaeus back to Sardes, which is besieged; Achaeus asks Ptolemy for the help of a naval relief-fleet.

Greece
Demetrius of Pharos, adviser to Philip of Macedon and anti-Roman ex-admiral in Illyria, is killed attempting to take over Messene.

Italy
Hannibal is approached during an unsuccessful siege of Cumae by five Tarentine nobles, ex-prisoners from Cannae, who promise the defection of their city when his army arrives; he marches to Naples and Nola and then quickly on to Tarentum, but finds that the Roman fleet from Brundisium has joined an enlarged garrison; the city does not revolt so he returns to Campania.

Adriatic
Philip leads a fleet of 120 ships into the Adriatic and takes Oricum; he then moves on to besiege Apollonia.

Laevinus, commander of Roman fleet and army at Brundisium against Macedon, receives reports that Philip's fleet has attacked Apollonia; he sails across the Adriatic, retakes Oricum, and sends Naevius Crista and 2000 men to relieve Apollonia. They arrive at night, unobserved from Philip's camp, and next day they sally to drive off besiegers; Philip panics and burns his fleet sooner than face naval battle, then evacuates his army back over the mountains to Macedon.

Laevinus establishes a base at Oricum but there is no more fighting.

213

Sicily
?March/April – Marcellus, continuing command as proconsul as the next consuls enter office in Rome, launches attack on Syracuse; he attacks the city by land and sea, with Roman galleys lashed together in pairs to carry scaling-ladders, which can be lifted up masts and placed against the sea-walls of the city at appropriate height; however, the philosopher Archimedes develops defensive engines to aid the besieged, including catapults to sink ships, giant 'claws' to lift them out of the water, and probably some sort of giant mirror to focus the rays of the sun and concentrate them on particular points to start fires; with the help of these machines all attacks are defeated, and the Romans are too nervous of the machines to approach the sea-walls again.

Leaving ex-praetor Appius Claudius in charge of siege, Marcellus takes part of his army off to reduce Syracuse's dependant towns; Himilco lands with 25,000 infantry and 3000 cavalry at Heraclea Minoa and marches to Agrigentum, and Marcellus fails to reach there first but catches Hippocrates bringing a Syracusan force to assist Himilco and destroys it.

Greece

Aratus of Sicyon is 'strategos' of Achaea for the final time, but by now is disapproving of his patron and supposed friend King Philip for his increasingly autocratic behaviour (and possibly his affair with Aratus' daughter-in-law, too). He dies, aged fifty-eight, later in the year.

Adriatic

(Into 212) Philip conquers the Dassaratae tribe and the southern part of the Illyrian kingdom of the Ardaei, and also overruns Athamania. He thus secures most of southern Illyria, and can then move on westwards along the Adriatic coast without risking a naval challenge to the Roman fleet.

Seleucids

Antiochus III besieges Achaeus in the citadel of Sardes, and it is stormed in a surprise attack as expert Seleucid troops (Cretans) climb up the steep rock unnoticed; the rebel is captured, mutilated, and executed. Antiochus fully restores Seleucid control over western Asia Minor.

212

Sicily

Early – During negotiations concerning prisoner-exchange outside Syracuse, a Roman officer calculates the height of the nearby wall by Galeagra tower so that scaling-ladders can be brought up; while the inhabitants are celebrating a festival of Artemis and getting drunk the Romans scale the wall at night, kill guards, and open the nearby Hexapylon gate; the main army is admitted and gains control of the main part of the 'new' city on the Epipolae heights overlooking the harbour, forcing Epicydes' defenders to withdraw into the older quarter of Achradina downhill by the harbour. The citadel of Euryalus, left isolated at the western end of the 'new' city, soon surrenders.

Italy

?February/March – There is resentment against Rome in Tarentum after some hostages from the city are executed in Rome for attempted escape; Philemenus and Nico lead a new conspiracy and go to Hannibal's winter camp during a hunting expedition to offer the city to him; negotiations secure Tarentum's right to self-government, freedom from garrison, and no tribute, Hannibal forms a force of 10,000 cavalry and infantry, which he leads swiftly to Tarentum while supposedly out foraging; the Roman commander Livius fails to realize what the spotting of some Numidian cavalry in the vicinity means, and at night while conspirator officers are distracting him with a party Hannibal moves up to the Temenid gate, which other plotters seize; Philemenus arrives at another gate with a boar after another supposed hunt and on his admission spears the guard, and the Carthaginians storm into the city and join conspirators at the forum; the populace is summoned and submits, but Livius holds the citadel and the Roman garrison at Metapontum joins him.

Sicily

Himilco and Hippocrates return with the main Carthaginian army too late to save most of Syracuse, and blockade the Romans while their ships break blockade at sea and reinforce the Ortygia citadel, the seat of power in city, in the harbour; however, plague breaks out in the Carthaginian camp on unhealthy marshy ground by the harbour and the many casualties include both Himilco and Hippocrates; the survivors withdraw.

Adriatic
Philip storms the citadel of Lissus, the most powerful stronghold on the central Adriatic coast, to secure domination of the region on land.

Sicily
Autumn – Bomilcar brings 700 merchantmen and 150 warships to relieve Syracuse, and is confronted by Marcellus' navy off Cape Pachynus; both fleets avoid battle while sheltering from gale, but Bomilcar then loses his nerve and sails direct to Hannibal at Tarentum leaving Syracuse to its fate; the garrison starts to lose hope and Epicydes flees to Agrigentum.

211

Sicily
The mercenary troops at Ortygia citadel prevent the surrender of Syracuse, which the Greek residents want, due to fear of execution by Romans, but Spanish officer Moericus arranges to admit a party of Roman soldiers; while Marcellus attacks Achradina to distract the garrison they are taken across the harbour by merchant-ship and admitted to the citadel through a gate. The citadel is stormed and its royal treasury seized; soon afterwards Achradina surrenders, and during the Roman plundering of the 'old city' Archimedes is killed, unrecognized by a soldier, despite Marcellus' orders to secure him alive. According to legend he was too busy studying a technical drawing in the dust on ground to respond to an arresting Roman soldier.

Marcellus moves against Hanno's Carthaginian army at Agrigentum, which has been joined by Muttines the Libyan and a force of expert Numidian raiders from Hannibal in Italy; encouraged by Muttines' successes against Roman-allied towns, Hanno moves up to the River Himera and the armies skirmish; Muttines wins some clashes, but is recalled to Heraclea Minoa after a mutiny and in his absence Hanno and Epicydes are defeated by Marcellus.

Late – Marcellus leaves Sicily with his plunder from Syracuse and allied cities including art-works; after his departure 8000 Carthaginian infantry and 3000 cavalry arrive in Sicily.

Winter 211–210

Greece
A Roman alliance with the Aetolian League in Greece, Philip's opponents, is organized by a Roman embassy led by Valerius Laevinus. Rome is to supply a naval force of twenty-five 'quinqueremes' to campaign, and Aetolians to have any territory conquered from Philip south of Corcyra and also the return of Acarnania; neither side is to make peace without the other's permission. Scopas and Dorimachus are the Aetolian negotiators, as old enemies of Macedon. Sparta, Elis, and Mantinea join alliance with Rome.

Valerius Laevinus' fleet, based at Corcyra, aids the Aetolian campaign against Philip and takes the island of Zacynthus. Philip realizes what is happening and attacks Oricum and Apollonia to secure the Adriatic coast from the Roman fleet, then takes Sintia to keep the Dardanians back. Hearing that he is on the north-west borders, Scopas as Aetolian 'strategos' invades Acarnania, but the inhabitants take an oath for all to resist to the death and appeal to Philip; as Philip reaches Dium en route south, Scopas retires to Aetolia.

210

Greece
Spring – Laevinus' fleet enters the Gulf of Corinth to aid Aetolians, and joins them to take Anticyra in Locris.

Sicily
Laevinus advances on Agrigentum, where Hanno has dismissed Muttines from command of the Numidian cavalry and given the post to his own son; Muttines angrily opens secret negotiations with Laevinus, and on his arrival the Numidians open a gate to the Roman army; Hanno and Epicydes flee by sea, leaving the city and most of troops to be captured.

Greece
Philopoemen returns to Achaea after a decade in Crete as a mercenary captain. He is elected the pro-Macedonian 'Hipparch' of Achaean League to command the cavalry, which he reforms. Later that year he is commanding when the Acheaans fight an Aetolian/Elis army, and kills the enemy commander Damophantus in single combat.

Philip drives the Aetolians out of Thessaly.

A Roman and Aetolian fleet takes the island of Aegina, which is handed to Rome's new ally, Philip's opponent King Attalus of Pergamum, and lands troops in Elis in the western Peloponnese.

Machanidas is regent of Sparta for young king, ?Pelops.

209

Italy
March – Fabius Maximus and Quintus Fulvius Flaccus are consuls; Fabius commands around Tarentum and Fulvius in Lucania. Fabius leaves four legions to watch Hannibal and leads his other ten against Tarentum while Bruttian irregular troops and soldiers from Sicily raid northwards from Rhegium against Hannibal's rear.

Carthalo's Carthaginian garrison of Tarentum is undermined by the infiltration of a Tarentine pretended deserter from Fabius' army who persuades his sister's Bruttian lover, a Carthaginian officer, to desert with his men when Fabius arrives; the Romans attack the walls, and the Bruttian and his men help them to scale their stretch of wall and enter Tarentum; the town is stormed and sacked and Carthalo is cut down trying to reach Fabius to surrender, and 30,000 inhabitants are sold as slaves as an example. Hannibal arrives too late, and unsuccessfully tries to tempt Fabius to march south into an ambush by sending him pretended traitors from Metapontum offering the town to Rome.

Seleucids
Antiochus III invades Parthia, and besieges the capital, Hecatompylus; the Parthians under King Priapatius surrender and become his vassals.

Greece

Attalus of Pergamum brings his fleet to Aegina to aid Rome, and in the autumn their general, Galba, arrives to join him.

Philpoemen is 'strategos' of Achaean League for the year, and reorganizes and expands the infantry, training them in new battle-tactics.

208

Greece

Pyyrhias is 'strategos' of the Aetolian League, along with honorary co-generalship for the League's new ally and funder Attalus of Pergamum.

Philip leads the Macedonian army through Greece to aid the Achaean League against an attack on Achaea by Machanidas, regent of Sparta, defeating Pyrrhias' Aetolians and 1000 Roman allies en route at two clashes near Lamia; he meets envoys from Athens, Rhodes, Chios, Ptolemy IV, and King Amynander of Athamania (south Epirus) at Phalara for their attempts at mediation. He accepts a thirty-day truce, uses it to strengthen Chalcis lest Attalus and his fleet attack it, and proceeds to Argos for the Nemean Games where he is voted in as their president.

Philip addresses the Achaean general assembly at Aegium, but the Roman fleet arrives at Naupactus under Publius Sulpicius and this inspires the Aetolians to demand that their allies, e.g. Scerdilaidas, get their lands back and Philip refuses and leaves. The Romans raid the Achaean coast and send troops to Cyllene to back up Aetolians and Elis troops there; Sulpicius then aids Aetolians and Elis in successful battle with Philip, who has to withdraw to Macedon in a hurry as the rebel Aeropus seizes Lychnidus in Orestis and incites Dardanians to invade. Attalus of Pergamum and his fleet fail to take Chalcis from Macedon; Sulpicius joins Attalus and his fleet at Aegina.

Achaeans under Philopoemen attack Sparta and kill regent Machinadas in battle at Mantinea; Nabis seizes control as 'tyrant', reforming the citizenship to open it to new entrants and reorganizing the army.

Seleucids

Antiochus III invades Bactria and besieges King Euthydemus in his capital, Bactra/Balkh.

207

Italy

March – Marcus Livius Salvinator and Tiberius Claudius Nero are consuls.

Summer – Battle of the River Metaurus: Hasdrubal, brother of Hannibal, and his reinforcements from Spain are destroyed as they arrive in Italy by Livius and Claudius; (Polybius) c.10,000 Carthaginians and 2000 Romans are killed; Hasdrubal is either killed or kills himself, and his head is taken south by returning Claudius and thrown into Hannibal's camp in Apulia.

Hannibal has now lost serious hope of reinforcement and is forced into defensive positions in Bruttia.

Greece

Summer – Sulpicius with twenty-five and Attalus with thirty-five ships establish a new Aegean base at Lemnos ready to raid Macedonian coasts, while Philip defends Macedonia against their expected raids and sets up camp at Demetrias; Menippus defends Euboaea against an allied landing. Philip raids Aetolia and burns the crops after they invite Attalus to address their council at Heraclea. Sulpicius and Attalus sack Oreus in Boeotia, but Attalus is nearly caught while sacking Opus as Philip arrives quickly from Thessaly and he has to re-embark and sail off. Attalus leaves for Asia Minor after the news that Philip's ally Prusias of Bithynia is invading his territory.

Philip invades Aetolia and takes Thronium, while his Achaean allies in the Peloponnese, led by general Philopoemen, defeat Rome and Aetolia's ally Sparta at Mantinea. Envoys from Ptolemy IV and Rhodes come to Philip at Elatea to mediate; he marches into the Peloponnese to Phlius en route to drive Machanidas off Achaea but the latter retreats before he can be caught. He then makes a brief foray from the Gulf of Corinth into Aetolia to attack Erythrae, sails to Corinth, and sends his army back via Boeotia to Macedon, while he goes to Chalcis to commend the garrison for defence against Attalus and sails to Demetrias.

Seleucids

Antiochus III makes peace with Euthydemus of Bactria, who recognizes his suzerainty and is allowed to stay as governor; the latter's son Demetrius marries Antiochus' daughter Theophila.

206

Greece

Aetolians agree to peace with Philip after mediation by Egypt and Rhodes, but Rome prepares for a new offensive now that more troops can be spared from Italy.

Seleucids

Antiochus III crosses the Paropamisadae/Hindu Kush to the upper Indus valley on a morale-boosting repeat of Alexander's march ('Anabasis'), to impress and secure treaties with the local Indian rulers. He then returns to Areia en route across Iran.

205

Italy

February/March – Scipio, son of the 218 consul and conqueror of Spain, is elected consul after promoting the idea of an invasion of Africa despite opposition led by Fabius; he is granted Sicily, with permission to cross to Africa if he deems it necessary.

Greece

Proconsul Publius Sempronius Tuditanus is sent with 11,000 men and thirty-five 'quinqueremes' to Epirus on a new expedition to fight Philip, and lands at Dyrrachium; Philip's army advances on Apollonia, and the Romans hasten to its defence but reject his attempt to force battle. With no new allies likely to fight in Greece and the Epirots offering to mediate, which Philip accepts, Sempronius opens negotiations with Philip and the

'Peace of Phoenice' (Epirot town) is agreed whereby the 'status quo' is accepted and Rome secures new possessions on the Illyrian coast. Rome's allies Scerdilaidas of Illyria (Ardiaei) and Longarus of the Dardani are confirmed in possession of their lands.

Achaea moves against the remaining Macedonian garrisons in Greece; Philip blames Philopoemen and tries to assassinate him.

Seleucids
Antiochus III returns to Seleucia in Mesopotamia after his long journey to the Indian frontier and back.

Sicily/Italy
Scipio reorganizes his army in Sicily, replacing the older veterans of the two Cannae legions there with new troops, and sends Laelius and around thirty ships to raid the African coast, alarm Carthage, and make contact with King Masinissa of Numidia.

204

Spring – Scipio invades Africa.

Greece
Nabis of Sparta attacks Achaea and starts a war over a refugee runaway groom of his being given sanctuary in Megalopolis.

Seleucids
?Antiochus III sails down the Persian Gulf to Gerra, near Ormuz.

Egypt
Autumn? – Death of Ptolemy IV, aged in his early thirties; he is succeeded by his five-year-old son Ptolemy V.

The late king's widow Arsinoe loses out to the ministers Agathocles (brother of the late king's mistress) and Sosibius in a struggle for power and is executed; they take over the regency.

203

Greece/Seleucids
A Roman embassy travels to Macedon for talks with Philip.

Antiochus III meets Philip to divide up 'spheres of influence'; Antiochus gives Philip a free hand in the Aegean and Ionia, probably with a view to concentrating on Egypt.

Egypt
28 November – After the death of co-regent Sosibius, his partner Agathocles takes over and belatedly announces the death of Ptolemy IV and the accession of Ptolemy V.

Italy
Late? – Hannibal and his army are evacuated from Bruttia to Carthage.

202

North Africa/Italy
Battle of Zama: Scipio decisively defeats Hannibal and destroys the Carthaginian army. Hannibal retires to Hadrumetum and Scipio, with more supplies now arriving, sends Laelius to Rome and sails up to Carthage with his fleet. The Carthaginian Senate's first embassy is sent away, but they are so demoralized that they have no option but to agree to the terms he announces.

Peace-terms are proposed by Scipio and later ratified by the Senate: all Roman prisoners and deserters and all elephants are handed over; Carthage loses all territory outside Africa and surrenders all but ten 'triremes' of the fleet; Masinissa is given the extended kingdom of Numidia; Carthage is to pay 10,000 talents as reparations in annual instalments over fifty years, and make no war outside Africa and there only with Rome's permission; prominent hostages are to be surrendered as surety for terms being carried out.

Greece
Philip takes various towns around the western Propontis and enslaves their inhabitants to terrify resistance; he is clearly aiming at Ionia so Attalus and Rhodes are nervous. At around this time Pleuratus (III) succeeds his father Scerdilaidas in Illyria, keeping up a Roman alliance.

Egypt
Chief minister/regent Agathocles is lynched in a riot in Alexandria as the native Egyptians revolt in the Delta; the government is paralysed and revolt spreads to Upper Egypt. Tlepolemus of Pelusium becomes chief minister.

201

Italy
The Senate ratifies the peace-terms and sends delegation to Carthage; all the proscribed Carthaginian warships are towed out of the harbour and burnt, and there are mass-executions of surrendered Roman deserters; Scipio returns to Rome for a grand triumph, assuming the sobriquet 'Africanus', and Hannibal probably commands what is left of the Carthaginian army and reputedly puts them to farming to help restore prosperity to the ravaged countryside.

Greece
Philip leads a naval expedition to Samos to take over the Ptolemaic naval base there, thus dominating the eastern Aegean and threatening Rhodes; Attalus of Pergamum helps the Rhodians to defeat Philip's fleet off Chios and save the nearby islands. Philip lands in Caria to overrun some mainland towns under Rhodian control.

Rhodes, as leading independent island in the Aegean and naval power, and Attalus send envoys to Rome to warn against Philip's aggression in Aegean and the Propontis area and seek military aid, and the Senate sends three envoys, including Sempronius Tuditanus, to Ptolemy V of Egypt (currently facing invasion by Antiochus III) for an alliance.

Consul Aelius sends Laevinus to take over the Sicilian fleet from Octavius and bring it to Dyrrachium; at the latter, Laevinus consults with Aurelius who is returning from talks with Philip in Macedonia and brings details of Philip's armies.

Philopoemen leads a picked force of volunteers to Messene without waiting for official Achaean approval and mustering of an army after Nabis of Sparta attacks it; they drive Nabis back.

Philip takes Maronea, on the Thracian coast, by land and admiral Heraclides takes his fleet parallel at sea; Callimedes surrenders Aenus to Philip, who reaches the Hellespont and besieges Abydos then executes two Acarnanians for 'blasphemy' in entering the sanctuary at Eleusis during the main annual festival there; their angry compatriots are stirred up to raid Attica by Philip.

Egypt

While rebellion continues in Upper Egypt, the Ptolemaic army is under-strength in Palestine and Antiochus III overruns it; the mercenary commander Scopas the Aetolian saves Gaza from Antiochus in a brilliant defence and after Antiochus retires for the winter Scopas is made chief minister by Ptolemy V.

Greece

Autumn – Attalus of Pergamum arrives at Abydos by sea as Philip is besieging it, ignores appeals for immediate help, and goes on to Athens with his Rhodian naval escort for talks to persuade Athens against Philip. The Rhodians overrun most of the Cyclades, and Attalus sets himself up at Aegina to watch developments; Philip returns home to Macedon.

The Hellenistic Era 2 –
The Triumph of Rome 200 to 145 BC

200

Italy/Greece

March – Publius Sulpicius Galba and Gaius Aurelius Cotta are elected as consuls. The Senate declares war on Philip, and Athens sends an appeal for aid against Philip's general Philocles' invasion; Sulpicius is granted command against Philip; Ptolemy V's regency sends envoys promising troops for Greece if Rome desires it; Attalus of Pergamum sends ships to assist in the defence of Athens.

Cycliadas elected pro-Macedonian annual 'strategos' of the Achaean League; Philopoemen leaves for Crete.

Sulpicius arrives in Epirus, and sends Caius Claudius Cento with twenty warships and 1000 men to relieve Philip's army's siege of Athens while Philip is at Abydus on Hellespont attacking Ptolemy's local garrisons; Philip ignores visiting Roman envoy Marcus Aemilius, en route back from Egypt, and outrages neutral Greek opinion by brutal sack and slaughter at Abydus.

Claudius, at Athens' port Piraeus with his ships, raids and destroys the Macedonian base at Chalcis on the Euboean straits, and in revenge Philip hastens south from Thessaly and nearly takes Athens by surprise; he besieges the city again and ravages countryside, but fails to lure the Achaean League's council at Argos into sending troops to assist him in return for his attacking their enemy Nabis of Sparta.

Philip ravages Attica but withdraws; Sulpicius, based near Apollonia in Epirus, sends Lucius Apustius to attack the Macedonian frontier, and Antipatreia is taken and Codrio surrenders; the Dardani tribe on Macedonian frontier and Pleuratus, leader of the Illyrians who were Roman allies in earlier war, send envoys to Sulpicius to join Roman coalition, and Roman envoy Purpurio and others from Philip and Athens all fail to secure a favourable decision on an alliance by the council of the Aetolian League.

Sulpicius marches into the Pindus Mountains towards Macedonia, plunders the territory of the Dassaretti, and skirmishes with Philip's army; he defeats Philip in a confused battle where the king is unhorsed and nearly killed, but fails to follow up pursuit enabling him to get away and campaigns into Orestis (south-western Macedonia), taking Celytrum and Pelion; meanwhile, Pleuratus' Illyrians and the Dardani raid Macedonia in support of Rome, and Aetolians belatedly decide to join the latter after hearing of Philip's reverses.

The Aetolians and their Athamanian allies sack Cercinium, and raid into Thessaly but are caught unexpectedly by Philip and routed. Apustius' Roman fleet joins Attalus and his navy at Hermione, the eastern tip of Peloponnese near Epidaurus, and they storm the island of Andros and other pro-Philip garrisons in the Aegean but fail in a raid on Cassandreia in Chalcidice.

Autumn – Oreus, on the north coast of Euboea, is taken with Aetolian help.

Seleucids/Egypt
Ptolemy's general Scopas defeats Antiochus in Palestine, but the latter then wins the battle of Panium near the Jordan; the Egyptians retreat to Gaza in disarray and are forced to stave off the invasion threat by ceding Palestine and Phoenicia to the Seleucid kingdom.

199

Italy/Greece
March – Lucius Cornelius Lentulus and Publius Villius Tapulus are elected as consuls; Villius is sent to Macedonia and Lentulus is to remain in Italy.

Villius deals with a mutiny of troops and campaigns indecisively in the Pindus against Philip who has fortified the passes around Antigoneia to block the frontier; Philip strengthens his alliance with Achaea.

Villius eventually moves up the Aous valley avoiding Macedonian defences, and ?wins a battle with Philip; however, he cannot enter Macedon.

198

Italy/Greece
March – Sextus Aelius Paetus and Titus Quinctius Flaminius are elected as consuls; Flaminius is granted command in Macedonia, and Aelius in Cisalpine Gaul. Attalus sends a delegation to warn that he is being attacked by Antiochus III in Asia Minor and would like his auxiliaries returned as soon as possible; the Senate sends envoys to Antiochus to request him to leave Rome's allies alone, and in April? Flaminius arrives with reinforcements in Corcyra, earlier than expected, to take over Villius' army.

As the Romans and Macedonians confront each other, Philip offers talks and he and Flaminius meet on the banks of the River Aous where Flaminius requires the removal of Philip's garrisons in Greek cities, evacuation of Thessaly, and return of plunder and Philip will only accept what arbitrators judge he should do, not Roman terms; Flaminius uses a local shepherd with knowledge of the mountain-paths to send a picked force to circumvent Philip's defences and when they signal that they are in place launches a frontal attack, which they assist; Philip is taken by surprise and flees to safety in the mountains, and with the road clear Flaminius advances through Lyncestis into Thessaly; the Aetolians and Athamanians join Romans in ravaging Thessaly, and Philip retires into Macedon.

Flaminius' brother Lucius Quinctius with fleet arrives in Athens and joins Attalus for assault on Euboea; Eretria is taken without Philip's commander Philocles (at Chalcis) intervening, and Carystus surrenders; Flaminius fails to take Atrax, near Larissa in Thessaly, and moves into Phocis to secure coastal towns for the landing of supplies from Corcyra; he takes Anticyra but is held up at Elatia.

After the Achaeans expel Cycliadas, leader of their pro-Philip faction, Flaminius is hopeful of securing an alliance and, arriving at Cenchrae to attack nearby Corinth, sends envoy Lucius Calpurnius to the Achaean council with Pergamene and Rhodian assistance;

the Achaeans vote to ally with Attalus and Rhodes, and for a treaty with Rome subject to its acceptance by the votes of the Senate and Assembly; Achaean troops join Flaminius and Attalus to besiege the Macedonian garrison in Corinth, but the garrison holds out and Philocles' Macedonian fleet brings reinforcements to Corinth so the siege abandoned; Argos deserts to Philip, but Elatia finally falls to Flaminius.

Winter – At Philip's request, Flaminius and Attalus, with representatives of their allies, meet him for peace-talks on the shore of the Malian Gulf; Flaminius requires the evacuation of Macedonian garrisons in Greece, surrender of prisoners and deserters, and the return of Illyrian areas seized from Rome since peace, and his allies put in claims for other places; a two-month truce is agreed, and Philip's proposals of which places he will cede (not all of those demanded) are relayed by a Roman/allied delegation to the Senate to obtain their reaction; the allies convince Senate that as long as Philip holds his current garrisons at key positions of Demetrias (Thessaly), Chalcis (Euboea) and Corinth, the 'fetters of Greece', he can advance elsewhere and intimidate Greece at will.

Philip sends envoys to Nabis of Sparta against Achaea, offering him Argos; Nabis is admitted to the city by Macedonians but at a subsequent truce-meeting with Flaminius and Attalus deserts to them instead.

197

Italy/Greece
March – Caius Cornelius Cethegus and Quintus Minucius Rufus are elected as consuls; due to tribunes' advice, the Senate agrees to continue with Flaminius in command in Macedonia until such time as the consuls, allocated to Italy for the new Gallic campaign, have finished war and one of them can go out to replace him.

Reinforcements are sent out to Greece; Cornelius fights Insubres in Cisalpine Gaul and Minucius suppresses a revolt in Liguria and ravages Boii territory to draw them off from the combined Gallic army.

Flaminius advances from Elatia into Boeotia, and joins Attalus at Thebes to secure an alliance with the Boeotian League at their council-meeting in the city, while Philip receives his unsuccessful envoys back from Rome and raises levies; Flaminius advances to Thermopylae and thence into Pthiotis, and Philip marches into Thessaly; Flaminius reaches Pherae, and the two armies manoeuvre in southern Thessaly until accidental confrontation at Cynoscephalae where the darkness of storm hides how close they are to each other.

Battle of Cynoscephalae ('The Dog's Head'): Philip has possession of an advantageous position on a ridge and drives the initial Roman attack back, but his men descend into the plain and their rigid 'phalanx' tactics are outmanoeuvred by skilful Roman and Aetolian attacks with the help of Rome's elephants, particularly when a tribune attacks Philip's right wing from the flank; c. 8,000 Macedonians are killed and 5000 prisoners (Polybius/Livy). Philip flees north.

Flaminius receives Philip's envoys at Larissa, and rejects Aetolian demands to depose him and seize his kingdom with irritation at their claims to have played major role in the victory, warning that if Macedonia is destroyed the northern tribes will pour through it into Greece; a truce is granted, and at a peace-conference held at the Vale of Tempe the Aetolians fail to secure their claim that the terms of their alliance with Rome in 211 mean that they should obtain the territory Rome has taken in war (i.e. Boeotia and Thessaly) and Rome should just have the loot; Philip surrenders his son Demetrius and other hostages and proposed terms, centring on Macedonian evacuation of Greek garrisons, are sent to the Senate.

The Rhodians send envoys to Antiochus, who is now besieging Coracesium during the campaign along the southern coast of Asia Minor against remaining Ptolemaic garrisons and allies there, and successfully threaten him into not sending his fleet west, thus preserving the independence of Caria and Lycia.

Autumn? – Death of Attalus of Pergamum after forty-four-year reign; he is succeeded by his son Eumenes.

196

Antiochus winters at Ephesus to threaten independent cities and rival powers' garrisons in western Asia Minor.

Italy/Greece
March – Lucius Furius Purpurio and Marcus Claudius Marcellus are elected as consuls; Marcellus' manoeuvres for command in Macedon are defeated and Flaminius' command is continued, while the proposed terms of peace with Philip are accepted in votes by the Senate and Assembly; it is agreed that Philip should evacuate all garrisons in Greece and some also in Asia Minor, surrender all deserters and all but five warships, reduce the army to 5000 (no elephants) and not wage war without Roman permission, and pay 1000 talents, half immediately and the rest in annual instalments; ten commissioners are sent to Greece to carry out the terms and decide on what to do about Demetrias, Chalcis, and Corinth. Both consuls are granted Italy as province.

Greek states ratify the treaty, with the exception of the angry Aetolians; Flaminius joins the commissioners and persuades them to return Corinth to Achaea but keep the other two positions in question until the threat of invasion by Antiochus is sorted out; his heralds announce the 'freedom of Greece' from occupation or tribute at the Isthmian Games, amidst enthusiastic scenes.

Antiochus' envoys are warned that he must not attack the lands of Philip, Ptolemy, or Greek states; the commission's settlement of Macedonian frontiers grants independence to the subordinate tribes of Orestis, Perrhaebia, and Dolopians who are in revolt, together with Thessaly, and on the western frontier Lychnidus is given to the Illyrians; on commissioner Cnaeus Cornelius' advice Philip sends envoys to Rome for alliance.

Antiochus besieges Lampsacus and Zmyrna and in spring crosses the Hellespont where he rebuilds the ruined city of Lysimacheia (ex-capital of Alexander's general Lysimachus' state c. 320–281), once capital of the Macedonian Thracian realm.

Lucius Cornelius, the Senate's envoy to mediate between Antiochus and Ptolemy, arrives at Lysimacheia with some of the commissioners from Greece; they demand that Antiochus evacuate places taken from Philip and Ptolemy and accuse him of intending to invade Europe, but he rejects them; a rumour that Ptolemy has died sends him off to Ephesus to prepare for a possible attack on Egypt, and on discovering that story is false he returns via Cyprus to Syria.

Egypt

Scopas the Aetolian and his fellow-exiles from Greece are rounded up and executed after their rival Aristomenes accuses them of plotting a coup; Aristomenes becomes chief minister.

Ptolemy V is crowned 'Pharoah' at Thebes with traditional Egyptian cultic ceremonies in a bid to improve his legitimacy with the majority population of the country.

195

Italy/Greece

The Senate receives report of the returning commissioners from Greece who warn that Antiochus and Nabis are both serious threats – as Antiochus is back in Syria Nabis is the more immediate threat, and it is left to Flaminius to decide what to do.

Commissioners are sent to Carthage to investigate complaints that Hannibal is in touch with Antiochus offering him support.

June? – Hannibal flees to the port of Cercina and secretly takes a ship to Tyre, en route to join Antiochus as he arrives at Ephesus.

Flaminius holds a conference of Greek states at Corinth where general opinion agrees with him about the need to curb Aetolians and Nabis, tells Antiochus' envoys to him to go to Rome, and leads an army against Argos with Aristaenus' Achaean army joining him; Flaminius' arrival fails to lead to revolt in Spartan-garrisoned Argos, so he invades Laconia with assorted Spartan exiles (including the expelled legitimate king, Agesipolis) joining him and Philip sending troops. The Roman fleet moves in on the coast as Rhodian ships and Eumenes' Pergamene fleet arrive, and Nabis summons Cretan aid to assist his mercenaries; Flaminius defeats a Spartan sally at the town of Sellasia, encamps at Amyclae outside Sparta, and devastates Laconia, and then he joins his brother Lucius Quinctius' fleet and the Pergamenes to besiege the port of Gytheum, which surrenders; Nabis sues for truce and unsuccessfully appeals to Flaminius on the grounds that Sparta has a treaty with Rome and Argos was Philip's ally against Rome, and is told that the treaty was with legitimate kings who he displaced; Rome's Greek allies are unwilling to launch a siege of Sparta, and terms are agreed whereby Nabis evacuates Argos and all his other garrisons outside Laconia, returns deserters, runaway slaves, and loot, and loses the Laconian coast and his navy; Nabis recovers his nerve and decides to reject terms and await aid from Antiochus, so Sparta is besieged and nearly falls in Roman attack on walls until Nabis' general Pythagoras sets buildings near the walls afire to halt Roman advance. Argos is seized by a revolt of citizens from those Spartans Nabis has left garrisoning it, and Nabis surrenders and accepts the peace-terms. The Aetolians object that Rome has left the tyrant in power and ignored his legitimate rival Agesipolis.

Hannibal arrives in Antioch to meet Antiochus' eldest son, Antiochus, at the Games there.

194

Greece

Flaminius, having wintered at Elatia, holds a Greek conference at Corinth and announces that he is leaving the country, evacuating Chalcis and Demetrias, and returning Corinth to Achaea; he proceeds via the two evacuations to Thessaly to install new local government by cities to replace the long Macedonian rule, and marches on to Epirus and Brundisium; back at Rome he holds a three-day triumph, with Philip's (younger) son Demetrius and Nabis' son Armenes among the parade of hostages.

194/3

Seleucids/Egypt
Antiochus III marries his daughter Cleopatra (I) to Ptolemy V of Egypt.

193

Italy/Greece
March – Lucius Cornelius Merula and Quintus Minucius Thermus are elected as consuls; the Senate receives a delegation from Antiochus, which refuses to give up his claims to the European provinces of Lysimachus' former realm (i.e. the Chersonese and Thrace) of which Antiochus has taken the Asian part or to liberate formerly independent cities in Ionia; the envoys of Greek and Ionian states complain to Senate about Antiochus' threat to their independence, and a delegation is sent to him to demand evacuation of European lands; envoys from Carthage warn Rome that Antiochus is preparing war with the aid of refugee Hannibal, and Rome is suspicious of how the city allowed Hannibal's detected agent Aristo to escape rather than arresting him at once; Scipio Africanus is among commissioners sent to Africa to adjudicate in border-dispute between Carthage and Masinissa.

Aetolians, led by Thoas, send envoys to Philip, Nabis, and Antiochus urging alliance against Rome and the Achaeans warn Rome as Nabis tries to cause revolt in his former Laconian coastal possessions; Nabis seizes the port of Gytheium and attacks Achaea but is repulsed.

Seleucids
Antiochus campaigns against the local tribes in Pisidia (south Asia Minor) and then goes on to Ionia.

Roman envoys Publius Sulpicius and Publius Villius arrive at Pergamum to consult Eumenes, and while illness delays his colleague Villius goes to Ephesus to meet Antiochus and (?accompanied by Africanus) meets Hannibal; talks at Apamea are delayed by the death of Antiochus' son Antiochus, and when Sulpicius arrives negotiations resume but meet no success; the Seleucid claim to the European territories of Lysimachus is maintained and Antiochus decides for war.

192

Italy/Greece/Seleucids
Flaminius' brother Lucius Quinctius Flaminius is elected as consul.

Praetor Atilius is sent to Greece with a fleet, followed by Flaminius and other envoys to secure troops from allies, while troops muster at Brundisium; Attalus, brother of Eumenes of Pergamum, brings the news that Antiochus has crossed into Europe; Flaminius' delegation secures adherence of the Thessalians, and then persuades the local Magnesians' meeting at Demetrias to reject overtures from the Aetolians who are claiming that Rome intends to return Demetrias to Philip; Thoas brings Antiochus' delegate Menippus to the

Aetolian conference which is debating war and secures an alliance with his master despite an appeal by Flaminius, and Aetolians (under Diocles) seize Demetrias; the Aetolians send Alexamenus with troops to supposedly aid Nabis at Sparta, but then to assassinate him and seize the city; Alexamenus kills Nabis at a military review, but furious Spartans slaughter him and his men and Philopoemen arrives from Achaea to secure an alliance with his League and Rome.

Failing in sieges of Lampsacus and Alexandria Troas on the Hellespont, Antiochus is told that Demetrias is in Aetolian hands and sails there with his army; he meets the Aetolian leadership at Lamia and is elected their commander, unsuccessfully attacks Chalcis, and sends delegates to the Achaean congress at Aegium; Flaminius persuades the Achaeans to stay loyal to Rome, but Chalcis falls to second attack and the rest of Euboea deserts to Antiochus.

191

March – Publius Cornelius Scipio Nasica and Marcus Acilius Glabrio are elected as consuls.

War with Antiochus is voted for by the Senate, and Glabrio is granted Greece and Nasica the war with Boii in Cisalpine Gaul; Flaminius' command in Spain is extended, and Aemilius Paullus (future conqueror of Macedonia and son of the consul killed at Cannae in 216) is among his praetors.

Antiochus visits Thebes to secure the adherence of the Boeotians; Epirus and the Athamanians send delegates for an alliance with him; he marches into Thessaly, fails to seduce the local cities or Philip from Rome, successfully attacks Pherae, and besieges Larissa until the approach of the Roman force under Appius Claudius and bad weather forces his withdrawal to Lamia.

May – Philip promises Rome money and troops and Ptolemy V promises money and grain.

Spring – Antiochus' troops muster at Chaeronea after a winter of lax discipline; he marches to Naupactus on the Gulf of Corinth via friendly Aetolia to invade Acarnania, but Cnaeus Octavius' arrival at Leucas off the west coast inspires locals to resist and he abandons the siege of Thyrraeum and retires; Marcus Baebius' army from Illyria and Philip with the Macedonians retakes towns in Thessaly.

Glabrio arrives in Thessaly, and Antiochus' Athamanian allies are defeated and surrender garrisons, after which Philip marches into and recovers Athamania as King Amynander flees. Glabrio marches south, and Antiochus moves up from Chalcis with an army of c.10,000 infantry and 500 cavalry (Livy) but fewer local allies than he expected; he camps at Thermopylae with the aid of c. 4,000 Aetolians who garrison the town of Heraclea and are told to seize the heights of Callidromus above the pass but do not do so in full strength as ordered. Glabrio moves to Thermopylae, and sends lieutenants Marcus Poricus Cato (Cato 'the Elder') and Lucius Valerius Flaccus to storm the heights.

Antiochus' (?smaller) army holds defensive walled positions across the narrows of the pass, and in the resultant battle the Seleucids hold out in the narrows until Cato secures his objective and descends to attack them in flanks and causes panic; Antiochus flees with cavalry via Elatia to Chalcis, leaving most of infantry to be caught by Glabrio during the pursuit. Phocis and Boeotia surrender to Roman advance, followed by Chalcis after

Antiochus' departure for Ephesus; Cato is sent to Rome with news of the victory; the Aetolians at Heraclea refuse to surrender to Glabrio so it is stormed, and Philip besieges Lamia until the Romans take over and it surrenders; the Aetolians, having sent envoys to Antiochus to assure they are ready to fight on before they hear of the fall of Heraclea, change their minds and send envoys to Glabrio, but are ordered to surrender their anti-Roman leaders and Amynander of Athamania and refuse; Glabrio advances into Aetolia to besiege Naupactus, while Flaminius, as Roman commissioner in Greece, answers an appeal from Messene against attack by the Achaeans by forcing the latter to withdraw and to hand over seized island of Zacynthus as well.

Caius Livius brings a new Roman fleet to Aegean to supersede Atilius as commander, while Antiochus sends Hannibal and admiral Polyxenidas to the Hellespont to resist Roman attack from Europe but decides to tackle the Roman fleet, now at Delos, instead.

Autumn? – Flaminius arrives at siege of Naupactus, and the Aetolians inside appeal to him as liberator of Greece to secure their pardon; he intercedes with Glabrio to negotiate their surrender and arrange for Aetolian delegation to go to Rome to negotiate terms, and the Senate returns Philip's hostage son Demetrius to him with thanks for his aid in the war.

Livius' Roman fleet joins up with Eumenes' Pergamene fleet at Phocaea, and defeats Polyxenidas' Seleucid fleet nearby, capturing thirteen ships; Antiochus leaves his eldest surviving son Seleucus (born 217?) in command in Aeolis while he raises troops inland in Phrygia, including the Celts of Galatia, and Hannibal is sent to Syria for more ships.

190

Early – Scipio Africanus' brother Lucius Cornelius Scipio and his ally Caius Laelius are elected consuls to finish the war with Antiochus.

The Aetolians' envoys try to negotiate easier terms but are told to choose between accepting whatever the Senate decides and paying 1000 talents and only having what friends and allies Rome allows; they return home. Lucius Scipio is granted command in Greece thanks to Africanus announcing that if that happens he will assist his brother's campaign, and Laelius is given Italy; the Aetolians seize the pass of Mount Corax to hold up the Roman advance to Naupactus, but Glabrio captures Lamia and attacks Amphissa.

Spring – Lucius Scipio and his brother arrive in Aetolia, fail to force Hypata to surrender, and join Glabrio at Amphissa where the Athenians intercede with Africanus for the Aetolians; Lucius Scipio repeats the Senate's terms despite Aetolian pleas of poverty concerning the amount of indemnity to be paid, and the Aetolians secure a six-month truce while they send envoys back to Rome; the Scipios lead an army across Macedon and Thrace to the Hellespont, aided by Philip, and Livius sails the Roman fleet up there to secure the crossing and attack Sestos; meanwhile, Polyxenidas, as a Rhodian exile, approaches the Rhodian fleet-commander Pausistratus pretending to be able to secure Antiochus' fleet for them and Rome if he is helped to be pardoned in Rhodes. Once he has lulled the Rhodians into a sense of security, he attacks their fleet and sinks most of it.

Prince Seleucus recovers Phocaea and Cyme for his father once Livius has sailed north.

Livius calls off the surrender-talks at Abydus to speed back to Ionia on news of the Rhodian disaster, reaches the survivors at Samos, and raids the Ephesus area where the Seleucid navy shuns battle; Aemilius Regillus takes over the fleet and demonstrates against

Ephesus again, while Livius and a smaller force raid Lycia and win the battle outside Patara but fail to take the town; Livius returns home.

Seleucus invades Pergamum and besieges the city, and Antiochus brings his Gallic levies down to the coast to camp at Sardes. The Roman and Rhodian fleets land at Elaea, and Antiochus advances to meet them, leaving the attempt on Pergamum to Seleucus; his envoys for truce and talks are told that nothing can be done until the consul arrives, and he marches to Adramyttium to intercept the Scipios as they march south from the Hellespont; Diophanes' Achaean reinforcements drive Seleucus off Pergamum.

Hannibal's fleet, en route from Syria, is intercepted and defeated off Side by the main Rhodian squadron under Eudamus; Antiochus fails to scare King Prusias of Bithynia into joining him against alleged intended Roman enslavement of all the Greek sovereigns, thanks to Africanus' reassurances to Prusias; Antiochus besieges pro-Roman Colophon, close to Ephesus, while Regillus takes his ships to stop the island of Teos giving supplies to the Seleucids, clashes with a squadron of pirates and pursues them to the promontory of Myonessus, and lands on Teos to plunder island until the inhabitants surrender their provisions; Polyxenidas brings his fleet to Teos in hope of trapping the Romans in harbour of Geraestus, but they move out in time and his ships are spotted hiding nearby.

Battle of Myonessus: fifty-eight Roman and twenty-two Rhodian ships defeat Polyxenidas' eighty-nine Seleucid ships (Livy), helped by the use of burning torches on prows. The Romans break the enemy line in the centre and then assist the Rhodians; thirteen Seleucid ships are sunk and thirteen captured. The Romans lose two ships.

Antiochus abandons his siege of Colophon and withdraws his garrison from Lysimacheia in the Chersonese, and while Lucius Aemilius Scaurus's squadron transports the Scipios' army over the Hellespont Regillus recaptures Phocaea. Proposals from Antiochus' envoy Hercaclides of Byzantium for a settlement based on Antiochus withdrawing remaining troops from various cities and paying half Rome's expenses are rejected and he is told Antiochus must free all Aeolis and Ionia; the Scipios advance via Ilium (Troy), where Africanus offers sacrifices, to the River Caicus where Eumenes of Pergamum joins them, and Antiochus retires from Thyatira to fortify camp at Magnesia-ad-Sipylum.

Battle of Magnesia: Antiochus' surprise weapon of scythed chariots is negated by Eumenes' Cretan archers showering them with missiles and causing horses to panic, and as neighbouring infantry are exposed by the chariots' flight and flee Roman attack the Seleucid armed 'Cataphracts' (heavy cavalry, ?of Persian origin) are exposed too; the Romans charge the disordered enemy line and rout them, though on the wing Antiochus with his cavalry outflanks and drives back the Roman auxiliaries and attacks the Roman camp behind them, which commander Marcus Aemilius (Lepidus) saves; Eumenes' brother Attalus brings his cavalry to the rescue, and Antiochus flees; c.50,000 Seleucid infantry and 3000 cavalry are killed (Livy) to c. 320 Romans.

Magnesia and Ephesus surrender, and Polyxenidas flees to Syria; the Scipios enter Sardes, and Antiochus sends envoys to negotiate terms.

Eumenes requests the granting of inland Asia Minor West of the Taurus range to him to prevent Antiochus threatening the area again. Meanwhile, Antiochus has marched into Galatia and Phrygia to establish his rule there and acquire new revenue and recruits (especially ferocious 'Celtic' Galatians), hoping Rome will accept it. The Roman army is based at Ephesus.

189

Early? – The Senate ratifies Scipio Africanus' proposal that Antiochus pays 15,000 Euboean talents as indemnity, including 1,000 p.a. for twelve years, and 400 talents are to go to Eumenes; Hannibal, Thoas the Aetolian, and other leading troublemakers are to be handed over to Rome; all Western inland Asia Minor to the Taurus is to be given to Pergamum, and Lycia and Caria to Rhodes; all Asia Minor tributaries of Attalus of Pergamum (d. 197) are to pay the same tribute to Eumenes, but Seleucid tributaries are to be free; other minor arrangements are made regarding specific cities. A Roman commission is sent out to supervise the arrangements.

March – Marcus Fulvius Nobilior and Gnaeus Manlius Vulso take office as consuls; Fulvius is sent to Aetolia, which has now overrun Athamania and Ambracia, and advances from Apollonia through Epirus to besiege Ambracia. Aetolian commander Nicander fails to relieve Ambracia and instead drives Philip's elder son Perseus back out of Amphilocia. Pleuratus' Illyrian fleet joins the Achaeans to ravage Aetolian coast on Gulf of Corinth. The Aetolians, surrounded with now no hope of rescue by Antiochus, hold a council and send Phaneas and Damoteles to Fulvius to sue for peace, and he tells them to pay 2000 talents (half at once), disarm, and accept only the same allies as Rome's without further argument. Negotiations at Ambracia are aided by Amynander of Athamania, and the town surrenders; the Aetolians agree to pay 500 talents (200 at once and the rest over six years) and return all prisoners and deserters, and Fulvius advances into Aetolia where their council agrees to peace.

Delegates are sent to the Senate to secure their approval, and terms are agreed despite Philip's complaints of the recent Aetolian attacks on his frontier: Aetolia is to have the same friends and enemies as Rome, surrender deserters and prisoners, and give no aid to any army hostile to Rome.

Summer – Manlius Vulso, with an army in Ionia, and Eumenes' brother Attalus campaign in Galatia to suppress Antiochus' Celtic tribal allies; various towns are taken, but the Tolostobogii, Tectosages, and Trocmi tribes retire into the mountains; Manlius drives out the Tolostobogii defending the Mount Olympus range and kills c. 10,000 and captures c. 30,000 (Livy), and moves to Ancyra where the other two tribes pretend to open peace-talks but use the delay to evacuate non-combatants over the River Halys and then ambush the consul; the attack is routed, and the tribes are defeated in another battle in mountains and flee over the Halys.

Fulvius Nobilior arrives in the Peloponnese from supervising the settlement of Cephallonia, and attends the Achaean League council at Argos; Achaean leader Philopoemen uses the excuse of alleged Spartan attacks over their new frontier against exiles based in the Laconian coastal towns to demand the extradition of those responsible, and furious Spartans kill pro-Achaean leaders in their city, renounce the alliance with Achaea, and send an appeal to Fulvius for Rome to take Sparta under its protection; he refers them to the Senate.

Bactria

?Death of Euthydemus, ruler of Bactria for past thirty years or so; his son by the Seleucid princess Theophila, Demetrius, succeeds to his kingdom. ?Antimachus, his younger son, rules the province of 'Great Margiane'.

188

Italy/Greece

Early? – The Roman reply to the rival claims of Achaea and Sparta does not alter the status quo, but is regarded as favourable by both sides; Philopoemen marches into Spartan lands to demand the handover of the anti-Achaean leaders, and Spartan negotiators sent to his camp end up being assaulted by aggrieved Spartan exiles in the Achaean army; Philopoemen requires Sparta to demolish its walls, abrogate the ancient laws of Lycurgus that make Sparta a distinctive community, and accept back all exiles; Rome does not intervene.

March – Marcus Valerius Messala and Caius Livius Salvinator are elected as consuls.

Seleucids

In Asia Minor, Manlius receives peace-envoys from the Celts of Galatia and from Antiochus' ally Ariathares of Cappadocia who is told to pay 600 silver talents; he marches into Pamphylia to collect supplies and 2500 talents promised by Antiochus, then back to Apamea on hearing that Eumenes has arrived from Rome; at Apamea the treaty with Antiochus is finalized. Antiochus is not to allow any armies that are hostile to Rome across his territory, surrender all his elephants and all but ten large and ten small warships, hand over all territory west of the Taurus Mountains as earlier arranged, pay 12,000 Attic talents to Rome and 350 to Eumenes, hand over 540,000 'modi' of wheat, and surrender Hannibal, Thoas the Aetolian, and others. Quintus Minucius Thermus takes the treaty to Antiochus to receive his oath of adherence, and Quintus Fabius Labeo takes the Roman fleet to Patara to receive and burn the Seleucid navy; Manlius and the Roman commissioners sort out the affairs of former Seleucid cities, and once all is settled Manlius leads the army back into Thrace where he is ambushed near Cypsela by tribesmen and Thermus is killed and some baggage looted.

Autumn – Manlius arrives at Apollonia.

Hannibal flees to Prusias of Bithynia, a ruler not included in the Treaty of Apamea.

Ariathares IV of Cappadocia has to apologize to Rome for backing Antiochus III, and marries his daughter Stratonice to Eumenes of Pergamum so the latter will speak up for him with Rome.

187

Italy/Greece

Marcus Aemilius Lepidus and Caius Flaminius are elected as consuls.

Lepidus, blaming Fulvius Nobilior for the delay in his consulship, promotes the cause of the Ambracian delegation, which arrives in Rome to accuse him of sacking and looting their city and enslaving the populace when they were at peace with Rome; Flaminius defends Fulvius' actions on the grounds that Ambracia was hostile, but the Senate resolves to restore Ambracian property. Manlius returns to secure a triumph and defeat charges that he had no right to attack the Galatians as the Senate and people had not declared war and that he incompetently allowed himself to be ambushed in Thrace.

Lucius Scipio is accused of accepting a bribe from Antiochus to improve the terms of peace-treaty and is fined ?four million 'sesterces' as part of rival nobles' attack on the Scipio brothers.

Seleucids

Death of Antiochus III, who is killed plundering a temple in Elymais (Persia) (aged around fifty-three) in search of treasure to rebuild his denuded treasury; succeeded by his elder son Seleucus (IV), who is around thirty.

Late summer – Achaea renews its alliance with the Seleucids at the request of the new king.

Egypt

The recapture of Thebes ends rebellion in Upper Egypt; the Ptolemaic army reaches the First Cataract frontier, but probably rebels escape up-river into Nubia ('Ethiopia') and are pursued there as war with that power follows in a year or two.

Bactria

?King Demetrius I, relieved from the threat of Seleucid attack by Antiochus III's death, takes the opportunity to detach Arachosia (Herat province) and Areia from the Seleucid kingdom and extends his power to the Paropamisadae/Hindu Kush. This is the probable end of Seleucid rule in eastern Iran.

186

Greece

Seleucus sends an embassy to Athens to renew friendship; Rome does not interfere.

185

Italy/Greece

Complaints reach the Senate about Philip's annexation of Athamania and advances in Thessaly, Perrhaebia, and Thrace, to which Eumenes of Pergamum adds warnings, and with the cities of Aenus and Maronea near the Hellespont under new Macedonian garrisons a senatorial commission goes out to investigate; the commissioners call a conference of those concerned at Tempe in Thessaly and hear complaints, and Philip defends his annexations on Thessalian and Perrhaebian frontiers as replying to neighbours' aggression but is told to restore the places in dispute; Philip insists on his right to Aenus and Maronea free from Roman interference as they are not covered by any treaties and reminds commissioners of his services to Rome.

Rome assists Eumenes of Pergamum with the war against Prusias of Bithynia; Hannibal commands the Bithynian fleet and in one battle has jars of snakes thrown over from his ships onto the Pergamene ones.

184

Italy/Greece

The Senate receives the commissioners' report.

March – Publius Claudius and Lucius Porcius are elected as consuls. Appius Claudius is sent out to see that Philip has evacuated the border-positions and does so at Aenus and Maronea as well. When Claudius arrives in Macedon Philip reluctantly evacuates the towns, but has his opponents in Maronea massacred first. Claudius demands that Philip send his agent in Maronea, Cassander, to Rome for questioning but the accused is mysteriously poisoned en route. Philip sends his younger son Demetrius to Rome to win support and hastens to annex more of Thrace.

?Philip sends to the tribes of Istria close to north-east Italy to ask them to invade Roman territory and distract his main enemy.

Claudius goes on to the Peloponnese to meet the council of Achaean League at Cleitor and accuses the Achaeans concerning Philopoemen's behaviour at Sparta, whose leading exiles are accompanying the Roman commissioners; Lycortas leads the Achaean defence of their actions.

India
?Death of the last Maurya king, Brinadratha, in a coup at capital of Pataliputra; the collapse of his disintegrating realm into anarchy encourages Greek king Demetrius of Bactria to cast covetous eyes on the upper Indus valley. The first Greek expedition since 305 to this region follows in a few years.

183

Italy/Greece
Complaints from Philip's neighbours, especially the Thracians and Eumenes, are delivered to the Senate and answered by Philip's son Demetrius; Eumenes complains about Prusias of Bithynia (Hannibal's host), and Spartan accusations against Achaea are renewed.

Messene revolts against the Achaean League, and the latter's attacking general Philopoemen is captured in an ambush in hilly country as he leads a force to Corone to take it before the Messenians get there; his horse falls on him as he is guarding his cavalry's rear in retreat. He is executed by poison, aged seventy; the Messenians are later overwhelmed and forced to rejoin the League.

Quintus Marcius Philippus is sent as commissioner to Macedon and the Peloponnese; Flaminius goes to Bithynia, and Prusias considers handing over Hannibal to appease Rome and puts his house under guard but Hannibal takes poison and dies, aged sixty-four. Prusias signs peace with Rome and Eumenes.

Philip returns the Thracian coastal positions that Rome demands, but as his son Demetrius returns to popular acclaim as the kingdom's saviour from Roman assault he becomes jealous of his son; he campaigns inland to retake Philippopolis and the Hebrus valley.

182

Complaints from Philip's neighbours multiply as he forcibly evacuates suspect inhabitants of coastal cities inland and replaces them with loyal Thracian colonists.

Quarrel between Philip's sons Perseus and Demetrius, the latter being accused of excessive partiality towards Rome the national enemy; Perseus alleges that his brother intends to murder him in concert with Roman agents (with Flaminius in Rome assisting them) to secure the throne.

Anatolia
Prusias (I) of Bithynia, Hannibal's ex-host, dies; he is succeeded by his son Prusias II.

181

Greece

Philip takes his army on a training-expedition into northern Thrace, and climbs Mount Haemus from which it is supposedly possible to see towards Italy (which Livy writes is his intended target for next campaign, of revenge on Rome). He has Demetrius sent home under escort from Didas, governor of Paeonia, who is told to win the young man's confidence and find out if he is plotting treason; supposedly, Demetrius discusses fleeing to Rome and asks Didas if he can help provide a safe exit from Macedon through his territory. Perseus, Didas' ally, is told then forges a friendly letter from Flaminius to Demetrius to show to his father who believes it. Later, Demetrius is sent off to receive some tribal hostages in a remote part of Paeonia and is poisoned by Didas at Heraclea on his father's orders.

Egypt

Death of Ptolemy V, aged twenty-eight; his widow Cleopatra (I), daughter of Antiochus III and sister of Antiochus IV, becomes regent for their elder son, Ptolemy VI, who is aged around six.

180

?There is peace between Pharnaces of Pontus and Eumenes.

Egypt

?Death of Aristophanes of Byzantium, head of the 'Great Library' of Alexandria; he is succeeded by Aristarchus of Samothrace.

Bactria /India

At around this date, Demetrius of Bactria crosses the Hindu Kush along Alexander's route to invade the upper Indus valley, which becomes new province of his extended kingdom. He rules this area, 'Gandhara' centred on Taxila, personally with his ?brother Apollodotus in the central Indus valley (probably extending down-river to its mouth within a few years); their general Menander is sent on into the Punjab. Demetrius' sons Euthydemus of Bactria and Demetrius II of the Hindu Kush rule the Western provinces.

179

Greece

?Philip discovers that the letter from Flaminius to Demetrius concerning a 'plot' that caused him to order his son's murder was forged by Perseus' men; he considers replacing Perseus as heir with his cousin Antigonus but before he can do anything dies at Amphipolis, aged fifty-nine; Perseus succeeds amidst suspicion of murder. He defeats the invasion by the Bastarnae tribe, and sends envoys to Rome to renew Philip's treaty of alliance.

178

Eumenes of Pergamum and his brothers visit Athens, and attend the Panathenaic Games where Eumenes' chariot wins a race. His brother Attalus stays on at the Academy for a philosophical course run by Carneades.

177

Anatolia
A Lycian embassy under Nicostratus is sent to Rome to complain about the oppression of local cities, e.g. Xanthus, by Rhodian rulers since 187; the Senate orders the furious Rhodians to behave better.

Seleucids/Greece/Anatolia
Seleucus IV marries his daughter Laodice to Perseus, and his Rhodian allies escort her to Macedon. This is followed by Perseus' sister Apame marrying Prusias II of Bithynia, possibly implying Perseus is building up an anti-Rome coalition.

India
?At around this date Menander commences the Greek conquest of the Ganges valley, in due course extending down-river to the Maurya heartland and the city of Pataliputra.

176

Egypt
Death of Queen and regent Cleopatra I, mother of Ptolemy VI and sister of Seleucus IV.

175

Greece
Perseus drives the Bastarnae out of Dardania.

Seleucids
3 September – Assassination of Seleucus IV in his capital, Antioch in Syria, aged around forty-three, by his treasurer Heliodorus who proclaims his small son Antiochus king. His adult younger brother Antiochus IV, currently in Athens, challenges this and sails to Pergamum where Eumenes backs him and lends him troops; the latter escort him home, and the new regime is swiftly overthrown. Seleucus's infant sons (Antiochus and Demetrius) are superseded and Antiochus IV marries his brother's widow. The talented but egocentric and religiously quirky new ruler soon develops a (politically unifying) cult of himself as a god personified, calling himself 'Theos Epiphanes' ('god manifest'). This may be influenced by the Eastern cults or by the 300s cult of Demetrius 'Poliorcetes' in Athens.

India
?At around this date, death of Euthydemus of Bactria; his probable brother Demetrius II succeeds to rule all of the Western lands of the Bactria/Indus/Ganges state, with a relative or lieutenant called Agathocles in Arachosia (Herat province) succeeded within a few years by Pantaleon.

174

Greece/Italy
Perseus suppresses the Dolopian tribes on his frontier, who are considering an approach to Rome for aid, and takes his army on to Delphi, which causes alarm among neighbouring

rulers such as Eumenes and warnings to the already suspicious Senate; he attempts to seduce the Achaean League by offering to return escaped slaves if they will rescind their law banning Macedonians from entering Achaean territory (which could enable his armies to enter Achaea during war with Rome); the Achaeans do not respond.

A Roman commission is sent to Aetolia to sort out civil disturbances among the factions in towns.

Palestine
?Death of 'High Priest' of Jerusalem, Onias; his brother Joshua, aka 'Jason' as he is a Hellenist enthusiast, pays the new Seleucid king Antiochus IV to be appointed his successor and vigorously promotes Greek culture in the city to the horror of the traditionalists. Some Hellenizers abandon circumcision over the next few years, and attend gymnasia for naked sport.

173

Italy/Greece
Appius Claudius is sent to Thessaly and Perrhaebia to sort out factional disturbances; Marcus Marcellus mediates between Aetolians while on a trip to Delphi, and addresses the Aegean League at Aegium to congratulate them for banning the kings of Macedon from their territory. Eumenes sends a warning of Perseus' preparations for war with Rome via his brother and ambassador Attalus, and a commission is sent to Pergamum to investigate and then go on to Egypt to renew the treaty with the regency government for Ptolemy VI (acceded 181); envoys led by Apollonius are received from Antiochus IV of the Seleucid kingdom to renew the treaty signed with his father and apologize for lateness in paying war-reparations due from 188.

172

Eumenes arrives in Rome and addresses the Senate on a list of Perseus' anti-Roman actions, including the overthrow of pro-Roman tribal rulers and attempt to seduce Achaeans, and his preparations for war; Perseus' envoy Harpalus denies it but assures that his master will defend himself if attacked; on his way home Eumenes is attacked on a visit to Delphi and nearly killed by stones rolled down the mountainside onto his party as he walks along a narrow part of the road. He is stunned, and the attackers think he is dead and run off up the mountains while he is rescued and taken to a ship and thence to Aegina to recover. Macedonian agents are blamed, and the returning Roman commissioner to Greece, Caius Valerius, collects evidence of the attack in Delphi and presents it to the Senate together with his findings about Perseus' preparations for war and allegations of Perseus' friend Lucius Rammius of Brundisium that on a visit to Perseus the latter asked him to arrange poisonings of Roman commanders. War is decided and troops are mustered by praetor Caius Sicinius and sent to Epirus.

Returning Roman commissioners who were sent earlier to Perseus, to demand reparations and observe the situation, report that he denied it all, treated them insolently, wants to re-negotiate the treaty with Philip, which he denounced as unequal, and secretly met Asian delegations; an Illyrian delegation sent to Rome by King Gentius is accused of spying for Perseus on their master's orders.

Commissioners return from Antiochus IV, Ptolemy V, and Eumenes saying that all three kings have rejected anti-Roman offers from Perseus.

171

Italy/Greece

January – Publius Licinius Crassus and Caius Cassius Longinus are elected as consuls; as they assume office they carry out the sacrifices necessary to precede declaration of war, and once the soothsayers pronounce favourable omens for quick action the Senate sends a motion for war to the Popular Assembly.

The Macedonian campaign is awarded to Licinius and Italy to Cassius, and four new legions are to be raised – two per consul, with Licinius' containing 6000, not the usual 5200 men.

Perseus sends envoys who declare that he is at a loss to understand the reasons for war, and the Senate is addressed by Spurius Carvilius, sent by their commissioners in Greece, on Perseus' attacks on Perrhaebia and Thessaly and tells the Macedonians that if their king wishes to make reparations he can do so to Licinius when he arrives with his army; commissioners Marcius Philippus, Aulus Atilius, the Corneli Lentuli brothers, and Lucius Decimius bring 1000 troops to Corcyra to tour Rome's allies and seek aid, Philippus and Atilius visiting Epirus, the Lentuli visiting Peloponnese and Geminius visiting the would-be neutral king Gentius of the Illyrians.

The Aetolians rally to Philippus and Atilius, who then go on to Thessaly; Perseus appeals to Philippus as their fathers were 'guest-friends', secures an interview on the River Peneus on frontier, and successfully requests a truce with a promise to send envoys to Rome, Philippus agreeing to his proposals in order to secure more time for mustering of armies; Boeotia decides to reject offers from Perseus' local supporters and hold to the Roman alliance, and arrests the pro-Macedonian leaders and sends them to the Roman commissioners as prisoners, but Coronea and Haliartus dissent from the Theban-led Roman alliance and try to secure troops from Perseus; Achaeans are requested to supply 1000 troops to Rome. Another Roman commission (Claudius, Postumius, and Junius) secures the adherence of Rhodes and the other Aegean islands, and Rhodians show them forty ships ready for war; the only lack of Roman success occurs with Decimius' mission to Illyria.

Late spring? – Perseus' embassy arrives in Rome, and Philippus and Atilius return to report on their commission's work and assure that Greece is ready for war. Some senators demur at Rome's bad faith towards Perseus at using delaying-tactics but not being prepared to negotiate once Rome is ready, in case he genuinely wants peace, but they are outvoted; the envoys are reminded of Perseus' crimes such as the attack on Eumenes and are sent home. Atilius is sent to garrison Larissa against a Macedonian attack on Thessaly, and Licinius is told to join his army from Italy and sail to Greece, while praetor Caius Lucretius takes fleet to Greece to link up with allied navy; Lucretius' brother Marcus impounds some Illyrian ships he finds en route.

Perseus sends the refugee ruler of the Ardaei in Illyria, Pleuratus, as envoy to Gentius of Illyria to urge alliance against Rome.

Egypt/Seleucids
Ptolemy VI's army fails in an invasion of Seleucid Palestine and Phoenicia.

170

Italy/Greece
January – Aulus Hostilius Mancinus and Aulus Atilius Serranus are elected as consuls.

The inhabitants of Chalcis, base of the assembling Roman fleet in Greece, complain of extortion, billeting, illegal slavery, and theft of art-treasures by praetor Caius Lucretius and his recent replacement Lucius Hortensius, and are promised redress and given presents; Lucretius is recalled, tried, and heavily fined.

Appius Claudius is sent with troops to the Illyrian/Epirot frontier at Lychnidus to watch Gentius, while Roman ships proceed to Illyrian coast; Claudius over-confidently tries to secure the Macedonian frontier town of Uscana but is surprised by a sally and driven back with heavy losses.

Egypt/Seleucids
War between Antiochus IV and Ptolemaic Egypt over Coele-Syria; Antiochus sends Meleager's embassy to Rome to seek support, Ptolemy VI sends Timotheus and Damon.

Greece
Hagesander and Agesilochus lead a Rhodian embassy to Rome to reassure the Senate about Rhodian support as the current struggle between pro- and anti-Perseus parties on the island leads to rumours of an imminent Macedonian alliance.

Seleucids
?Death of Antiochus IV's elder son and heir, Antiochus.

169

Italy/Greece
January? – Perseus retakes Uscana from a Roman garrison, which he promises to free if they surrender but does not; he marches into Illyria to take allied towns and encourage Gentius to join him, and sacks Oaeneum; Gentius refuses to join war, but after Perseus has left Cloelius' Romans unsuccessfully attack Uscana.

January – Quintus Marcius Philippus and Cnaeus Servilius Caepio are elected as consuls.

Caius Popilius and part of army winter in Ambracia.

Ariston is elected as pro-Roman 'strategos' for the year 169–8 in Achaea.

March? – Perseus marches into Aetolia expecting support, but a Roman garrison under Popilius is hurried into the main town, Stratus, before he can arrive and Diophantus' Aetolian cavalry join them, not Perseus; the King has to give up his hopes of alliance and return home as supplies are low; however, his local allies harass Claudius during the latter's advance to assist Popilius.

April? – Philippus and the fleet-commander, Caius Marcius Figulus, cross from Brundisium to Actium in Ambracia with their forces; Philippus marches overland to Thessaly to take over the army there. The future historian Polybius is an Achaean envoy to Philippus in Thessaly, sent at 'strategos' Archon's suggestion to ask him when and where the Romans would like their troops to report.

When Marcius brings up the fleet from Chalcis the generals invade Macedonia where Perseus is encamped on the coast at Dium. The Roman force manages to cross the mountains near Lake Ascuris on difficult paths, engages Hippias' waiting Macedonian force, which Perseus fails to assist, and then struggles down the steep mountains to emerge on the coast near Dium, to Perseus' rear, where they are not expected. The Romans are now cut off from their other troops and supplies across the main passes by Perseus' remaining garrisons around Dium, but Perseus panics and flees north to Pydna; Philippus temporarily occupies Dium before moving to Phila to link up with the fleet and receive supplies.

Philippus avoids an advance and immediate battle amidst grumbling; Popilius storms the nearby Macedonian fort at Heracleum; Popilius besieges Meliboea on slopes of Mount Ossa but is driven off by the Macedonian general Euphranor.

Prusias of Bithynia and the Rhodians send unsuccessful embassies to the Senate for peace with Perseus; the Rhodians' recital of all their services to Rome, complaint at war's disruption of their trade, which is Rome's fault for requiring them to break relations with Perseus, and threat to attack whichever party prevents peace annoy their hearers. Eumenes leaves the Roman camp in Macedonia for the winter after developing a bad relationship with Philippus, and suspicion of his lack of support rises.

Egypt/Seleucids

Envoys of the new young King Ptolemy VIII ('Euergetes', nicknamed 'Physcon' – 'Fat Belly'), who has recently deposed his elder brother Ptolemy VI, arrive in Rome to plead for help against Antiochus IV who has invaded Egypt to restore (his sister Cleopatra I's son by Ptolemy V) Ptolemy VI and is besieging Alexandria; Antiochus cannot take Alexandria, but on his withdrawal he leaves Ptolemy VI at the old capital Memphis in control of the rest of Egypt.

Ptolemy VI negotiates his brother's surrender in return for their becoming joint sovereigns.

Seleucids

Antiochus IV carries off the sacred treasures from the Temple in Jerusalem to help pay off his 188 war-indemnity debts to Rome; the ex-'High Priest' Jason and his anti-Seleucid supporters attack Jerusalem, and besiege pro-Seleucid 'High Priest' Menelaus in the Temple until Seleucid troops arrive to expel them.

168

Italy/Greece

January – Aemilius Paullus and Caius Licinius are elected as consuls.

Ptolemy VIII's envoys arrive in Rome appealing for help against Antiochus and Caius Popilius Laenas is sent with a mission to warn the Ptolemies to agree to mutual peace, the defaulter to be regarded as unfriendly to Rome.

Eumenes, alarmed at Roman power spreading, tries to negotiate a settlement that would leave Perseus with his kingdom, and sends secret envoys to ask Perseus for 500 talents in return for his not sending Rome military aid and 1500 for negotiating peace; Rome becomes suspicious of him.

Greece

Ptolemy's envoys arrive in Achaea to try to hire mercenaries and ask for a commander to assist against Antiochus – Lycortas or Polybus are suggested.

Gentius of Illyria finally arrives at Dium to aid Perseus, but the latter's attempt to win over Eumenes fails as his price is too high; Perseus is offered help by the Gauls/Celts inland from Illyria and marches to the Axius River to meet them, but their demands for pay are too high and they go home.

Aemilius Paullus is granted two legions to take to Macedonia; praetor Cnaeus Octavius is to command the fleet and Lucius Anicius to succeed Claudius at Lychnidus; the levy is held.

Early April – The consular army leaves Rome; the Romans arrive in Epirus, and Anicius joins Claudius and marches against Gentius to relieve siege of Bassania and take Lissus; he chases Gentius up the coast to his base at Scodra, besieges it, and forces him to surrender; Gentius and his relatives and leading nobles are rounded up and deported to Rome.

Paullus and Perseus confront each other on the banks of the River Elpeus near Pydna, where the narrow coastal strip and mountains inland mean that the Macedonian defensive position cannot be outflanked; Paullus launches a frontal attack to keep Perseus occupied while troops under Scipio Nasica and his own son Quintus Fabius Maximus (so-called as adopted by a childless member of the Fabii Maximi) secretly march inland to cross passes in the Olympus range into Perrhaebia and emerge in Perseus' rear; Scipio's men succeed and take Pytheum to Perseus' rear, and the Macedonians retire to Pydna, allowing the Roman army to advance.

21 June – The eclipse of the moon precedes 22 June. Battle of Pydna: the Macedonian phalanx is attacked at different points by Roman 'spearheads' rather than being allowed a straight infantry clash with the opposing line, which is to its advantage, and the elephants and Latin allies on the Roman right rout the Macedonian left wing, after which the Second Legion breaks through the phalanx in the centre. The Macedonian cavalry under Perseus flee, and c. 20,000 are killed and 11,000 captured (Livy). Paullus' younger son Publius Scipio (Aemilianus) is among the Roman cavalry in the pursuit.

Perseus flees to Pella, his capital, and thence Amphipolis whence he sends envoys to ask for terms but goes on to the island of Samothrace, and Pella and the other cities and districts of Macedonia submit; Paullus enters Pella to assume control of all Macedonia and sends his son Fabius to announce the victory to Rome.

Octavius brings the Roman fleet to Samothrace. Perseus, accused of impiety to an important shrine there by murdering his friend Evander who was evading trial over the 172 attack on Eumenes at Delphi, has to flee the island. He and his son Philip fail to reach their boat and the royal pages, offered amnesty by Octavius in return for surrender, identify their whereabouts; Perseus has to surrender and is taken to Paullus' camp on the mainland and received honourably.

Anicius marches into Epirus, and Phanote and other towns surrender; he takes up winter quarters at Scodra in Illyria.

The Senate appoints ten commissioners to settle affairs of Macedonia and five for Illyria.

Egypt/Seleucids

Popilius' commissioners, en route to Egypt, call in at Rhodes to complain about the hostile behaviour of assorted Rhodian politicians, and the scared island Assembly votes to condemn to death anyone found guilty of conspiring against Rome; they go on to Alexandria, where Antiochus IV is now demanding the surrender of the Pelusium area and Cyprus from the restored Ptolemy VI and sails to Pelusium at the eastern mouth of the Nile to invade the country.

Achaeans and Athens send envoys to Antiochus at Pelusium for peace with Ptolemy VI, and blame the ill-will that Antiochus says Ptolemy's regime has shown to him on the chief minister Eulaeus, for whose behaviour he should not blame the young king. Antiochus claims that his illustrious predecessors Antigonus 'Monopthalmus' and Seleucus I were accepted as rulers of Coele-Syria by the Ptolemies and the region was not a dowry for Ptolemy's mother Cleopatra I as the Egyptians claim.

Popilius arrives at Antiochus' camp at Eleusis, four miles from Alexandria, and delivers the Senate's decree demanding withdrawal; Antiochus says he will consult the council before replying, and traditionally Popilius draws a circle in the sand round the King with his staff and demands a reply before he steps out of it; Antiochus agrees to withdraw and the commission goes on to Cyprus to send the Seleucid fleet home. This is seen subsequently as emblematic of haughty Rome taking control over the Greek Eastern Mediterranean rulers' destinies.

Macron, Ptolemaic governor of Cyprus, defects to Antiochus IV.

Anatolia

There is a tribal Galatian revolt against Pergamum, backed secretly by Rome to weaken Eumenes; it is suppressed after campaigns of about a year.

167

Italy/Greece

January – Marcus Junius and Quintus Aelius are elected as consuls; Junius is to have Liguria and Aelius Cisalpine Gaul.

Delegations bringing congratulations from across the East for the downfall of Perseus are received in Rome, and it is agreed to install 'free' republics in Macedonia and Illyria, each country to be divided into independent districts under the protection of Rome, which receives half the taxes normally paid to the deposed kings; there are four districts in Macedonia, three in Illyria.

Attalus leads his brother Eumenes' Pergamene delegation to Rome, delivering an appeal for commissioners to be sent to Galatia to deal with the anti-Pergamene revolt.

The Rhodian delegates, Philophron and Astymedes, are refused normal courtesies of 'friends and allies' on account of their countrymen's equivocal behaviour over the war, but praetor Marcus Juvenius Thala's attempt to have war declared on Rhodes is defeated; however, Rhodes loses its formal allied status and is required to evacuate Lycia and Caria, which it does.

Delos is handed to Athens on condition that it is made a 'free port'; this stimulates trade there at Rhodes' expense, annoying the latter, which already resents having to evacuate Caria and Lycia.

Paullus tours through Greece, and in autumn calls a Macedonian conference at Amphipolis where the division of the state into four republics is announced – going from east to west, the areas are to have as capitals Amphipolis, Thessalonica, Pella, and

Pelagonia. 'Senators' are appointed to run each district and Paullus organizes a new administration and laws, but the popular reduction of taxes is offset by the new difficulties for commerce across the formerly unified country. The Greek states send delegations to Paullus to list and accuse their anti-Roman leadership, plus assorted victims of political spite by the triumphant pro-Roman parties, and they are sent on to Rome; Paullus holds celebratory Games at Amphipolis, and then marches back through Epirus to the Adriatic coast, requiring the leaders of surrendered pro-Perseus towns in Epirus to collect their gold and silver, which is then seized before the towns' walls are pulled down.

Caius Claudius Pulcher and Cnaeus Domitius Ahenobarbus are sent to Achaea to deliver Roman terms: Achaea is required to send 1000 suspected anti-Romans it has named to Rome as hostages; they include the future historian Polybius of Megalopolis, who becomes a friend of Aemilius Paullus and his 'Hellenophile' circle of eminent Romans open to Greek ideas (which includes Paullus' teenage youngest son, who as 'Scipio Aemilianus' later becomes the conqueror of Carthage).

Anatolia

Prusias of Bithynia visits Rome to congratulate the Senate on victory, hand over his son Nicomedes (effectively as a hostage) for Roman education, and appeal unsuccessfully for the lands of Antiochus' former realm in Asia Minor, which were not given to anyone by Rome in 187 but have since been seized by Galatians to be given to him.

Bactria/India

Eucratides overthrows and kills Demetrius I, king of the Indus valley state and overlord of Bactria and the Ganges valley, but is defied both by the latter's general Menander, ruler of the Ganges region, and by Apollodotus (?brother of Demetrius) in the upper Indus valley ('Gandhara'). The position and longevity of Demetrius I's son Demetrius II of Bactria/Hindu Kush is unclear, but probably Eucratides removes him within a year or two.

Palestine

December – Antiochus IV enters Jerusalem with an army to install a garrison and build a temple of Zeus in the 'Temple' precinct in a mixture of security-concerns and aggressive Hellenism, thus touching off the Maccabean revolt.

166

Italy/Greece

Perseus of Macedonia dies under house-arrest at Alba Longa near Rome.

Seleucids

?Spring – Antiochus IV holds grand games at Antioch's suburb Daphne, in imitation of Roman celebrations, for his Egyptian and Bactrian wars and satisfies Tiberius Sempronius Gracchus' mission of inspection to see that he is keeping to the terms of his father's treaty with Rome.

Antiochus invades Armenia.

Palestine

There is an outbreak of guerrilla war in the Judaean hills against the Seleucid regime and their 'Hellenizing' vassals in Jerusalem at the Temple, led by the militant nationalist Temple priest Mattathias ('Maccabeus') and his sons, especially Judas; they proclaim the current Temple rituals 'unclean' and want the return of traditional, non-Greek ways. Mattathias is soon killed and Judas takes over the resistance-movement.

165

Judas Maccabeus' Jewish rebels defeat several Seleucid armies in guerrilla war around Jerusalem, killing the general Antiochus.

Anatolia

Prusias sends an embassy under Python to complain to Rome of encroachments by Pergamum; other Asian embassies also encourage the Senate to believe that Eumenes is treating with Antiochus against them; Astymedes' Rhodian embassy secures restoration of alliance.

164

Palestine

Jonathan Macabbeus defeats Antiochus' general Lysias at the battle of Beth-Sur; he then defeats generals Ptolemy and Gorgias in battle at the main Seleucid base, Emmaus. Antiochus agrees terms whereby the Seleucids hold onto a garrison in Jerusalem and the rebels are allowed to reside in the city and worship at the Temple.

December – Jonathan breaks the treaty by leading his followers to 'purify' the Temple, expelling their 'Hellenizing' enemies, and blockades the Seleucid garrison.

Seleucids

Autumn – Antiochus IV dies at Tabae in western Iran, near Ecbatana, on a Parthian expedition, allegedly struck by insanity after despoiling a local shrine; he is succeeded by under-age son Antiochus V under the regency of minister Lysias; the Senate rejects his nephew Demetrius' (aged around twenty?) appeal to be allowed to return to rule as their client, and sends Cnaeus Octavius, Spurius Lucretius, and Lucius Aurelius to 'assist' the regency for Antiochus V.

163

Egypt

Early – Ptolemy VI of Egypt, deposed from co-rule by his younger brother Ptolemy VIII again the previous year, goes to Rome to request moves for his restoration and arrives in ostentatious poverty with a few servants to show his state. With the help of Seleucus IV's son Demetrius, a hostage in Rome for Antiochus IV's good behaviour, he secures the granting of a Senatorial commission to go to Egypt and mediate.

May – An Alexandrian revolt expels Ptolemy VIII before they return; the latter goes to Rome for help (163/2) and the Senate is told by his elder brother's agents and Roman supporters that he was so hated in Alexandria he barely escaped with his life so he would be useless as a ruler. The Senate agrees for Ptolemy VIII to rule, in Cyprus, as his brother's junior colleague, and Titus Torquatus and Cnaeus Merula escort him there. He is told to wait in western Egypt while they negotiate his peaceful installation. However, while they are vainly trying to talk Ptolemy VI into accepting it he hears of a revolt by mercenary troops at Cyrene and tries to use them to gain Cyrene instead; the populace hate him on account of his autocratic misrule in Alexandria as king earlier and successfully resist. Luckily, the Senate now quarrels with Ptolemy VI and orders that Ptolemy VIII be given Cyrene to keep the kingdom divided and weak.

Anatolia
Ariathares V succeeds Ariathares IV in Cappadocia.

Bactria
Euthydemus declares independence of the Seleucid realm. ?Treaty of peace between him and his foe Menander, ruler of northern India, and around this time Apollodotus of 'Gandhara' either dies or is expelled by Euthydemus.

162

Seleucids
Octavius the Roman commissioner is murdered at Laodicea in Syria by a group led by Leptines, and despite the assurances of Lysias' regency that they were not involved Rome suspects them.

Lysias defeats Judas Maccabeus in battle near Jerusalem, but agrees to a treaty (possibly as he fears he will soon face invasion from Demetrius and needs peace) and agrees to an autonomous Maccabean regime in Jerusalem and the sacking of unpopular 'High Priest' Menelaus as pro-Greek and not sufficiently Jewish in his rituals.

Demetrius escapes from Rome with the connivance of Polybius the historian, an exiled Achaean politician living there as hostage, and the assistance of Ptolemy VI's ambassador Menyllus who provides a ship; his local friends lay a false trail on his supposed holiday trip to Circeii to account for him being missing so he has five days' start. He sails back to Syria where he lands at Tripoli and marches inland to the army headquarters at Apamea. The army defects to him, and he overthrows Antiochus V; the Senate sends Gracchus, Lucius Lentulus, and Servilius Glaucia east to watch the developing situation and report back. Demetrius defeats rebel Timarchus of Babylon.

161

?Gracchus reports favourably on Demetrius' loyalty, and the new Seleucid regime is accepted with Demetrius sending gifts and Octavius' killer to Rome.

Rome accepts an embassy from Judas Maccabeus led by his brother Simon, as rebels against the Seleucids, showing it intends to undermine Demetrius. There is a treaty between Judas Maccabeus and Rome for an alliance against Demetrius, who refuses to accept Maccabean autonomy; there is war between Jews and Demetrius with the latter's numbers gradually prevailing.

?Demetrius marries off his cousin Nysa, daughter of Antiochus IV, to new ally Pharnaces of Pontus. It is from this marriage that later Mithridates VI will claim his Seleucid /Asia Minor inheritance against Rome.

160

Palestine

Judas Maccabeus is defeated and killed by Demetrius' general Bacchides; the Seleucid army occupies Jerusalem, but Judas' brothers Jonathan and Simon flee across the Jordan to build up a new army in the desert.

159

Anatolia

Death of Eumenes of Pergamum; he is succeeded by his brother Attalus, who is regarded as more trustable by Rome.

Bactria/India

?Eucratides of Bactria is killed in battle, and is succeeded by his son Heliocles; probably the general Menander, viceroy of the upper Indus and upper Ganges by this point, becomes independent.

158

Anatolia

Ariarathres of Cappadocia, deposed in revolt by Orophernes, visits Rome to secure help; Orophernes sends a rival embassy.

157

The Senate orders the division of Cappadocia between Ariarathres and Orophernes; the latter refuses to accept it.

156

Orophernes of Cappadocia is murdered; Ariarathres returns home as King with Pergamene military assistance.

Egypt/Rome

After an attempt by his brother's men to assassinate him, Ptolemy VIII flees to Rome and asks for help for deposing him, and displays his scars to the Senate; he fails to get support, partly due to the opposition of Cato 'the Elder'.

155

Greece

The heads of the principal philosophical schools in Athens (excepting the Epicureans) visit Rome with an embassy that is sent to secure remit of a Senate fine for Athens sacking the town of Oropus; Diogenes the Stoic and Critolaus the Cynic are received with enthusiasm by Hellenophile young nobles and teach classes of students, but Carneades the Sceptic is less popular for saying that if the Romans wanted to be truly virtuous they would return their conquests.

Achaean mission under Xenon and Telecles fails to have their hostages allowed home; Claudius Cento, Lucius Hortensius, and Caius Aurunculieus are sent to Pergamum to halt the war but are unsuccessful and on return they blame Prusias for treating them badly.

155/4

Egypt
Archias, Ptolemy VI's governor of Cyprus, plans to defect to Demetrius but is arrested and put on trial; he commits suicide before condemnation.

Ptolemy blames Demetrius for the plot and joins his foes, linking up with Attalus and Ariathares.

154

Anatolia
Attalus invades Bithynia but is driven out by Prusias; ?he takes up the cause of a pretended son of Antiochus IV living in Smyrna, Alexander Balas (who has recently had a favourable reception on visit to Rome), to the Seleucid throne against the hostile Demetrius, crowns him at Pergamum, and assists his cause.

Egypt
Ptolemy VIII appeals to Rome for aid against his elder brother Ptolemy VI.

153

Anatolia
Ten Roman commissioners visit Attalus to warn him against an attack he is planning on Bithynia with the aid of Pontus and Cappadocia, and then go on to Prusias who rejects most of their demands but changes his mind after they leave; peace is settled on Roman terms, namely the territorial 'status quo' and Prusias paying Attalus 500 talents in twenty years with twenty warships.

Seleucids
?Alexander Balas visits Rome to secure support with his adviser Heracleides, addresses the Senate, and despite failing to satisfy them is recognized as the legitimate son of Rome's ally Antiochus IV and allowed to recruit mercenaries to attack Demetrius.

Greece
The Achaean hostages in Italy are finally allowed to return home.

152

Seleucids
Autumn – Alexander Balas and his mercenary army land at Ptolemais/Acre and march inland to fight Demetrius over Syria; Jonathan Maccabeus joins the invaders and agrees treaty of autonomy/alliance.

Palestine
Jonathan Maccabeus becomes 'High Priest' of Jerusalem by grant of his new ally Alexander Balas, still technically his overlord, combining political and religious leadership for the precarious new state.

150

Seleucids
Summer – Alexander Balas defeats Demetrius who falls in battle; and takes the Seleucid kingdom. He executes his foe's widow Laodice and eldest? son, but is generally merciful. Ptolemy VI agrees an alliance with him and sends him one of his two daughters (by Cleopatra II), Cleopatra Thea, as his wife.

   Alexander Balas, as 'Theos Epiphanes', is dominated by his increasingly unpopular chief minister Ammonius.

Anatolia
(or 151) Attalus gets Prusias' son Nicomedes, sent to Rome as his ambassador to get a fine for mid-150s aggression remitted, to revolt as the suspicious King's orders to his mission in Rome to kill the Prince are revealed to the target by defecting Andronicus. Nicomedes is to take over Bithynia as a Pergamene ally; a Roman mission sent to mediate arrives too late to save Prusias who is defeated and killed.

Greece
May? – Belligerent demagogue Diaeus is elected as the annual general commanding the Achaean League.

   Andriscus of Adramyttium (Troad, north-west Asia Minor), a pretender who claims to be the late King Perseus' son who died in Italy in c. 164 and has already made one recent attempt to revolt in Macedon, goes to Thrace after his patron Demetrius' overthrow and persuades King Teres to lend him troops for an anti-Roman revolt.

149

Greece
Invasion of Macedon by rebel exile Andriscus, the 'Pseudo-Philip', with an army of Thracians; he wins victory over the forces of the easternmost republic on the east side of the Strymon River, and crosses to defeat the scattered forces of the other republics one by one; Scipio Nasica II is sent there by the Roman Senate to organize resistance.

   An Achaean dispute with Sparta over the latter's special legal status leads to Achaean demagogue Diaeus and Callicrates going on an embassy to Rome, which is unsuccessful in securing Roman support for their position on Sparta. On their return, Diaeus proposes a military attack on Sparta, without waiting for permission from Rome, which should be consulted as Sparta's protector but is too preoccupied to send immediate reply to Achaea as the latter requested.

148

In Macedon, Andriscus defeats a Roman army whose praetor commander Juventius Thalna falls in battle; Carthage sends the rebels a delegation.

The Senate orders Achaea to leave Sparta alone, and requests that their League grant full independence (i.e. in making foreign policy) to two of their most powerful members, Corinth and Argos. Caecilius Metellus leads a large Roman army to Macedon, and defeats and kills Andriscus; Macedon is turned into a Roman province under permanent Roman military occupation, which alarms some Greeks (especially the Achaeans).

Metellus proposes the reduction of Achaean League's centralized powers, leaving the new Roman province and army dominating Greece; it leads to fears of a 'divide and rule' policy and rising hostility in Achaea where Diaeus promotes a war with Rome.

Seleucids
?Parthians overrun Media and drive Seleucids out of the Iranian plateau.

Africa
Roman siege of Carthage commences.

India
?Death of Menander, ruler of the Ganges valley and Punjab with the upper Indus; succeeded by son Strato under the regency of the boy's maternal uncle Agathocles, governor of Arachosia (Herat province).

147

Greece
The dispute between the Achaean League and Sparta leads to the belated despatch of a conciliatory Roman embassy to investigate, suspending the earlier request to the League to 'free' members Corinth and Argos.

Following a stormy reception given to Roman ambassador Aurelius Orestes at the meeting of Achaean League council where Achaeans led by Critolaus accused Rome of wanting to break up the League, Rome sends a second embassy under Sextus Caesar; they call discussions with Achaea and Sparta at Tegea, and after the hostile behaviour of Achaean representative Critolaus they judge Achaea at fault in the dispute with Sparta and send reports to the Senate and to new governor Metellus in Macedonia. Metellus' delegates Cnaeus Papirius, Popilius Laenas the younger, Aulus Gabinius, and Caius Fannius go to the Achaean assembly at Corinth but are shouted down by hostile Achaeans, led by Critolaus, who believe Rome is too preoccupied with Carthage to respond aggressively.

May? – Critolaus is elected as the annual Achaean 'strategos' and imposes taxes on the richer citizens to help raise an army, including freed slaves.

Seleucids
Demetrius's young son Demetrius II, probably thirteen, is placed at the head of an anti-Alexander Balas conspiracy then an invasion, by Ptolemy VI; Lasthenes the Cretan leads a mercenary army to invade Cilicia with Demetrius II and Egyptian support.

Demetrius II invades Phoenicia and is joined by Jonathan Maccabeus, who fights Balas' governor of Coele-Syria, Apollonius; the realm is split in two.

146

Italy/Greece

Cnaeus Cornelius Lentulus and 'novus homo' Lucius Mummius are elected as consuls. Mummius is sent to Greece to deal with the Achaean League. Aemilianus is voted continued command in Africa for duration of the war.

Critolaus leads an Achaean expedition to besiege revolted member Heraclea-ad-Oetum in Malis, near Thermopylae; Metellus advances to defeat him and relieve the town, and the Achaeans retreat into allied Boeotia where the insurrectionary lower classes have taken up their cause against Rome.

Death of Critolaus, but his successor Diaeus is even more hostile to Rome and organizes an army of freed slaves to assist resistance while disturbances in cities lead to executions of leading pro-Romans.

Metellus marches south and reaches the isthmus of Corinth where Mummius arrives to take over his army; he defeats the Achaeans outside Corinth after which Diaeus kills himself, occupies the city, and has it demolished as an example to Greece; its inhabitants are enslaved and art-treasures are carried off to Rome. Achaean states of the Peloponnese are turned into an unofficial Roman province together with Attica, Boeotia, Malis etc. as the Boeotian and Phocian leagues are disbanded – the states are officially autonomous but are dependent on the Roman governor of Macedonia, whose province annexes some nearby areas.

Africa

Scipio Aemilianus takes and destroys Carthage.

145

Seleucids/Egypt

Summer – Alexander Balas, the Seleucid ruler, asks for help from Egypt. Ptolemy VI lands in Syria and marches to Antioch; the allies quarrel after Ptolemy demands that Balas hand over his chief minister Ammonius for alleged murder-plot, and Ptolemy seizes Antioch; Ammonius is lynched in a riot.

Ptolemy turns down offer of the throne, probably due to fear of Rome, and agrees to recognize Demetrius II in return for Coele-Syria and Pheonicia.

Ptolemy defeats Balas in battle of the River Oenoparas near Antioch but is mortally wounded there, aged around forty-two; Balas is killed in retreat by an Arab chieftain.

Demetrius II gains the Seleucid realm and marries Cleopatra Thea; Ptolemy VIII arrives in Egypt from Cyrene to depose Ptolemy VI's son by Cleopatra II (Ptolemy, usually referred to as Ptolemy VII as he is king of Egypt for several months); he then marries Cleopatra II. A few days later he has the boy murdered at a banquet.

(?Late summer 145) A revolt against Demetrius and his plundering Cretan mercenaries at the army headquarters at Apamea in Syria is led by the local officer Diodotus 'Tryphon', who elevates a son of Alexander Balas called Antiochius (VI), aged two, to the throne as his puppet in a civil war.

Palestine

Demetrius II sends troops to stop Jonathan Maccabeus blockading his garrison in the Jerusalem citadel, and is recognized as his overlord. The city and district of Samaria are given to Jonathan Maccabeus by Demetrius II as an ally.

Bibliography

Section One 560 to 479 BC

Primary Sources

Diodorus Siculus, *Library of History*, tr. Russell Geer (Harvard UP, 2004 ed): Book 11, chapters 1–40 (Greco-Persian and Sicilian-Carthaginian wars).

Herodotus, *The Histories* (Penguin Classics edition, 1970):

Book One: 6–56, Lydia to the Persian Conquest; 56–68 the early Greeks; 95–140, the rise of Cyrus of Persia, 140–77 Ionia and its Persian conquest,177–200, the conquest of Babylon, 201–16 the final years of Cyrus.

Book Three: 1–15, Cambyses' conquest of Egypt; 16–38, final years of Cambyses; 39–60, sixth century Greece; 61–79, murder of Cambyses and accession of Darius; 89–97 the Perisan Empire. 120 ff the end of Polycrates of Samos; 134 ff, Persia in the Mediterranean; 139 ff. fall of Samos; 150 ff revolt of Babylon.

Book Four: 83 ff. Darius' Scythian expedition; 145–67 the Greeks in Cyrene.

Book Five: 1–27 Persian conquest of and early Greeks in the eastern Balkans.

Book Five, ch. 28 to Book Six, ch. 42: the Ionian Revolt. Includes Vi, ch. 34–41 on Miltiades' family.

Book Six: 43–8 Persian demands for Greek submission; 49–93, Sparta, Athens and Aegina; 94–120 the Marathon campaign; 121–40 factions at Athens.

Book Seven: 1–4, revolt of Egypt at accession of Xerxes; 7, suppression of revolt; 19–25 preparations to attack Greece; 26–138 advance into Europe; 138–71 Greek preparations, including 153–78 Sicilian wars; 188 ff, battles of Thermopylae and Artemision.

Book Eight: 27–99 campaign in central Greece, occupation of Athens, battle of Salamis; 100–44 withdrawal of Xerxes and diplomacy of Mardonius in winter 480/79.

Book Nine: 1–89, Mardonius occupies Athens then withdraws, and battle of Plataea; 90–116 campaign of Mycale amd new Ionian revolt.

Thucydides, *History of the Peloponnesian War*, tr. Rex Warner (Penguin Classics, 1954) pp. 442–4 on Athens in the 510s BC.

Plutarch, *Lives: The Rise and Fall of Athens*, tr. Ian Scott-Kilvert (Penguin Classics 1960): Themistocles (pp. 77–94); Aristides (pp. 109–40); Cimon (pp. 141–55).

Secondary Sources

Books

Boardman, J, with N G L Hammond, D M Lewis, and M Ostwald, *The Cambridge Ancient History vol iv: Persia, Greece and the Western Mediterranean* (Cambridge UP 1988).

Burn, A R, *The Lyric Age of Greece* (London 1960).

Cook, J M, *The Persian Empire* (New York 1983).

De St. Croix, G E M, *The Origins of the Peloponnesian War* (London 1972).

Dunrabin, T, *The Western Greeks* (Oxford 1948).

Finley, M I, *Ancient Sicily* (London 1979).

Forrest, W G, *The Emergence of Greek Democracy* (London 1966).

Forrest, W G, *A History of Sparta* (London 1968).

Green, J, *The Year of Salamis 480–479 BC* (London 1970).

Grundy, G B, *The Great Persian War and its Preliminaries* (London 1901).

Hammond, N G L, and J Boardman, *Cambridge Ancient History, vol iii: The Expansion of the Greek World, Eighth to Sixth Centuries* (Cambridge UP 1982).

Hansen, M C, *The Athenian Ecclesia* (Copenhagen 1983).

Hignett, C, *A History of the Athenian Constitution to the End of the Fifth Century* BC (Oxford UP 1952).

Jones, A H M, *Athenian Democracy* (Oxford 1957).

Lenardon, R J, *The Saga of Themistocles* (London 1978).

Lewis, D K, and J Boardman, JK Davies, M Ostwald, *The Cambridge Ancient History, vol v: The Fifth Century* (Cambridge UP 1992).

Articles

Alexander, J W, 'Was Cleisthenes an Athenian archon?' in *Classical Journal*, vol 54 (1958–9), pp. 307–14.

Alexander, J W, 'More remarks on the archonship of Cleisthenes' in *Classical Journal*, vol 55 (1959–60) pp. 220–221.

Allison, F G, 'The original Marathon runner' in *Classicla Weekly*, vol 24 (1931) p. 152.

Andrewes, A, 'Athens and Aegina, 510–480 BC' in *Journal of the British School of Archaeology at Athens*, vol 37 (1936–7) p. 18.

Baillie Reynolds, P K, 'The shield signal at the battle of Marathon' in *Journal of Hellenic Studies*, vol 49 (1929) pp. 160 ff.

Beazley, J D, 'The death of Hipparchos' in *Journal of Hellenic Studies*, vol 68 (1948) pp. 26–8.

Bicknell, P J, 'The command structure and generals of the Marathon campaign' in *Antiquite Classique*, vol 39 (1970) pp. 427 ff.

Bicknell, P J, 'Cleisthenes as politician: an exploration' in *Studies in Athenian Politics and Genealogy, in Historia*, vol 19 (London 1972).

Bicknell, P J, 'The date of Miltiades' Persian expedition' in Antiquite Classique vol 41 (1972) pp. 225 ff.

Boardman, J, 'Herakles, Peisistratus and sons', in *Revue Archaeologique* (1972) pp. 57–71.

Brunt, P A, 'The Hellenic League against Persia' in *Historia*, vol 2 (1953) pp. 135–63.

Buck, R J, 'The reforms of 487 BC in the selection of archons' in *Classical Philology*, vol 60 (Oxford 1965) pp. 95–150.

Burn, A R, 'Hammond on Marathon: a few notes' in *Journal of Hellenic Studies*, vol 89 (1969) p. 118.

Burstein, S, 'The recall of the ostracised and Themistocles' decree' in *Californian Studies in Classical Antiquity*, vol 4 (1971) p. 978.

Develin, R, 'Miltiades and the Parian expedition' in *Antiquité Classique*, vol 46 (1977) pp. 571 ff.

Ehrenberg, V, 'The origins of democracy' in *Historia*, vol 1 (1950) pp. 515–48.

Eliot, CW, and McGregor, M F, 'Kleisthenes: eponymous archon, 525/4' in *Phoenix*, vol 14 (1960) pp. 27–35.

Evans, J A S, 'The final problem at Thermopylae' in *Greek, Roman and Byzantine Studies*, vol 5 (1964) pp. 231 ff.

Evans, J A S, 'Notes on Thermopylae and Artemision' in *Historia*, vol 18 (1969) pp. 318 ff.

Forrest, W G, 'The tradition of Hippias' expulsion from Athens' in *Greek, Roman and Byzantine Studies*, vol 30 (1969) pp. 277–86.

Fornara, C W, 'The cult of Harmodios and Aristogeiton' in Philologus, vol 114 (1970) pp. 155–80.

Frost, F J, 'Themistocles' place in Athenian politics' in *California Studies in Classical Antiquity*, vol I (1968) pp. 105 ff.

Grant, J R, 'Leonidas' last stand' in *Phoenix*, vol 15 (1961) p. 14 ff.

Hammond, N G L, 'Studies in the chronology of the sixth and fifth centuries BC' in *Historia*, vol 4 (1955) pp. 371–411.

Hammond, N G L, 'The battle of Salamis' in *Journal of Hellenic Studies*, vol 76 (1956) pp. 32–54.

Hammond, N G L, 'The campaign and battle of Marathon' in *Journal of Hellenic Studies*, vol 88 (1968) pp. 13–57.

Hammond, N G L, 'The extent of Persian occupation in Greece' in *Chiron*, vol 10 (1980) pp. 53–66.

Hodge, A T, 'Marathon to Phaleron' in *Journal of Hellenic Studies*, vol 93 (1975) pp. 169 ff.

Hodge, A T and L Losada, 'The time of the shield signal at Marathon' in *American Journal of Archaeology*, vol 74 (1970) p. 31 ff.

Hope Simpson, R, 'Leonidas' decision' in *Phoenix*, vol 26 (1972) pp. 1–11.

Hudson, H G, 'The shield signal at Marathon' in *American Historical Review*, vol 12 (1937) p. 43.

Jeffrey, L H, 'The campaign between Athens and Aegina in the years before Salamis' in *American Journal of Philology*, vol 82 (1962) pp. 44 ff.

Kelly, D H, 'The Athenian Archonship 5076–487/6' in *Antichthon*, vol 12 (1978) pp. 1–17.

Kinzl, K H, 'Notes on the exile of the Alcmaeonidai' in *Rhinisches Museum*, vol 119 (1976) pp 311–14.

Lang, M, 'The murder of Hipparchos' in *Historia*, vol 3 (1954–5), pp. 395–407.

Lateine, D, 'The failure of the Ionian Revolt' in *Historia*, vol 31 (1982) pp. 129 ff.

Leonardon, R J, 'The archonship of Themistocles, 493/2' in *Historia*, vol 1 (1956) pp. 401–9.

Leonardon, R J, 'The chronology of Themistocles' ostracism and exile' in *Historia*, vol 8 (1959) pp. 23–48.

Lesby, D M, 'The Spartan embassy to Lygdamis' in *Journal of Hellenic Studies*, vol 77 (1957) pp. 272–5.

Lewis, D M, 'The archon of 497/6' in *Classical Review*, new series vol 12 (1962) p. 201.

Lewis, D M, 'Cleisthenes and Attica' in *Historia*, vol 12 (1967) pp. 22–40.

Loenen, D, 'The Peisistratids: a shared rule' in *Mnemosyne*, series 4, part 1 (1948) pp. 81–9.

McCargar, D J, 'The archonship of Hermokrean and Alkmaion: a further consideration' in *Rhinisches Museum*, vol 119 (1976) pp. 315–23.

McCargar, D J, 'The relative dates of Kleisthenes' legislation' in *Historia*, vol 25 (1976) pp. 385–95.

McGregor, M F, 'The pro-Persian party at Athens from 510 to 480' in *Harvard Studies in Classical Philology*, supplement 1 (1940) pp. 71–95.

Maurice, F, 'The size of the army of Xerxes at the time of the invasion of Greece 480 BC' in *Journal of Hellenic Studies*, vol 50 (1930), pp. 210–35.

Maurice, F, 'The campaign of Marathon' in *Journal of Hellenic Studies*, vol 52 (1932) pp. 13 ff.

Munro, J A, 'Some observations on the Persian Wars: 3. The campaign of Plataea' in *Journal of Hellenic Studies*, vol 24 (1904) pp. 44–65.

Oliver, J K, 'Reforms of Cleisthenes' in *Historia*, vol 9 (1960) pp. 503–7.

Pritchett, W, 'New light on Plataea' in *American Journal of Archaeology*, vol 61 (1957) pp. 9–13.

Pritchett, W, 'New light on Thermopylae' in *American Journal of Archaeology*, vol 62 (1958), pp. 203 ff.

Pritchett, W, 'Towards a restudy of the battle of Salamis' in *American Journal of Archaeology*, vol 63 (1959) p. 261.

Raubitshchek, A, 'The ostracism of Themistocles' in *American Journal of Archaeology*, vol 51 (1947) pp. 257–62.

Robertson, A S, 'The Thessalian expedition of 480 BC' in *Journal of Hellenic Studies*, vol 96 (1976) p. 100ff.

Robinson, C, 'The struggle for power at Athens in the early fifth century BC' in *American Journal of Philology*, vol 60 (1939) pp. 232–7.

Robinson, C, 'Athenian politics 510–486 BC' in *American Journal of Philology*, vol 66 (1945) pp. 243–54.

Seager, R, 'Herodotus and "Athenian Politics" on the date of Cleisthenes' reforms' in *American Journal of Philology*, vol 84 (1963) pp. 287–9.

Shrimpton, G, 'The Persian cavalry at Marathon' in *Phoenix*, vol 54 (1980) pp. 20 ff.

Thompson, W E, 'The archaeology of Cleisthenes' in *Classical Journal*, vol 55 (1959—60) pp. 217–24.

Wade-Gery, H T, 'Miltiades' in *Journal of Hellenic Studies*, vol 71 (1951) pp. 212–51.

Wade-Gery, H T, 'Themistokles' archonship' in *Bulletin of the School at Athens*, vol 37 (1940), pp. 263–70.

Walters, K, '400 ships at Salamis?' in *Rhinisches Museum*, vol 124 (1981) pp. 199 ff.
Williams, G E M, 'Athenian poltics 508/7–480 BC: a reappraisal' in *Ahenaeus*, vol 60 (1982) pp. 521–44.

Section Two 478 to 432 BC

Primary Sources
Diodorus Siculus, *Library of History*: book 11, chapters 41–62 (470s–60s in Athens);chapters 63–92 (Athens and Greeks vs Persia 450s BC); book 12, chapters 1–21 (Athens 450–30s BC) and 22–40 (outbreak of Peloponnesian War).
Thucydides, *The Peloponnesian War*, tr. Rex Warner (Penguin Classics, edition, 1954): the Penteconteitia, 478–35 BC (pp. 87–103); Pausanias and Themistocles 470s–60s BC (pp. 108–17); Epidamnus 435–3 BC (pp. 49–53); Corcyra 433–2 BC (pp. 53–67); Epidamnus 432 BC (pp. 58–61); countdown to war 432 BC (pp. 103–7).
Plutarch, *The Rise and Fall of Athens*, tr. Ian Scott-Kilvert (Penguin Classics, 1960): lives of Themistocles (pp. 95–108), Cimon (pp. 155–64), Pericles (pp. 165–99).

Secondary Sources

Books
Anderson, J K, *Xenophon* (London 1974).
Cambridge Ancient History, vol v, as above.
Connor, W, *The New Politics of Fifth Century Athens* (Princeton UP, 1971).
Cook, op. cit.
Deane, P, *Thucydides' Dates, 465–431 BC* (Don Mills, Ontario, 1972).
De St. Croix, op. cit.
Dover, J K, *Thucydides* (Oxford UP 1973).
Dunrabin, op. cit.
Ehrenberg, Victor, *Sophocles and Pericles* (Oxford UP 1954).
Ehrenberg, Victor, *The Greek State* (Oxford UP 1960).
Finley, op. cit.
Finlay, J H, *Thucydides* (Cambridge, Mass., 1942).
Finlay, J H, *Three Essays on Thucydides* (Cambridge, Mass., 1967).
Forrest, op. cit.
Hammond, N G L, *A History of Greece to 322 BC* (Clarendon Press,1987 edition).
Hansen, op. cit.
Hignett, op. cit.
Hornblower, S A, *A Commentary on Thucydides: Vol I, Books I–III* (Oxford UP 1997).
Kagan, Donald, *The Outbreak of the Peloponnesian War* (Cornell UP, 1989).
Jones, A H M, op. cit.
Jones, A H M, *Sparta* (Oxford UP 1966).
McQuinn, T B, *Athens and Samos, Lesbos and Chios, 478–404 BC* (Manchester 1981).
Meiggs, Russell, *The Athenian Empire* (Oxford UP 1972).
Rhodes, P J, *The Athenian Boule* (Oxford UP 1972).

Articles
Adcock, F E, 'The breakdown of the Thirty Years' peace, 445–431 BC' in *The Cambridge Ancient History*, volume 5 of original edition, pp. 165–92 (Cambridge 1940).
Alexander, J A, 'Thucydides and the expedition of Callias against Potidaea, 432 BC' in *American Journal of Philology*, vol 83 (1962) pp. 265–87.
Andrewes, A, 'The Melian debate and Pericles' last speech' in *Proceedings of the Cambridge Philological Society*, vol 186 (1960) pp. 1–10.

Andrewes, A, 'Thucydides and the causes of the war' in *Classical Quarterly*, new series, vol 9 (1959) pp. 229–39.

Andrewes, A, 'The opposition to Pericles' in *Journal of Hellenic Studies*, vol 98 (1978) pp. 1–8.

Badian, E, 'The peace of Callias' in *Journal of Hellenic Studies*, vol 107 (1987) pp. 1–39.

Barns, J, 'Cimon and the first Athenian expedition to Cyprus', in *Historia*, vol 2 (1953–4) pp.163–76.

Beaumont, R L, 'Corinth, Ambracia, Apollonia' in *Journal of Hellenic Studies*, vol 72 (1952) pp. 62–73.

Brunt, P A, 'The Megarian decree' in *American Journal of Philology*, vol 72 (1951) pp. 269–82.

Chambers, Mortimer, 'Thucydides and Pericles' in *Harvard Studies in Classical Philology*, vol 62 (1957) pp. 79 ff.

Cole, J B, 'Cimon's dismissal, Ephialtes' revolution and the Peloponnesian Wars' in *Greek, Roman and Byzantine Studies*, vol 15 (1974) pp. 269–85.

Dickins, Guy, 'The true cause of the Peloponnesian War' in *Classical Quarterly*, vol 5 (1911) pp. 2238–48.

Dickins, Guy, 'The growth of Spartan policy' in *Journal of Hellenic Studies*, vol 32 (1912) pp. 1–42.

Frost, F J, 'Thucydides, son of Melesias, and Athenian Politics before the War' in *Historia*, vol 13 (1964) pp. 385–99.

Frost, F J, 'Themistocles' place in Athenian politics' in *Californian Studies in Classical Antiquity*, vol I (1968) pp. 105 ff.

Hammond, N G L, 'The origins and nature of the Athenian alliance of 478–7 BC' in *Journal of Hellenic Studies*, vol 87 (1967) pp. 41–61.

Badian, E, 'Towards a chronology of the Pentekonteitia down to the renewal of the Peace of Callias', in *Echoes du Monde Classique*, new series, vol 7 (1988) pp. 289–320.

Drewes, R D, 'Diodorus and his sources' in *American Journal of Philology*, vol 83 (1962) pp. 383–94.

Du Boer, W, 'Political propaganda in Greek chronology' in *Historia*, vol 5 (1956) pp. 163–77.

Ehrenberg, V, 'The foundation of Thurii' in *American Journal of Philology*, vol 69 (1948) pp. 149–70.

Fornara, C W, 'On the chronology of the Samian War' in *Journal of Hellenic Studies*, vol 99 (1979) pp. 7–19.

Forrest, W, 'Themistocles and Argos' in *Classical Quarterly*, new series, vol 10 (1960) pp. 221–41.

Jackson, A H, 'The original purpose of the Delian League' in *Historia*, vol 18 (1969) pp. 12–16.

Lamire, H B, 'Pausanias and Persia' in *Greek, Roman and Byzantine Studies*, vol 11 (1970) pp. 295–305.

Leonardon, R, 'The chronology of Themistocles' ostracism and exile' in *Historia*, vol 8 (1959) pp. 23–48.

Libourd, J M, 'The Athenian disaster in Egypt' in *American Journal of Philology*, vol 92 (1971) pp. 605–15.

Mattingly, H B, 'The peace of Kallias' in *Historia*, vol 15 (1965) pp. 273–81.

Mattingly, H B, 'Periclean imperialism' in Badian, E, ed., Mattingly, H B Ancient Societies and Institutions Mattingly, H B, pp. 193–224.

Meiggs, Russell, 'The growth of Athenian imperialism' in *Journal of Hellenic Studies*, vol 63 (1943) pp. 21–34.

Meiggs, Russell, 'The crisis of Athenian imperialism' in *Harvard Studies in Classical Philology*, vol 67 (1963) pp. 1–36.

Milton, M, 'The date of Thucydides' synchronization of the siege of Naxos with the flight of Themistocles' in *Historia*, vol 28 (1979) pp. 257–75.

Oliver, J H, 'The peace of Callias and the Pontic expedition of Pericles' in *Historia*, vol 6 (1957) pp. 254–5.

Pritchett, W K, 'The transfer of the Delian treasury' in *Historia*, vol 18 (1961) pp. 17–71.

Raubitschek, A E, 'The peace policy of Pericles' in *American Journal of Archaeology*, vol 70 (1966) pp. 37–42.

Reece, D W, 'The battle of Tanagra' in *Journal of Hellenic Studies*, vol 70 (1950) pp. 75–6.

Reece, D W, 'The date of the fall of Ithome' in *Journal of Hellenic Studies*, vol 82 (1962) pp. 111–20.

Robertson, N D, 'The true nature of the "Delian League", 478–451 BC' in *American Journal of Ancient History*, vol 5 (1980) pp. 64–96, 110–33.

Rhodes, P J, 'Thucydides on Pausanias and Themistocles' in *Historia*, vol 19 (1970) pp. 387–400.

Sealey, R, 'The great earthquake in Lacedaemon' in *Historia*, vol 6 (1957) pp. 357–71.

Smart, J D, 'Kimon's capture of Eion' in *Journal of Hellenic Studies*, vol 92 (1972) pp. 128–46.

Smart, J D, 'Athens and Egesta' in ibid, pp. 146 ff.

Stockton, D, 'The death of Ephialtes' in *Classical Quarterly*, new series, vol 32 (1982) pp. 227–8.

Wallace, W, 'The Egyptian expedition and the chronology of the decade 460–450 BC' in *Transactions of the American Philological Association*, vol 67 (1936) PP. 252–60.

Walsh, J, 'The authenticity and the dates of the peace of Callias and the congress decree' in Chiron, vol 11 (1981) pp. 31–63.

Westlake, H D, 'Thucydides and the Athenian disaster in Egypt' in *Classical Philology*, vol 45 (1950) pp. 209–16.

Westlake, H D, 'Thucydides and the Penteconteitia' in *Classical Quarterly*, new series, vol 5 (1955) pp. 55–67.

White, M E, 'Some Agiad dates: Pausanias and his sons' in *JKS*, vol 84 (1964) pp. 140–52.

Section Three 431 to 404 BC

Primary Sources

Diodorus Siculus, *Library of History*: book 12, chapters 41–84 (420s Peloponnesian War); book 13, chapters 1–19 (Syracuse and Athens 415–13 BC), 19–64 (Peloponnesian War after 411 BC), 65–90 (end of the career of Alcibiades from 406 BC, and Carthage vs Greek Sicily in 400s BC), 91–114 (Peloponnesian War ends 406–4 BC, and rise of Dionysius I in Sicily 406–5 BC).

Thucydides, *The Peloponnesian War*, as above: 431 BC (pp. 119–51); 430 BC (pp. 151–68); 429–8 BC (pp. 168–93); Mytilene campaign and other events 428–7 BC (pp. 194–245); 426–5 BC (pp. 246–74); Pylos 425 BC (pp. 265–90); 425–4 BC (pp. 291–318); Delium campaign 424 and Macedonia 424–3 (pp. 318–34); 423 BC (pp. 423–47); 422–1 BC (pp.348–63); inter-war years 421–16 BC (pp.363–400); Melos 416 BC (pp. 400–08); Sicily 415 BC (pp. 414–42. 446–65); 414 BC (pp. 465–88); 413 BC Sicilian disaster (pp. 488–537); 412–11 BC (pp. 538–62); 411 BC constitutional crises (pp. 562–605).

X enophon, *A History of My Times* (i.e. the 'Hellenica'), tr. Rex Warner (Penguin Classics, 1966): 411–07 BC (pp. 53–73); 406 BC (pp. 74–97); 405 BC (pp. 98–104); 404 BC (pp. 105–23).

Plutarch, *The Rise and Fall of Athens*, as above: lives of Pericles (pp. 199–206), Nicias (pp. 207–43); Alcibiades (pp. 247–83); Lysander (pp. 287–301).

Secondary Sources

Books

Anderson, op. cit.
Bommaeler, J, *Lysandre de Sparte* (Paris 1981).
Cambridge Ancient History, vol v, as above.
Connor, op. cit.
Cook, op. cit.
Dover, op. cit.
Finley, op. cit.
Finlay, op. cit.
Forrest, op. cit.
Hammond, N G L (1987 edition), op. cit.
Hansen, op. cit.
Hatzfeld, J, *Alcibiades* (Paris 1951).
Hignett, op. cit.
Kagan, Donald, *The Archidamian War* (Cornell University Press 1974).

Kagan, Donald, *The Peace of Nicias and the Sicilian Expedition* (London 1987).
Kagan, Donald, *The Fall of the Athenian Empire* (Cornell University Press 1987).
Jones, op. cit.
McQuinn, op. cit.
Matyzak, Philip, *Expedition to Disaster: the Athenian Misson to Sicily in 415 BC* (Pen and Sword 2012).
Meiggs, op. cit.

Articles
Amit, M, 'The disintegration of the Athenian Empire in Asia Minor (412–405 BC)' in *Scripta Classica Israelica*, vol 2 (1975) pp. 38–71
Andrewes, A, 'The Melian debate and Pericles' last speech' in *Proceedings of the Cambridge Philological Society*, vol 186 (1960) pp. 1–10.
Andrewes, A, 'The Arginusae trial' in *Phoenix*, vol 28 (1974) pp. 112–22.
Bloeday, E, 'Alicibiades re-examined' in *Historia*, vol 21 (1973).
Brunt, P A, 'Thucydides and Alcibiades' in *Revue des Etudes Grecques*, vol 65 (1952) pp. 59–96.
Cloche, P. 'L'Affaire d'Arginusae (406 avant JC)', in *Revue Historique*, vol 130 (1919) pp. 5–68.
Ehrhart, C, 'Xenophon and Diodorus on Aegospotamai' in *Phoenix*, vol 24 (1970) pp. 225–8.
Ferguson, W, 'The constitution of Theramenes' in *Classical Philology*, vol 21 (1926) pp. 72–5.
Halladay, A, 'Athens' strategy in the Archidamian War' in *Historia*, vol 27 (1978) pp. 399–427.
Harding, P, 'The Theramenes myth' in *Phoenix*, vol 28 (1974) pp. 101–11
Kelly, T, 'Thucydides and Spartan strategy in the Archidamian War' in *American Historical Review*, vol 87 (Feb 1982) pp. 25–54.
Lewin, A M and D, 'Notes on the peace of Nicias' in *Journal of Hellenic Studies*, vol 77 (1957) pp. 177–80.
McGregor, M, 'Kleon, Nikias and the trebling of the tribute' in *Transactions and Proceedings of the American Philological Association*, vol 66 (1935) pp. 146–64.
McGregor, M F, 'The genius of Alcibiades' in *Phoenix*, vol 19 (1965) pp. 27–46.
Meritt, B D, 'The chronology of the Peloponnesian War' in *Proceedings of the American Philosophical Society*, vol 115 (1971) pp. 97–124.
Poole, J C F, 'Thucydides and the plague of Athens' in *Classical Quarterly*, new series, vol 29 (1979) pp. 282–300.
Quinn, T J, 'Political groups at Chios 412 BC' in *Historia*, vol 18 (1969) pp. 22–30.
Rhodes, P J, 'The Four Thousand in the Athenian revolutions of 411 BC' in *Journal of Hellenic Studies*, vol 92 (1972) pp. 115–27.
St. Croix, G E M, 'The constitution of the Five Thousand' in *Historia*, vol 5 (1956) pp. 1–23.
Seaman, M G, 'The Athenian expedition to Melos in 416 BC' in *Historia: Zeitschirift fur alte Geschichte*, vol 6, part 4 (1997) pp. 385–418.
Smart, J D, 'Athens and Egesta' in *Journal of Hellenic Studies*, vol 12 (1972) pp. 128–46.
Strauss, Barry, 'Aegospotamai reexamined' in *American Journal of Philology*, vol 114 (1983) pp. 24–35.
West, A B, 'Pericles' political heirs' in *Classical Philology*, vol 19 (1924) pp. 124–46, 201–18.
Westlake, H D, 'Alicibiades, Agis and Spartan policy' in *Journal of Hellenic Studies*, vol 58 (1938) pp. 31–40.

Section Four 403 to 360 BC

Primary Sources
Diodorus Siculus, *Library of History*: Book 14: chapters 1–18 (404–387 BC), 19–31 (expedition of the Ten Thousand 401–399 BC), 32–9 (390s wars of Agesilaus vs Persia), 40–78 (Carthage vs Dionysius I in 390s BC), 79–112 (Greece and Sicily to 387 BC); Book 15: chapters 1–56 (Greece to 371 BC), 57–95 (wars of the 360s BC, to Mantinea).
Plutarch, *The Rise and Fall of Athens*, as above: lives of Alcibiades (pp. 284–5), Lysander (pp. 301–18).
Plutarch, *The Age of Alexander*, tr. Ian Scott-Kilvert (Penguin Classics, 1973): Agesilaus (pp. 25–68); Pelopidas (pp. 69–103); dion (pp. 104–50).

Xenophon, *A History of My Times*, as above: Athens, 403–2 BC (pp. 124–35); 401–399 BC (pp. 139–47); 398–7 BC (pp. 148–63); 396–4 BC (pp. 164–206); 393–0 BC (pp. 207–21); 389–6 BC (pp. 222–55); 385–0 BC (pp. 256–78) ; 379–2 BC (pp. 279–316); 371–66 BC (pp. 317–82); 366–2 BC (pp. 383–403).
Xenophon, *The Persian Expedition* (i.e. 'Anabasis'), tr. Rex Warner (Penguin Classics, 1949).

Secondary Sources

Books
Buckler, J, *The Theban Hegemony 371–362 BC* (Cambridge, Mass/London 1980).
Cargill, J, *The Second Athenian League* (Berkeley, California/London 1981).
Cartledge, P A, *Sparta and Lakonia* (London 1979).
Cartledge, P A, *Agesilaos and the Crisis of Sparta* (London 1987).
Cook, op. cit.
Gray, V G, *The Character of Xenophon's Hellenica* (London 1989).
Hammond, N G L (1987 edition), op. cit.
Jones, A H M, *Athenian Democracy* (Oxford 1969).
Krentz, P, *The Thirty at Athens* (Cornell University Press 1982).
Ryder, T T B, *Koine Eirene* (London 1965).
West, A B, *The History of the Chalcidian League* (Madison, Wisconsin, 1973).

Articles
Anderson, J K, 'The battle of Sardes in 395 BC' in *Californian Studies in Classical Antiquity*, vol 7 (1974) pp. 27–53.
Bruce, I A F, 'Internal politics and the outbreak of the Corinthian War' in *Emerita*, vol 28 (1960) pp. 75–86.
Buckler, J, 'Dating the peace of 375/4 BC' in *Greek, Roman and Byzantine Studies*, vol 12 (1971) pp. 353–71.
Buckler, J, 'The Alleged Theban alliance of 386 BC' in *Eranos*, vol 78 (1980) pp. 179–85.
Burnett, A B, 'Thebes and the expansion of the second Athenian confederacy' in *Historia*, vol 11 (1962) pp. 1–17.
Cawkwell, G, 'The common peace of 366/5 BC' in *Classical Quarterly*, new series, vol 11 (1961) pp. 80–6.
Cawkwell, G, 'Notes on the peace of 375/4' in *Historia*, vol 12 (1963) pp. 84–93.
Cawkwell, G, 'Epaminondas and Thebes' in *Classical Quarterly*, new series vol 22 (1972) pp. 254–78.
Cawkwell, G, 'The imperialism of Thrasyboulus' in *Classical Quarterly*, new series vol 26 (1976) pp. 270–7.
Cawkwell, G, 'The decline of Sparta' in ibid., pp. 62–84.
Cawkwell, G, 'The foundation of the second Athenian confederacy' in *Classical Quarterly*, new series, vol 28 (1978) pp. 43–60.
Cawkwell, G, 'The King's peace' in *Classical Quarterly*, new series, vol 31 (1981) pp. 69–83.
Fuks, A, 'Notes on the rule of ten at Athens in 403 BC' in *Mnemosyne*, vol 6 (1953) pp. 198–207.
Gray, V G, 'The years 375–371 BC: a case study in the reliability of Diodorus and Xenophon' in *Classical Quarterly*, new series, vol 30 (1980) pp. 306–26.
Grayson, C, 'Did Xenophon intend to write history?' in Levick, B M, ed., *The Ancient Historian and His Materials: Essays in Honour of C E Stevens* (Farnborough, 1975) pp. 31–43.
Griffiths, G T, 'The union of Corinth and Argos (392–386 BC)' in *Historia*, vol 1 (1950) pp. 236–56.
Hamilton, C D, 'Spartan politics and policy, 405–401 BC' in *American Journal of Philology*, vol 91 (1970) pp. 294–314.
Hatzfeld, J, 'Notes sur la chronologie des Helleniques' in *Revue des Etudes Anciennes*, vol 25 (1933) pp. 387–95.
Kaller, L, 'Iphikrates, Timotheos and Athens, 371–360 BC' in *Greek, Roman and Byzantine Studies*, vol 24 (1983) pp. 329–52.

Kelly, D H, 'Agesilaus' strategy in Asia Minor, 396–395 BC' in *Liverpool Classical Monthly*, vol 3 (1978) pp. 97–8.

Macdonald, J, 'A note on the raid of Sphodrias' in *Historia*, vol 21 (1972) pp. 38–44.

Mosley, D J, 'The Athenian embassy to Sparta in 371 BC' in *Proceedings of the Cambridge Philological Society*, vol 188 (1962) pp. 41–6.

Mosley, D J, 'Theban diplomacy 371 BC' in *Revue Etudes Grecques*, vol 85 (1972) pp. 312–18.

Parke, H, 'The development of the second Spartan empire (405–371 BC)' in *Journal of Hellenic Studies*, vol 50 (1930) pp. 37–79.

Pedech, P, 'La date de la bataille de Leuctra' in *Rivista d'Istoria Anticca*, vol 2 (1972) pp. 2–6.

Perlman, S, 'The causes and outbreak of the Corinthian War' in *Classical Quarterly*, new series vol 14 (1964) pp. 64–81.

Rice, D G, 'Agis, Agesipolis and Spartan politics, 386–379 BC' in *Historia*, vol 23 (1974) pp. 164–82.

Roos, A G, 'The peace of Sparta of 374 BC' in *Mnemosyne*, series 4, vol 2 (1949) pp. 265–85.

Roy, J, 'Arcadia and Boeotia in Peloponnesian affairs, 370–362 BC' in *Historia*, vol 20 (1971) pp. 569–99.

Ryder, T T B, 'Athenian foreign policy and the peace-conference at Sparta in 371 BC' in *Classical Quarterly*, new series, vol 13 (1963) pp. 237–41.

Ryder, T T B, 'Spartan relations with Persia after the King's peace: a strange story in Diodorus book 15, ch. 9' in *Classical Quarterly*, new series vol 13 (1963) pp. 105–9.

Sanders, L J, 'Diodorus Siculus and Dionysius I of Syracuse' in *Historia*, vol 30 (1981) pp. 394–411.

Seager, R, 'Lysander and the Spartan empire' in *Classical Philology*, vol 43 (1948) pp. 145–56.

Seager, R, 'Thrasyboulus, Conon, and Athenian imperialism, 396–386 BC' in *Journal of Hellenic Studies*, vol 87 (1967) pp. 95–115.

Seager, R, 'The King's peace and the balance of power in Greece, 386–362 BC' in *Athenaeum*, vol 52 (1974) pp. 36–63.

Seager, R, 'Agesilaus in Asia: propaganda and objectives' in *Liverpool Classical Monthly*, vol 2 (1977) pp. 18–4.

Smith, R, 'The opposition to Agesilaus' foreign policy, 394–371 BC' in *Historia*, vol 4 (1953) pp.274–88.

Thompson, W E, 'The politics of Phlius' in *Eranos*, vol 68 (1970) pp. 224–30.

Thompson, W E, 'Arcadian factionalism in the 360s' in *Historia*, vol 32 (1983) pp. 149–60.

Tuplin, C J, 'The date of the union of Corinth and Argos' in *Classical Quarterly*, new series vol 32 (1982) pp. 75–83.

Thompson, W E, 'Timotheus and Corcyra: Problems in Greek History 375–373 BC' in *Athenaeum*, vol 62 (1984) pp. 337–68.

Usher, S, 'Xenophon, Critias and Theramenes' in *Journal of Hellenic Studies*, vol 88 (1968) pp. 128–40.

Westlake, H D, 'The sources of Plutarch's "Pelopidas"' in *Classical Quarterly*, vol 33 (1939) pp. 117–22.

Whitehead, R, 'Sparta and the Thirty Tyrants' in *Ancient Society*, vols 13–14 (1982–3) pp. 106–30.

Wiseman, J, 'Epaminondas and the Theban invasions' in *Kiro*, vol 51 (1969) pp. 277–99.

Section Five 359 to 323 BC

Primary Sources

Arrian, *The Campaigns of Alexander*, tr. Aubrey de Selincourt (Penguin Classics, 1971 edition): Book One (assassination of Philip 336 BC to Alexander at Gordium 333 BC); Book Two (to the fall of Gaza 332 BC); Book Three (to the capture of Bessus 329 BC); Book Four (to the Rock of Aornos 326 BC); Book Five (to Alexander's decision on the Beas to return to Europe 325 BC); Book Six (to the arrival back in Persia 324 BC); Book Seven (to the death of Alexander 323 BC and the theories about his death being murder or not).

Austin, M M, *The Hellenistic World From Alexander to the Roman Conquest: a Selection of Ancient Sources in Translation* (Cambridge UP 1981).

Diodorus Siculus: *Library of History*: Book 16: chapters 22–39 (Philip II and Greece in the 350s BC), 40–65 (revival of Persia and the end of the Sacred War to 346 BC), 66–95 (career of Timoleon in Sicily and the wars of Philip vs the Greeks, ending with Philip's assassination in 336 BC); Book

17: chapters 1–16 (Alexander in Greece to 334 BC), 17–39 (Alexander in Asia, to the battle of Issus 333 BC), 40–63 (to the battle of Gaugamela, 331 BC), 64–80 (to the death of Parmenion 330 BC), 81–103 (to India 325 BC), 104–18 (to the death of Alexander 323 BC).

Polybius, *The Histories*, tr. by Robin Waterfield (Oxford World Classics, Oxford UP 2010): Book Twelve, in this edition, pp. 427–31 on Callisthenes and Alexander, pp. 431–45 on Timaeus' history of Timoleon.

Secondary Sources

Books

Adams, W L, and Borza, E, Philip II, *Alexander the Great and the Macedonian Heritage* (Lanham, Maryland 1982).

Bosworth, A B, *From Arrian to Alexander* (Oxford 1988).

Bosworth, A B, *Conquest and Empire: the Reign of Alexander the Great* (Oxford UP 1988).

Bosworth, A B and Baynham, E J, *Alexander the Great in Fact And Fiction* (Oxford UP 2006).

Bosworth, C, *A Historical Commentary on Arrian's History of Alexander*, Books 1–3 (Oxford UP 1980).

Bradford, A S, *Philip II of Macedon: A Life from the Ancient Sources* (Westport, Connecticut 1992).

Buckler, J, *Philip II and the Sacred War* (Leiden 1989).

Carey, C, *Aeschines* (Austin, Texas, 2000).

Cargill, op. cit.

Cawkwell, G L, *Philip of Macedon* (London 1978).

Cartledge, P, *Alexander the Great: The Hunt for a New Past* (London 2003).

Ellis, J R, *Philip II and Macedonian Imperialism* (London 1976).

Errington, R M, *A History of Macedonia* (Berkeley/Los Angeles, 1990).

Fuller, J F C, *The Generalship of Alexander the Great* (New Brunswick 1960).

Green, P, *Alexander of Macedon* (Harmondsworth 1974).

Hamilton, J R, *Plutarch's Alexander: a Commentary* (Oxford UP 1969).

Hammond, N G L, *A History of Macedonia*, vol 1 (Oxford UP 1972).

Hammond, N G L, *Alexander the Great: King, Commander and Statesman* (London 1980).

Hammond, N G L, *Three Historians of Alexander the Great* (Cambridge UP 1983).

Hammond, N G L, *A History of Greece to 322 BC* (Clarendon Press, 1987 edition).

Hammond, N G L, *The Macedonian State: The Origins, Institutions and History* (Oxfiord UP 1989).

Hammond, N G L and G Griffith, *A History of Macedonia: vol 2* (Oxford 1979).

Hansen, M H, *The Athenian Democracy in the Age of Demosthenes* (Oxford UP 1991).

Hatzopoulos, M B, and Loukopoulos, L, eds, *Philip of Macedon* (London 1980).

Heckel, W, and Tritel, L A, eds, *Crossroads of History: The Age of Alexander the Great* (Claremont, 2003).

Herzfeld, E, *The Persian Empire* (Paris 1948)

Lane Fox, R, *Alexander The Great* (Penguin 1973).

Marsden, E W, *The campaign of Gaugamela* (London 1964).

Olmstead, A T, *History of the Persian Empire* (London 1948)

Pearson, L, *The Lost Histories of Alexander the Great* (American Philological Association, 1960).

Ryder, op. cit.

Sacks, K, *Diodorus Siculus and the First Century* (Princeton UP 1990).

Sealey, Robin, Demosthenes and his Time: A Study in Defeat (Oxford UP 1993).

Sprawski, S, *Jason of Pherae* (Krakow 1999).

Talbert, R J, *Timoleon and the Revival of Greek Sicily 344–317 BC* (Cambridge 1974).

Tarn, W W, *Alexander the Great*, 2 vols (Cambridge UP 1948).

Tuplin, C, ed., *Xenophon and His World* (Stuttgart 2004).

West, A B, op. cit.

Westlake, H D, *Thessaly in the Fourth Century BC* (London 1935).

Worthington, I, ed., *Demosthenes: Statesman and Orator* (London 2000).
Worthington, I, *Alexander the Great: Man and God* (London 2004).
Worthington, I, *Philip II of Macedonia* (Yale UP 2008).

Articles
Adams, W L, 'The royal Macedonian tomb at Verghina: a historical interpretation' in *Ancient World*, vol 3 (1980) pp. 67–72.
Andronikos, M, 'The finds from the royal tombs at Verghina' in *Proceedings of the British Academy* 65 (1979) pp. 355–67.
Badian, E, 'The eunuch Bagoas' in *Classical Quarterly*, new series vol 8 (1958) pp. 144–57.
Badian, E, 'The death of Parmenion' in *Transactions and Proceedings of the American Philological Association*, vol 91 (1960) pp. 324–38.
Badian, E, 'Harpalus' in *Journal of Hellenic Studies*, vol 81 (1961) pp. 16–43.
Badian, E, 'The death of Philip II' in *Phoenix*, vol 17 (1963) pp. 244–50.
Badian, E, 'Agis III' in *Hermes* (1967), pp. 67–92.
Badian, E, 'The battle of the Granicus: a new look' in *Ancient Macedonia*, vol 2 (1977) pp. 271–93.
Balsdon, J P, 'The "divinity" of Alexander' in *Historia*, vol 1 (1950) pp. 363–88.
Battersby, C, 'What killed Alexander the Great?' in *The Australian and New Zealand Journal of Surgery*, vol 77 (1007), pp. 85–7.
Bloedow. E, 'Why did Philip and Alexander launch a war against the Persian Empire?' in *L'Antiquite Classique*, vol 72 (2003) pp. 261–74.
Borza, E N, 'Alexander and the return from Siwah' in *Historia*, vol 16 (1967) p. 369.
Borza, E N, 'Fire from heaven: Alexander at Persepolis' in *Classical Philology*, vol 67 (1972) pp. 233–48.
Bosworth, A B, 'The death of Alexander the Great: rumour and propaganda' in *Classical Quarterly*, new series vol 21 (1971) pp. 112–36.
Bosworth, A B, 'Errors in Arrian' in *Classical Quarterly*, new series vol 26 (1976) pp. 17–39.
Bosworth, A B, 'A missing year in the history of Alexander the Great' in *Journal of Hellenic Studies*, vol 101 (1981) pp. 17–39.
Bosworth, A B, 'Alexander the Great and the decline of Macedon' in *Journal of Hellenic Studies*, vol 106 (1986) pp. 164–81.
Bosworth, A B, 'Nearchus in Susiana' in J Heinrichs, ed., *Festschrift G Wirth zum 60 Geburtstag am 9.12.86* (Amsterdam 1988) pp. 546–67.
Brown, T S, 'Callisthenes and Alexander' in *American Journal of Philology*, vol 70 (1949) pp. 225–48.
Buckler, J, 'Philip II's designs on Greece' in W R Wallace and E Harris, eds., *Transitions in Empire: Essays in Honour of E Badian* (Norman, Oklahoma 1996) pp. 77–96.
Burn, A R, 'Notes on Alexander's campaigns 332–330 BC' in *Journal of Hellenic Studies*, vol 72 (1952) pp. 81–92.
Burstein, S M, 'The tomb of Philip II and the succession of Alexander the Great' in *Echoes du Monde Classique*, vol 26 (1982) pp. 141–63.
Carney, E D, 'Olympias' in *Ancient Society*, vol 18 (1987) pp. 35–62.
Cawkwell, G L, 'Aeschines and the peace of Philocrates' in *Revue Etudes Grecques*, vol 73 (1960) pp. 416–38.
Cawkwell, G L, 'The defence of Olynthus' in *Classical Quarterly*, vol 12 (1962) pp. 122–40.
Cawkwell, G L, 'Eubulus' in *Journal of Hellenic Studies* 83 (1963) pp. 47–67.
Cawkwell, G L, 'Demosthenes' policy after the peace of Philocrates I and II' in *Classical Quarterly*, vol 13 (1963) pp. 120–3 and 200–13.
Devine, A M, 'Grand tactica at Gaugamela' in *Phoenix*, vol 29 (1975) pp. 374–85.
Dmitriev, S, 'Alexander's exiles decree' in *Klio*, vol 86 (2004) pp. 34–81.
Ehrhart, C, 'Two notes on Philip of Macedon's first interventions in Thessaly' in *Classical Quarterly*, vol 17 (1967) pp. 296–301.
Ellis, J R, 'The order of the Olynthiacs' in *Historia*, vol 16 (1967) pp. 108–11.
Ellis, J R, 'The stepbrothers of Philip II' in *Historia*, vol 22 (1973) pp. 350–4.

Ellis, J R, 'Amyntas, Perdikkas, Philip II and Alexander the Great' in *Journal of Hellenic Studies*, vol 91 (1971) pp. 15–24.

Ellis, J R, 'The assassination of Philip II' in H J Dell, ed., *Ancient Macedonian Studies in Honour of C F Edson* (Thessaloniki, 1981) pp. 99–137.

Fears, J R, 'Pausanias the assassin of Philip II' in *Athenaeum*, vol 53 (1975) pp. 111–35.

Frederiksmayer, E A, 'Divine honours for Philip II' in *Transactions and Proceedings of the American Philological Society*, vol 109 (1979) pp. 39–61.

Griffiths, G T, 'Alexander's generalship at Gaugamela' in *Journal of Hellenic Studies*, vol 67 (1947) pp, 77–89.

Griffiths, G T, 'Philip of Macedon's early intervention in Thessaly' in *Classical Quarterly*, new series vol 20 (1970) pp. 67–80.

Hamilton, J K, 'The letter of Darius at Arrian (book) 2. (chapter) 14' in *Proceedings of the Cambridge Philological Society*, vol 14 (1968) pp. 33–48.

Hamilton, J K, 'The cavalry battle at the Hydaspes' in *Journal of Hellenic Studies*, vol 76 (1956) pp. 26–31.

Hammond, N G L, 'Alexander's campaign in Illyria' in *Journal of Hellenic Studies*, vol 94 (1974) pp. 61–87.

Hammond, N G L, '"Philip's Tomb" in historical context' in *Greek, Roman and Byzantine Studies*, vol 19 (1978) pp. 331–50.

Hammond, N G L, 'The battle of the Granicus river' in *Journal of Hellenic Studies*, vol 100 (1980) p. 73–88.

Hammond, N G L, 'Some passages in Arrian concerning Alexander' in *Classical Quarterly*, vol 30 (1986) pp. 455–76.

Hammond, N G L, 'The royal journal of Alexander' in *Historia*, vol 37 (1988) pp. 129–50.

Hammond, N G L, 'The battle between Philip and Bardylis' in *Antichthon*, vol 23 (1989) pp. 1–9.

Hammond, N G L, 'The sources of Justin on Macedonia to the death of Philip' in *Classical Quarterly*, vol 41 (1991) pp. 496–508.

Heckel, W, 'The conspiracy against Philotas' in *Phoenix*, vol 31 (1977) pp. 9–21.

Heckel, W, 'The flight of Harpalus and Taurrikos' in *Classical Philology*, vol 72 (1977) pp. 133–5.

Heckel, W, 'Kleopatra or Eurydike?' in *Phoenix*, vol 32 (1978) pp. 155–8.

Heckel, W, 'Philip and Olympias (337/6 BC)' in Shrimpton, D S, and McCargar, D J, eds., *Classical Contributions: Studies in Honour of M F McGregor* (Locust Valley, New York, 1981).

Heskel, J, 'Philip II and Argaios: a pretender's story' in Wallace, R W, and Harris, E, eds., *Transitions in Empire: Essays in Honour of E Badian* (Norman, Oklahoma, 1996) pp. 37–56.

Jones, T B, 'Alexander the Great and the winter of 330/29 BC' in *Classical World*, vol 28 (1935) pp. 124–5.

Kelly, D, 'Philip II and the Boeotian alliance' in *Antichthon*, vol 14 (1980) pp. 64–83.

Lehman, P W, 'The so-called tomb of Philip II: a different interpretation', in *American Journal of Archaeology*, vol 84 (1980) pp. 537–31.

Markle, M M, 'The strategy of Philip II in 346 BC' in *Classical Quarterly*, vol 24 (1974) pp. 253–68.

O'Neill, J, 'Political trials under Alexander the Great and his successors' in *Antichthon*, vol 33 (1999) pp. 28–47.

Parke, H W and Boardman, J, 'The Struggle for the tripod and the first sacred war' in *Journal of Hellenic Studies*, vol 77 (1957) pp. 276–82.

Pearson, G N, 'The diary and the letters of Alexander the Great' in *Historia*, vol 3 (1954–5) pp. 429–39.

Perlman, S, 'Greek diplomatic tradition and the Corinthian League of Philip II' in *Historia*, vol 34 (1985) pp. 153–74.

Rahe, P A, 'The annihilation of the Sacred Band at Chaeronea' in *American Journal of Archaeology*, vol 85 (1981) pp. 84–7.

Roebuck,C, 'The settlement of Philip II with the Greek states in 338 BC' in *Classical Philology*, vol 43 (1948) pp. 73–92.

Ruzicka, S, 'A note on Philip II's Persian War' in *American Journal of Ancient History*, vol 10 (1985) pp. 84–95.

Ryder, T T B, 'Demosthenes and Philip's peace of 338/7 BC' in *Classical Quarterly*, vol 26 (1976) pp. 85–7.

Schep, L,'The death of Alexander the Great: reconsidering poison' in Whaeatley, P and Hannah, R *Alexander the Great: Essays From the Antipodes* (Regina, 2009), pp, 227–36.

Sprwaski, S, 'Philip II and the Freedom of the Thessalians' in *Electrum*, vol 9 (2003) pp. 61–4.

Sprwaski, S, 'All the king's men: the Thessalians and Philip II's designs on Greece' in Musial, D, ed., *Society and Religions: Studies in Greek and Roman History* (Torun, 2005).

Westlake, H D, 'Friends and successors of Dion' in *Historia*, vol 32 (1983) pp. 161–72.

Section Six 323 to 200 BC

Primary Sources

Diodorus Siculus, *Library of History*: Book 18, chapters 1–25 (the Successors, 323–2 BC), 26–75 (the Successors, to 317 BC); Book 19, chapters 1–9 (the rise of Agathocles in Sicily to 317 BC), 10–48 (Antigonus vs the other generals to 315 BC), 49–65 (the rise of Cassander and Greece in the 310s BC), 66–100 (Greece in the early 300s BC), 101–10 (Agathocles in the later 310s BC and the death of Alexander IV 311/10 BC); Book 20: chapters 1–18 (Sicily 310–02 BC), 19–44 (Agathocles vs Carthage in the early 310s BC), 45–72 (the careers of Agathocles, continued, and Demetrius in the early 310s BC), 73–90 (Demetrius 309–5, especially vs Rhodes), 91–113 (Antigonus vs the other Successors to Ipsus 301 BC); Book 21 (Greece and the Successors 301–285 BC, incomplete); Book 22 (the Gauls in Greece 280–77 BC, incomplete); Books 23 and 24 (the First Punic War, incomplete, to 241 BC); Book 26 (the Second Punic War in Sicily, incomplete); Book 27 (the career of Nabis of Sparta and other late 200s BC Greek events, incomplete); Book 28, opening section (Philip V vs Greece in the late 200s BC).

Livy, *The War with Hannibal* (Books 21–30 of *The History of Rome from Its Foundations*), tr. by Aubrey de Selincourt (Penguin Classics, 1965): Book 24, chs. 20–40 (pp. 255–81) on Sicily and Greece in 214 BC; Book 25, Books 8–11 (pp. 303–11) on southern Italy in 212 BC; Book 25, chapters 25–31 (pp. 325–38) on Sicily in 212 BC; Book 26, chapters 20–2 (pp. 380–5) on Sicily 211 BC, chapters 24–6 (pp. 386–9) on Greece in 210 BC, chapters 39–41 (pp. 405–9) on Tarentum and Sicily 210 BC; Book 17, chapters 15–16 (pp. 446–50) on southern Italy 209 BC, chapters 30–3 (pp. 468–72) on Greece 208 BC; Book 18, chapters 5–8 (pp. 501–7) on Greece in 207 BC.

Livy, *Rome and the Mediterranean* (Books 31–45 of *The History of Rome From Its Foundation*), tr. by Henry Bettenson (Penguin Classics, 1974): Book 31, chapters 1–4 on 201 BC, chapters 5–49 on 200 BC; Book 32, chapters 1–7 on 199 BC, chapters 8–27 on 198 BC, chapter 28 – Book 33, chapter 24 on 197 BC; Book 34, chapters 1–42 on 196 BC; chapter 43 – Book 34, chapter 45 on 195 BC; chapters 46–56 on 194 BC; chapter 57 – Book 25, chapter 22 on 193 BC; chapters 23–51 on 192 BC: Book 26, chapters 1–45 on 191 BC; Book 27, chapters 1–56 on 190 BC: Book 28, chapters 1–36 on 189 BC, chapters 37–42 on 188 BC, chapter 43 – Book 39, chapter 7 on 187 BC; Book 39, chapters 8–22 on 186 BC, chapters 23–32 on 185 BC, chapters 33–45 on 184 BC, chapters 46– 2 on 183 BC; Book 40, chapters 1–19 on 182 BC, chapters 20–34 on 181 BC, chapters 35–44 on 180 BC, chapters 45–57 on 179 BC; Book 41, chapters 19–20 on 175 BC, chapters 21–6 on 174 BC; Book 42, chapters 1–6 on 173 BC, chapters 11–28 on 172 BC, chapter 29 – Book 43, chapter 3 on 171 BC; Book 43, chapters 4–12 on 170 BC, chapter 13 – Book 44, chapter 18 on 169 BC; Book 44, chapter 19 – Book 45, chapter 12 on 168 BC; Book 45, chapters 17–44 on 167 BC.

Polybius, *The Histories*, tr. by Robin Waterfield (Oxford World Classics, Oxford UP 2010): Book One (First Punic War, to 241 BC); Book Two (Greece and Macedon, plus the other Hellenistic kingdoms, to 222 BC); Book Three (Second Punic War to 216 BC, little on the Greeks); Book Four (Greece and Macedon 221 BC to the start of 218 BC); Book Five (Greece and Macedon/Second Punic War 218–16 BC); Book Six (a little on Greek constitutional affairs but mostly Rome).

Secondary Sources

Books

Adams, W L, *Alexander the Great: Legacy of a Conqueror* (Longmans, London 2004).

Bennett, B, and Roberts, M, *The Wars of the Successors, in Commanders and Campaigns*, vol 2 (Pen and Sword 2008/2009).

Berthold, R, *Rhodes in the Hellenistic Age* (Cornell UP 1984).

Bevan, E R, *The House of Seleucus*, 2 vols (London 1902).

Billows, R, *Antigonus the One-Eyed and the Creation of the Hellenistic State* (University of California Press 1990).

Bury, J B, *The Cambridge Ancient History*, original edition: vols 6–8 (Cambridge UP 1927–30).

Carey, M, *A History of the Greek World from 323 to 146 BC* (Methuen, 1972 edition).

Carney, E, *Olympias: Mother of Alexander the Great* (Routledge 2006).

Champion, J, *Pyrrhus of Epirus* (Pen and Sword 2009).

Cross, G N, *Epirus* (Cambridge 1932).

Ellis, W, *Ptolemy of Egypt* (Routledge, London 1994).

Gabbert, J, *Antigonus II Gonatas: a Political Biography* (Routledge, London 1997).

Grainger, J, *The League of the Aetolians* (Leiden 1999).

Grainger, J, *Alexander the Great Failure: The Collapse of the Macedonian Empire* (Continuum, London/New York 2007).

Habicht, C, *Athens from Alexander to Antony*, tr. D Schneider (Harvard UP 2007).

Hammond (1979), op. cit.

Hansen, E V, *The Attalids of Pergamon* (Ithaca, New York, 1947).

Heckel, W, *The Marshals of Alexander's Empire* (Routledge, London, 1992).

Lund, H, *Lysimachus: A Study in Early Hellenistic Kingship* (Routledge, Lodon 1992).

O'Sullivan, D, *The Regime of Demetrius of Phalerum in Athens, 317–307 BC* (Leiden 2009).

Shimron, B, *Late Sparta: the Spartan Revolution 243–146 BC* (Buffalo, New York 1972).

Tarn, W W, *Antigonus Gonatas* (Oxford 1933).

Tarn, W W, *The Greeks in Bactria and India* (Cambridge, 1951 edition).

Walbank, F W, *Aratus of Sicyon* (Cambridge 1933).

Walbank, F W, *Philip V of Macedon* (Cambridge 1940).

Waterfield, R, *Dividing the Spoils: the War for Alexander the Great's Empire* (Oxford UP 2011).

Articles

Adams, W L, 'The dynamics of internal Macedonian politics in the time of Cassander' in *Ancient Macedonia*, vol 3 (1983), pp. 3–30.

Adams, W L, 'Antipater and Cassander: generalship on restricted resources in the fourth century', in *Ancient World*, vol 10 (1984) pp. 79–88.

Adams, W L, 'Cassander, Alexander IV and the tombs at Verghina' in *Ancient World*, vol 22 (1991) pp. 27–33.

Adams, W L, 'The successors of Alexander' in Tritle, L, ed., *The Greek World in the Fourth Century* (Routledge, London 1997) pp. 228–48.

Anson, E, 'The date of Triparadeisus' in *American Journal of Philology*, vol 107 (1986) pp. 208–17.

Anson, E, 'Antigonus, the satrap of Phrygia' in *Historia*, vol 37 (1988) pp. 471–7.

Anson, E, 'The evolution of the Macedonian army assembly (330–315 BC)' in *Historia*, vol 40 (1991) pp. 230–47.

Anson, E, 'The chronology of the Third Diadoch War' in *Phoenix*, vol 60 (2006) pp. 226–35.

Ashton, N, 'The Lamian War – a False Start?' in *Antichthon*, vol 17 (1983) pp. 47–63.

Ashton, N, 'Craterus from 324 to 321 BC' in *Ancient Macedonia*, vol 5 (1993) pp. 125–31.

Ashton, N and Parkinson, S, 'The death of Alexander the Great: a clinical reappraisal' in Tamis, A M, ed., *Macedonian Hellenism* (Melbourne, 1990) pp. 27–36.

Badian, E, 'The treaty between Rome and the Achaian League' in *Journal of Roman Studies*, vol 42 (1952) pp. 76–80.

Badian, E, 'Notes on Roman policy in Illyria (230–201 BC)' in *PBSR*, vol 20 (1952) pp. 72–93.

Bayliss, A, 'Antigonus the One-Eyed's return to Asia in 322: a new restoration for a rasura in IG II 682', in *Zeitschrift fur Papyrologie und Ephigrafik*, vol 155 (2006) pp. 208–26.

Baynham, E, 'Antipater: manager of kings' in Worthington, I, *Ventures into Greek History* (Oxford UP 1994) pp. 331–56.

Boiy, T, 'Royal and satrapal armies in Babylon during the Second Diadoch War. The "Chronicle of the Successors" on the events during the seventh year of Philip Arrhidaeus (= 317/16 BC)' in *Journal of Hellenic Studies*, vol 130 (2010) pp. 1–13.

Bosworth, A B, 'Philip III Arrhidaeus and the Chronology of the Successors' in *Chiron*, vol 22 (1992) pp. 56–81.

Bosworth, A B, 'Perdiccas and the kings' in *Classical Quarterly*, new series vol 43 (1993) pp. 420–7.

Bosworth, A B, 'Ptolemy and the will of Alexander' in Bosworth and Baynham, E, eds., *Alexander the Great in Fact and Fiction* (Oxford UP 2000) pp. 207–41.

Bosworth, A B, 'Why did Athens lose the Lamian War?' in Palagia, O, and Tracy, S, *The Macedonians in Athens 322–229 BC* (Oxford UP 2003), pp. 14–22.

Breebart, A, 'King Seleucus I, Antiochus, and Stratonice' in *Mnemosyne*, series 4, vol 20 (1967) pp. 154–64.

Briscoe, J, 'The Antigonids and the Greek states' in Garnsey, P, and Whitaker, C R, eds., *Imperialism in the Ancient World* (Cambridge 1971).

Brunt, P. 'Alexander, Barsine and Heracles' in *Rivista di Filologia e d'Instruzione Classica*, vol 103 (1975) pp. 22–34.

Burstein, S, 'Lysimachus and the Greek cities of Asia: the case of Miletus' in *Ancient World*, vol 3 (1980) pp. 73–9.

Burstein, S, 'Lysimachus and the Greek cities: the early years' in *Ancient World*, vol 14 (1986) pp. 19–24.

Carney, E, 'The curious death of the Antipatrid dynasty' in *Ancient Macedonia*, vol 6 (1999) pp. 209–16.

Carney, E, 'The trouble with Philip Arrhidaeus' in *Ancient History Bulletin*, vol 15 (2001) pp. 63–89.

Carney, E, 'Women and military leadership in Macedonia' in *Ancient World*, vol 35 (2004) pp. 184–95.

Collins, N, 'The various fathers of Ptolemy I' in *Mnemosyne*, series 4, vol 50 (1997) pp. 436–76.

Daubies, M, 'Cleomene III, les helotes et Selassie' in *Historia*, vol 20 (1971) pp. 665–95.

Delev, P. 'Lysimachus and the Third War of the Successors (314–311 BC)' in Angelova, H, ed., *Thracia Pontica*, vol VI. 2 (Sofia, 2003) pp 63–76.

Devine, A M, 'Diodorus' account of the Battle of Gaza' in *Aca Classica*, vol 27 (1984) pp. 31–40.

Devine, A M, 'Diodorus' account of the Battle of Paraitacene (317 BC)' in *Ancient World*, vol 12 (1985) pp. 75–86.

Devine, A M, 'Diodorus' account of the Battle of Gabiene' in ibid., pp. 87–96.

Dow, S, and Edson, L F, 'Chryseis: a study of the evidence in regard to the mother of Philip V' in *Harvard Studies in Classical Philology*, vol 48 (1937) pp. 127–80.

Dmitriev, S, 'The last marriage and death of Lysimachus' in *Greek, Roman and Byzantine Studies*, vol 47 (2007) pp. 135–49.

Errington, R M, 'Philip V, Aratus and the conspiracy of Apelles' in *Historia*, vol 16 (1967) pp. 19–36.

Errington, R M, 'From Babylon to Triparideisos: 323 to 320 BC' in *Journal of Hellenic Studies*, vol 90 (1970) pp. 49–77.

Errington, R M, 'Diodorus Siculus and the chronology of the early Diadochi' in *Hermes*, vol 105 (1977) pp. 478–504.

Ferguson, W S, 'Demetrius Poliorcetes and the Hellenic League' in *Hesperia*, vol 17 (1948) pp. 112–36.

Fine, J N A, 'The background of the Social War of 220–217 BC' in *American Journal of Philology*, vol 61 (1940) pp. 129–65.

Greenwalt, W, 'The search for Arrhidaeus' in *Ancient World*, vol 10 (1984) pp. 69–77.

Greenwalt, W, 'Argead name changes' in *Ancient Macedonia*, vol 6 (1999) pp. 453–62.

Gruen, E, 'Aratus and the Achaean alliance with Macedon' in *Historia*, vol 21 (1972) pp. 609–25.

Hammond, N G L, 'Illyria, Rome and Macedon in 229–205 BC' in *Journal of Roman Studies*, vol 58 (1968) pp. 1–20.

Hammond, N G L, 'Alexander's veterans after his death' in *Greek, Roman and Byzantine Studies*, vol 25 (1984) pp. 51–61.

Hauben, H, 'On the chronology of the years 313–311 BC' in *American Journal of Philosophy*, vol 94 (1973) pp. 256–63.

Hauben, H, 'The First War of the Successors (321 BC): chronological and historical problems' in *Ancient Society*, vol 8 (1977), pp. 85–120.

Hauben, H, 'Rhodes, Alexander and the Diadochi from 333/2 to 304 BC' in *Historia*, vol 26 (1977) pp. 307–39.

Heckel, W, 'The career of Antigenes' in *Symbolae Osloenses*, vol 57 (1982) pp. 57–67.

Heckel, W, 'The politics of Antipatros, 324–319 BC' in *Ancient Macedonia*, vol 6 (1999) pp. 489–98.

Hope Simpson, R, 'The political circumstances of the peace of 311 BC' in *Journal of Hellenic Studies*, vol 74 (1954) pp. 25–31.

Hope Simpson, R, 'Ptoleamaus' invasion of Greece in 313 BC' in *Mnemosyne*, series 4, vol 8 (1955) pp. 34–7.

Hope Simpson, R, 'Antigonus, Polyperchon and the Macedonian regency' in *Historia*, vol 6 (1957) pp. 371–3.

Kertesz, I, 'Ptolemy I and the battle of Gaza', in *Studia Aegyptica* (1974) pp. 231–41.

Laix, R de, 'Polybius' credibility and the triple alliance of 230/229 BC' in *Californian Studies in Classical Antiquity*, vol 2 (1969) pp. 65–83.

Larsen, J R, 'Phocis and the Social War of 220–217 BC' in *Phoenix*, vol 19 (1965) pp. 116–28.

Macurdy, G, 'Alexander IV and Roxane in Epirus' in *Journal of Hellenistic Studies* 52 (1932) pp. 256–61.

Meeus, A, 'The power struggle in Babylonia in 323 BC' in *Ancient Society*, vol 38 (2008) pp. 39–82.

O'Sullivan, L, '"Le Roi Soleil": Demetrius Poliorcetes and the dawn of the Sun King', in *Antichthon*, vol 42 (2008), pp. 78–99.

Seyrig, H, 'Seleucus I and the foundation of Hellenistic Syria' in Ward, W A, ed., *The Role of the Phoenicians in the Interraction of Mediterranean Civilizations* (Beirut 1988), pp. 53–63.

Shimron, B, 'Polybius and the reforms of Cleomenes III' in *Historia*, vol 13 (1966) pp. 147–58.

Tarn, W W, 'The first Syrian War' in *Journal of Hellenic Studies*, vol 46 (1926) pp. 154–62.

Tarn, W W, 'The new dating of the Chremonidean War' in *Journal of Hellenic Studies*, vol 54 (1934) pp. 26–39.

Wheatley, P, 'The date of Polyperchon's invasion of Macedonia and murder of Heracles' in *Antichthon*, vol 32 (1998) pp. 12–23.

Wheatley, P, 'The chronology of the third Diadoch war' in *Phoenix*, vol 52 (1998) pp. 257–81.

Wheatley, P, 'The Antigonid campaign in Cyprus, 306 BC' in *Ancient Society*, vol 31 (2001) pp. 133–56.

Section Seven 199 to 100 BC

Primary Sources

Diodorus Siculus, *Library of History*: Book 28, concluding section (Philip V vs Greece and the Romans, to 193 BC); Book 29 (Greece, the Seleucids, and Rome to 172 BC); Book 30 (the second Rome vs Macedonia war, 171–168 BC); Book 31 (Rome and Asia Minor to 153 BC); Book 32 (Rome, Greece, Macedonia and the Seleucids/Ptolemies to 145 BC).

Secondary Sources

Books

Allen, R, *The Attalid Kingdom: a Constitutional History* (Oxford UP 1983).

Auston, M M, *The Hellenistic World from Alexander to the Roman Conquest* (Cambridge 1981).

Bevan, op. cit.

Bevan, *A History of Egypt under the Ptolemaic Dynasty* (Methuen London 1927).

The Cambridge Ancient History: vol VIII, ed. Aston E, Walbank F W, Frederiksen M W, and Ogilvie, R M (Cambridge UP 1989).

Carey, op. cit.

College, M A R, *The Parthians* (New York 1967).

Ferguson, W S, *Hellenistic Athens* (London 1911).

Fraser, G M, *Ptolemaic Alexandria*, 3 vols (Oxford 1972).

Hansen, op. cit.

Jansen, H L, *Die Politik Antiochos IV* (Oslo 1943).

Skeat, T, *The Reigns of the Ptolemies* (Munich 1954).

Walbank (1940), op. cit.

Whitehorne, J, *Cleopatras* (Routledge, London 1994).

Woodstock, G, *The Greeks in India* (London 1966).

Articles

Bellinger, A, 'The end of the Seleucids' in *Transactions of the Connecticut Academy of the Arts and Sciences*, vol 38 (1949) pp. 51–102.

Bikerman, E, 'Notes on Seleucid and Parthian chronology' in *Berytus*, vol 8 (1944) pp. 73–83.

Bunge, J, 'Antiochus Helios' in *Historia*, vol 24 (1975) pp. 164–88.

Bustein, S M, 'The aftermath of the peace of Apamea' in *American Journal of Ancient History*, vol 5 (1986) pp. 1–12.

Dell, H J, 'Antiochus III and Rome' in *Classical Philology*, vol 62 (1964) pp. 94–103.

Derow, P, 'Polybius and the embassy of Kallikrates' in *Essays Presented to C M Bowra* (Oxford 1970) pp. 12–24.

Derow, P, 'Polybius, Rome and the East' in *Journal of Roman Studies*, vol 69 (1979) pp. 1–15.

Errington, R M, 'The alleged Syro-Macedonian pact and the origins of the Second Macedonian War' in *Athenaeum*, vol 49 (1971) pp. 336–54.

Fuke, A, 'The Bellum Achaicum and its social aspect' in *Journal of Hellenic Studies*, vol 80 (1970) pp. 78–89.

Helliesen, J M, 'Demetrius I Soter: a Seleucid King with an Antigonid Name' in Dell, H, ed., *Ancient Macedonian Studies in Honour of Charles F Edson* (Thessaloniki 1981).

Holleaux, M, 'Le mort d'Antioch IV Epiphanes' in *Revue Etudes Anciennes*, vol 18 (1916) pp. 76–102.

Houghton, A, 'The second reign of Demetrius II of Syria at Tarsus' in *American Numismatical Society Museum Notes*, vol 24 (1979) pp. 211–16.

Macdonald, A H, 'The treaty of Apamea (188 BC)' in *Journal of Roman Studies*, vol 57 (1967) pp. 1–8.

Paltiel, E, 'Antiochus IV and Demetrius of Syria' in *Antichthon*, vol 15 (1979) pp. 42–7.

Paltiel, E, 'Antiochus Epiphanes and Roman politics' in *Latomus*, vol 41 (1982) pp. 229–54.

Swain, J W, 'Antiochus Epiphanes in Egypt' in *Classical Philology*, vol 39 (1944) pp. 73–94.

Dynastic Tables

Kings of Sparta

Name	Accession	Death/dep.	Years ruled
Agids			
Polydoros	c. 700	c. 665	c. 35
Eurycrates	c. 665	c. 640	c. 25
Anaxander	c. 640	c. 615	c. 25
Eurycratides	c. 615	c. 590	c. 25
Leon	c. 590	c. 560	c. 30
Anaxandridas	c. 560	c. 515	c. 45
Cleomenes	c. 515	(491? dep. & soon k.)	c. 24?
Leonidas (brother)	491?	480	11?
Pleistarchus (son) (Regent: Pausanias, cousin, c.480–73)	480	458?	22?
Pleistoanax (son of Leonidas' brother)	458?	444	14?
Pausanias (son)	444	394	40
Agesipolis (son)	394	380	14
Cleombrotus (brother)	380	371	9
Agesipolis II (son)	371	369	2
Cleomenes (brother)	369	309	60
Areus (grandson)	309	264	45
Acrotatus (son)	264	262?	2?
Areus II (son)	262?	254	8?
Leonidas II	254	(242 dep.)	12
Cleombrotus II	242	241	1
Leonidas II	241	235	6
Cleomenes II	235	221	14
Agesipolis III	219	215	4
Eurypontids			
Theopompus	c. 710	c. 675	c. 45
Anaxandridas	c. 675	c. 645	c. 30
Zeuxidamus	c. 645	c. 625	c. 20
Anaxidamus	c. 625	c. 600	c. 25
Archidamus I	c. 600	c. 575	c. 25
Agasicles	c. 575	c. 550	c. 25
Ariston	c. 550	c. 515	c. 35
Demaratus (Damaratus deposed by arrangement of his fellow-king Cleomenes.)	c. 515	(491? dep.)	c. 24?

Name	Accession	Death/dep.	Years ruled
Leotychidas (?second cousin)	491?	469 (exile 478/6)	22?
Archidamus II (i) (grandson)	469	427	42
Agis II (son)	427	400/399	27/8 (age: 40s?)

(Agis' son Leotychidas disinherited due to suspicion of his mother's relations with the visiting Athenian exile general Alicibiades.)

Name	Accession	Death/dep.	Years ruled
Agesilaus II (half-bro.)	400/399	361	38/9 (age: c. 84)
Archidamus II (ii) (son)	361	338	23 (age: >70)
Agis III (son)	338	331	7
Eudamidas (brother)	331	c. 300	c. 31
Archidamus IV (son)	c.300	c. 270	c. 30
Eudamidas II (son)	c. 270	245?	c. 25?
Agis IV (son)	245?	241	4 (age: 20s)
Eudamidas III	241	228	13
Archidamus V	228	217	11
Lycurgus	219	210	9
Pelops	210	206	4
Nabis	206	192	14

Rulers of Macedon

Name	Date of birth	Accession	Death/dep.	Years r.	Age
Alcetas		c. 570	c. 540	c. 30	
Amyntas (son)		c. 540	c. 492	c. 48	
Alexander I (son)		c. 492	c. 450	c. 42	
Perdiccas II (son)		c. 450	414	c. 36	
Archelaus (son)	c. 448?	414	399	15	c. 49?
Orestes (son)	c. 410	399	397/6	2/3	c. 13/14
Aeropus (uncle)	c. 445?	397/6	July 394	2/3	c. 51?
Amyntas II (cousin)		394?	393?	1?	
(Pausanias, son, superseded but reigns briefly in 393/2)					
Amyntas III (i) (grandson of Perdiccas' brother)	c. 420?	393?	(392? dep.)	1?	
Amyntas III (ii)		391?	late 370	21?	c. 50?
Alexander II (son)		late 370	368	1/2	
Ptolemy (brother-in-law, possibly son of Amyntas II)		368	365	3	
Perdiccas II (brother of Alex.)	c.388?	365	359	6	c.29?
Amyntas IV(son)	c.364?	359	(359/8 dep.) k. 336	<1	(c. 5 dep.) c. 28
(Regent: Philip, uncle, 359–9/8)					
Philip II (uncle)	383	359/8	Sum 336 (k)	22/3	46/7

Name	Date of birth	Accession	Death/dep.	Years r.	Age
Alexander III 'the Great' (Egypt from 332; Persia from 330) (son)	Jul? 356	Sum 336	10 Jun 323	12, 10? m.	32, 11? m.

(Due to Alexander's and his successors' absence in Asia, the general Antipater ruled Macedonia as regent from 334 to 319.)

Name	Date of birth	Accession	Death/dep.	Years r.	Age
Philip III Arrhidaeus (also King of Asia) (half-bro.)	c. 355?	Jun 323	317 (k)	5/6	c. 37?
Alexander IV (also King of Asia) (son of A. III)	Aug? 323	Aug? 323	311/10?	12/13?	12/13?

(Regents: Antipater 323–19, Polyperchon 319–18, Queen Olympias 317–16)
(Philip III was killed by his stepmother, Alexander's mother, Olympias, who was killed by Cassander; the latter probably killed Alexander IV too.)

Name	Date of birth	Accession	Death/dep.	Years r.	Age
Cassander (regent 317) (married to Philip II's daughter)	c. 358?	311/10	Late 298	12/13 (effect. 19)	c. 60?
Philip IV (son)	c. 318	298	spring? 297	4 m.	c. 21
Antipater (brother)	c. 315	297	(295 dep.)	2	(c. 20 dep.)
Alexander V (brother)	c. 313	297	294 (k)	3	c. 19

(294: Alexander evicts Antipater but falls victim to the adventurer Demetrius, naval warlord of the Aegean and Ionia and married to Cassander's sister Phila.)

Name	Date of birth	Accession	Death/dep.	Years r.	Age
Demetrius 'Poliorcetes' (married to Cassander's sister)	337	294	(288 dep.) d. 283	6	(49 dep.) 54

(288: Demetrius evicted by his neighbour, Lysimachus, King of Thrace.)

Name	Date of birth	Accession	Death/dep.	Years r.	Age
Lysimachus (Eastern M.) (Western M. 284–1) (Thrace from 322)	c.358	288	281(k)	7	c. 77
Pyrrhus, King of Epirus (Western M.) (i)	319	288	(284 dep.) 272 k.	4	(35? dep.) 47

(281: Lysimachus, now ruling from Macedonia to Western Anatolia, is killed in battle by Seleucus. Interregnum; kingship claimed by Seleucus, founder of the Seleucid realm, q.v..)

Name	Date of birth	Accession	Death/dep.	Years r.	Age
Ptolemy 'Ceraunus' (son of Ptolemy I of Egypt, q.v., and daughter of Antipater)	c. 315	280	279 (k)	1	c. 36
Meleager		279	279	<1	
Antipater II (grandson of A.)		279	279	42 days	

(Interregnum during Celtic invasions.)

Name	Date of birth	Accession	Death/dep.	Years r.	Age
Antigonus 'Gonatas' (i) (son of Demetrius; grandson of Antipater)	319?	278	(275 dep.)	3	(44? dep.)
Pyrrhus (ii)		275	(274 dep.) k. 272	1 (Total: 5)	(45 dep.) 47
Antigonus 'Gonatas' (ii)		274	239	35	80?
Demetrius II (son)	c.275	239	229	10	c. 46

Name	Date of birth	Accession	Death/dep.	Years r.	Age
Antigonus II 'Doson' (grandson of Demetr. I)	c. 267	229	221	8	c. 46
Philip V (son of D. II)	238	221	179	42	59

(197/6: Philip loses his Southern Greek dominions and Thessaly following defeat by Rome, whose dependent ally he becomes.)

Name	Date of birth	Accession	Death/dep.	Years r.	Age
Perseus (son)	210	179	(168 dep.) d. 166	11	(42 dep.) 44

(Macedonia broken up into four republics by Rome; Perseus deported to Italy.)

Kings of Epirus

Name	Birth	Accession	Death/dep.	Years r.	Age
Tharrhypas		c. 425?	c. 400?	c. 25?	
Alcetas		c. 400?	c. 380?	c. 20?	
Neoptolemus I (son of T.)		c. 380?	c. 360?	c. 20?	
Arrybas (brother)		c. 360?	342	c. 18?	
Alexander (son of N.)	c. 375?	342	331	9	c. 45?
Neoptolemus II (i) (titular to 317) (son)	c. 334	331	(313 dep.)	18	(c. 21 dep)
Aecidas (son of Arr.)		331	317	14	
Alcetas II (brother)		313	307	4	
Pyrrhus (i) (son)	319?	307	(302 dep.)	5	(17? dep.)
Neoptolemus II (ii)		302	295	7	c. 39
Pyrrhus (ii) (and Macedonia 288–4, 275–4)		295	272	23	47?
Alexander II (son)	c. 295?	272	239?	33?	c. 56?
Pyrrhus II (son)		239?	237?	2?	
Ptolemy (brother)		237?	233?	4?	

Seleucid Kings

Name	Birth	Accession	Death/dep.	Years r.	Age
Seleucus I 'Nicator'	c. 357	Apr 311	Sep? 280 (k)	31 5? m.	c. 77
Antiochus I (son)	c. 323	Sep? 280	261	19	c. 62
Antiochus II 'Theos' (son)	c. 286	261	246	15	c. 40
Seleucus II 'Callinicus' (son)	c. 268	246	226	20	c. 42
Seleucus III (son)	c. 245	226	223	3	c. 22
Antiochus III 'Restitutor Orbis' (brother)	243/2	223	187	36	55/6
Seleucus IV 'Philopator' (son)	217	187	175 (k)	12	41/2
Antiochus IV 'Epiphanes' (brother)	c. 205	175	late164 (k)	11	c. 41
Antiochus V 'Eupator' (son)	c. 170	late 164	162	<2	c. 12

(Regent: Lysias, 163–2.)

Name	Birth	Accession	Death/dep.	Years r.	Age
Demetrius I (son of S. IV)	c. 185	162	150	12	c. 35
Alexander 'Balas' (rival king; pretended son of Ant. IV)	c. 172	152	145 (k)	7	c. 27
Antiochus VI (son) (*Regent: Diodotus 'Tryphon'*)	148/7	145	142	3	5/6
Demetrius II 'Nicator' (rival king) (son of D I)	c. 160	147	(139 dep.)	8	(c.21 dep.)
Antiochus VII 'Sidetes' (brother)	c. 157	139	129	10	c. 28
Demetrius II (ii)		129	125	4	c. 35
Seleucus V (son)	c. 144?	125	125	<1	c. 19?
Antiochus VIII 'Grypus' 'Philometor' (brother)	c.142?	125	96	29	c. 46?
Antiochus IX 'Cyzicenus' (son of A. II)	c. 133?	115	95	20	c. 38?
Seleucus VI 'Epiphanes Nicator' (son of A. VIII)		96	95	1	
Philip I (brother)		95	83?	12?	
Demetrius III 'Philopator' (brother)		95	88	7	
Antiochus X 'Eusebes Philopator' (brother)		95	88?	7?	
(Conquest of most of Syria by Tigranes of Armenia; some revival on his defeat by Rome 69/8.)					
Antiochus XI		68	67	1	
Antiochus XIII (son of Ant. X)		66?	64	2?	
Philip III (rival King)		66?	65		

Ptolemaic Dynasty of Egypt

Name	Birth	Accession	Death/dep.	Years r.	Age
Ptolemy I 'Soter'	c. 364	322	283	39	c. 81
(Ptolemy disinherited his elder son, Ptolemy 'Ceraunus', who ended up Macedonia, q.v.)					
Ptolemy III 'Euergetes' (son)	c. 277	Jan 246	Jan 221	25	c. 56
Ptolemy IV 'Philopator' (son)	235?	Jan 221	Nov 205	16, 10 m.	30?
Ptolemy V 'Epiphanes' (son)	209	Nov 205	Spr 180	24, c. 5 m.	28/9
(Regent: Arsinoe, mother, 205–3)					
Ptolemy VI 'Philometor' (i) (son)	188?	Spr 180	(164 dep.)	16	(24? dep.)
Ptolemy VIII 'Euergetes' 'Physcon' (i) (brother)	c. 184	164	(163 dep.)	1	(c. 21 dep.)
Ptolemy VI (ii)		163	Sum 145(k)	18	43?

Name	Birth	Accession	Death/dep.	Years r.	Age
Ptolemy VII 'Eupator' (son)	c.164	Sum 145	Sum? 145	weeks	c.19)
Ptolemy VIII (ii)		Sum? 145	(130 dep.)	15	(c. 54 dep.)
Cleopatra II (wife and sister)	c.186?	130	(129 dep.) d. 115	1	(c. 57? dep.) c. 71?
Ptolemy VIII (iii)		129	116	13	c. 68
Cleopatra III (wife and niece)	c. 161?	116	101	15	c. 60?
Ptolemy IX 'Soter' 'Lathyrus' (i) (son)	142	116	(109 dep.)	7	(33 dep.)
Ptolemy X Alexander (i) (brother)	c. 140	109	107	2	c. 51
Ptolemy IX (ii)		107	(101 dep.)	6	(41 dep)
Ptolemy X (ii)		101	89	12	(c. 51 dep)
Ptolemy IX (iii)		89	80	9	62
Berenice III (daughter)	c.120	80	80	< 6 m?	c.40
Ptolemy XI Alexander (son of P. X)	c. 100	80	80	1 m.	c. 20
Ptolemy XII 'Neos Alexander' 'Auletes' (i) (son of P. VIII)	c. 107	80	(58 dep.)	22	(c. 49 dep.)
Cleopatra VI (wife)		58	57	1	
Berenice V (daughter)	c. 80?	58	55	3	c. 25?
(55: Rome forcibly restores Ptolemy XI. Partial Roman military occupation thereafter.)					
Ptolemy XII (ii)		55	51	4	c. 56
Ptolemy XIII (son)	c. 64	51	Spr 47 (dr.)	3/4	c. 17
(47: Julius Caesar intervenes in civil war between Ptolemy XII and Cleopatra VII in the latter's favour.)					
Cleopatra VII (sister)	70	51	Aug 30 (suic.)	20/1	39/40
Ptolemy XIV (brother)	c. 61	Spr 47	44	2/3	c. 17
Ptolemy XV Caesarion (son of C.)	Early 46	44	Aug 30 (k)	13/14	16

Index